The Woodwinds

The Woodwinds: Perform, Understand, Teach provides comprehensive coverage about the woodwind family of musical instruments for prospective instrumental music teachers. What sets this book apart is its focus on *how to teach* the instruments. Preparing students in the *how* of teaching is the ultimate goal of the woodwind class and the ultimate goal of this book, which organizes information by its use in teaching beginning instrumentalists.

In developing performance and understanding, pre-service teachers are positioned to learn to *teach through performance*—contrasted with an "old-school" belief that one must first spend much time tediously trying to understand how things work *before* playing the instruments.

The book is organized in three parts: Preliminaries, Teaching the Instruments, and Foundations. Chapters in Teaching the Instruments are organized by instrument (flute, clarinet, saxophone, oboe, bassoon) and, within each instrument, according to how an effective teacher might organize experiences for novice learners. Basic embouchure and air stream are covered first, followed by instrument assembly, then hands and holding. Embouchure coverage returns in greater depth, then articulation, and finally "the mechanism," which includes sections on the instruments of the family, transposition, range, special fingerings, tuning and intonation, and reeds. In Foundations, topics are situated in big picture contexts, calling attention to the broad applicability of information across instruments.

James L. Byo is Carl Prince Matthies Professor of Music Education at Louisiana State University in Baton Rouge.

The Woodwinds
Perform, Understand, Teach

James L. Byo
Carl Prince Matthies Professor of Music Education
at Louisiana State University

NEW YORK AND LONDON

First published 2016
by Routledge
711 Third Avenue, New York, NY 10017

and by Routledge
2 Park Square, Milton Park, Abingdon, Oxon, OX14 4RN

Routledge is an imprint of the Taylor & Francis Group, an informa business

© 2016 Taylor & Francis

The right of James L. Byo to be identified as author of this work has been asserted by him in accordance with sections 77 and 78 of the Copyright, Designs and Patents Act 1988.

All rights reserved. No part of this book may be reprinted or reproduced or utilized in any form or by any electronic, mechanical, or other means, now known or hereafter invented, including photocopying and recording, or in any information storage or retrieval system, without permission in writing from the publishers.

Trademark notice: Product or corporate names may be trademarks or registered trademarks, and are used only for identification and explanation without intent to infringe.

Library of Congress Cataloging in Publication Data
Names: Byo, James L., author.
Title: The woodwinds : perform, understand, teach / James L. Byo.
Description: New York, NY ; Abingdon, Oxon : Routledge, 2016. | 2016
Identifiers: LCCN 2015043409 | ISBN 9781138123007
Subjects: LCSH: Woodwind instruments—Instruction and study.
Classification: LCC MT339.5 .B96 2016 | DDC 788.2—dc23
LC record available at http://lccn.loc.gov/2015043409

ISBN: 978-1-138-12300-7 (hbk)
ISBN: 978-1-138-12301-4 (pbk)
ISBN: 978-1-315-64911-5 (ebk)

Typeset in Bembo, Nelvetica Neue, and Kabel
by Florence Production Ltd, Stoodleigh, Devon, UK

Contents

List of Illustrations   viii
Preface   xiii

PART 1   PRELIMINARIES   1

1   Woodwinds in Diverse Contexts   3

How Woodwind Instruments Work   3
The Contexts of Woodwind Performance and Teaching in Schools   5
How People Learn   6
How You Learn   10
Instrument Selection and Assignment   12

PART 2   TEACHING THE INSTRUMENTS   17

2   Flute   19

Flute Tone and Early Stage Embouchure   19
Flute Assembly, Disassembly, and Care   26
Flute Hand Position   27
Flute Tone Development   30
Flute Tonguing   37
The Flute Mechanism   40
Study Questions   46
Performance Testing of University Students on Secondary Instruments   48
Flute Fingering Chart   50

3   Clarinet   52

Clarinet Tone and Early Stage Embouchure   52
Clarinet Assembly, Disassembly, and Basic Care   62

Clarinet Hand Position 64
Clarinet Tone Development 66
Clarinet Tonguing 73
The Clarinet Mechanism 76
Study Questions 96
Performance Testing of University Students on Secondary Instruments 98
Clarinet Fingering Chart 100

4 Saxophone 102

Saxophone Tone and Early Stage Embouchure 102
Saxophone Assembly, Disassembly, and Basic Care 112
Saxophone Hand Position 114
Saxophone Tone Development 115
Saxophone Tonguing 120
The Saxophone Mechanism 122
Study Questions 132
Performance Testing of University Students on Secondary Instruments 134
Saxophone Fingering Chart 136

5 Oboe 138

Potential for Success in Oboe Study 138
Oboe Tone and Early Stage Embouchure 139
Oboe Assembly, Disassembly, and Basic Care 140
Oboe Posture, Hands, and Holding 142
Oboe Tone Development 143
Oboe Tonguing 150
The Oboe Mechanism 150
Initial Playing Material 164
Study Questions 170
Performance Testing of University Students on Secondary Instruments 171
Oboe Fingering Chart 173

6 Bassoon 175

Potential for Success in Bassoon Study 175
Bassoon Tone and Early Stage Embouchure 176
Bassoon Assembly, Disassembly, and Basic Care 179
Bassoon Posture, Hands, and Holding 186
Bassoon Tone Development 189
Bassoon Tonguing 195
The Bassoon Mechanism 196
Initial Playing Material 211

Study Questions   217
Performance Testing of University Students on Secondary Instruments   219
Bassoon Fingering Chart   221

PART 3 THINKING FOUNDATIONALLY ABOUT THE WOODWINDS AND WOODWIND TEACHING   225

7 Using Foundations for Perspective   227

Foundations of Tone Quality   227
Foundations of Teaching   230
Foundations of Assembly and Disassembly   236
Foundations of Instrument Care   237
Foundations of Posture, Hands, and Holding   241
Foundations of Tonguing and Articulation   243
Foundation of the Mechanism   246
Foundations of Tuning and Intonation   252
Foundations of Reed and Mouthpiece   254
Foundations: Professional Organizations and Periodicals   256

Notes on the Author   257
Index   259

Illustrations

FIGURES

1.1	Harmonic Series Overtones	5
2.1	Head Joint with Plugged End	20
2.2	Lip Over Embouchure Hole	21
2.3	Lip Over Embouchure Hole	21
2.4	Teaching/Learning Sequence: Head Joint Practice	24
2.5	Alignment of Foot Joint and Body of Flute	26
2.6	Embouchure Hole Aligned with Row of Keys	26
2.7	Flute Hand Position	28
2.8	Line of Lips Parallel with Line of Flute	32
2.9	Line of Lips Not Parallel with Line of Flute	32
2.10	Small Aperture (Middle School Musician)	32
2.11	Small Aperture (Middle School Musician)	32
2.12	Small Aperture (High School Musician)	32
2.13	Aperture Naturally Off-Centered	32
2.14	Lip-Across Exercise	34
2.15	Rhythmic Pulsations for Vibrato Development	36
2.16	Backward Approach to Teaching Tonguing	38
2.17	Isolate Tongue Movement	39
2.18	Flute Range	41
2.19	Alternate B-flat and F-sharp	42
2.20	Third Octave Fingerings	42
2.21	Flute Trills	43
2.22	Harmonics	44
2.23	Flute Tuning Notes	44
2.24a	Flute Fingering Chart page 1	50
2.24b	Flute Fingering Chart page 2	51
3.1	Small Piece	52
3.2	Steadied Hand with Ligature	54

3.3	Correctly Positioned Screw Heads	54
3.4	Incorrectly Positioned Screw Heads	54
3.5	"Goal Posts" in Reed Position Adjustment	54
3.6	Curvature of the Mouthpiece (Fulcrum)	55
3.7	Embouchure (Middle School Musician)	58
3.8	Embouchure (High School Musician)	58
3.9	Teaching/Learning Sequence: Small Piece Practice	60
3.10	Bell and Lower Joint Assembly	63
3.11	Lower and Upper Joint Assembly	63
3.12	Clarinet Hand Position	65
3.13	Left Thumb in the 2 O'clock Position	65
3.14	Imperfect Embouchure but Good Sound	67
3.15	Negative Embouchure Example	67
3.16	Embouchure Checkpoints	71
3.17	Ascending Major 6th Checkpoint	72
3.18	Backward Approach to Teaching Tonguing	74
3.19	Isolate Tongue Movement	75
3.20	Clarinet Range and Register	78
3.21	Throat Tones	79
3.22	Right-Hand Fingers in the Right-Hand-Down Technique	79
3.23	Marking a Right-Hand-Down Passage	79
3.24	The Use of the Register Key to Produce 12ths	80
3.25	Labeled Pinky Keys on the Lower Joint	80
3.26	Cross-Fingerings: How to Figure Them Out	82
3.27	Cross-Fingering Examples	83
3.28a	Clarinet Trill Fingerings page 1	84
3.28b	Clarinet Trill Fingerings page 2	85
3.29	Clarinet Tuning Notes	86
3.30	The Single Reed Labeled	89
3.31	The Mouthpiece Labeled	94
3.32a	Clarinet Fingerings page 1	100
3.32b	Clarinet Fingerings page 2	101
4.1	Steadied Hand with Ligature	103
4.2	Correctly Positioned Screw Heads	104
4.3	Incorrectly Positioned Screw Heads	104
4.4	"Goal Posts" in Reed Position Adjustment	104
4.5	Front View of Embouchure (Middle School Musician)	107
4.6	Side View of Embouchure	108
4.7	Teaching/Learning Sequence: Small Piece Practice	110
4.8	Shape of Left Hand in Instrument Hold	114
4.9	Side View of Embouchure (High School Musician)	115
4.10	Negative Embouchure Example	116
4.11	Backward Approach to Teaching Tonguing	121

4.12	Isolate Tongue Movement	122
4.13	Saxophone Range and Register	125
4.14	Short-Tube Notes	125
4.15	Right-Hand-Down Technique	125
4.16	Articulated G-sharp	126
4.17	Alternate Fingerings	126
4.18	The Palm Key Notes	127
4.19	Trill Fingerings	128
4.20	Saxophone Tuning Notes	128
4.21	Adding Keys for Pitch Adjustment	130
4.22a	Saxophone Fingering Chart page 1	136
4.22b	Saxophone Fingering Chart page 2	137
5.1	Oboe Hand Position	143
5.2	First Notes: Call and Response	144
5.3	First Notes: Disguised Long Tones	144
5.4	Rote Study for Oboe	145
5.5	Front View of Embouchure	146
5.6	Side View of Embouchure	146
5.7	Oboe Range and Octaves	152
5.8	Half-Hole and Octave Key Notes	153
5.9	Regular F, Fork F, and Left F Fingerings	153
5.10	Fork F in Context	153
5.11	Left F in Context	154
5.12	F Fingerings in Context	154
5.13	Oboe in Beginning Band Method Books	154
5.14	Right E-flat and Left E-flat Fingerings	155
5.15	Left E-flat in Context	155
5.16	The A-flat Major Scale	155
5.17	Articulated G-sharp/A-flat	156
5.18	Oboe Trill Fingerings	156
5.19	Oboe Tuning Notes	157
5.20	Labeled Oboe Reed	163
5.21	Unlabeled Oboe Reed	163
5.22	Oboe Left-Hand Exercises	165
5.23	Oboe Right-Hand Exercises	166
5.24	Oboe Second Octave Exercises	167
5.25	Oboe Left-Hand Chromatics	168
5.26	Oboe Right-Hand Chromatics	169
5.27a	Oboe Fingering Chart page 1	173
5.27b	Oboe Fingering Chart page 2	174
6.1	Front View of Embouchure	177
6.2	Side View of Embouchure	178
6.3	Parts of the Bassoon	179

6.4	Seat Strap at Front Edge	180
6.5	Small Hole to the Right in Assembly	180
6.6	Tenor Joint to Boot Joint	181
6.7	Bass Joint to Boot Joint	181
6.8	Thumb Keys Alignment	181
6.9	Unlocked Mechanism	182
6.10	Locked Mechanism	182
6.11	How to Grasp the Bocal	182
6.12	Front View of Instrument Hold	183
6.13	Side View of Instrument Hold	183
6.14	Reed Case	185
6.15	Left-Hand Thumb Keys Labeled	187
6.16	Lean of Instrument against Index Finger	187
6.17	Boot Joint Thumb Keys Labeled	188
6.18	First Notes: Call and Response	189
6.19	First Notes: Disguised Long Tones	190
6.20	Rote Study for Bassoon	190
6.21	Bassoon Range	197
6.22	Whisper Key Range	198
6.23	Half-Hole Notes	199
6.24	Left-Hand Thumb Keys Labeled	199
6.25	C-sharps	199
6.26	Thumb or Pinky?	200
6.27	Flick Key Notes	201
6.28	Flick Key Passages	201
6.29	Alternate Fingerings for E-flat	201
6.30	Tenor Clef	201
6.31a	Bassoon Trill Fingerings page 1	202
6.31b	Bassoon Trill Fingerings page 2	203
6.32	Bassoon Tuning Notes	203
6.33	Bassoon Reed Parts	208
6.34	Bassoon Reed Tip Opening	209
6.35	Bassoon Left-Hand Exercises	212
6.36	Bassoon Right-Hand Exercises	213
6.37	Bassoon Second Octave Exercises	214
6.38	Bassoon Left-Hand Chromatics	215
6.39	Bassoon Right-Hand Chromatics	216
6.40a	Bassoon Fingering Chart page 1	221
6.40b	Bassoon Fingering Chart page 2	222
6.40c	Bassoon Fingering Chart page 3	223
7.1	Stimulus Notes and Fingerings	249
7.2	First Octave Notes and Their "Overblown" Counterparts	250
7.3	Clarinet 1st Finger up Major Sixth	250

TABLES

1.1	The Sound Factors of Woodwind Instruments	4
1.2	Needs Assessment Chart	13
2.1	Performance Test: Flute Head Joint Sequence	25
3.1	Performance Test: Clarinet Embouchure	61
4.1	Performance Test: Saxophone Embouchure (mouthpiece and neck)	111
7.1	Artist Performers as Models of Tone Quality	229

Preface

The Woodwinds: Perform, Understand, Teach was written primarily for university students preparing to teach instrumental music in schools and university instructors who teach these students in a woodwind techniques course. It is relevant also to the needs of school and private music teachers who teach woodwind instruments. Its contents are essential and therefore vital to the success of the instrumental music teacher and student.

Twenty years ago as a teacher of the college woodwind techniques course, I was a bit puzzled and a lot stifled by a disconnect between the well-respected woodwind textbook I used and the in-class experiences I felt were necessary and good for my students (and soon-to-be professional music teachers). I wanted to teach in a setting where textbook reading and in-class experience were complementary, not askew, *and* at the risk of expecting too much, I wanted the college woodwind class experience to be consistent with well-founded pedagogy for 5th grader Jasmine, 8th grader Kayla, and 11th grader Blake. After all, my students were looking to put Jasmines and Kaylas and Blakes into the empty seats pictured on this book's cover—by teaching them well!

The Woodwinds is marked by an unrelenting focus on effective pedagogy, on rubbing shoulders with the greater reality that is effective teaching. Far from a collection of isolated facts, issues, and "tricks," this book provides comprehensive coverage of the instruments while keeping attention on the how of teaching in group settings. Preparing students to teach is the ultimate goal of the university woodwind class, a goal that can be reached by addressing teaching and musicianship intentionally, systematically, and consistently rather than selectively or haphazardly.

I conceived this book in the context of the university woodwind techniques course involving all five primary instruments—flute, clarinet, saxophone, oboe, and bassoon. This, however, does not preclude its usefulness in other course configurations. Having seen the need for a book that provides essential information and organizes it in ways consistent with principles of good teaching, I became focused on how effective teachers of the woodwind instruments think. What do they know, listen to, and look for in class or rehearsal? How do they make decisions and organize experiences for learners ranging from rank beginners to experienced high school musicians?

ORGANIZATION

The Woodwinds is organized in three parts.

Part 1, "Preliminaries," is designed to function as a warm-up for the semester. Conceptualized as the semester's first week experience, it gets students thinking about how the instruments work, the contexts under which woodwinds are taught in schools, how people learn, and instrument selection and assignment.

Part 2, "Teaching the Instruments," provides comprehensive coverage of essential matters pertaining to the woodwind family of musical instruments. Other books of this type also make this claim. What sets *The Woodwinds* apart is its focus on how to teach the instruments. Preparing students in the how of teaching is facilitated by book and class experiences that organize and contextualize the information around its use in teaching beginning instrumentalists.

Good teaching prioritizes active learning and therefore those who use this textbook, beginning in Week 2, are led to play the instruments. Performance supplemented by good instruction leads to understanding. With performance and understanding developing in tandem, pre-service teachers are positioned to learn to teach. This contrasts with the traditional belief that one must first understand how things work as well as name things (instruments of the family, instrument parts, registers, transpositions) before having the opportunity to play the instruments. It also stands in contrast to a false belief that the instruments can be learned without spending meaningful time performing on them.

The details of each instrument are organized by instrument according to how an effective teacher might organize experiences for novice instrumentalists. The following order of topics is strategic in that it involves learners in knowledge and skill *when* this knowledge and skill are most essential:

1. Basic embouchure and air stream.
2. Instrument assembly.
3. Hands and holding.
4. Embouchure in greater depth.
5. Articulation.
6. The mechanism—for example, instrument family, transposition, range, reeds.

Notice in the order how embouchure, hence tone production, is prioritized; it is first *and* it returns in greater depth in 4. Also notice that the many issues of knowing *about* the instruments (6), important as they are to a comprehensive knowledge, are presented *after* the primary issues of instrument performance and pedagogy are developed.

To be sure, details are plentiful. I wish, however, to avoid obscuring big ideas, principled ways of thinking, and conceptual thinking (the forest) with what is otherwise too easily viewed as a collection of isolated facts and issues (the trees). I call the forest "Foundations," and they are presented in Part 3.

Part 3, "Using Foundations for Perspective," widens the lens and provides perspective on what's essential. And Foundations can serve as an intended and much-needed review of essential matter. Teachers of woodwinds class might consider using Foundations on an as-needed basis. Foundations to a large extent are present in the details; they are just not as apparent as they are in the Foundations chapter.

Functional performance experiences for university students learning to play secondary flute, clarinet, and saxophone in class settings can be found in any number of published beginning band method books. Therefore, *The Woodwinds* does not include performance material for these instruments. University students learning the secondary instruments in one semester need a sequence of performance materials that, for practical as well as pedagogical reasons, is not different from that which is appropriate for 5th or 6th grade beginners. The concert B-flat key orientation of these beginning method books, however, is not conducive to good initial performance experiences on oboe and bassoon. For this reason, I provide five sets of performance material intended to introduce and orient the university student in a "friendly" way to oboe and bassoon.

FEATURES

1. Content organized and sequenced in ways that mirror how effective teachers think, make decisions, plan, observe, and assess in class woodwind teaching.
2. Essential information presented in two ways: 1) In necessary detail and 2) condensed into Foundations that widen the lens and provide bigger-picture perspective.
3. How people learn: Although the information provided is far from exhaustive, I like the idea of bringing a piece of the psychology course into the secondary instrument course to show, if nothing else, that when the aim is teaching and learning, the two subject areas—psychology and woodwinds—are in fact one.
4. Embouchure coverage separated into two sections: 1) Early stage issues in class instruction (small piece practice, first sounds on instrument, potential for success) and 2) tone development (what to look and listen for, teaching strategies for specific targets, reeds, vibrato). The complexities of instrument assembly, hand position, and holding, situated between the two embouchure sections, serve as distractions in early stage embouchure work—so too in beginning instruction in the schools. It is therefore wise to return to a focus on embouchure following these distractions. Furthermore, with this arrangement I wish to reinforce thinking that draws a distinction between introducing and refining. By following the step-by-step procedures suggested for making first sounds, the teacher has merely introduced embouchure and air stream. To introduce students to embouchure—to provide first day experiences in embouchure—is not to refine embouchure. The introduction is simply the first in a series of similar experiences over time that combined with much detailed observation may result in the teacher having taught and the student having learned a characteristic embouchure.
5. Performance testing and a few sample tests that help teachers teach and students learn.
6. Instrument care that extends to key functionality and quick-fix pad replacement.
7. Single and double reeds. Given the large effect that reeds have on tone, response, and pitch, the coverage of technical and practical information is ample.
8. Performance material for oboe and bassoon.
9. Study questions in each instrument chapter.

Content and ways of thinking are consistent with the pedagogical approach in *The Habits of Musicianship: A Radical Approach to Beginning Band*, a method book by Robert Duke and me. In *The Woodwinds*, I make occasional references to *The Habits of Musicianship*. To acclimate to this approach, an *Introductory Text for Teachers* is available at https://cml.music.utexas.edu/online-resources/habits-of-musicianship/introduction/.

When reading and studying the content of this book, keep in mind that all flaws in instrumental performance, whether committed by beginners or advanced students, find their solutions in a focus on the fundamental habits of expressive performance. So to know and understand the information in this book is to know and understand much about woodwind performance and teaching at all levels of sophistication.

HOW COLLEGE TEACHERS MIGHT USE THIS BOOK

In my woodwinds classes, I divide the semester into four or five segments; that is, students get direct experience with four or five woodwind instruments. Four provides a little more time per instrument; five a little less. More time is good; one fewer instrument experienced is not good. Clearly, we have to make choices. The primary in-class activity is instrument performance, with the class set up like a beginning band class.

I like the heterogeneous arrangement of instruments because of the teaching and management challenges it mirrors from many K–12 instrumental settings. This arrangement also takes into consideration the numbers of school-owned instruments we have for secondary instrument use.

The primary outside-of-class activity for students is readings from this book coupled with brief assignments and tasks designed to highlight selected content and hold students accountable for reading. Typically I assign one reading per week. Students read the assigned chapter or topic appropriate for the instrument they play in class at that time.

In the brief experience that one semester in anything provides, it is important for college teachers to be clear-headed about priorities. What information and skill is essential? Of the information provided in a book, what do you choose to highlight and develop, what do you "mention," and what doesn't make into your class at all?

"Preliminaries" is a good first week endeavor—all of it or some of it. You will find information in this section that makes a compelling first-day class experience, even before the students acquire the book. By the end of Week 1 and certainly the start of Week 2, students have secondary instruments in hand.

Among the sections in "Teaching the Instruments," Early Stage Tone, Tone Development, and Mechanism are mainstay readings. Much of the information in these readings is new to my students and important enough to be learned well. If you, the teacher, adopt the pedagogical approaches presented in the book, readings and in-class activities will complement each other. This consistency makes sense to my students; what makes sense generates buy-in from them.

You may find it unnecessary to assign readings of Assembly/Disassembly, Hand Position, and Tonguing because these processes are suitably dealt with experientially in class. The information is available in written form in each instrument chapter, but I use it and encourage its use only on an as needed basis or for review during the semester or during future teaching.

I find space in the syllabus for class coverage and readings on the single and double reeds (found in the Mechanism sections of each chapter), given the large effect that reeds have on tone, response, and pitch in woodwind study.

I spend extra class time with select sections; for example, Refining Flute Tone, the various Tuning and Intonation sections, Clarinet Cross-Fingerings coupled with Range and Register, and Potential for Success (oboe and bassoon).

Rather than make all of the "Foundations" required reading, I pick and choose foundations on which to focus and use these portions of the book in class as a way to highlight and reinforce.

ACKNOWLEDGMENTS

I have been incredibly fortunate to cross paths with people who have inspired and shaped my thinking about many things musical and pedagogical. Relative to *The Woodwinds* I owe a debt of gratitude to: Joseph Edwards, Alexander (Sandy) Stuart, and my father Donald Byo, all outstanding musicians and teachers associated with Youngstown (OH) State University; Clifford Madsen, Bob Duke, and my sweet wife Jane Cassidy, all outstanding musicians and teachers associated with the Florida State University; DaLaine Chapman, Janice Crews, Christian Gonzalez, Brant Karrick, Javier Rodriquez, Katy Strickland, and Mark Waymire, who were willing users of this book in previous forms; the terrific student musicians of the Wooster (OH) City Schools with whom I worked and learned so much from as a young teacher from 1978 to 1985; the many wonderful music majors with whom I have worked at Louisiana State University, 1988–present; Paige Jarreau and Abby South, photography; Danielle Emerich and Andrew Owen, music notation; and Constance Ditzel, senior editor with Routledge, whose guidance through the publication process was invaluable.

James Byo
October 2015

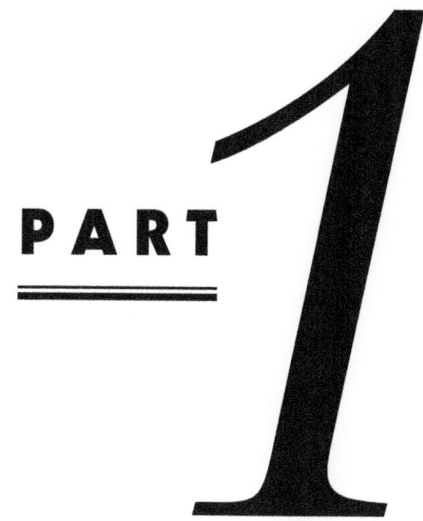

PART 1

Preliminaries

CHAPTER 1

Woodwinds in Diverse Contexts

We begin with relatively brief coverage of five topic areas, which I hope will provide a helpful, bigger-picture perspective before we dive into the details of the instruments and teaching. I view these topics as entry points. The first, "How Woodwind Instruments Work," is an entry point in acoustics. The second, "The Contexts of Woodwind Performance and Teaching in Schools," asks you to consider the great many circumstances under which instruments are taught in the schools and how this variety is both a challenge and a potential joy to the teacher. The third, "How People Learn," is intended to prime your pump, so to speak, about how teaching works best when it is consistent with what we know about how learners learn. The fourth, "How *You* Learn," asks you to be a bit reflective about how you might best teach yourself in the woodwind class. Last, "Instrument Selection and Assignment" provides some background to the practical matters of getting students on instruments, but also opens a line of thought into the processes of creating and sustaining student interest in instrumental music.

HOW WOODWIND INSTRUMENTS WORK

If your non-musical but curious grandfather were to ask "What makes a saxophone sound like a saxophone and not like another instrument?" what would you say? To satisfy his curiosity, you'd like to have an answer that is accurate without being overly complex. Wade through just a bit of complexity with me. In a few pages, when you come out the other end, you'll be in a position to impress your grandfather. Here we go.

Acoustically, a wind instrument sounds as it does because of its shape (cylindrical or conical), the nature of its pipe (closed or open), its fixed and variable lengths (length varying according to fingering used), the diameter of the bore, the sound source (edge tone, single reed, double reed), and the material of which the instrument is made. Interestingly, the impact of material on tone quality is less about the material itself (wood, brass, plastic) and more about the capacity of the material to be shaped to precise specifications in the construction process. Material is no more than a secondary factor in explaining why wind instruments sound as they do.

You see in Table 1.1 that the flute is the only open pipe within the woodwind family. The flute when played is open at both ends. The other woodwinds have one end open (the bell) and the other end closed, the reed end being closed by the player's embouchure.

Tone is produced when low-pressure, atmospheric air inside the bore of an instrument is activated by high-pressure air supplied by the player. The edge of the flute embouchure hole separates the air

TABLE 1.1 The Sound Factors of Woodwind Instruments

Instrument	Shape	Pipe	Sound Source	Body Material
Flute[1]	Cylindrical	Open	Edge	Solid silver Nickel silver[2]
Clarinet	Cylindrical	Closed	Single reed	Grenadilla Rosewood Plastic[3]
Saxophone[4]	Conical	Closed	Single reed	Brass[5]
Oboe	Conical	Closed	Double reed	Grenadilla Plastic
Bassoon	Conical	Closed	Double reed	Maple Plastic

Notes
1. To beautify and prevent corrosion, flutes are finished with nickel or silver plating.
2. Nickel silver metal is an alloy of copper, nickel, and zinc.
3. Plastics (thermoplastic and polypropylene) are formed from resins that become plastic when heated and cooled.
4. Saxophones are finished with acrylic lacquer or silver plating.
5. Brass is an alloy of copper and zinc.

stream in two, with tightly alternating episodes of air going in and out of the head joint, creating what we know as vibration. Likewise, the thin and thus malleable tip of a reed responds to tension in the embouchure and speed of air stream by oscillating back and forth against the facing of a mouthpiece (single reed) and blade to blade (double reed). The interaction of high-pressure air (the air stream) and low-pressure air (the atmosphere inside the mouthpiece or double reed) causes the reed opening to close. This increasingly smaller opening changes the nature of the air pressure inside the mouthpiece, which causes the reed to open again. These alternating pressure differences cause the reed to close and open very rapidly. If the clarinet or saxophone reed is not dampened properly by the embouchure (i.e., if embouchure pressures are not correct or at least "ballpark" correct), the reed may vibrate at its own resonant frequency, producing what we recognize as a squeak.

Timbre (pronounced *tamber*) refers to quality of sound. What distinguishes clarinet timbre from flute timbre? One tone, any tone, is really a combination of many tones that sound together in a unique combination of individual-tone strengths to form what we hear as one tone or one timbre. This combination of many tones occurs in a prescribed pattern of intervals that form a harmonic series. A harmonic series on the fundamental C is presented in Figure 1.1. It shows 16 harmonics.

About the individual-tone strengths, the cylindrical bore of the clarinet is closed at one end, thus making odd numbered partials sound louder than even numbered ones. The cylindrical bore of the flute is open at both ends, thus having a different effect—the even numbered partials are stronger than they are for clarinet. The conical bore and closed pipe of the saxophone produce still another distribution of even and odd numbered partial strengths. Why do instruments sound as they do? Primarily because shape of bore (cylindrical or conical), nature of pipe (closed or open), and source of vibration (single reed and mouthpiece, double reed, or edge) affect in different ways the strength of the individual partials.

Vibrato is applied as a standard technique to both enhance and project tone on the flute, saxophone, oboe, and bassoon, and stylize tone on jazz clarinet. A diaphragmatic vibrato is commonly used on flute, oboe, and bassoon. Jaw vibrato is common on the saxophone. Vibrato is not viewed as a standard

FIGURE 1.1 Harmonic Series Overtones

technique for classical clarinet in the United States, though it is used judiciously by some players. Clarinet vibrato in classical music finds greater acceptance outside the United States.

You might be thinking that understanding how tone happens is no big deal when one views characteristic tone as *one* thing—for example, characteristic saxophone tone. What's a saxophone sound like? A saxophone, of course. But Griffin Campbell gets a "characteristic" saxophone tone that is quite different from Debra Richtmeyer's "characteristic" tone. There are distinct timbre differences in both of these characteristic tones. Likewise, the tone of an artist-level French oboist is very different from that of an artist-level American oboist. How can this be when there are so many common factors among musicians—bore shape, pipe condition, bore diameter, material, sound source?

Answer: Different timbres exist in large part because one performer's use of embouchure and air stream inhibits or stimulates certain partials within the range allowed by the instrument more so than another performer's, and because the common factor of sound source—for example, the single reed and mouthpiece—is not such a common factor after all. That is, one reed style and mouthpiece setup can be very different from another.

What should a player do to get a better sound or a different sound? Stimulate certain partials or dampen certain partials or change reed style.

To your grandfather's question "What makes the saxophone sound like a saxophone?" you might say: The saxophone is shaped like a gradually expanding cone. When played, it is closed at the reed end with the player's mouth creating the close. These two things—conical shape and one closed end—make the saxophone sound very different from a flute, which has two open ends, and a clarinet, which has a cylindrical shape. Back to the saxophone—conical shape, closed end, and a single reed sound source combine to give the saxophone its characteristic sound among all wind instruments. When high-pressure air blown by the player interacts with low-pressure air inside the mouthpiece, the reed vibrates, causing the instrument to respond as only a saxophone does.

THE CONTEXTS OF WOODWIND PERFORMANCE AND TEACHING IN SCHOOLS

Woodwind teaching in K–12 schools happens in an amazing variety of contexts. Changing context and the concomitant need for teachers to adapt are facts of a teaching life. What teachers know and do one way will often need to be adjusted to fit a number of different teaching contexts. There are parallels in other professions. A pro baseball player whose been squaring up every fastball thrown his way will eventually see a steady diet of off-speed pitches from wily pitchers. In this off-speed context, the batter will have to make adjustments in order to succeed—a fact of baseball life. Adjustment is a fact of woodwind teaching life.

While reading this textbook, remind yourself from time to time that your teaching will be most effective when it is adaptable. What you learn in this book and in class will be most useful when you take the fundamentals presented one way—for example, the fundamentals of flute tone production—and consider that they become slightly to very different things when experienced by 6th grader Allison, 6th grader Loren, 6th grader Jason, and in various other contexts. Check out these contexts for flute tone production:

- in a class of six beginning flute players
- in a full band of 55 beginners
- in a low SES urban school
- in a wealthy suburban school
- in a 30-minute group flute lesson once per week
- on five 50-minute full band rehearsals per week
- in a 90-minute block
- when she has private lessons
- when she does not
- on a well-adjusted instrument
- on a borrowed instrument with leaky pads
- with a perceptive, motivated student
- with a student who needs you to teach them to be perceptive and motivated
- in a minute before class as you "steal" time with one beginner.

You can imagine how across these 14 contexts, the fundamental aspects of flute embouchure stay the same, but students' personal interactions with embouchure and tone production vary. The teacher who is ready to address this variety is adaptable. *How* do we teach embouchure when the student does not practice? *How much* flute embouchure can we cover in a rehearsal of a full band? *How fast* can we move through embouchure on one rehearsal per week? *When* do we move on to the next step in the sequence when some students seem ready and others do not?

Can you imagine coaching a saxophone quartet? A clarinet choir? A mixed woodwind trio? The sax section of a jazz band? How does a woodwind quintet seat itself? What are the challenges of the woodwind section of a school orchestra? A fine high school flutist is preparing the Chaminade Concertino. How can you be helpful? Same question for the bassoonist preparing the first movement of the Mozart Concerto. What do you do on Day 1 of the 6th grade clarinet class? Yes, there is an amazing variety of teaching contexts to look forward to as an instrumental music teacher.

In a music teacher preparation program where there is a finite amount of time and opportunity, you cannot possibly experience directly more than a handful of the various contexts that confront music teachers daily. Keep in mind, however, that contexts exist in and around you no matter where you are—in class, in rehearsals, in lessons, in master classes, in fieldwork, in student teaching. Keep your eyes open for them. Be aware. Notice. Imagine yourself applying what you know in different situations.

HOW PEOPLE LEARN

Having spent many years as a student in classes, lessons, and rehearsals, you might think that the meat of teaching is in what the *teacher* does:

- The teacher demonstrates the embouchure on the flute head joint.
- The teacher, with a watchful eye and keen ear, observes clarinet tone and hand position.

- The teacher organizes instruction into logical and consistent sequences of student activity.
- The teacher addresses the group, but also makes numerous individual contacts to assess progress.
- The teacher determines the nature and amount of repetition necessary for skill development.
- The teacher knows and applies various teaching strategies necessary to solve performance problems.
- The teacher . . . The teacher . . . The teacher.

What about the student? We seem to think much less about how students or people in general learn. Perhaps we should call them learners instead of students as a reminder that effective teachers look to connect teaching techniques with the intellectual, skill-based, and social *needs* of learners. This seems an obvious fact of education, but too often it is violated as teachers prioritize "teaching" and place far secondary importance on how people learn.

In reading this text, you may in fact perceive an emphasis on how to *teach*; how people *learn* is addressed more implicitly than explicitly. Consider that the teacher actions described in the above bulleted points are *informed by* how people learn. However, because the focus has been on teacher actions (and your focus is on becoming an effective teacher), you might not notice this how-people-learn underpinning.

Playing an instrument involves what psychologists call procedural memory, the memory involved in organized body movements (e.g., making a tone on the clarinet). Procedural memory is about "knowing how" to do things, which is different from declarative memory's knowing of facts, information, concepts, rules. Playing an instrument involves motor skills (procedural memory). These motor skills are supported and informed by the "knowing" involved in declarative memory. So how do children learn in contexts that involve both procedural and declarative memory?

What follows is a selection of ways that people learn, all germane to woodwind teaching, and all related or derived from the first one—people learn by doing. Abundant credit goes to Johann Heinrich Pestalozzi (1746–1827), the progressive Swiss educator, whose fundamental ideas remain current in today's playing field of pedagogical thought.

People learn by doing

Obvious, right? But remember classes in your past that were dominated by teacher talk and little student doing, other than sitting, listening, taking notes, and memorizing. In these classes, you weren't necessarily "doing" the subject matter; you were taking notes. You weren't doing science in the way that scientists do science or history in the way that historians do history.

There is lots of evidence that, although we learn by doing, teachers find it attractive to try to "talk" students into learning. So to know that people learn by doing and to devise class and rehearsal experiences consistent with this aphorism is no trivial thing!

For example, in leading novice clarinet players through a sequence of embouchure formation steps, that is, in having them do the components of embouchure in a sensible order, at first slowly, thoughtfully, reflectively, and repeatedly across many days, you "do" them into positive tone quality habits. The alternative is dominated by teacher talk. The teacher takes students through the step-by-step sequence a few times across the first days, then, expecting them to "know it by now," reminds and cajoles and corrects and encourages; in other words, tries to *talk* them into doing.

Think about this. Notice the not-so-subtle and important difference between these two approaches. In the first, the teacher structures repeated experiences in organized and thoughtful doing, putting a premium on correct repetitions while students are in the teacher's presence. In the alternative, the class experience is quite random as the teacher "puts out fires" as they arise. The teacher tells students,

"We did this yesterday. Remember? You can do this. . . . No, no, Jonathan you have to sit up the whole time and make sure your teeth are on top of the mouthpiece. Cecilia, your reed's on crooked. Jennifer, put more mouthpiece in your mouth. Michael, don't touch Steven."

This is not to say that teacher talk is always a bad thing. In the lecture approach, it is a way to get lots of good information disseminated quickly. Some amount of lecture (teacher talks/students listen) is basic to all formalized teaching. The point here is that there is a tendency for teachers to over-talk and for students to under-do. Let's ask ourselves: "When is teacher talk necessary and when is it not?" When can we minimize talk by structuring do-oriented experiences that rely on some teacher guidance, cuing, and non-verbal communication rather than many words of explanation? Many of the procedures in this text are conceptualized this way.

People Learn by Experiencing Things before Understanding Things (Experience *before* Theory)

Sound illogical? This is about timing. When should students be taught the understanding part of what they do? In many instances, students learn best when the teacher gets them to *do* something *before* explaining the "theory" of what they are doing. The explanation may come 5 minutes or 5 days from now; regardless, the explanation will not "reason" students into doing the thing in question. When the explanation comes after rather than before the doing, it tends to be "stickier" (slang for "I understand"). The experience provides the context needed for understanding the explanation.

The "backward approach" to teaching tonguing, presented in the clarinet and saxophone chapters, is an example of "experience before theory." A series of structured activities leads students to finding the tip of the reed with the tip of the tongue and achieving a legato tongue almost without realizing that they are using their tongues to articulate. This contrasts with a more typical approach in which teachers explain and explain about tonguing with no student action until the end of the experience, oftentimes resulting in multiple failed attempts at starting notes with the tongue. A good deal of backtracking is necessary to get many students up to speed.

People Learn in a Structured Environment

Well, they also learn in an unstructured environment. But since you'll be teaching students in large, often heterogeneous groups, let's come down on the side of more rather than less structure. In a structured environment, teaching/learning experiences are organized in ways that make sense. People learn when the process makes sense. The teaching/learning sequence for flute head joint practice, presented in the flute chapter, is ordered sensibly—in a way that, if used consistently, leads to multiple correct repetitions, which in turn leads to correct habit formation.

People Learn in an Environment Free of Interference

Needless interference or distraction complicates. You know this, having been distracted by a misbehaving student in class. You woodwind majors have been distracted by a bad reed, you brass majors by a rangy part, you string majors by a nasty shift, or you percussion majors by many measures of rest in the part. Less obvious and often overlooked is the interference unwittingly produced by the teacher. Some/many students cannot screen out what is unimportant or irrelevant, so they can't access what's important. Inconsistency or lack of clarity in teacher approach distracts. Too much teacher talk distracts. Too many skills or thoughts at one time interfere. Lack of appropriate and necessary expressive nuance in teacher speech interferes. Feedback mistakes on the part of the teacher interfere. Children learn by having opportunity to establish new information and skill in working memory before other information has a chance to get mixed up with or push aside the target information or skill.

People Learn Best When Approached as Individuals

Avoid labels that standardize children; for example, the middle school child. There is no standard middle school child. They are all different in terms of what they bring to class and what they need from class. Some will need more repetitions, more explanations, more opportunities, more time than others. Expect this. This is one place where you will show your skill as a teacher. How will you reach individuals in the group environment? Ask and answer the question, "What do I want my students to know and do, ultimately without my assistance?" Then ask, "What do I want Lisa to know and do, ultimately without my assistance?" By answering these questions, you have your goals; now work like a dog to accomplish them. Throughout this paragraph, you see elements of Russian psychologist Lev Vygotsky's scaffolding, a condition under which the teacher provides necessary support for the student en route to creating an independent learner, one who ultimately operates effectively without that support.

People Learn When Complex Skills are Separated into Their Component Skills

Clarinet embouchure is a complex skill. People learn this big skill by first succeeding with its component skills. Component skills develop and then merge through small approximations, practice opportunities (including those in the presence of the teacher), and shaping (teacher feedback provided to individual students).

People Learn through Correct Repetition

They learn when repetition has been done mindfully. As a teacher, what must you do, how must you *be* to establish conditions that promote mindfulness? How much repetition or experience is necessary to lift the skill or knowledge out of the fragile category? Repetition of an action or thought can lead to automaticity. Automatic behavior is often desirable. We aim to create conditions that enable the bassoon player to immediately and automatically (without thinking) form the ideal embouchure. There is, however, an undesirable side of automaticity, that is, when that automatic bassoon embouchure doesn't leave room for the flexibility necessary to change the embouchure when it must adjust for the naturally sharp pitch of half-hole G.

People Learn/Remember When They Have Learned Well in the First Place

Most things are forgotten because they were never firmly learned. The best way to enhance memory is to make sure students know and can do the essential features of the task or skill. This necessitates frequent assessment of understanding and skill development, and re-teaching.

People Learn Not Only When Material is Introduced but When It is Re-taught

Re-teaching, or that which happens *after* the introduction of material, is at the heart of teaching. This is when the teacher makes numerous brief individual contacts to reinforce and correct and provides frequent opportunities for correct repetition. I like re-teaching over review because review carries with it the connotation that "my students should know this because I taught it to them already." The problem with this thinking is that students are not ready to review what they have mastered so little of. If new material was recently introduced, it is smart to assume that it has not been learned; therefore, it has not been taught.

People Learn Best That Which They Put to Use

I'll explain by telling a story. "Little Bird" is a melody I wrote for beginning band. You can find the score on page 92 at https://cml.music.utexas.edu/assets/pdf/habits/Habits-Music-SCORE.pdf.

Very soon after my 6th graders are able to "find their way" through the notes and rhythms, I ask "What does the title mean?" It's about a bird—a little bird. A pre-flight little bird in a nest. The score provides *graceful* as a descriptor. How does one play in "little bird in a nest" style? What do we do to create a graceful sound? This is not just the old stand-by *legato*; it's *graceful*! We get a good conversation going about conveying to an audience that idea in our playing.

We focus on the five four-measure phrases. As students explain their thinking, they seem to understand the phrases as complete thoughts, each needing to be played as a unified whole and with direction. Without being told, they demonstrate a good sense for where it would be appropriate (and inappropriate) to take a breath. The last four measures provide interesting options for expressive performance. I try to take advantage of the programmatic nature of the melody. In this setting my students do as well or better than I as they function as their own teachers. I guide just a little bit.

Students are *using* the concepts and ideas presented in the melody by thinking about them, talking about, interacting with each other and me about them, experimenting with them, and then working to reproduce the concepts and ideas in sound for the benefit of real or imaginary listeners and for our own pleasure.

People Learn from Their Peers

In 5th and 6th grade, students are becoming less dependent on their parents and more dependent on their peers for support. Teachers should not remain on the "sidelines" concerning peer interactions. Don't leave this important area to chance. Foster positive, friendly peer interactions. When you rehearse the saxophones alone, do you *really* want everyone else fingering through their parts, or do you want them learning from their peers? How could you "structure" this learning? Really think about that!

When considering how children learn, one would hope to come to grips with the age-old aphorism, that teachers should teach *children*, not music or clarinet or math or English. You get it, right? Actually, teachers teach children's brains. Hmm. How does the brain learn?

HOW *YOU* LEARN

Having just considered how students learn, it's a good time to think about how *you* learn, that is, how you might best learn in a 15-week university course in which you will want to develop skill playing the woodwind instruments and acquire knowledge important for effective music teaching.

How *do* you learn? Well, you know better than I. Let the following serve as reminders.

1. Skills develop through practice—consistent, correct practice. So just do it. Respect the instruments. Respect the class. Respect yourself. Show that you are disciplined, organized, and capable of leading yourself, which is unquestionably a prerequisite for leading others.

2. Start early. Don't wait to get serious about practicing until the second week of a semester segment. By then, you may be too far behind to catch up.

3. Don't underestimate the amount and quality of secondary instrument practice that will be necessary for you to play each instrument well at an intermediate level. This is not a "show and tell" appreciation class. This is where you learn your craft; it's about your future if what you want to do is teach instrumental music.

4. Don't limit your practice to big blocks of time in your schedule. Big practice blocks are great, but you won't have enough of them. Take advantage of brief moments. You've got 20 minutes now. Don't waste it. Get the clarinet out and immediately launch into thoughtful work on keeping the lower lip firm against the teeth while tonguing.

5. What's your plan? Do you have a plan for this practice session? Are you working on something, or just winging it (pretend practice)? For this class, what's important?

    - You must make a characteristic tone with embouchure and air stream fundamentals in place.
    - You must hold the instrument correctly.
    - You must articulate with relative ease (legato and staccato).
    - You must control tone while playing loud and soft.
    - You must play accurately and expressively within a two-octave range of correctly fingered notes.

6. Practice, beyond playing through what you can already play well, is about decision making, problem preventing, and problem solving. Teaching is about decision making, problem preventing, and problem solving. So is rehearsing. So is being a leader of people. Perhaps the best indicator of whether you've got the stuff to be a good teacher, rehearsal conductor, and leader is your ability to practice effectively when you're alone in a room with an instrument you can't play right now. How can you "practice" others if you can't "practice" yourself? So what are you going to do *right now* to move yourself forward on this instrument?

7. Do you have practice discipline? Only the best among you have this. Can you develop it if it's not already there?

8. Got a legitimate persistent problem you can't solve on your own? Get help now from your instructor or a knowledgeable other. Don't wait.

9. It is important to be able to play the notes, but good secondary instrument practice is about much more than just notes. Unfortunately, many college music majors don't know what to do in practice if it's not about note-chasing. Which leads to this—much of your practice should be about tone development (details of embouchure, use of air stream, and tonguing). Tone has a major impact on intonation. There is nothing more important in instrumental performance than tone quality.

10. Do you play the secondary instruments with the same concerns you have when you play your primary instrument? You should.

    - Do you play with a convincing legato tongue?
    - Do you play with an eye toward phrases in music? Or are you breathing in the middle of a four-measure phrase?
    - Are you shaping the phrase according to what the notes "tell you to do," or are you "just playing?" Can you show that you can play the range of *piano* to *forte* on the secondary instruments?

- Are you playing the piece at an appropriate tempo?
- Are you hearing intonation deficiencies in your playing? What are you doing about them?
- Is your rhythm accurate?
- Have you worked out the awkward fingering?

These are *constants* in music. They apply always. They matter always.

11. The semester may "begin" five times for you in this class. There are five instruments to be learned. This is different from other courses, where you begin once, get a feel for what's going on, find a routine, and then ride it out to the end. So accept the challenge. Be disciplined. Be persistent. Lead yourself. Teach yourself.

12. On cognitive concepts such as transposition, flute lip-across technique, the lower lip in the clarinet embouchure, cross-fingerings, double reed crow, tuning and intonation, and more, test your knowledge by explaining it out loud to yourself or a friend. This reveals both clear and muddled thinking.

INSTRUMENT SELECTION AND ASSIGNMENT

"Instrument Selection and Assignment" is a traditional and cryptic reference. I used to like it. Today, I prefer this title: Creating and Sustaining Student Interest is a Process.

By process, I mean teacher thought and action that are focused, aware, opportunistic, and ongoing. It's our job to drum up business—make customers for instrumental music. In this section, we will think about:

- the beginning (and other) instruments
- a process for needs assessment
- attrition as a motivator
- choice or selection of instrument as a factor in retention and attrition
- instrument demonstration and follow-up activities.

The Beginning (and Other) Instruments

In school band settings, where students are taught in groups, the beginning woodwind instruments are, most appropriately, the flute, clarinet, and alto saxophone. The piccolo, oboe, bassoon, low clarinets, and low saxophones are not typical beginning instruments in schools. The double reed instruments pose reed and, in the case of bassoon, size challenges. Low clarinet and low saxophone players are typically converted from clarinet and alto saxophone. Piccolo players first become good flute players.

When students add or switch to these other instruments in the second or third year of study, after having had a solid start on a beginning instrument, they come to the new instrument with the advantages of a developed embouchure and air stream. They are also bigger and more mature young people. Ordinarily, students who play oboe, bassoon, and the low reeds use school-owned instruments, of which there is a finite supply. The music program cannot afford to have non-contributors on these instruments—those who are not committed to or capable of succeeding on the instrument. To this end, it is wise to make decisions about who should switch to what instrument based on a student's one- to two-year track record on a beginning instrument.

TABLE 1.2 Needs Assessment Chart

	Fl	Ob	Cl	BCl	Bsn	AS	TS	BS	Hn	Trpt	Trb	Euph	Tuba	Perc
5th	21	0	31	0	0	13	0	0	0	24	10	2	0	17
6th	15	2	25	1	1	10	1	0	3	18	9	3	2	13
7th	14	1	18	1	2	9	1	1	4	10	7	2	2	9
8th	14	0	17	2	1	8	1	0	3	9	8	1	1	10
9th	10	0	12	2	2	6	2	1	3	9	8	2	1	8
10th	5	1	6	0	1	3	0	0	2	7	4	2	2	5
11th	4	2	7	2	1	4	2	1	3	3	2	1	1	5
12th	4	1	4	1	1	3	1	1	4	5	3	1	2	4

A Process for Needs Assessment

The needs assessment chart shown in Table 1.2 is a way to keep track of the numbers of students playing instruments in each grade. The numbers are collected system-wide from printed programs of year-ending concerts. As an example, this is an arbitrary program that started 118 beginning students in 5th grade and has two high school bands. The chart provides a picture of attrition, changes in numbers based on instrument switches, areas of numerical strength, and areas of need. Notice in this example, the healthy nature of the bassoon area. Assuming that all continue to play into high school, three years from now there will be six bassoonists from grades 9 through 12. With two high school bands, these numbers are good. In oboe, however, three years from now there will be only three players, and two of them will be freshmen. Work needs to be done to recruit an oboe player or two from the current 8th or 9th grade class.

Attrition as a Motivator

Consider also that the numbers in the chart indicate 70% attrition from grade 5 through grade 12. Though the example is arbitrary, a 70% attrition rate is not out of line with reality. Many school instrumental music programs show 70% or more attrition across six or seven years. Use this unpleasant fact as motivation to be good at creating and sustaining interest in band. Young people opt out of band for many reasons, some very legitimate. We teachers should work hard to create conditions (those we control) that reduce this 70% attrition figure substantially.

Choice or Selection of Instrument as a Factor in Retention and Attrition

The approach advocated in this book is one that exhorts teachers to understand the importance of and take real responsibility for getting young people started on the "right" beginning instrument, such that the pleasure typically associated with the first weeks of instrument study extends into subsequent months and years. Why has the pleasure been extended? Because students, having been solidly grounded in the habits of musicianship made possible in part by personally "friendly" instruments, recognize and take pleasure in their ability to play with beautiful tone, facile articulation, and ample range and finger technique.

For the instrumental music experience to be rewarding to larger numbers of students, teachers must be centrally involved in matching student to instrument. Advise parents, and make this advice specific to their child. Subtly guide students to "choose" the instrument for which you see them having the most potential. Student choice has a wide-ranging definition—from choice that is uninformed or feebly informed to that which has been shaped by a knowledgeable and skillful music teacher. Students and parents can be "taught" to prefer and feel like they had choice in the matter. Student choice counts; it is legitimate, and often students choose a good instrument for themselves. But in fact too many students are allowed too much free rein in determining what instrument they play. They "choose" instruments that pose immediate or eventual challenges that limit their ability to be successful. There would be far fewer mistakes (right child–wrong instrument) if teachers were to have less faith in the "practice can overcome just about anything" aphorism. No doubt, to play an instrument well requires effort and practice, but something's not right if "tedious" is how the first days, weeks, and months are described because the student can't make a small enough flute aperture or get close to a good clarinet embouchure.

The selection and assignment of instruments is a topic that falls under the recruiting umbrella. Recruiting is not a once a year thing. Recruiting happens always. You are recruiting when you make a student feel good by successfully teaching him something or by having an upbeat chat with him in the hallway or by taking advantage of the fun in music education—positive recruiting. You are also recruiting when you are not able to teach something successfully or you have an unpleasant exchange with a student—negative recruiting. If the "word on the street" about you is a positive one, parents will want their children to be a part of your program. And the word *will* get out! Your students will talk to their parents, to their friends, and to their siblings about you in one of three ways—positive, neutral, or negative. How do you want to be viewed? Decide, then make it happen! View recruiting as an everyday thing.

Instrument Demonstration and Follow-Up Activities

Collecting the troops

Middle school 6th graders are best considered for band in the spring of the 5th grade so that schedule makers know who needs to be scheduled for band class. So in March of the 5th grade year, do an *instrument demonstration* for every 5th grader. You may demonstrate the instruments yourself. You may do it in combination with high school or middle school band students (individuals or small ensembles or the whole marching band!). Or music stores are eager to provide a person to do the demonstrating for you. If you have or can predict low interest for a certain instrument, structure your demonstration to highlight this instrument. Advertise. Send a recruiting letter home with students—one that relates the benefits of music participation and includes a summary of the music program, beginning level through high school. Make this information available on a website.

Instrument selection or assignment

Make *individual contact* with all prospective instrumental students. For example, you might pull five 5th graders out of class at a time, and take them to a room with a display of new beginning instruments. One at a time, ask what they are interested in playing, and try them out on one or more instruments. Spend a few minutes with each student teaching him/her to get a small piece sound (flute head joint, clarinet mouthpiece and barrel, saxophone mouthpiece and neck). You have three concerns—student preference, goodness-of-fit between student and instrument, and balanced instrumentation. If you detect a physical condition that might predict lack of success on the preferred instrument, encourage the student to consider a different instrument. If a student appears physically set for more than one instrument, encourage him or her in the direction of where you need players for a balanced instrumentation.

Instrument recommendations

Communicate with parents your instrument recommendations for each student. Include information about instrument rental, what method book to buy, when school lessons begin, and a return stub for parents to sign if the student plans on joining the program in the fall.

Instrument selection/assignment—again

Ideally, there is a second layer of instrument selection/assignment that takes place during the first several weeks of school lessons. In the approach advocated in this text and *The Habits of Musicianship* (Duke & Byo), the first several weeks involve no music stands and no method book from which to play exercises and melodies. These weeks instead place a premium on small piece practice as a necessary and vital precursor to playing the fully assembled instrument. The time spent playing on small pieces is informative regarding individual students' abilities and tendencies. As long as students are playing only on these small pieces, those who continue to struggle without success are often more amenable to consider trying a different, and perhaps more suitable, small piece. "I've never actually tried to play a flute, but I can tell from this head joint that I'm not happy. Let me blow into something else and see how it works."

Small piece practice leads to first experiences with the fully assembled instrument that again involve no method book or music reading. Instead, initial work with the instrument is designed to lead students to the "real" first notes of top line F for flute, chalumeau register G for clarinet, and 4th line D for sax. Unconventional, perhaps even radical, these first notes are strategic. By starting on these "longer-tube" notes (and in the key of F concert), the instruments demand that students use a more rather than less correct embouchure, air stream, and hand position. All instruments start with notes that require use of both hands.

Short-tube notes can happen on less than optimal air stream and embouchure quotients, leading to incorrect habits of performance that have to be corrected later when the "more demanding" register is introduced. Approached as such, the first several weeks continue to provide evidence of a student's suitability for the instrument. Ease of playing these starting notes is another indicator of which instrument is most appropriate for the beginner. Rather than students selecting instruments based only on sound, appearance, and a brief trial, students experience an extended trial period that provides substantial information about goodness-of-fit.

So let's return to your role as interest creator and sustainer. You build interest in the large-scale instrument demonstration, keep it alive in the personal contact setting, make it palpable in your contacts with parents, and set the stage for sustaining it with the choice of a kid-friendly instrument.

PART 2
Teaching the Instruments

CHAPTER 2

Flute

FLUTE TONE AND EARLY STAGE EMBOUCHURE

Small Piece

Teaching embouchure in the early stage involves the small piece of the flute. The small piece is the head joint. It requires no assembly. The instrument case should be placed correct-side up on the lap or on the floor. On the floor, it is sometimes easier for young, small students who kneel or sit. Open the case. Remove the head joint. Close the case.

Embouchure Characteristics

1. Line of lips is parallel to line of flute.
2. Flute forms a right angle to the face.
3. Lower lip covers one-third of the embouchure hole.
4. Small aperture.
5. Lower lip is relaxed.
6. Upper lip is slightly firm.
7. Minimal head joint pressure against lip.
8. Jaw down (causing mouth corners to resemble a pouting shape).

Air Stream Characteristics

1. Blow *straight ahead* toward the opposite edge of the embouchure hole. The edge splits the air stream. The flute's tone is described as an edge tone.
2. Blow *fast* air through a small aperture.

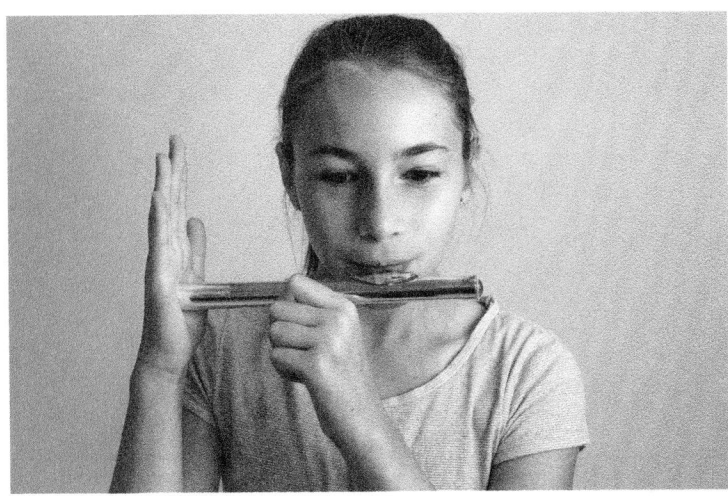

FIGURE 2.1
Head Joint with Plugged End
(Produced by Paige Jarreau at Paige's Photos)

Teaching Embouchure

Early embouchure work should involve the head joint alone and characteristics 1 through 7 listed above. Jaw down can be introduced later. As shown in Figure 2.1, first sounds are made with the end of the head joint covered (or plugged) by the palm of the hand. This should produce an approximate A 440.

For ballpark placement, center the embouchure hole on closed lips with the head held erect. Then role the head joint out until the hole is "looking at" the ceiling, but with about one-third of the hole covered by a relaxed lower lip. Aim the air stream so that approximately half of the air goes into the hole and half goes across the hole.

For more precise head joint placement, that is, to find the sweet spot, experiment by moving the head joint slightly up or down, right or left, or by rolling it slightly in or out. The student produces a tone with each adjustment, and the teacher and student determine the quality of each tone, aiming to find the most characteristic of head joint tones. Do not underestimate the need for this type of experimenting in the beginning stages. Too often teachers are easily satisfied with a flute tone that is breathy or hollow when a little experimentation and persistence could result in more focus and a richer resonance.

In working with a group of beginning flutists trying to make first sounds, your approach might consist of the following sequence of instruction. Embedded within this sequence are specific strategies (in italics) designed to jump-start success.

Sequence for Making First Sounds in Group Instruction

Note that the first three activities are done without the head joint. In a class of mixed instruments, all students can do numbers 1 through 3.

1. Without the head joint, demonstrate a sustained silent P consonant by holding the head erect and blowing a cooling soup stream of air at the palm of the hand held in front of the face. The air stream is begun with the P consonant. The air speed and lip shape should be roughly the same as when one cools hot soup. Following your lead, students imitate. During repetitions, *focus student attention* on the pop of the P consonant (the air stream blows the lips open) and on small aperture (not allowing the lips to open big). The lower lip should be quite relaxed (soft).

2. Demonstrate *blowing cool air up an arm* held vertically in front of the face by sliding the lower lip out against a stationary upper lip. Students imitate. Repeat until students get the right idea. Keep the head erect and still. The soft lower lip moves out in response to increased air speed. This strategy is good for establishing a soft lower lip and slightly firm upper lip. It is good for setting up the lip position necessary to play in the flute's second and third octaves.

3. Facing the same direction as the students, demonstrate the hold of the head joint. With the *left hand in position to wave at yourself*, rest the head joint on the base of the left index finger. Fingers and thumb should grasp loosely. With the right palm, plug the end of the head joint. Students imitate (see Figure 2.1).

4. Demonstrate placement of the head joint by *centering the embouchure hole on closed lips*—head erect. Next, roll out the head joint so that the hole points to the ceiling. Students imitate. This is not a precise placement; it is "ballpark" only. Ask students to feel for centeredness. In time, they will be able to sense centered placement without having to go through this step. They should be weaned of this "place and roll" step as soon as its usefulness has expired.

5. Say to your students. "Some of your lower lip should hang over the embouchure hole. Look at my lower lip." Students imitate. Students should be able to *feel the edge of the head joint hole making contact with the bottom of their lower lip*. On a lip of average thickness, the contact point is near the line of demarcation between lip and skin of chin; on a larger lip, the contact point is higher—*on* the lip itself. Check and adjust individual placements. Figures 2.2 and 2.3 show two different players with lip over the embouchure hole.

6. At a moderate tempo, demonstrate 4 beats of a sustained pitch (an approximate A 440) beginning with the pop of the P consonant. Without losing a beat, students imitate. Continue this alternation of teacher and students in a *4 beats on/4 beats off* pattern. Even if some students get no tone in their initial attempts, encourage them to *sustain the air stream*. Make sustained blowing a habit. As you the teacher demonstrate and the students respond, notice what the students are doing and how they are sounding. Much more on this later.

7. Make contact with individual students.

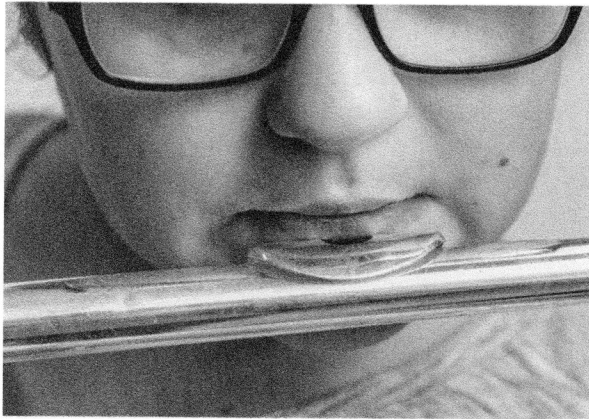

FIGURE 2.2 Lip Over Embouchure Hole
(Produced by Paige Jarreau at Paige's Photos)

FIGURE 2.3 Lip Over Embouchure Hole
(Produced by Paige Jarreau at Paige's Photos)

Teacher Demonstration

Notice in the above "Sequence for Making First Sounds" the prevalence of teacher demonstration. You have your own head joint in order to demonstrate. Do not underestimate the power of demonstration as a teaching tool. At this stage, students need some ideal combination of teacher talk (explanation) and teacher demonstration. With instrument in hand, you will find great value in showing and demonstrating. Young people need opportunities to see, then do. Much of what you will say in the above sequence is, "Do this," "do it again," and "watch me." The teaching, at least in part, is in the demonstrating!

More about the Small Piece

There are three different pitches, useful to beginning flutists, which can be produced on the head joint alone with plugged end, open end, and lip across. Experience with them facilitates embouchure development.

While students are becoming increasingly more skillful with the plugged-end experience, think about when you will introduce the open-end experience (an octave higher A). Playing with the end open is more akin to playing on the fully assembled instrument. As with the plugged-end pitch, work toward an increasingly clear tone (position of head joint on lip, relaxed lower lip, small aperture). Students should be able to consistently produce and sustain moderately clear plugged-end and open-end pitches before progressing to the third head joint pitch, which we will call the *lip-across pitch*.

To produce the lip-across pitch, return to the plugged-end sound. While sustaining it, blow the lower lip forward, intent on covering more of the embouchure hole. In other words, *allow* the relaxed lower lip to be blown forward by the fast air stream. Control of and help in the forward positioning of the lip comes from the corners of the mouth and/or the upper lip. You might sense that the corners or upper lip serve to somewhat "squeeze" the lower lip forward. As the lip moves closer to the strike wall, there is a point at which the pitch jumps up a 12th to an approximate E. This is the embouchure that will be used to produce high notes, specifically, some of the second octave (roughly top line F and above) and all of the third octave of the flute's range. The effective teacher is able to demonstrate this lip movement for students to see up close. Demonstration is a vital teaching tool here because the lip-across technique is not an easy one for some students. It is not necessary to produce this third head joint pitch before moving on to the fully assembled flute. With persistent effort on the part of teacher and student, in time most students can succeed with the lip-across technique.

The lip movement involved in the lip-across technique for producing high notes is the same as that used for the *air up arm* teaching strategy explained above. This strategy is a good and necessary precursor to introducing the lip-across technique. Lip-across practice is great for developing the lip flexibility needed to play with good tone and accurate intonation in the upper register of the flute. For intonation adjustment, incrementally more lip across the hole raises the pitch. Less lip across the hole lowers the pitch.

Expect students' first attempts with the lip-across technique to be unsuccessful, even frustrating. At first, when they push the lip forward the tone may stop. Encourage them to continue blowing and pushing the lip forward *through* this break in the tone. It's a good idea to plant the lip-across seed before it is a necessity. Early in flute study, a seed planted is enough; no need to grind away at lip across through multiple failed attempts. Return to it another day. As you listen to individuals, you will begin to recognize when students are close to getting it right. You will hear the faint beginning of the upper pitch. At this point, the lip needs to cover just a bit more of the embouchure hole and/or the air stream needs to be pushed faster for complete success.

Some students will think that they are extending the lip forward when in fact they are not. You can make this apparent by having them look at themselves in a mirror. Some students will be able to produce the higher pitch without lip movement. You will notice that they are instead making the aperture smaller. This is not a problem. Encourage these students, however, to develop the lip-across technique. Some students are not physically able to make a small enough aperture without the assistance of the lip-across technique.

For those who struggle inordinately with early lip-across attempts, the upper register can be achieved by placing the embouchure hole such that more lip covers the hole from the start. In other words, start with the lip already across. Continue efforts to develop the flexibility inherent in the lip-across technique.

Avoid having students believe that the upper register is produced by simply blowing harder. Blowing harder will yield high notes, but they will be sharp in pitch, strident in tone, and impossible to play at soft dynamic levels. In addition, rolling the head joint in will create easy high notes, but will cause tone and pitch problems.

Teaching/Learning Sequence: Head Joint Practice

Repetition of desired behaviors can be organized by a process we will call a teaching/learning sequence. Note the following teaching/learning sequence used in work with the head joint alone.

1. Left hand.
2. Right hand.
3. Sit tall.
4. Head joint to you.
5. Lower lip.
6. Line of lips.
7. Right angle.
8. P.

The sequence is an abbreviated form of a step-by-step process used in early embouchure work. The substance of each step is already established by the teacher in students' minds. It is at this point that students need only brief reminders of what comes next in the sequence, hence the 1–8 list above.

Students know, based on your demonstration, instruction, and guided experiences, that *left hand* refers to the proper hold of the head joint in the left hand, and that *right hand* refers to plugging the end of the head joint. They know what *sit tall* means, and that *head joint to you* means to bring the head joint to an erect head rather than moving the head forward and down to meet the head joint. They know that *lower lip* refers to the process of searching for (feeling for) ideal placement of the head joint on the lower lip. Ideal placement is of course determined by quality of sound. *Line of lips* refers to the parallel relationship of lip line and head joint. *Right angle* is a reminder to create a right angle between the head joint and the face. *P* is a reminder to start the tone with closed lips.

This instructional sequence is a checklist of what one thinks about and does in preparing to make a tone on the head joint. At the beginning level, students who repeatedly fail to do one or more of the steps fail not because they are incapable of doing the behaviors. They fail because the brain does not tell the body the right information. The teaching/learning sequence represents a proactive approach in that it organizes student thought and action up-front—from the beginning. If properly rehearsed, it promotes good habits before bad ones have a chance to take hold.

24 TEACHING THE INSTRUMENTS

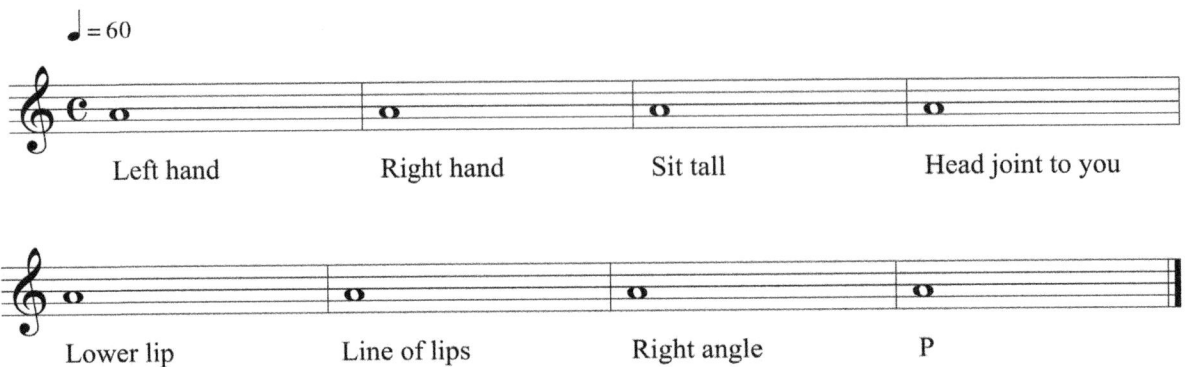

FIGURE 2.4 Teaching/Learning Sequence: Head Joint Practice

In effect, this sequence breaks down into individual steps what an accomplished flutist does all at once—in one big step. The accomplished flutist would simply put the head joint to their mouth and produce a beautiful tone. This is also the goal for your beginners, but they can't start there. This teaching/learning sequence breaks "embouchure" into constituent parts. The parts can be rehearsed at a deliberate pace and eventually at a faster pace such that eight separate steps begin to meld together and become one big action. This idea can be promoted by rehearsing the sequence rhythmically. As illustrated in Figure 2.4, each step is chanted by the teacher in 4-beat durations during which students respond accordingly.

At appropriate times, the pace from step to step can be accelerated by chanting in 2-beat, then 1-beat durations per step at roughly quarter note equals 60. With enough in-class repetition, most students will memorize this sequence seemingly without trying. To ensure that everyone memorizes and habitually does the sequence, the effective teacher will consider testing students on it.

Performance Testing: Head Joint

The test presented in Table 2.1 can be administered using a video recorder. Set up a recorder in a practice room. Students, one at a time, unobtrusively leave class in a pre-arranged order to take the test. Each student enters the practice room, sits in a chair in view of the recorder (which is recording continuously), and demonstrates the head joint sequence. When finished, the student unobtrusively returns to class/rehearsal as the next student, waiting outside the practice room, enters the test room. At a later, convenient time, view the recording, complete the following test form, and assign grades.

There is no reason for young flute players to be playing with poor posture, a drooping head, a drooping flute, or an incorrect lower lip position in March of the school year. In fact, there is no reason for any of these conditions to exist beyond September of the first year. If they do exist, it is primarily the fault of the teacher who has failed to organize information logically or doesn't provide enough opportunities during lessons for students to do what is right or is oblivious to what students are doing, thus allowing bad habits to creep in. To avoid being one of these teachers, you must know, organize, demonstrate, provide opportunities, observe, provide more opportunities, observe, provide more opportunities, correct, remind, provide more opportunities—you get the point.

All students are able to sit tall *one time* when asked. The goal, though, is to get them to sit tall *every time* when playing the flute—without you having to ask! All students can make the flute parallel with

TABLE 2.1 Performance Test: Flute Head Joint Sequence

Name:		
Date:		
	Yes	No
1. You rested head point on left-hand contact point. Your fingers and thumb grasped loosely.		
2. You plugged the end of the head joint with open palm.		
3. You sat tall.		
4. You brought the head joint to your erect head.		
5. You searched for ideal placement of head joint on lower lip.		
6. Line of lips was parallel to line of head joint.		
7. Head joint formed a right angle to your face.		
8. You started the tone with a P consonant.		
9. You sustained the tone for at least 4 seconds.		
10. You did 1-9 in the correct order.		
Grade:		

Note: 9-10 Yes = A (Proficient), 8 Yes = B (Developing), 6-7 Yes = C (Novice)

the line of the lips one time when reminded. The goal is to get them to do it *every time*—and to remind themselves. Rehearsal of teaching/learning sequences and performance testing are tools that promote doing things a certain way, doing things the same way each time, doing things thoughtfully, and attending to the details. This way of thinking about testing presents it as a teaching tool—a teacher's aid, so to speak—not a punitive measure.

Potential for Success in Flute Study

Probably the best indicator of whether a student is suited for flute study is the ability to make a ballpark accurate sound on the head joint. This entails achieving a relatively small aperture and relatively clear tone (with emphasis on *relatively*) in a several minute, one-on-one session with a knowledgeable teacher. Not being in the ballpark after 3 minutes does not mean that the student is incapable of playing the flute. It means only that the student may experience difficulty in tone production in the early stages. The question is: "Can the student with the help of a teacher overcome this difficulty before losing interest in the instrument?" With many students, the answer to this question is yes. If it appears, however, that the student might progress faster on another instrument, the teacher might be wise to encourage the student in that direction instead of the flute.

Some people have a Cupid's bow formation to their upper lip, which usually has a deleterious effect on tone quality. In this condition, when forming an aperture, the center of the upper lip follows a downward path, which obstructs the airflow from the aperture. It in effect cuts the air stream in two parts. The Cupid's bow condition, if it exists, is apparent in the first attempt to make a tone on the head joint. The observant and thoughtful teacher reflects on two questions: a) Will the Cupid's bow create problems that will prevent success and discourage the student? If so, steering the student toward another instrument is a good option. b) Am I working with a student who is driven to play the flute and is likely to be a good sport in working tediously to find an "off-centered" position of the head joint on the lip thus opening the door for success on the instrument? Other flutists have overcome the Cupid's bow challenge.

Children of small stature can have difficulty holding and fingering the flute while maintaining embouchure contact. This is one reason that starting flutists as 5th and 6th graders is perhaps more appropriate than starting them as 4th graders.

Students with disabilities (physical, cognitive, emotional, sensory) should be given a more comprehensive evaluation than that described above concerning potential for success. Consult with the student's team of teachers/counselors, as well as his parents, to develop a full knowledge of the student's capabilities.

Difficulties and disabilities aside, a student with a strong desire to succeed on an instrument can sometimes overcome major obstacles.

FLUTE ASSEMBLY, DISASSEMBLY, AND CARE

Assembly Sequence

FIGURE 2.5 Alignment of Foot Joint and Body of Flute
(Produced by Paige Jarreau at Paige's Photos)

FIGURE 2.6 Embouchure Hole Aligned with Row of Keys
(Produced by Paige Jarreau at Paige's Photos)

1. Remove the body of the flute from the case by sliding the ring finger into one of its ends and lifting.
2. Remove the foot joint.
3. Place the part of the foot joint that has no keys into the palm of the right hand and, with the thumb, close the keys near the bottom end of the joint. Note: Closed keys will not bend when pressure is applied in the assembly process.
4. With the left hand, grasp the body in a place that depresses keys and avoids the key that sticks out (G-sharp).
5. With small back and forth turns, assemble foot joint and body *so that the rod of the foot joint points to the center of the last key on the body.* Note: As shown in Figure 2.5, rod of foot joint should not line up with rod of the body. It's counterintuitive.
6. Grasp the head joint.
7. Grasp the non-keyed upper part of the body with one hand. Insert the head joint with small back and forth turns. Push it in until it stops, then pull it out about 1/8 inch (3mm). Note: The flute is designed to play in tune (A = 440) when the head joint is pulled out 1/8 inch (3mm). As shown in Figure 2.6, align the embouchure hole with the row of keys on the body.

Disassembly and Swabbing

Disassemble the flute in reverse order as follows.

1. Grasp head joint and body (where there are no keys), and with small back and forth turns remove the head joint.
2. Swab the head joint.
3. Swab the body and foot joint as one piece.
4. Remove the foot joint by grasping body and foot joint as described in assembly. Use small back and forth turns.

To swab, insert the corner of a handkerchief through the eye on the cleaning rod. Wrap it over the "eye" and down the length of the rod. Insert into head joint. Then insert into body/foot joint unit. Cut the handkerchief to proper size, if need be. For storage in the case, spread the handkerchief on top of the disassembled flute.

FLUTE HAND POSITION

Left Hand

1. The flute rests on the base knuckle of the left index finger with the finger wrapping around the flute to its key (the second key in the line of keys; see Figure 2.7). Don't be surprised if this aspect of hand position gives students some trouble. A common mistake is to place the base knuckle to the side of the instrument rather than underneath. You'll notice in Figure 2.7 that there is a to-the-side look to this proper position but in reality there is some portion of knuckle under the instrument.

FIGURE 2.7 Flute Hand Position
(Produced by Paige Jarreau at Paige's Photos)

2. The left thumb depresses the B-natural lever. As you look at the two thumb keys with the instrument held in playing position, the B-natural lever is on the right.

3. With thumb and first finger depressed, skip a key, then depress fingers 2 and 3 on adjacent keys.

4. The left-hand pinky hovers above the G-sharp key, which protrudes.

5. The left wrist should be bent so that the back of the hand forms a north–south line, not east–west line. This allows finger 3 and pinky to curve and make proper contact with the keys.

Right Hand

6. From the left-hand finger 3, skip two keys.

7. The side of the right thumb (not the thumb print) makes contact under the flute, opposite finger 1.

8. Right-hand fingers 1, 2, 3 depress the last three round-shaped keys.

9. A C-shape should be created by this thumb and finger 1. Attention to this C-shape while maintaining a fairly straight right wrist prevents students from leaning on the rod with the base of finger 1.

10. The right-hand pinky operates the E-flat key on the foot joint, which is depressed for most notes on the flute.

Balancing the Instrument

It may be better to think of the flute hold as less about holding and more about balancing among three constant contact points—the lower lip, the base knuckle of the left index finger, and the right thumb. The left index finger provides light pressure in toward the player. I emphasize *light* inward pressure. This is countered by the right pinky on the E-flat key that pushes slightly forward (away from the player). This way, with all fingers raised except the right pinky (a C-sharp), the flute remains secure.

This final point is worth repeating. When students finger the aforementioned C-sharp or C-natural (left index finger and right pinky only), they often feel like they are going to drop the instrument. An active right pinky optimally placed on the E-flat key prevents this from happening. Figure 2.5 shows this active pinky making contact toward the end of the key more so than across the key.

Marking Finger Placement for Flute

Of all the woodwind instruments, where to put your fingers is least clear or intuitive on the flute. When finger placement is first introduced, students often go home and forget which finger goes where. To avoid this, the teacher will find it useful to apply small stickers on keys to show where the fingers go. Marking the placement of left-hand finger 1, the left knuckle contact point, and right thumb contact point is often all that is necessary. Marking is probably not necessary in settings where students have band every day of the week.

What to Look for in Flute Hand Position

1. Is the flute contacting the base knuckle of the left index finger?
2. Is the right thumb making contact under finger 1?
3. Is there a backward C-shape between right thumb and finger 1?
4. Is the right wrist straight?
5. Is the rod of the foot joint centered with the key of right-hand finger 3 such that the pinky contacts the E-flat key naturally?
6. Is the left wrist bent to create a north–south line with the back of the hand?

The most common faults among beginning flute players are a reluctance to rest the flute on the base knuckle of the left index finger and a tendency to lean the base of the right index finger on the rod of the flute. To prevent the latter, keep the right wrist in a fairly straight line—back of hand through wrist to forearm.

Attempting to play the note C exposes holding/balance problems. If the flute wants to fall inward, get more left knuckle under the instrument and adopt a more "active" right pinky. Notice in Figure 2.5 that the tip of the pinky makes contact toward the end of the key. Applying some light pressure to the key with the pinky will keep the instrument upright when fingering C.

Because the flute is held in a transverse manner, seating in a band can affect holding and hand position. If flute players are crowded together, they cannot maintain the parallel relationship of lip line and flute line. The flute droops. Flutists need room to their right sides. To create room, alternate the positions of their seats—one slightly forward and one slightly back. Player 1's flute will extend slightly in front of player 2's body. Player 2's flute will extend behind player 3's body. No line of sight problems exist in this arrangement.

FLUTE TONE DEVELOPMENT

Refining Flute Tone

What you understand about what you've read so far will not make good flute players. You making a good tone and tonguing well on the flute will not make good flute players. You getting an A in this class will not make good flute players. The way you know embouchure and hand position and teaching/learning sequence right now, while important and in many ways fundamental, is only introductory in nature. You don't know or haven't thought about what happens *after* the introduction—after the first few days of doing and saying all the things you know to do and say about the flute. What will your flute instruction look like in October and November?

What will you do with the very real fact that there is not one embouchure? Notice that I write about only one in this book. There are as many embouchures as there are children to make them, some variations from ideal being troublesome and some not. Which is troublesome? Which is not?

What will you do with the very real fact that there are as many ways for students to perceive and interpret what you say and have them do as there are children? You say "make a small aperture" and four flute novices make four different-sized apertures. You are preparing for a life in teaching where the targets move, sometimes predictably and sometimes at random, like you're poised with a hammer to play Whac-A-Mole. Really.

With so many facets and details in flute performance, it's easy (or convenient) to overlook that students have needs that extend beyond the introduction of new stuff, no matter how good you are at introducing it. It's easy to overlook because "to answer your question, Byo, in October and November, we will move forward by playing more lines in the method book. And we will be getting ready for the first concert." More new things to introduce—notes, meters, rhythms, articulations, dynamics, watching the conductor, listening—and likely distract attention away from the fundamentals of flute performance.

What tends to get lost in this whirlwind of activity is the meat of pedagogy—the act of *refining* what you introduce. Quality matters. Yes? How students do things matters. Yes? And quality must matter now (at the beginning stage), because the alternative is to have students forming bad habits that become difficult to undo.

Good teachers don't think in terms of introducing, then refining. They mix the two in various doses depending on what students need now and what they're capable of handling now with success. Good teachers think of refining, not introducing, as the meat of teaching. They are always considering the *effects* of their instruction and how to proceed from there. What happens when I say this or demonstrate that? Good teachers focus on the results of their instruction because those results provide hints about what and how to refine. There is a lot of noticing that goes into good teaching. How observant are you? There is a lot of thinking that goes into good teaching. How good of a thinker are you?

So your mission as a future professional music teacher is not just about knowing the information, it's about using the information effectively and being tuned in to students such that you have entry points from which to make decisions about how to use the information you know. It's easier said than done, because "tuned in to students" means tuned in to *individuals*—every one of them. It's tough, but it's do-able. And it can be great fun! Some students' challenges are easy to figure out. Some are hard. The hard ones don't have easy answers, but all students deserve a teacher who, in the face of not having an answer for a problem, goes to work trying to find that answer. What makes good players is a teacher attitude that says failure is not an option. Sure, the student is also responsible, but we teachers are most in control of ourselves, so fundamentally, this section is about your attitude.

Try being systematic about getting to individuals each class. If you have individuals play only briefly, enough for you to know what's going on, followed by what I like to call a "10-second lesson," you could interact meaningfully with four students in less than 2 minutes. Considering that you have a classroom of students sitting idly during this time, this is fair. It's not too much to expect them to sit quietly for 2 minutes. And if you make it your job to create some interest in what you do with the individuals, the others may even sit attentively. That's the goal. Anything requiring more than a brief comment or demonstration and one or two tries by a student ("10-second lesson") needs to be dealt with across multiple days or outside of class time.

In this individual time, you've heard students play alone and, importantly, they've heard themselves play alone. You've created a setting where you can provide personalized feedback (the best kind), make opportunities for and celebrate correct repetition, and put on public display your teaching skill while never losing sight of the need for attaining an optimal distribution of group, section, and individual performance. By knowing how individuals are doing, you can identify personalized "themes" that, once things get going in the right direction, need only brief in-class reminders.

I invite you to think in terms of what to look for in flute embouchure and what to listen for in flute embouchure. In pointing your attention to specific aspects of embouchure and sound, you put yourself in a position to refine. To actually refine, you must get on the inside of your teaching situation, which is different from existing only on the outside. "Teacher outsiders" have lots of things to tell and show their students, but are not invested in the details of how individual students respond. "Teacher insiders" get mixed in with the detail of individual students' responses. They roll up their sleeves. They notice. They go to work *making* things happen sooner rather than later.

At one end of the spectrum in problem solving and refining, you've tried everything you know to do in the group setting. At the other end, you move a student closer to the target by getting up close to see the embouchure (head joint placement, lip position, lip tension, aperture), trying to re-produce on your instrument the flawed sound the student is getting, and learning from that how you might advise the student. You try things, all the while noting the effect. You rule out certain options and see the potential in others. You avoid getting frustrated with failed attempts (yours and theirs). Failure and educated guesses are just part of the process. Give yourself and the student credit for persisting in the face of adversity. Live to see another day when continued effort might come up with a promising idea or approach. Certainly, you can ask for advice from flute majors or experienced band directors and read articles about embouchure, and you should. But I urge you to trust yourself and your instincts to work to your advantage when you put yourself in a position to become a master assessor. Your instincts and ability to use your knowledge skillfully stay on the sideline if you're not mixing things up at the noticing level—intent, even driven, to figure out the puzzle that the student brings.

What to Look for in Flute Embouchure

1. Is the head erect and facing forward?
2. Is the flute parallel with the line of the lips? Figure 2.8 shows this parallel relationship. Figure 2.9 is a negative example. There is no parallel relationship.
3. Is the flute held forming a right angle to the face? In Figure 2.6 above, follow the flute from foot joint to head joint and notice the right angle of the instrument to the player's face.
4. Does some lower lip hang over the embouchure hole?
5. Are the lips, at a minimum, aligned? Better yet, is there the sense that the lower lip protrudes some?

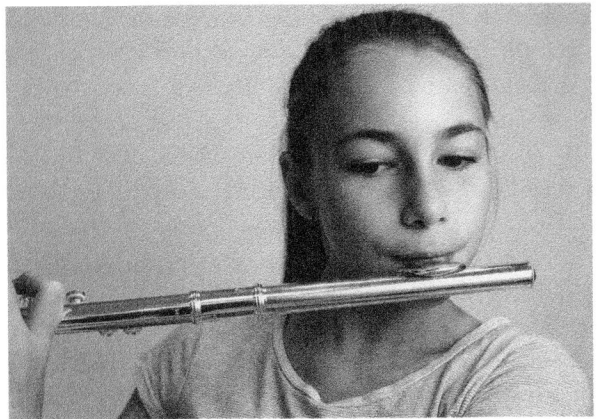

FIGURE 2.8 Line of Lips Parallel with Line of Flute
(Produced by Paige Jarreau at Paige's Photos)

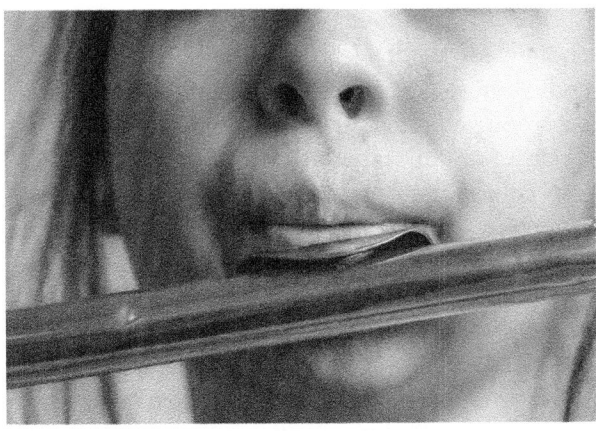

FIGURE 2.9 Line of Lips Not Parallel with Line of Flute
(Produced by Paige Jarreau at Paige's Photos)

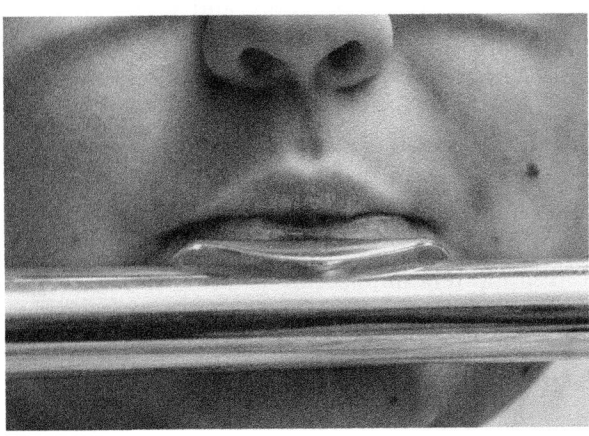

FIGURE 2.10 Small Aperture (Middle School Musician)
(Produced by Paige Jarreau at Paige's Photos)

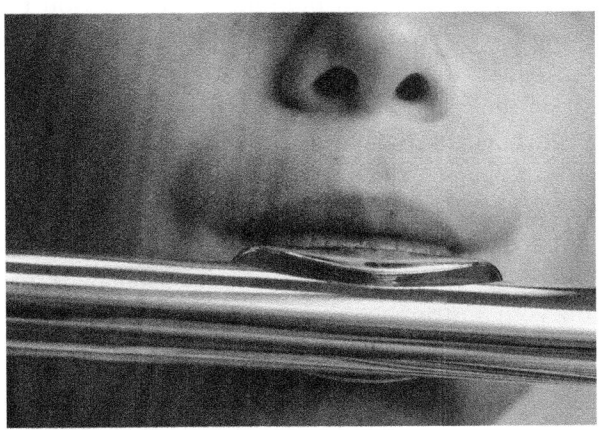

FIGURE 2.11 Small Aperture (Middle School Musician)
(Produced by Paige Jarreau at Paige's Photos)

FIGURE 2.12 Small Aperture (High School Musician)
(Produced by Paige Jarreau at Paige's Photos)

FIGURE 2.13 Aperture Naturally Off-Centered
(Produced by Paige Jarreau at Paige's Photos)

6. Is the lower lip relaxed?

7. Is the aperture small enough? In Figures 2.10 and 2.11 small apertures are made by 7th graders. In Figure 2.12 this high school senior makes a small aperture and because the instrument is cold and the air stream warm, you'll notice a V-shaped vapor trail—an indicator of proper aperture size and shape. Figure 2.13 is interesting in its depiction of a 7th grader who is getting a good sound by playing with a naturally off-centered aperture.

Numbers 1, 2, and 3 above involve actions that are very do-able. If students know about them and teachers know to look for them in the process of correct habit formation, all or nearly all novice flute players can do them successfully. The actions become difficult, however, when we try to get students to do them as corrections to bad habits. In other words, when a student gets comfortable playing with the head down, it is difficult to get her to play with the head erect. When one gets accustomed to playing with a sagging flute (lazy arm), doing otherwise is not easy. So work hard to get students to do things the right way early and often, so that bad habits don't establish themselves. To succeed with the items on this list, students need frequent correct repetition—both the thinking part of it and the doing part of it.

Numbers 4 and 5 (lower lip hang and lip alignment) work somewhat together. If students have one they're likely to have both. Numbers 6 and 7 (relaxed lower lip and small aperture), if they don't come naturally to your students, are somewhat more difficult to achieve. You are not likely to create a more relaxed lower lip by saying, "Relax your lower lip." You are not likely to fix an aperture that is too large by saying, "Make the aperture smaller." The teaching is in getting the student to do, not in the teacher talking about what needs to be done. Refer to "Embouchure Teaching Strategies" below for help with relaxed lower lip and small aperture.

What to Listen for in Flute Embouchure

1. Tone quality. In the early stages, you want the tone to be sustained, relatively clear, and unwavering. Memorize this list—sustained, relatively clear, and unwavering. It defines "ballpark" tone. Possible causes of a breathy tone are: a) too little lower lip over the embouchure hole; b) too large an aperture; c) the head joint turned out too far; and d) the air stream not centered with the embouchure hole. Notice an observational relationship here—your *listening* (breathy tone) leads to *look* (too large an aperture?).

2. Volume. In the early stages, you want students to blow a fast (*fortissimo*) air stream. Ask yourself, "Is the student blowing a sufficiently fast air stream? Is the aperture small enough to create a fast air stream?"

3. Pitch. On the head joint, the pitch should be an approximate A concert. If the pitch is noticeably flat, ask yourself, "Is the head joint turned inward such that the air is going too much into the hole?"

4. Overblowing and sharp upper register. The second and third octaves can be reached by simply blowing hard, but the tone will distort and the pitch will be sharp. To play these octaves with characteristic tone, accurate pitch, and controlled dynamics, the student must do one of the following: Extend the relaxed lower lip across the embouchure hole, make a smaller aperture, or both. The exercise in Figure 2.14 is good for practicing the lip-across technique.

FIGURE 2.14 Lip-Across Exercise

Get a best possible tone on second line G. I repeat: Get a best possible tone on second line G. Then slur to the octave G by allowing the lower lip to move forward to cover more of the embouchure hole. Add a bit more air speed in the process. Think of allowing the air to blow a relaxed lower lip across until the upper octave occurs. Also think of blowing the air stream *up your nose* to achieve the same result. The D above the staff will speak by lifting the first finger of the left hand. This D will pop out very willingly if the lip is across the embouchure hole for the previous G.

The air stream that strikes the edge of the embouchure hole must be pressurized. In other words, it must be sufficiently fast to allow the head joint to function optimally. It is good that students think in terms of pushing fast air, but fast air alone will not do the job. Fast air must be combined with, and in large part result from, a small aperture. Fast air with too large an aperture will result in breathy tone, much wasted air, and frustrated students. The moral of the story is that if the teacher emphasizes the use of a fast air stream or big breath without emphasizing or knowing how to lead students to the necessary small aperture, both teacher and students will be frustrated. See the small aperture teaching strategies listed below.

Dizziness from Hyperventilation

Dizziness is the result of hyperventilation, which is caused by too large an aperture. Too large an aperture allows air to be expelled at a rapid rate thus decreasing the carbon dioxide in the blood. If dizziness occurs (and it will with beginners), have students cease playing until the dizziness subsides. It will subside for good once students develop a small enough aperture that air is used efficiently.

What to Feel for in Flute Embouchure

Head joint pressure. Teacher pulls the closed end of the head joint away from the lip of an unsuspecting student as he plays. If it slams back, the pressure is too great. The head joint should simply pull away and stay away. Note that it is impossible to have a relaxed lower lip when the head joint is being pressed firmly into it.

Embouchure Teaching Strategies

To Achieve a Relaxed Lower Lip and Slightly Firm Upper Lip

Blow cool air up and down your vertically positioned arm by sliding the lower lip alternately out and in. Keep the head erect and still. Good for setting up the lip position necessary to play in the second and third octaves.

To Achieve a Small Aperture

1. As if cooling soup.

2. Sustained silent P consonant. Focus on the pop made by the P consonant. Do this first without the head joint, then with the head joint. First sounds should begin with P because by starting with the lips shut rather than open, a smaller rather than larger opening is encouraged. If you include a vowel in your thinking about "silent" P, let it be PIH, not POO. Avoid a blowing-into-a-coke-bottle sound, which is produced by starting with the lips open.

3. Reduce an aperture that is too large by pushing downward with the center of the upper lip while sustaining a pitch. The firmness of the center of the upper lip is an important aperture-controlling factor.

4. Reduce an aperture that is too large by squeezing shut (or pressing together) from the mouth corners during sustained air or sustained tone.

5. As if spitting a grain of rice off the end of your tongue.

To Achieve a Parallel Relationship Between Line of Flute and Line of Lips

1. Encourage students to judge for themselves by looking in a mirror while playing the flute or on the head joint.

2. Have students, in bringing the flute up to playing position, reach out fully extended to the right, then bring the flute to the mouth. This strategy is necessary when you notice students whose heads are turned to the left as they play. The head should face forward.

To Test for Head Joint Pressure against Lip

Teacher pulls screw end of head joint away from lip of unsuspecting student during a sustained note. If it slams back, the pressure is too great. Head joint should simply pull away and stay away.

To Achieve Jaw Down (Pout)

1. Close mouth, drop jaw (open teeth) while keeping lips shut; maintain this feel while making a small aperture.

2. Stifled yawn feel.

Vibrato

Vibrato is applied as a standard technique to both enhance and project tone on the flute, oboe, bassoon, and saxophone. A so-called diaphragmatic vibrato is commonly used on the flute. It is more probable that the abdominal muscles, not the diaphragm, are the active agents in this type of vibrato. To get the feel, say an accented "Hah!"

When for Vibrato?

In the school setting, vibrato can be introduced late in the middle school years, though there should be no hurry to do so. Vibrato should not be introduced before a student has had ample time to develop a well-supported and stable straight tone. One approach is to leave the teaching of vibrato to the private teacher. The students who study privately will tend to be ahead of the others in terms of tonal development, finger technique, and tongue technique. These students will likely occupy the top chairs. When vibrato is most advantageous—that is, during solo work—these students will be in a position to use it.

Teaching Vibrato

1. Say "Hah!" Repeat slowly to experience the initial "source" and feel of a vibrato. Then remove the vocalization, that is, "Hah" to expel air, not vocal tone. Repeat.

2. Repeat "Hah" without vocalization but with a "cooling soup" embouchure. Hold your hand in front of your mouth, take a big breath, and slowly pulse the air with repeated "Hah"s so that you feel it on your hand.

3. Do the same thing into the flute on an easy to produce note (e.g., B). Start with slow, large, rhythmic pulsations as represented in Figure 2.15. As you learn to control the evenness of the pulsations, increase speed of pulsation as shown.

FIGURE 2.15 Rhythmic Pulsations for Vibrato Development

4. Gradually across practice sessions and multiple lessons, increase the speed of the pulses. Resist the urge to pulsate fast too soon. Concentrate on a controlled, rhythmic pulsing. Avoid the fast "shake" of a bleating goat.

5. Apply the above pulse rhythms to a simple tune of whole, half, and quarter notes done at a slow pace—for example, "Hot Cross Buns." Continue making the pulses rhythmic, even mechanical sounding.

6. Once this becomes a more natural act, refine by rounding the edges of the pulses. Work for a more fluid vibrato, less abrupt. This often happens as a result of a practice technique involving 4, 5, 6, and 7 pulses per beat at quarter note equals 60.

Provide the opportunity for young flutists to hear good vibrato through live and recorded performances. For a good demonstration of a process involved in teaching vibrato, see the James Galway master class on vibrato at www.youtube.com/watch?v=u0yCw9xm0E4.

FLUTE TONGUING

Pre-tonguing Activity, Contact Point, and Vowel Shape

During initial embouchure development, the consonant P is used to begin sustained tones.

Flute tonguing involves touching the tip of the tongue to the roof of the mouth near the teeth line, as if saying "TU." The tip of the tongue refers to a location on top and just back from the actual tip.

Among professional flutists, there is increasing acceptance of "forward tonguing" or "French tonguing." One tongues through the lips, touching the tongue to the bottom of the top lip. You may have students who naturally gravitate toward this. If so, it is acceptable.

Teaching Tonguing: Two Alternatives

Traditional Approach to Teaching Tonguing

The traditional approach to teaching tonguing, to use terminology from psychology, is a holistic approach. Tonguing is kept intact; it is not broken into its component parts. Modeling by the teacher, with voice and instrument, is integrated with the following steps. In response to the model:

1. Students say "TU" (or some appropriate variant) using their speaking voices.
2. Students form an aperture (as if cooling soup) and start a sustained air stream as if saying "TU."
3. Students legato tongue a series of "TU"s on a continuous stream of air through this aperture.
4. On the instrument, students finger a mid-range note, form an embouchure, position the tip of the tongue against the roof of the mouth near the teeth line and initiate the start of a tone as if saying "TU." Sustain.
5. On the instrument, students do a series of four "TU"s, tip of tongue to roof of mouth. They tongue a continuous airstream.

Backward Approach to Teaching Tonguing

The traditional approach works for many students. It doesn't for others. The problem is that they are unable to coordinate air stream, embouchure, and tongue. They can't put it all together at once. Or they unknowingly articulate from the throat (glottal tonguing). The *Backward Approach* teaches tonguing by starting with something that we know students can do successfully, that is, start a tone with a pre-tonguing technique (the P consonant for flute, a breath attack for other woodwinds), and progressing into unknown tonguing territory. Keep in mind that the approach in this book is one that begins with tone production as an isolated element. Tone is not integrated with tonguing. Tonguing is introduced *after* a ballpark accurate embouchure and tone are achieved. Read each step below and compare to steps in Figure 2.16.

1. As shown in Figure 2.16, the student plays a mid-range note using the pre-tonguing articulation to initiate tone, sustains for 2 beats, on beat 3 *stops* the tone by simply stopping the air stream. Repeat as necessary in order to allow the student to *find beat 3*.

POO----	POO---T	POO TOO-----	POO TOO TOO TOO	TOO----------
Step 1 Find beat 3	Step 2 Tongue stops tone	Step 3 Keep air moving	More of Step 3	Step 4 Tongue start of note

FIGURE 2.16 Backward Approach to Teaching Tonguing

2. The student plays, sustains for 2 beats, on beat 3 *stops* the tone by touching the tip of of the tongue against the roof of the mouth near the teeth line (POO—T). Repeat this process several times in order to allow the student to *find the spot where the tongue goes.*

3. Student repeats Step 2 but when the tongue touches the roof of the mouth, it touches for only an instant. It is immediately pulled away (imagine touching a hot surface) while the air stream keeps going (POO—TOO—). Extend this process by tonguing successive quarter notes in legato tongue fashion (POO—TOO—TOO—TOO).

4. Start the tone with the tongue in traditional manner (TOO—).

Step 3 reiterated. Work hard to get students to legato tongue here. They should keep the air moving while tonguing. They will want to treat each note as a separate entity rather than a part of a series of notes that should be played as a line of music. Some will want to breathe after every note. Some will want to re-set their embouchure after every note. Don't let these faults creep in now; they are hard to correct later.

Assessment and Tonguing

I considered calling this section Addressing Problems in Tonguing, but it's actually about something bigger and more far reaching in your development as a music teacher. We'll call it assessment. Don't confuse this form of assessment with making up, giving, and grading tests. Assessment as I intend it here is one thing that good teachers do that makes them good.

Simply, assessment is collecting information. When I'm about to leave my office to walk across campus, I look outside my window to determine whether I should take an umbrella. I assess with my eyes. At my desk, my back is turned to the window, so frequently I hear thunder or rain before I see the visible effects. I assess with my ears. Assessment is something that people do all the time in order to get along in life. In the music room and rehearsal hall, effective teachers are keen observers, taking in information, some obvious and some subtle, in order to make wise moment-to-moment decisions about what to do. This recurring cycle of collect–decide–act is fundamental to the structured teaching/learning setting. The teacher's skills of observation and assessment are greatly enhanced when she knows what to look for and listen for relative to tonguing.

Things the Teacher Can See

1. Is the jaw moving? Jaw movement is caused by large tongue movements. Confine movement to the front of the tongue—as if saying "d-d-d-d" at a fairly rapid pace. Articulate with little outward sign of movement, like a ventriloquist. To fix excessive jaw movement, the teacher must slow the student down, isolate the problem, and do some detailed work. The exercise in Figure 2.17 should be played on an easy-to-produce note. Use a legato tongue (do not stop the air between notes). Ask yourself: Is the tongue shaped as if saying "OO." On contact, is the tip of the tongue touching above the teeth as if saying "TOO"? Is the tongue moving only slightly away from the contact point? Is the jaw still?

FIGURE 2.17 Isolate Tongue Movement

2. Glottal tonguing. Be on the lookout for glottal tonguing (starting the sound in the throat), which can been seen and heard. Some beginners will unknowingly "tongue" from the throat. They think that they are tonguing correctly, not realizing their error.

Things the Teacher Can Hear

1. No tongue at all, a sort of huffing or puffing.
2. A "THU"-like sound. If the articulation sounds like "THU," the tongue is not pressing firmly enough against the teeth just prior to the release of the air.
3. Lack of coordination between tongue and fingers in fast passages or involving certain awkward note pairs regardless of tempo. The student must slow down! Isolate the specific problem (e.g., a two-note sequence) and slow the tempo enough for an errorless performance across successive trials. Increase the tempo in small increments while maintaining errorless performance. Coordination problems can be fixed also by starting at a very slow tempo, playing each note short, fingering each note just a bit *before* tonguing it, and continuing this process while increasing the tempo in small increments. At a certain tempo, it becomes impossible to finger *before* tonguing, so at this point the practice procedure has reached its limit.

Multiple Tonguing

Multiple tonguing (double and triple tonguing) is possible on all woodwind instruments. It is a standard performance technique on the flute. Many accomplished high school players double and triple tongue with relative ease.

- *Double tongue.* Use an alternating "Tah-Kah" articulation. For a less percussive effect, use "Dah-Gah."
- *Triple tongue.* Use "Tah-Tah-Kah (Dah-Dah-Gah)" or "Tah-Kah-Tah (Dah-Gah-Dah)."

THE FLUTE MECHANISM

Brief History

The present-day fingering system for the flute was patented by Theobald Boehm in 1847. The earliest indicators of the existence of the "transverse flute" (held horizontally) were in wood carvings dated in the 10th century. The first evidence of the instrument being connected with any type of written music was in the late 13th century. Players gravitated away from wooden flutes and toward metal instruments during the mid-19th century.

Family and Transposition

All flutes in the family have the same basic fingerings. Of all the instruments in the family, only the flute is a beginning instrument.

Piccolo

1. Built in the key of C, it sounds up one octave. Piccolo in D-flat, found in older band scores, sounds up a minor 9th. A piccolo in D-flat part played on a piccolo in C must be read up a half step.
2. Has no foot joint; therefore the lowest note is D.
3. Made of wood, metal, or plastic. The darker sound of wood blends better than the brighter sounding metal. Metal is durable and projects well in a marching band.
4. Intonation is a greater problem on the piccolo than it is on the flute. It is wise to have a plan of attack with regard to warming the instrument in cases where the concert repertoire does not use the piccolo on every selection.

Flute

Built in the key of C, it sounds as it is written.

Alto Flute

1. Built in the key of G, it sounds down a perfect 4th.
2. Requires a greater volume of and slower air; more bottom lip over embouchure hole.

Bass Flute

Built in the key of C, it sounds down one octave.

Instrument Manufacturing

The present-day flute is made of solid silver (professional model) or nickel-silver (student model) and has a cylindrical bore. Closed-hole instruments (tone holes covered by keys) are intended for beginning through intermediate level players. Open-hole (French model) instruments are used by more advanced and professional-level players. Open-hole flutes offer more control over tone quality and more alternate fingerings.

Closed-hole flutes are recommended for beginners, but when an open-hole flute must be used, the ring keys can be filled with cork or plastic inserts by an instrument repair technician. This in effect makes the instrument a closed-hole flute. The corks may be removed at a later time.

A curved head joint is available for beginners. For small children, flutes with curved head joints are easier to hold than those with traditional head joints, though the vast majority of young flute students experience only minor, if any, problems holding the traditional instrument.

Be aware of distinctions between professional and student line models. Most manufacturers produce both; in other words, one name (e.g., Gemeinhardt) comprises different types of flute (piccolo, flute, alto flute, bass flute), models of flute (relatively inexpensive to expensive), and options (C or B foot joint, open or closed holes, silver plating or solid silver). New student model instruments start at roughly $500.00. If for rent, they run about $30 per month. Good-quality used instruments can be purchased for less. Professional model instruments can range from $2500 to $10,000 and beyond.

When flute players acquire a *step-up* instrument, it is wise to change from a closed-holed model to an open-holed model with a solid silver head joint, which produces a clearer tone than silver plating, and a B foot joint, which extends the range a half step and enhances the pitch and tone quality of the high register.

Haynes makes perhaps the most well-known professional quality flute. The following lists of instrument manufacturers are not exhaustive. They are provided to make you aware, not to recommend.

- Professional model instruments are made by manufacturers Haynes, Powell, Gemeinhardt, Muramatsu, Yamaha, and others.
- Student model instruments are made by manufacturers Armstrong, Artley, Evette, Gemeinhardt, Jupiter, Pearl, Yamaha, and others.

Range

Figure 2.18 shows the range of flutes extending to low B (B foot joint) or C (C foot joint).

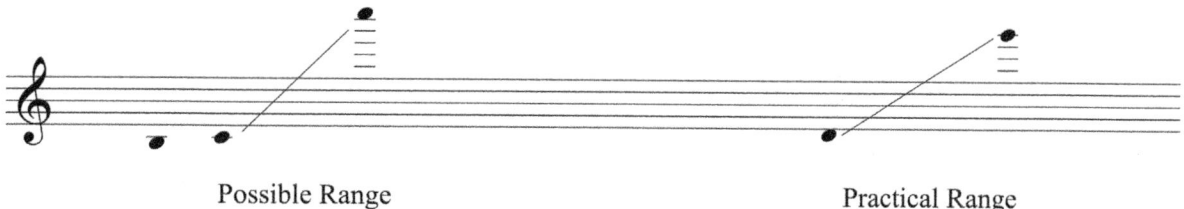

Possible Range   Practical Range

FIGURE 2.18 Flute Range

Fingering Issues

Thumb B-flat and Alternate F-sharp

Two alternate fingerings find frequent use at the intermediate level—thumb B-flat and alternate F-sharp. Primary B-flat (thumb on the key to the right plus 1–1–E-flat key) should be taught first in the beginning stages. Thumb B-flat (thumb on the key to the left plus 1 and E-flat key) is used in Figure 2.19, Examples

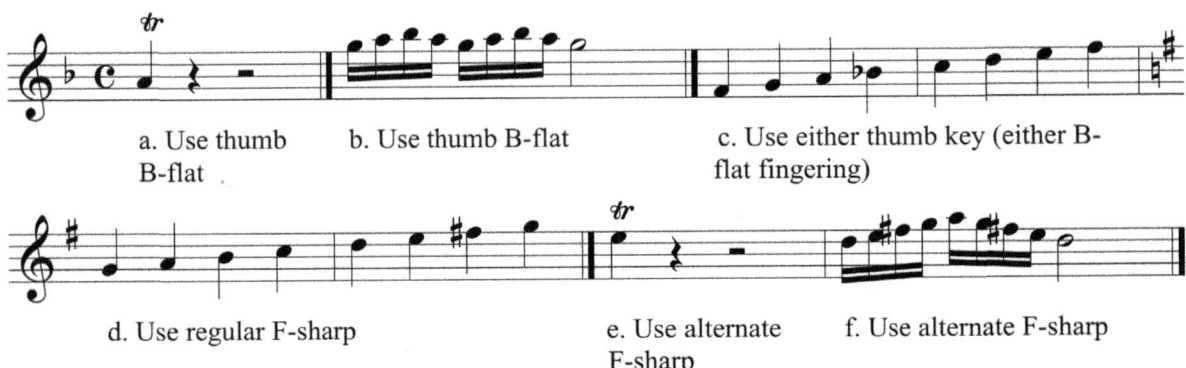

FIGURE 2.19 Alternate B-flat and F-sharp

a and b. Try both of these examples, first with one B-flat fingering, then the other. You'll see why thumb B-flat is preferred.

It is important to understand that the two thumb keys can be used interchangeably for almost every note on the flute except B and third octave F-sharp. For example, Example c can be played with either thumb key depressed for the entire scale. However, Example d with its B-natural should be played with the right-side key depressed for the entire excerpt. If the left-side key were to be depressed, B-flat would sound. Sliding the thumb from one key to the other in mid-excerpt should be avoided.

The primary fingering (and the one taught first) for F-sharp involves right-hand finger 3. The alternate fingering, using right-hand finger 2 instead of 3, is useful for the E trill in Example e and the passage in Example f, where the sequence of notes involving F-sharp lies such that using right-hand finger 2 is easier.

Third Octave Fingerings

Third octave fingerings, considered in isolation, seem complicated. Considering them in comparison to known second octave fingerings may reduce the complexity. In Figure 2.20, the numbers above the

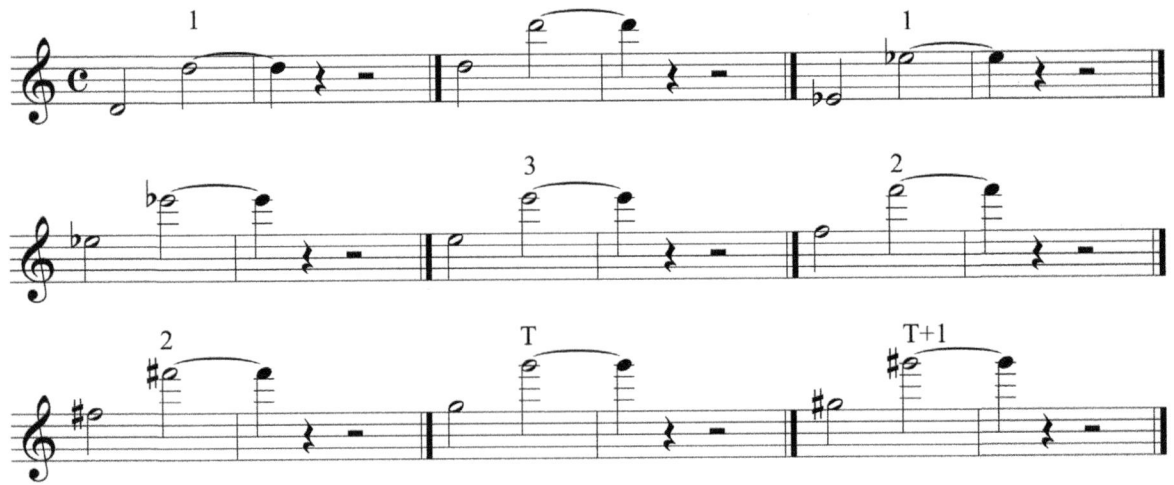

FIGURE 2.20 Third Octave Fingerings

notes indicate the finger(s) to raise in order to make the high note *from* the low note fingering. In addition, third octave notes require more lip across the embouchure hole than do second octave notes. High E-flat has all fingers down, including the left pinky on the G-sharp key. Figure 2.20 is not a slurring exercise.

Some Trill Fingerings

Figure 2.21 shows select trill fingerings involving something other than the normal fingerings for the two notes. The grey key(s) should be trilled. More comprehensive and collections of trill fingerings are available on the Internet. Note: Of the two right-hand trill keys (see small ovals to the side of the main keys), the top one (between the F and E keys) involves right-hand finger 2 and the bottom one involves right-hand finger 3.

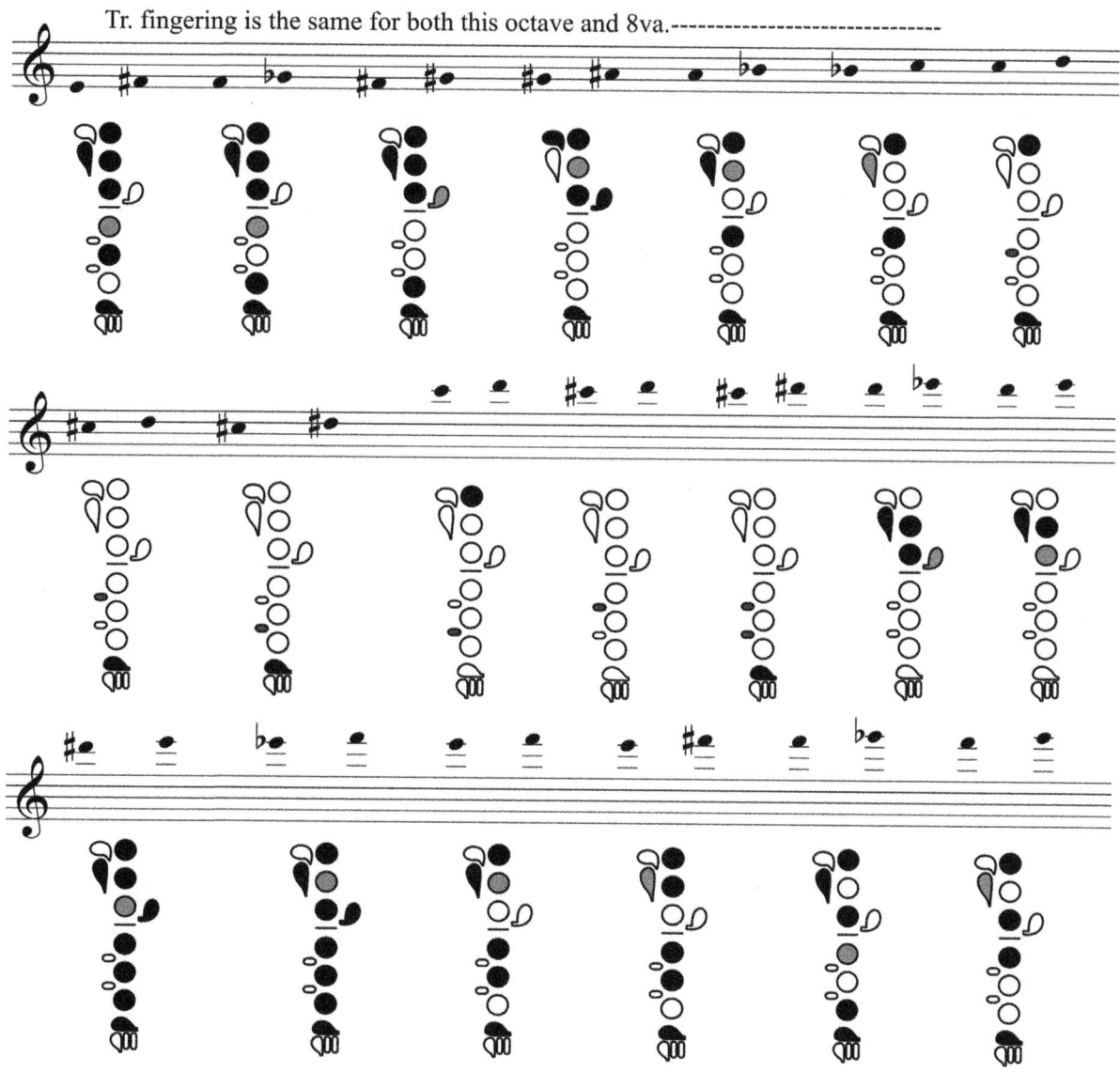

FIGURE 2.21 Flute Trills

Harmonics

Harmonics are pitches that are produced by fingering a fundamental note (e.g., the low D in Figure 2.22) and overblowing such that pitches in the harmonic series result. All notes in the first octave can be used as fundamentals. To overblow, make the aperture smaller, the air stream faster, and blow more across the embouchure hole using the lip-across technique. The small circles in Figure 2.22 mean to use harmonic fingerings to produce the notes.

Harmonics have a more pure tone quality or timbre than the same notes fingered in the regular manner. Contemporary composers exploit the variety in tone color made possible by this special effect. Harmonics are stable in pitch at the *pianissimo* level, whereas the same third octave notes fingered regularly are difficult to sustain at *pianissimo* without going flat. It is thought that regular practice of harmonics is good for developing flexibility and control in the embouchure.

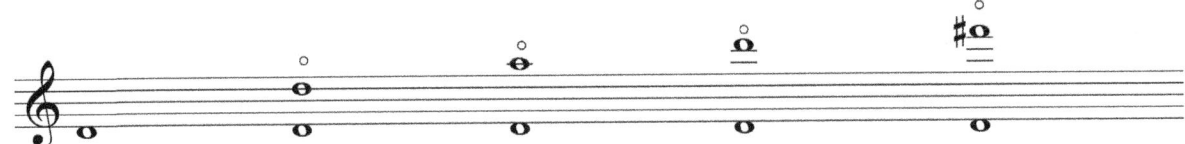

FIGURE 2.22 Harmonics

Tuning and Intonation

Basic Information

1. The flute is designed to play in tune when the head joint is pulled out 1/8 inch (3mm).

2. The cleaning rod doubles as a *tuning rod*. On occasion the cork (or plug) in the head joint will move out of optimal position. To check for this, note that the tuning rod has a line etched into one of its ends. Insert this end into the head joint. If the line on the rod does not appear in the center of the embouchure hole, the cork is not optimally placed. If the cork must move toward the open end of the head joint for the line on the rod to be centered, loosen the screw and push in until the position is corrected. If the cork must move toward the closed end, tighten the screw until the cork is pulled enough to correct its position or use the tuning rod to push it into place.

3. Tune the flute by pulling or pushing the head joint. Any amount of pull beyond a half inch (12mm) indicates a problem with embouchure, air stream, or both. Pulling beyond a half inch does not get to the root of the problem.

4. Standard tuning notes are presented in Figure 2.23.

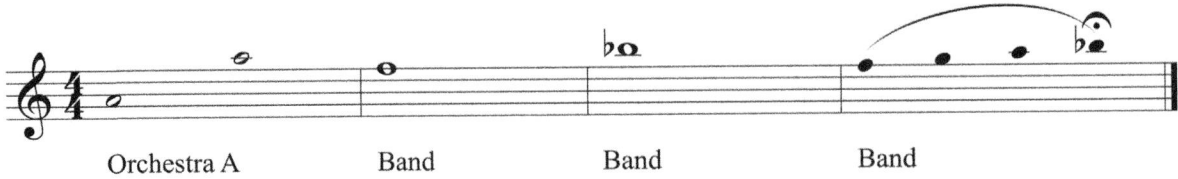

FIGURE 2.23 Flute Tuning Notes

Pitch Tendencies

Every wind instrument has pitch tendencies; certain notes, because of the design of the instrument, tend to be sharp, flat, or unstable (sharp and flat). By knowing the pitch tendencies of the flute, the effective music teacher is able to predict what might happen with regard to pitch before it actually happens in the lesson or rehearsal. Your job in rehearsal is to listen and decide if in fact student performance is consistent with the tendencies. If it is, you must know what to do to solve the pitch problems.

Flat Tendency

1. Cold temperature.
2. Low register.
3. Soft volume (including *decrescendo*).
4. Pad height too low.

Solutions for Flatness

One of the following combined with a discerning ear will remedy flatness.

1. Direct the air more across the embouchure hole (move the lower lip across the hole).
2. Raise the head.
3. Roll the flute out. Rolling has been used by band directors as a standard solution to flute pitch problems for years. This practice, however, is frowned upon by professional flutists, who are concerned about changes in tone quality, not just pitch, that result from rolling. It is better to change pitch by manipulating the lip so that it covers more or less of the embouchure hole, thus controlling the direction of the air stream.

Sharp Tendency

1. Upper register.
2. Loud volume (including *crescendo*).
3. C-sharp in the 2nd and 3rd octaves.
4. Pad height too high. Key (or pad) height for the row of keys involving fingers 1 through 3 in both hands should be uniform. On occasion, you will notice one key that raises up higher (or lower) than the rest. Adjustments may necessitate an instrument repair technician.
5. Leaky pad. A leaky pad can be detected by sound (a single note that is sharp or more fuzzy sounding than its neighboring notes), by feel (it will be reluctant to speak), and by sight (you may be able to see that a pad is not shutting uniformly around its circumference with normal finger pressure). Many times the problem is a simple fix involving an adjustment screw. Other times, the pad needs to be replaced or re-seated by an instrument repair technician.

Solutions for Sharpness

One of the following combined with a discerning ear will remedy sharpness.

1. Direct the air more into the embouchure hole.
2. Lower the head.
3. Roll the flute in.
4. The sharp C-sharp can be fixed by blowing more into the embouchure hole and by adding fingers 1, 2, and 3 of the right hand. For many flutists, the standard fingering for these notes includes the right hand down.

Tuning and Intonation Summary

- Assembly
  - Start with head joint pulled out 1/8 inch (3mm).
- Tuning notes (orchestra/band)
  - Play with best embouchure and at *f* dynamic level
  - Pull or push head joint
- Pitch tendencies
  - Temperature (cold = flat)
  - Register (low = flat; high = sharp)
  - Volume (soft = flat; loud = sharp)
  - Bad notes (most notorious: short-fingered C-sharp)
- Solutions
  - Lower lip more or less over the hole
  - Head raised and lowered
  - Roll instrument out or in (last resort)
  - For C-sharp, in addition to the above solutions, add the right-hand finger.

STUDY QUESTIONS

1. Describe the condition of each of the following in a characteristic flute embouchure: Line of lips, flute angle to face, lower lip, aperture, lower lip, upper lip, head joint pressure, jaw.
2. In the "Sequence for Making First Sounds in Group Instruction," find and list specific teaching strategies. A strategy, in this case, is a) an activity related to the real thing that is intended to promote the real thing (e.g., feeling the expansion of the stomach in teaching proper breathing) or b) a metaphorical way of presenting something (e.g., breathing as if stifling a yawn).
3. Describe the lip-across technique in head joint work.
4. How do you determine a child's potential for success on flute?

5. As a teaching and learning technique, describe the teaching/learning sequence. What are the advantages to student and teacher?
6. The flute is designed to play in tune when . . .
7. There is one peculiarity about positioning the foot joint on the body of the flute. What is it?
8. Demonstrate flute swabbing.
9. Demonstrate your knowledge of how to adjust the cork in the head joint.
10. While demonstrating, explain the details of optimal flute hand position.
11. When you practice the flute, are you thinking and doing the details listed under "What to Look for in Flute Embouchure" so that you are better able to use this information in your observational role as teacher?
12. When you practice, how would you describe your tone—breathy, clear, or somewhere in between? Are you achieving the second octave by blowing hard or by the lip-across technique? Is your aperture small enough to play a phrase without running out of breath?
13. How is high D fingered in relation to G?
14. What causes dizziness during flute playing?
15. When you play, how would you describe the amount of head joint pressure against your lower lip?
16. Create a list of small aperture teaching strategies.
17. Demonstrate the test for head joint pressure.
18. Have you produced vibrato in the methodical way described in the chapter? Try it on a third line B.
19. Before tonguing is introduced, how should beginning flute players start the tone? Why?
20. Other than being smaller, the piccolo is different from the flute in four ways. How so?
21. On a staff, write the flute's possible range.
22. Demonstrate the differences in fingerings between:
    - Primary B-flat and thumb B-flat
    - Primary F-sharp and alternate F-sharp.
23. From the explanation about harmonics, play one or more harmonics on the flute.
24. Demonstrate the flute tuning sequence done in concert bands.
25. Indicate pitch tendencies for the following conditions: Low register, soft volume, upper register, loud volume, C-sharp in the 2nd and 3rd octaves.
26. How does a flutist fix a flat tendency?
27. How does a flutist adjust the pitch of C-sharps?

PERFORMANCE TESTING OF UNIVERSITY STUDENTS ON SECONDARY INSTRUMENTS

A rubric is an evaluative tool. The rubric that follows makes clear the expectations of the university student playing the flute as he or she approaches the end of an intensive three to four weeks of study. Students may use the criteria to prepare for performance testing and to self-evaluate. Teachers may use the criteria to structure feedback.

1.	Assembled and disassembled (incl. swabbing) the instrument properly	Yes	No
2.	Maintained acceptable hand position:		
	a. Three contact points	Yes	No
	b. Curved fingers	Yes	No
	c. Fingerprints over the center of the keys	Yes	No
	d. Fingers remain close to the keys at all times	Yes	No
	e. Right thumb under finger 1, the two forming a C	Yes	No
	f. Left wrist bent so that hand approaches flute from underneath	Yes	No
3.	Formed a basic embouchure:		
	a. Line of lips parallel with line of flute	Yes	No
	b. Flute at 90° angle to face	Yes	No
	c. Lower lip covering one-third of the embouchure hole	Yes	No
	d. Soft lower lip	Yes	No
	e. Minimal head joint pressure	Yes	No
	f. Small aperture	Yes	No
4.	Covered more of the embouchure hole for 2nd octave notes	Yes	No
	Covered still more for 3rd octave notes	Yes	No
5.	Breathed through the mouth, leaving lower lip contact in place	Yes	No
	Breathed according to phrase	Yes	No
6.	Sustained a clear and unwavering tone on the instrument	Yes	No
7.	Directed air stream in a downward direction and dropped the jaw for low register response	Yes	No
8.	Recalled and played fingerings from low D to C above the staff	Yes	No

9.	Used right-hand-down technique appropriately	Yes	No
10.	Tongued unmarked notes and first notes of slurs	Yes	No
	Legato tongue was convincing	Yes	No
11.	Play expressively by varying volume and tempo as indicated or dictated by the notes	Yes	No
12.	Performance showed evidence of sufficient practice	Yes	No

FLUTE FINGERING CHART

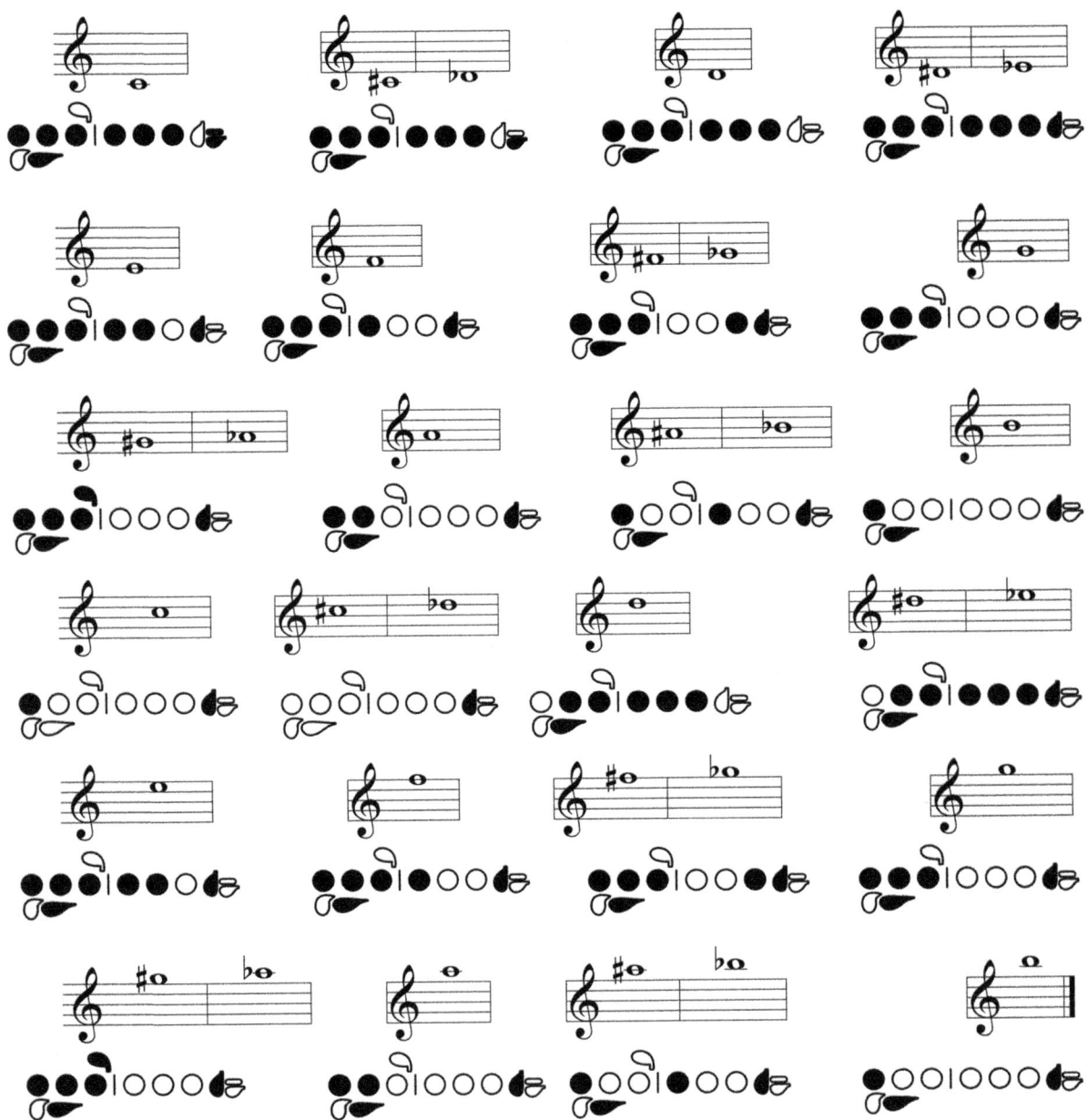

FIGURE 2.24A Flute Fingering Chart page 1

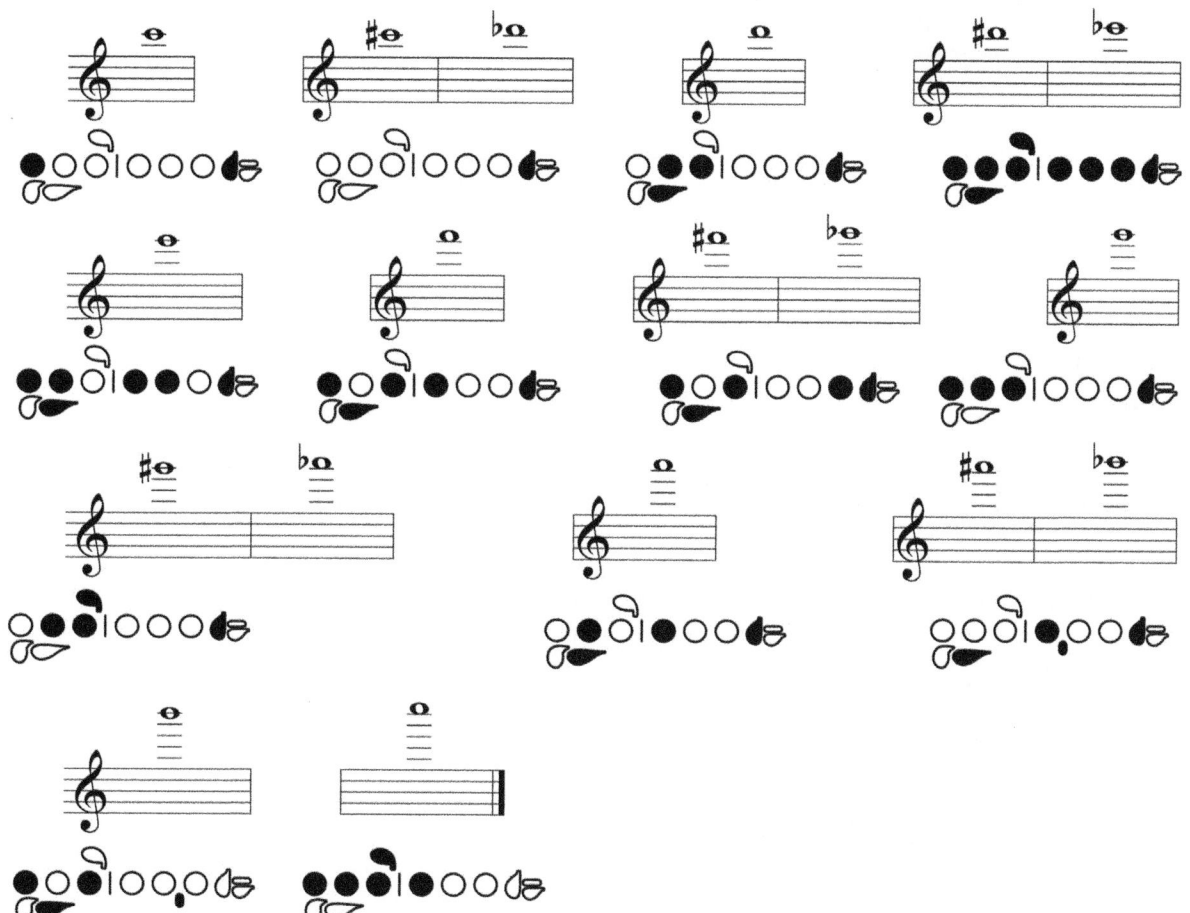

FIGURE 2.24B Flute Fingering Chart page 2

CHAPTER 3

Clarinet

CLARINET TONE AND EARLY STAGE EMBOUCHURE

Small Piece

Your first order of business as a student is assembling the small piece and as a teacher teaching assembly of the small piece. Assembly of the clarinet and saxophone small pieces is more complicated and time-consuming than that for the other woodwind instruments.

The small piece of the clarinet consists of the mouthpiece and barrel with reed and ligature. When embouchure pressures and air stream are correct, the small piece pitch will sound a concert F-sharp. The student pictured in Figure 3.1 is doing exactly that. Assembly and disassembly are presented below

FIGURE 3.1 Small Piece
(Produced by Paige Jarreau at Paige's Photos)

in lesson plan format complete with objective and step-by-step procedures. Assuming a group setting, several lessons may be necessary to thoroughly guide students through assembly of the small piece, initial embouchure formation, first sounds, and disassembly of the small piece.

Embouchure: Early Stage

Small Piece Assembly and Disassembly

Objective: Students will assemble and disassemble the clarinet small piece.

Before class: Teacher soaks students' new reeds in tap water and applies cork grease to joints that need it.

Procedures:

1. Teacher provides a reed, *all* of which has been soaked in water. While holding the reed at the side, students place the tip end in the mouth, flat side on tongue.

2. Before students open cases, teacher checks to see that instrument cases are situated with the correct side up. *Note*: It is sometimes easiest for many young people to place the case on the floor and sit or kneel beside it. For the following, I will assume chairs are being used.

3. Assembly of small piece. First, model and talk through the essential parts of 3a–h below, with students watching and listening. Second, lead students through 3a–e. Check/monitor individuals to the extent possible without unduly interrupting the group flow of activity. Third, lead students through 3f–h, 4, and 6. If there is time, do number 5.

    a. Remove mouthpiece, ligature, and barrel from case. Place on floor. Leave mouthpiece cap in case. Close case. Place case under chair.

    b. Remove ligature from mouthpiece by loosening the screws three to four turns. In other words, the mouthpiece should be naked.

    c. Assemble mouthpiece and barrel using back and forth motions. *Note*: If possible, the teacher should apply cork grease *prior to* the lesson. If dealt with during the lesson, this is a big time waster.

    d. Take reed out of mouth. While holding it on the side with tip-end up, place the flat side against the opening of the mouthpiece. Line up reed with mouthpiece at tip, on sides, and at bottom. Tip of reed should be even with end of mouthpiece. *Note*: The reed need not be aligned perfectly at this stage; we will take a more detailed look at alignment in step g below. While holding the small piece in the palm of one hand, keep the reed in place with thumb of that same hand.

    e. Inspect the ligature. The end with the larger circumference is the bottom. With the screws facing you, fit the larger circumference end over the mouthpiece. Guide the ligature down toward the stock end of the reed.

    Note 1: Pay attention to what you are doing here. As shown in Figure 3.2, steady your hand by placing the back of the ligature against the back of the mouthpiece, then pivoting the ligature over the reed. If the ligature makes contact with the tip of the reed, perhaps because of an unsteady hand, the reed is likely to be damaged.

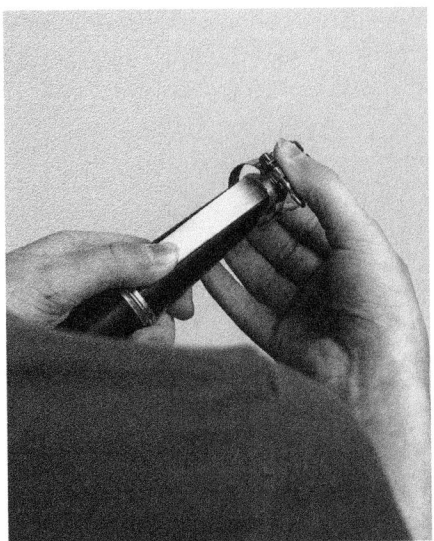

FIGURE 3.2 Steadied Hand with Ligature
(Produced by Paige Jarreau at Paige's Photos)

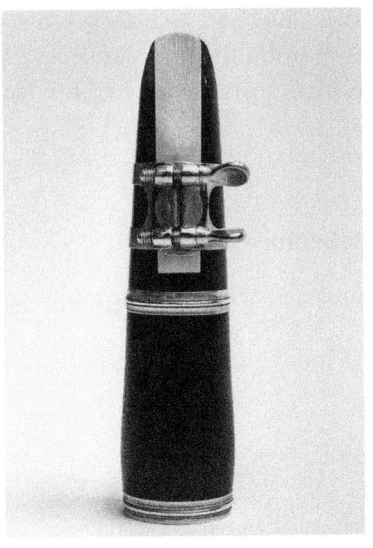

FIGURE 3.3 Correctly Positioned Screw Heads
(Produced by Paige Jarreau at Paige's Photos)

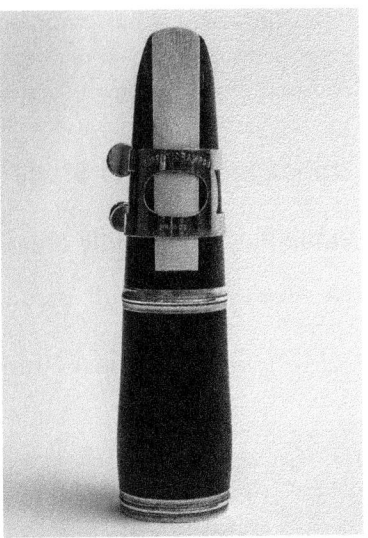

FIGURE 3.4 Incorrectly Positioned Screw Heads
(Produced by Paige Jarreau at Paige's Photos)

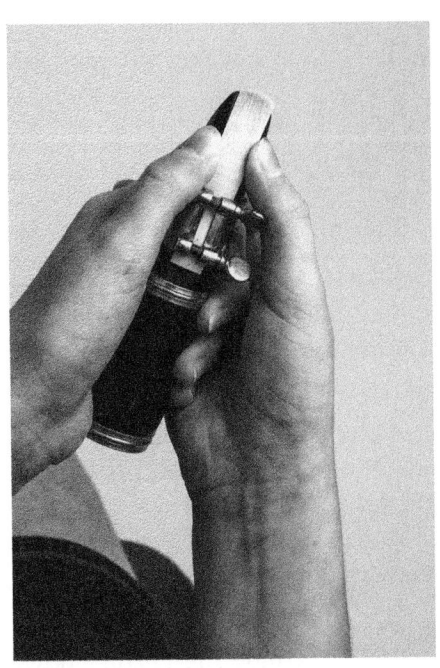

FIGURE 3.5 "Goal Posts" in Reed Position Adjustment
(Produced by Paige Jarreau at Paige's Photos)

Note 2: Ligatures are available in regular and inverted styles. On regular ligatures the screw(s) are located on the player side of the mouthpiece. On the inverted style, the screw(s) are located on the far side of the mouthpiece in relation to the player. To determine which is which, remember that the screw head(s) should be situated to the right as the player looks at the clarinet in playing position. Do not allow students to use one style of ligature as the other. In Figure 3.3 the screw heads are positioned correctly. In Figure 3.4 they are positioned incorrectly.

f. Pull the ligature down so that it is slightly below the top scribe line on the mouthpiece. If the mouthpiece has no scribe line, the ligature should be low enough that no part of it protrudes above the angle on the back of the mouthpiece.

g. Cradle the small piece in your palms, establishing your thumbs as *goal posts*. Use the thumbs to further align the reed with the mouthpiece at the tip, sides, and bottom. In Figure 3.5, notice the thumbs as goal posts.

h. Tighten the screws until snug. They are snug enough if you cannot pull the ligature off when trying to do so.

4. Check reed alignment and ligature position on each mouthpiece.

5. Initial embouchure work (not developed here).

6. Disassembly of small piece:

    a. Open instrument case.

    b. Loosen the ligature screws three to four turns.

    c. While holding the bottom end of reed in place with thumb, carefully remove the ligature. Place it on your lap.

    d. Remove reed. Hold on side.

    e. Using thumb and index fingers, wipe off excess moisture.

    f. Place flat side of the reed against the flat surface of a reed guard, plastic container, or cardboard container. Place in the instrument case.

    g. Disassemble mouthpiece and barrel using back and forth motions. Place the barrel in case.

    h. Re-assemble the ligature on the mouthpiece for storage. Cover the mouthpiece with a cap. Place in the case.

Follow this plan daily with you leading and controlling until habit formation begins to develop. Monitor individuals. Gradually give responsibility to students to do this independently, but remain observant.

You have noticed that swabbing has not been covered. This is intentional for several reasons: Time constraints, mental capacity (the above is enough new information for now), and limited attention spans (swabbing at this point would distract or take away from a focus of attention on *what's most important now*). There will be a time and place for swabbing—after instrument assembly and disassembly, after initial embouchure work, and after introduction of hand position.

Characteristics of Embouchure and Air Stream

Embouchure

1. Lower lip tight against the front of the lower teeth. Typically, this is beneficial in three ways: a) to establish the active, firm nature of the lower lip as a platform for the reed, b) to place *some* lip over the teeth, and c) to move the lower jaw forward slightly such that the bottom and top teeth are aligned.

2. Lower lip contacts reed at the fulcrum. The fulcrum is the point at which the mouthpiece begins its curve away from the reed. The amount of mouthpiece in the mouth is critical. How much? To the fulcrum. Figure 3.6 shows the curvature of the mouthpiece.

3. Upper teeth contact the mouthpiece.

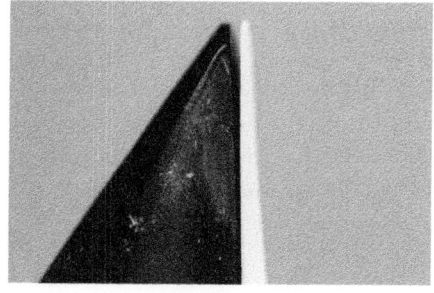

FIGURE 3.6 Curvature of the Mouthpiece (Fulcrum)

(Produced by Paige Jarreau at Paige's Photos)

4. Lips and cheeks against the teeth. This results in firm corners. Don't think "close the mouth"; think "close the lips against teeth."

5. Jaw is down. Jaw is situated as if saying "OH"; tongue as if saying "IH."

Air Stream

1. Blow straight ahead, not down.

2. Blow fast air.

3. Shape inner mouth cavity as if saying "IH." The tongue is high in the back. Feel the molars with sides of the tongue.

Sequence of Instruction for Making First Sounds in Group Instruction

This sequence of instruction with a group of beginning clarinet players is divided into several chunks of activity, each of which should be approached with careful consideration by both teacher and students. While reading the text, be aware of what is quoted material and what is not quoted.

First Chunk

1. Teacher demonstrates a thumb and fingertips hold of the small piece. Students imitate. The small piece hold is demonstrated in Figure 3.1 above.

Second Chunk

2. Without small piece, teacher to students: "Sit tall, head erect." Students do.

3. Without small piece, teacher to students: "Open mouth slightly. Pull lower lip tight against your teeth." Teacher demonstrates. Students imitate. Repeat several times. Check individuals. *Note*: Lip tight against teeth should put some lower lip over the lower teeth.

Don't be in a hurry to move on to the next chunk. Take some deliberate time with the second chunk. Build habit strength in sitting tall with erect head. See how students develop by having multi-class experiences with lip against teeth.

Third Chunk

1. With the nail of your index finger, show how much reed should be in the mouth. The fingernail shows the point on the reed (the fulcrum) that makes contact with the lower lip. Teacher to students: "Place your fingernail on this part of your reed, the fulcrum. This is the part of your reed that rests on your lower lip. Notice how much reed goes inside your mouth."

2. With small piece, teacher to students: "Sit tall. Open your mouth. Pull the lower lip against teeth. Place the reed at the fulcrum on the lower lip." Teacher demonstrates. Students imitate. Repeat this sequence several times: 1) Sit tall, 2) open mouth, 3) lip against teeth, 4) place reed at fulcrum. Check individuals for amount of reed in mouth. This is a good time to have students make a roughly 35° angle—small piece to face.

3. With small piece, the teacher continues: With reed at fulcrum, "Place your teeth on top." In other words, close the mouth just enough to allow the upper teeth to contact the top of the mouthpiece. Have students do this without closing their lips around the mouthpiece. At this point, you should be able to see the teeth making contact—a stabilizing contact, not a biting contact.

4. On the teacher's deliberately paced command, rehearse: 1) Sit tall, 2) open mouth, 3) lip against teeth, 4) place reed at fulcrum, 5) teeth on top. Check individuals.

It goes without saying that without a mirror I cannot *see* how much reed I have in my mouth. Using the side view of reed and mouthpiece to find the fulcrum provides a visualization of imagined mouthpiece placement on the lower lip. The students know what the goal is. And, importantly, finding the fulcrum provides a way to make a "mountain" out of something that is often overlooked in beginning clarinet—how much reed goes in the mouth. As their teacher, help them with the part they cannot see by making individual contacts and by providing mirrors. Peers can help each other in finding the optimal amount of mouthpiece in the mouth. There is a tendency to put too little in the mouth, which makes for a small sound.

Notice in the third chunk the choice of the word *place*. *Place* the fulcrum on the lip. *Place* rather than start at the tip of the reed and *push in*. Pushing or sliding the reed against the lower lip drags lip with it. Too much lip over the teeth dampens tone quality and can cause squeaking.

Fourth Chunk

1. Teacher demonstrates for students: 1) Sit tall, 2) open mouth, 3) lip against teeth, 4) place the reed, 5) teeth on top, 6) close the lips without pushing them forward and without raising the jaw. Step 6 is new. The lips should close around the reed and mouthpiece while staying *against* the teeth. Have students do the steps on the teacher's deliberately paced command. Repeat. Check individuals.

2. Teacher to students: "Blow fast air straight ahead!" Teacher demonstrates. Students sustain a first sound.

In the clarinet embouchure, the lips and cheeks stay close to the teeth. The lips (top, bottom, and sides) should be active, not passive, in the clarinet embouchure—active in the sense of pulling against the teeth. This lip activity provides support for the reed/mouthpiece. The jaw should stay down, though this aspect of clarinet embouchure need not be dealt with in the first days of study.

In Figures 3.7 and 3.8, notice these embouchure characteristics: Erect head, 35° angle—small piece to face, amount of mouthpiece in the mouth, lips and cheeks *against* teeth, and jaw down. The female is a 7th grader, the male an 11th grader, both making excellent sounds.

The ultimate goal with small piece practice is for students to produce an F-sharp concert at *forte* dynamic and with resonant tone. F-sharp concert is a sign that the embouchure—the parts of it that can be seen by the teacher *and* the parts of it that are inside the mouth—is either correct or well on its way to being correct. Don't be surprised if early small piece work by beginners yields F-concert (a half step too low) instead. This is typical. One aspect of embouchure development is getting the student to raise this F to an F-sharp over the first month of study. More on this below in "What to Listen for in Embouchure."

FIGURE 3.7 Embouchure (Middle School Musician)
(Produced by Paige Jarreau at Paige's Photos)

FIGURE 3.8 Embouchure (High School Musician)
(Produced by Paige Jarreau at Paige's Photos)

Initial Embouchure Work: A Closer Look

Notice that the first sounds sequence above makes no reference to the jaw down and arched tongue characteristics of embouchure. There is good reason for this. When I prepare to introduce embouchure, I ask myself, "What can I accomplish with a group of beginning clarinet players in the time available? What is a reasonable expectation on my part?" Over the next several weeks, I will be happy if my students are *in the ballpark* in terms of embouchure. Ballpark accuracy leaves the teacher in position to refine embouchure and air stream.

With these questions and desires as a backdrop, I make decisions about how to proceed based on *what is necessary now*. The issues that are pertinent now are: a) holding the small piece a certain way; b) sitting tall with head erect; c) pulling the lower lip against the teeth and paying attention to how much lower lip is over the teeth; d) aligning lower and upper teeth; e) placing the fulcrum on a firm lip; f) setting the teeth on top of the mouthpiece; g) closing the lips without pushing them forward; and h) blowing fast air. For 11- and 12-year-old students, these are do-able things. And this is plenty of challenge for the first several lessons. After several lessons, I want them to be well on the way toward doing these things on their own—habitually—without reminders from me. I do not want to have beginning clarinetists who in October of the school year do not play with their teeth on top, or who play with the head bowed, or who play with too little mouthpiece in the mouth, or who blow with a weak air stream. So students need opportunities to do these things many times correctly *in my presence* in order that October be reserved for refining embouchures.

Back to jaw down and arched tongue. Though not directly introduced to students to this point, I am aware of their importance. I'm noticing who among my students naturally gravitate to a jaw that is down. About these students, I'm saying to myself "Hurray!" I'm also noticing which students' small piece sounds sound like the tongue is arched.

For those students, who are not natural on these two issues, I'm thinking about how and when to address it. Letters a through h in the above paragraph, if done correctly, are conducive to jaw down and arched tongue. So providing ample experience in and good feedback about a–h is critical. But in the class setting, embouchure flaws are inevitable in some students. A soft lower lip, a flat tongue, and a bunched up chin not only affect quality of sound, they create more problems when tonguing and the clarion register are introduced. Ideally, the time to deal with major embouchure flaws is between ample experience with a–h and the introduction of tonguing and/or the clarion register.

Potential for Success in Clarinet Study

Probably the best indicator of whether a student is suited for clarinet study is his ability to get in the right ballpark concerning the small piece pitch and tone. This can reveal itself in an instrument selection experience involving a several minute, one-on-one session with a teacher. Is the student able to sustain a tone while keeping the head erect, while keeping the teeth on top of the mouthpiece, while avoiding puffing the cheeks, and without pressing the jaw upward in exaggerated fashion? If the answer is no to some or all of these questions, clarinet may not be a wise choice for this student. This being said, it is also possible for this student, with the help of a good teacher, to overcome initial deficiencies. The question is: "Can this happen before the student loses interest?"

Students with disabilities (physical, cognitive, emotional, sensory) should be given a more comprehensive evaluation than that described above concerning potential for success. The music teacher should consult with the student's team of teachers/counselors, as well as his parents, to develop a full knowledge of the student's capabilities.

Teaching/Learning Sequence: Small Piece Practice

As your students are working toward a ballpark-accurate small piece tone, practice of desired behaviors can be organized in a process I call the teaching/learning sequence. Note the following teaching/learning sequence for small piece work.

1. Sit tall.
2. Head erect.
3. Small piece to you.
4. Lower lip.
5. Fulcrum.
6. Teeth on top.
7. Lips to teeth,
8. Angle.
9. Fast air.

The sequence presented in Figure 3.9 is an abbreviated form or skeleton of a step-by-step process for getting ready to make a tone on the small piece. The substance of each step has already been established by you in the minds of the students. It is at this point that students need only brief reminders of what comes next in the sequence. Students know based on your instruction and guided experiences what *sit tall* and *head erect* mean. They know that *small piece to you* means to bring the small piece to the head rather than moving the head to meet the small piece. They know that *lower lip* means to pull it tight against the teeth. *Fulcrum* is a reminder to place it on the lower lip. *Teeth on top* is a reminder to place the teeth on top of the mouthpiece. Lips to teeth is what one does when closing around the reed—don't reach out with lips; instead keep them packed in against the teeth. *Angle* refers to the 35° angle of small piece with head. *Fast air* is a reminder to be aggressive with the air stream. If the head is erect, fast air will be pushed straight ahead, which is highly desirable and necessary if the goal of F-sharp concert is to be reached.

This instructional sequence is a checklist of what one thinks about and does in preparing to make a tone on the small piece. You might remember an earlier admonition to conjure a mental checklist of embouchure traits prior to producing a tone. Here it is at the beginning level. A student who repeatedly fails to do one or more of the steps in this sequence is not unsuccessful because he is incapable of doing the behaviors. He doesn't do them because his brain doesn't tell him to do them. The teaching/learning sequence represents a proactive approach to teaching and learning in that it organizes student thought and action up-front—from the beginning. If properly rehearsed (and this is a big if), it promotes good habits before bad ones have a chance to take hold.

In effect, the sequence breaks down into individual steps what an accomplished clarinetist would do all at once, as one big action. We must rehearse the parts at a deliberate pace, and eventually hasten the pace such that nine separate steps begin to meld together and become one big action. This idea can be promoted by rehearsing the sequence rhythmically. Each step is chanted by the teacher in 4-beat durations during which students respond accordingly.

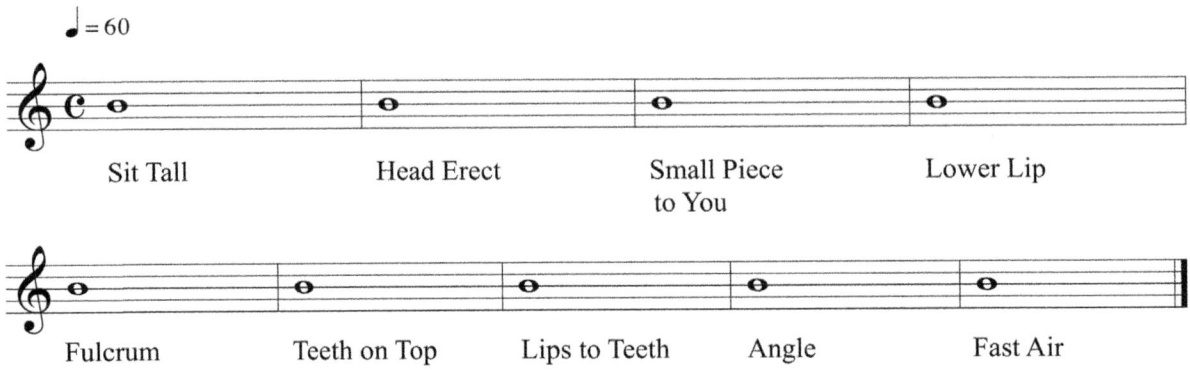

FIGURE 3.9 Teaching/Learning Sequence: Small Piece Practice

At appropriate times, the pace from step to step can be accelerated by chanting in 2-beat durations, then 1-beat durations per step at roughly quarter note equals 60. With enough in-class repetition, most students will memorize this sequence seemingly without trying. To ensure that everyone memorizes and does this sequence as a habit, the effective teacher will consider testing students.

Performance Testing

The performance test shown in Table 3.1 is no more than the "Small Piece Teaching/Learning Sequence" arranged in test format. Set up a video recorder in a practice room. Students, one at a time,

TABLE 3.1 Performance Test: Clarinet Embouchure

Name:		
Date:		
	Yes	No
1. You sat tall.		
2. Your head was erect.		
3. You brought the small piece to your erect head.		
4. You pulled your lower lip tight against your teeth.		
5. You placed the fulcrum on the lower lip.		
6. You rested your teeth on top of the mouthpiece.		
7. You pulled the lips and cheeks against teeth when closing the mouth.		
8. You made a 35° angle between small piece and head.		
9. You blew a fast air stream while sustaining the pitch.		
10. Your small piece pitch was concert F-sharp.		
Grade:		

Note: 10-point test; −1 if order is incorrect. 9–10 Yes = A (Proficient), 8 Yes = B (Developing), 6-7 Yes = C (Novice)

unobtrusively leave class in a pre-arranged order to take the test. Each student sits in a chair in view of the recorder, which is recording continuously, and demonstrates the small piece sequence. When finished, the student unobtrusively returns to class as the next student, waiting outside the practice room, enters the test room. Later, you view the recording, complete the test form, and assign grades.

All students are able to sit tall one time when asked. The goal, though, is for them to sit tall *every time* when playing the clarinet—without having been asked! All students can put enough mouthpiece in the mouth one time when reminded. The goal is to get them to do it every time—and to remind themselves! Rehearsing teaching/learning sequences and performance testing are tools that promote doing things the same way each time, doing things as a matter of habit, and attending to the details.

Notes to teacher:

1. For this test, situate the video recorder, as much as possible, so that you are able to view a close-up of the student's head from an oblique angle (part frontal and part side view).

2. As you can see on the grading scale, the student must do all or nearly all steps correctly in order to receive an A or B grade. The expectations are high because students were provided many opportunities to perform the sequence, and hence the test, in lessons/rehearsals.

Ideally, students would not be introduced to the assembled instrument until embouchure work on the small piece had resulted in most students achieving a reliable ballpark embouchure and air stream. Instrument assembly, instrument care, and hand position are explained here now, although there is more to be dealt with concerning embouchure development.

CLARINET ASSEMBLY, DISASSEMBLY, AND BASIC CARE

Assembly Sequence

1. Lay the closed case on a flat surface (a student's lap; the floor if lap is small). Check that the case is situated correct side up.

2. Complete assembly of the small piece (see "Small Piece Assembly" above). *Note*: There are two types of ligatures—traditional (the screws are located on the player side of the mouthpiece) and inverted (the screws are located on the side away from the player). No matter which type, the screw heads *always go to the player's right* (see Figure 3.3 above). If they protrude to the player's left, the ligature was put on incorrectly. Turn it around.

3. Remove the bell and lower joint from the case. With the protruding cluster of keys facing up and as shown in Figure 3.10, grasp the lower joint by placing the side that has no keys in the palm of the left hand and wrapping fingers around such that thumb and base of thumb shut the two open keys nearest the bottom end. Put the bell on the lower joint using small back and forth turns.

4. Remove the upper joint from the case. With the protruding cluster of keys facing down, situate the upper joint by placing the side that has few keys in the palm of the left hand. As shown in Figure 3.11, wrap fingers such that the middle finger closes the covered key, which raises the bridge key. *The bridge key must be raised during assembly in order to avoid bending the bridge key mechanism.* Grasping the lower joint at its bottom (where there are few keys) with the right hand, adjoin upper and lower joints with small back and forth turns. *Look at the bridge key area during assembly.* Back and forth turns that are too large will bend keys. The joints must align at the bridge keys.

5. Grasping the upper joint at its top (where there is only the closed register key) and the small piece at the barrel, adjoin the two with small back and forth turns. Align the mouthpiece such that the reed forms a straight line with the register key.

Disassembly and Swabbing

1. Remove the small piece. Loosen the ligature screws three to four turns each. Remove the ligature carefully while holding the base of the reed in place with the thumb.

2. Remove the reed (avoid handling at the tip). Wipe off excess moisture with thumb and index finger. Place the flat back of the reed (called the table) against the flat surface of a reed guard, plastic container, or cardboard container. Though it is impractical in the school environment, placing the reed with table side up on a surface in open air is ideal. This allows the reed to dry while avoiding warping and the formation of mildew.

3. Disassemble mouthpiece and barrel. Wipe the inside of the mouthpiece with the swab by using a finger to guide the swab in wiping the tone chamber and by rolling the swab in order to get inside the bore of the mouthpiece. When swabbing is complete, place the ligature on the mouthpiece, the cap over the mouthpiece, and store in the case. Pulling the swab through the mouthpiece frequently can damage the mouthpiece.

4. Swab the barrel. Wipe moisture on tenons and in receivers.

5. Insert the swab through the bell and pull through the assembled bell, lower joint, and upper joint.

FIGURE 3.11 Lower and Upper Joint Assembly
(Produced by Paige Jarreau at Paige's Photos)

FIGURE 3.10 Bell and Lower Joint Assembly
(Produced by Paige Jarreau at Paige's Photos)

6. Disassemble upper and lower joints and bell in reverse order of assembly. Take care to grasp the upper joint such that its bridge key is raised. Wipe moisture on tenons and in receivers.

Care

In the first weeks of clarinet study, knowledge of the following instrument care issues by teacher and students is sufficient. Additional information about instrument care is provided below in the section titled "Foundations of Instrument Care."

1. Apply cork grease for ease of assembly. Don't over-do it. If you see white on the tenon corks, too much grease is being used.

2. During swabbing, watch that swabs are small enough to be pulled through the joints. Do not allow students to force a swab through a joint. The moment the swab feels tight in the bore, stop! The swab can be pulled in the reverse direction to get it out. If the swab becomes stuck, more than likely the services of an instrument repair technician will be necessary. The swab should be pulled through from large end to small end of instrument or joint.

3. Watch that students get in the habit of removing the reed from the mouthpiece after lessons and rehearsals in order to swab the mouthpiece. Otherwise, the mouthpiece will become very dirty. It can be washed with lukewarm water. Hot water will cause it to warp.

4. If the instrument must be laid down on a chair, do so in two pieces (separated at the mid point) and with keys up. Do not stand it vertically on its bell.

5. Under extremes of temperature, wood will crack. Do not place or store woodwind instruments in extremes of hot or cold temperatures (on a heater or left in a car in cold weather).

CLARINET HAND POSITION

Right Hand

1. The right thumbprint should contact the body of the instrument under the thumb rest. The side of the thumb contacts the thumb rest about halfway between the tip and first knuckle.
2. The right thumb and index finger should form a backward C. The index finger should *not* lean into and help support the instrument.
3. The right-hand fingers, while curved, point nearly straight across the instrument.
4. The right pinky should hover just above the F/C key.

Left Hand

5. The left thumb should cover its hole at a *2 o'clock* angle. The corner of the left thumb should extend above the hole just enough to overlap the bottom edge of the register key. The register key will be depressed by rocking the thumb, not by sliding it.
6. The left thumb and index finger should form a modified C shape.
7. The left-hand fingers, while curved, point nearly straight across the instrument..
8. The left pinky should hover just above the E/B key.

The front view of Figure 3.12 shows several aspects of hands and holding: Angle of fingers straight across instrument, naturally curved fingers, and pinky fingers hovering over their respective keys. The side view of Figure 3.13 shows the top hand thumb at a 2 o'clock angle, and one can somewhat make out the backwards C shape of the bottom hand thumb and index finger.

Teaching/Learning Sequence: Hands and Holding

To get students in the right ballpark with initial hand position, a teaching/learning sequence for hands and holding can be structured as follows.

1. Thumb rest.
2. 2 o'clock.
3. 1–2–3–1–2–3.
4. Wrists in straight line.
5. Instrument to you.
6. Form embouchure.
7. Angle.
8. No lean.

FIGURE 3.12 Clarinet Hand Position
(Produced by Paige Jarreau at Paige's Photos)

FIGURE 3.13 Left Thumb in the 2 O'clock Position
(Produced by Paige Jarreau at Paige's Photos)

Students know, based on teacher instruction and guided experiences, that:

1. *Thumb rest* refers to proper positioning of right thumb. Is the thumbprint contacting the body of the clarinet? Is thumb rest resting halfway between the tip of thumb and first knuckle?

2. *2 o'clock* refers to the angle of the left thumb. It may help to do this and step 3 together as one.

3. *1–2–3–1–2–3* means to depress silently each finger (left hand 1–2–3, then right hand 1–2–3) at a slow pace determined by the teacher. Are the fingers relaxed and rounded? Are the fingerprints centered with the key holes? Students are advised to *feel for* hole coverage rather than to *look for* it.

4. Are the wrists in a mostly straight, natural line from forearms? (See Figure 3.12.)

5. *Instrument to you* means bring the instrument to your mouth rather than moving the head toward the clarinet.

6. *Form embouchure.* Embouchure is not the focus of this sequence. It simply provides a contact point to enable steps that follow.

7. *Angle* refers to the angle of the clarinet to the body. Is it at approximately 35°?

8. *No lean* refers to the position of the thumb and index finger of both hands. Is there a modified C-shape in the left hand and a backward C in the right hand?

These are the constituent parts of good hand position, which can be rehearsed initially at a deliberate, rhythmic pace. Each step is chanted by the teacher in 4-beat durations and, when appropriate, in 2-beat, then 1-beat durations during which students respond accordingly. With enough in-class repetition, most students will memorize this sequence. The effective teacher knows that enough correct repetition of this sequence in his or her presence will make this approach to hand position a habit of student performance.

Be aware that the typical beginning band method book does not progress to the notes of the right hand for quite some time. In this setting, your students have little incentive to position the right hand correctly. Instead, position of the thumb will get sloppy, the fingers will not stay spread over the keys, and the hand will lean into the side keys in order to help support the weight of the instrument. Though the method book may delay right-hand work, the teacher need not do likewise. Once holding has been introduced, it is time for student to *do* holding repeatedly. Have them do silent work, holding the clarinet in play position and depressing and raising keys in both hands (without looking) on teacher cues. To promote good right-hand position and to prepare for the day when the right hand will be used often, model and have students imitate brief sequences of slurred notes that provide practice in hole coverage. Ultimately, a descending F major scale, slurred slowly and thoughtfully, reveals the extent of success with hole coverage.

CLARINET TONE DEVELOPMENT

What to Look for in Clarinet Embouchure

1. Is the head erect?
2. Is there enough mouthpiece in the mouth?
3. Is the angle of the small piece correct?
4. Is the lower lip active—pulled against the teeth?
5. Is there too much or too little lip over the teeth?
6. Are the lips and cheeks against the teeth?
7. Are the teeth on top? You must check for this often during the early stages.
8. Are bottom and top teeth aligned—or very nearly so?
9. Is the jaw down?

For most beginning clarinet players, these steps involve actions that are do-able. They become hard, however, when we try to get students to do them as *corrections* to bad habits. In other words, when a student gets comfortable playing with the head down, it is difficult to play with the head erect. When one gets accustomed to playing without teeth on top, playing with the teeth on top is not so easy.

So work hard to get students to do things the right way early and often, so that bad habits don't establish themselves. To be successful with the items on this list, students need frequent correct repetition—both the thinking part of it and the doing part of it.

Number 6. Keeping the lips and cheeks against the teeth is included here not as a way to urge students to avoid puffing their cheeks. It is a legitimate clarinet embouchure characteristic. It promotes lip and corner firmness that is necessary for characteristic tone quality. Jaw down is characteristic of all wind instrument embouchures. You want the clarinet reed and mouthpiece to be supported by active lips, not the jaw pushing upward. Some clarinet teachers ask for a flat, pointed chin. Other experts say it is sufficient simply to have the jaw down.

The side views in Figures 3.7 and 3.8 show a number of desirable embouchure characteristics: Erect head, sufficient amount of mouthpiece in the mouth, a 35° angle of instrument with head, lips of cheeks against teeth, and jaw down. The embouchure in Figure 3.14 is a signal that embouchures can sometimes deviate from an idealized look and still work. The jaw in this photo does not appear to be down; however, the student at the time of the photo was getting a big, resonant sound. In fact, in the photo she is playing C above the staff!

FIGURE 3.14 Imperfect Embouchure but Good Sound
(Produced by Paige Jarreau at Paige's Photos)

Figure 3.15 shows a negative example. The chin is bunched up; the jaw is oriented in an upward, not downward, direction. Too much skin is making contact with the reed. There appears to be too much lower lip *in* the mouth.

What to Listen for in Clarinet Embouchure

1. Volume. Is the student playing *forte*? Is he blowing with fast air? From the beginning, encourage students to blow big!—to make a big sound—to play *f* always. You want the tone to be free and vibrant, which it won't be if students are not blowing with aggressive air streams.

2. F-sharp. Is the student producing F-sharp concert (or very near it) on the small piece? The small piece F-sharp is both an embouchure-teaching and embouchure-evaluating tool. Learn this technique well. It has the potential to invoke the student's ear in teaching and learning, and anything that involves the student's musical ear is good. Raise an E or F to F-sharp by a) using a fast-enough air stream, b) creating an "IH" shape in the tongue, c) increasing lip firmness, and d) and as a last resort changing to a harder reed.

FIGURE 3.15 Negative Embouchure Example
(Produced by Paige Jarreau at Paige's Photos)

3. Squeaking. Squeaking can be caused by too much reed in the mouth, too much lower lip over the teeth, too soft a lower lip, too much upward pressure from the jaw, reed out of alignment, finger coverage problem, or a warped reed or mouthpiece. When squeaking occurs, suspect first that there is too much mouthpiece in the mouth. Suspect second too much lower lip over the teeth and/or too soft a lower lip.

4. Small sound. Is the student producing a small, pinched sound? This is caused by not enough mouthpiece in the mouth, too much lower jaw pressure, or too slow a speed of air. It is not uncommon for a teacher to ask a student to put a bit more mouthpiece in the mouth and for the student's tone quality to improve and volume increase noticeably. There is a tendency among amateur clarinet players to put too little mouthpiece in the mouth.

5. Squawky, uncontrolled, unfocused, flat, no-energy sound. This is caused by not enough lip support or too low a tongue position.

What to Feel for in Clarinet Embouchure

Teeth on top. Grasp the barrel while the student plays and move it side to side. If it feels mushy, the upper teeth are not making contact with the mouthpiece.

What to Do When a Note Will Not Speak

When a note will not speak or speaks with difficulty, it is helpful for the teacher to have an organized plan of attack designed to diagnose the problem.

1. Check finger coverage. Are the tone holes covered? The player should *feel for* rather than look for correct placement. The teacher does the looking. If this doesn't work . . .

2. Turn the instrument around at the bottom of the barrel so that student can blow while you finger the instrument. If everything works, you know that the problem is in the student's fingers.

3. Have the student sustain an easily obtained note with good tone quality. Slur toward the problem note by adding one finger at a time. For example, if low G is the problem note, start on middle C (if in fact this is an easily obtained note) and add one finger at a time down to low G—slurred. (If finger coverage is the problem, this will reveal the finger that is the culprit.) Now start on low G. If this doesn't work . . .

4. Check the embouchure. If this doesn't work . . .

5. Try the instrument yourself. Are the bridge keys aligned? Is the reed worn, chipped, warped, misaligned, too soft, too hard? Is the mouthpiece chipped? Is there a leaky pad? Suspect a leaky pad if all else seems okay, and a note squeaks frequently or sounds fuzzy when it does speak.

Often the only way to know what the student is experiencing or feeling in terms of a note response problem or reed quality/strength issue is for the teacher to play the student's equipment. It is both good practice and good public relations for the teacher to sterilize the mouthpiece and reed in question both before and after using it. *Sterisol Germicide* is advertised to sanitize mouthpieces and reeds without causing damage to materials or finish.

Embouchure Teaching Strategies

Embouchure in General

The combination of mouthpiece, reed, and barrel alone (the small piece) and a fast air stream, if all else is correct, should result in an F-sharp concert. If the pitch is flat to this standard, one or more of the following could be the reason (diagnose in 1 through 6 order):

1. Head is down, meaning that the air is not blown straight ahead; it should be blown straight ahead.
2. Teeth are not on top.
3. Air stream is too slow.
4. Too little mouthpiece is in the mouth.
5. Embouchure is too relaxed.
6. Reed is too soft.

If the pitch is sharp to the standard (an infrequent occurrence with beginners), it is likely due to a pinched or too tight embouchure.

When you do small piece pitch work, you are in effect *tuning the embouchure*. The goal in small piece work is for students to memorize the *feel* of the embouchure when F-sharp is being produced, then reproduce this feel when playing the fully assembled clarinet. How much correct repetition of a sustained small piece pitch do you think is necessary to memorize the feel and then transfer it to the fully assembled instrument? Answer: A lot!

Fast Air Stream

1. Blow aerosol can air, not toothpaste tube air. In other words, push down—if seated, as if pushing through the chair (Tom Ridenour, www.ridenourclarinetproducts.com).
2. Push the air such that you feel the clarinet pushing back at you.
3. Push the air through to the bell of the clarinet, not just into the mouthpiece.
4. Create an "IH" position of the tongue while blowing.

Amount of Mouthpiece in the Mouth

1. Realize the tendency to put too little in the mouth.
2. Fulcrum on lower lip.
3. Intentionally put too much mouthpiece in the mouth in order to get a squeak. Then back it out a little at a time until squeak disappears.

Amount of Lip over the Lower Teeth

1. No lip showing outside the embouchure *may* mean too much lower lip is in the mouth.
2. Do not allow students to slide the mouthpiece/reed into the mouth. Open mouth and *place* reed on lip.
3. Pull lower lip against teeth without over-doing the amount of lip that goes over the teeth.

Teeth on Top

While the student is sustaining a pitch, grasp the barrel and move it side to side. If teeth are not making contact, it will feel mushy.

Firm Lips, Lips and Cheeks Against Teeth, and Jaw Down

1. Make a firm whistle formation, drop jaw, and maintain. The same can be achieved by saying "WHO" with drop of jaw.
2. Plug the end of the small piece with the palm of your hand and simulate the action involved in sipping a thick milkshake through a straw. Maintain this position. Think about what happened. Your lips firmed. Your lips and cheeks met up with your teeth. Your jaw moved down, if you allowed it to do so.
3. With mouthpiece/reed on the lower lip and teeth on top, say an exaggerated "EE," then meld into "OO" (but not quite all the way). Maintain while blowing. "EE" flattens the surface of the lower lip. The partial "OO" closes the corners, but does not change the flattened lower lip.
4. Have the student, while sustaining a pitch, try to push the upper lip down toward the mouthpiece. This will automatically lower the jaw.
5. Instead of approaching the embouchure by placing the reed on the lower lip first, as is typical, open the mouth and place the mouthpiece against the upper teeth first. Then put some lower lip over the bottom teeth. Then close the mouth from bottom up. This focuses student attention on gripping less than usual with the lower jaw.
6. Open the mouth about one inch (2.5cm), move the jaw forward so that bottom and top teeth are parallel, lip over teeth, place the mouthpiece on the lower lip, close around the reed/mouthpiece. The jaw forward aspect of this approach orients the jaw in a forward rather than upward (as in biting) direction.

Firm, Flat Lower Lip

1. Close the lips and push the index finger into the mouth against the resistance of the lips muscles. The action involved in creating the resistance firms and flattens the lower lip.
2. While sustaining open G, have the student place his index fingers just beneath the lower lip to the left and right of the reed (to free the hands, have the student support the clarinet by placing the bell on a leg). Direct the student to pull the lower lip down and away from the reed with the fingers. This should allow more of the reed to vibrate, causing more resonance in the tone.

Eliminate Puffed Cheeks

1. Have the student play a tone with puffed cheeks. As he sustains this tone, have him retract the cheeks. In other words, fix the problem by doing the problem, then during sustain, retract the cheeks.

2. Have the student, while sustaining a pitch, raise the tongue into an "IH" position. This high or arched position of the tongue is correct voicing on the clarinet and makes it difficult if not impossible to puff the cheeks.

Embouchure Checkpoints

Use the checkpoints presented in Figure 3.16 as an aid to evaluating embouchure quality.

FIGURE 3.16 Embouchure Checkpoints

1. Small piece pitch. F-sharp concert should result if air speed is *ff*, embouchure pressures correct, and reed strength appropriate. If the pitch is F-sharp, the embouchure is *in tune*.

2. Open G (or thumb and 1 E) on the instrument. Use these notes to transfer the feel of the embouchure on the small piece to the fully assembled instrument.

3. Slur the F major scale slowly descending to low F. You may begin using the right hand earlier than method books typically allow. If the student is not producing F-sharp on the small piece or not transferring this feel to the instrument, this scale allows the knowledgeable and observant teacher to notice flatness in pitch and/or tone quality. A tone that is flat in pitch, tone quality, or both is an indication of an embouchure that is too loose, air speed that is too slow, mouthpiece that is not enough in the mouth, tongue that is too low in the mouth (see "Voicing" below), or a reed that is too soft.

4. Slur low F to clarion C. Does the addition of the register key allow C to speak? If the F is solid (meaning *ff*, sustained, and no problem with finger coverage), but C is difficult to produce, the embouchure may be too loose. More precisely, the lips and cheeks may not be firm enough against the teeth or the lower lip may be too soft. As a checkpoint, there is good reason to produce 3rd space C long before the method book does. The clarinet embouchure is arguably the most difficult of woodwind embouchures to teach. It can be deceiving, that is, it can look good on the outside, but be flawed on the inside (embouchure pressures). Added to this, the typical first notes (open G down a 5th to middle C) of the method book do not make some embouchure flaws readily apparent, except to experienced teachers of the clarinet. Third space C is revealing. This register gives you some idea of what's happening on the inside of the embouchure. If the C pops right out easily, feel

good—the student is doing well! *Note*: For a first experience with clarion C, the teacher can depress the register key while the student plays a sustained low F.

5. Slur the C major scale slowly (clarion C to high C). If the tone cuts out on G or A, and the embouchure and air stream are okay, the reed may be too soft. Try a different reed of the same strength or increase strength by a half. Or the lips and cheeks may not be firm enough against the teeth, or the lower lip may be too loose, or the air speed too slow. The C major scale in this register is an excellent checkpoint for determining proper reed strength.

There is no reason that young clarinet players should be playing with head down, without teeth on top, without enough mouthpiece in the mouth, or without a fast air stream in March of the school year. In fact, there is no reason for any of these conditions to exist in September of the first year. If they do exist, it is primarily the fault of the teacher who does not know what to teach, or has failed to organize the information logically, or has not provided enough opportunities during lessons for students to do what is right, or has been oblivious to what students are doing, thus allowing bad habits to develop. To avoid being one of these teachers, you must know, organize, demonstrate, provide opportunities, look, notice, provide more opportunities, listen, notice, provide more opportunities, correct, provide more opportunities, remind, provide more opportunities. You get the idea.

When students are able to play in the clarion register with some ease, a good final "checkpoint" is high D played as a derivative of clarion F. As noted in Figure 3.17, establish a solid F, then slur to D by lifting the index finger of the left hand and depressing the top pinky key of the right hand (the E-flat key). This key in effect "tunes" the D (brings it up to pitch). If the D responds easily, the embouchure is in good shape. A lack of response may indicate too much upward jaw pressure or not enough mouthpiece in the mouth.

FIGURE 3.17
Ascending Major 6th Checkpoint

Other Important Factors in Clarinet Tone Development

Voicing

Have the student, while sustaining a pitch, raise the tongue into an "IH" position. This high or arched position of the tongue is correct voicing on the clarinet. It is an antidote to a typical beginning tone that, on the surface, sounds like a clarinet, but on close scrutiny is flat in pitch, tone quality, or both.

Reeds

Some unknowing students play on reeds that are too soft or too hard. Soft reeds will produce a bright, blatty, or thin tone. They will not respond readily in the upper register, making clean tonguing difficult. They will tend to play flat. Hard reeds will sound rough, unrefined, and sharp.

Take aside a student whose sound indicates a soft reed and do one or more of the following:

1. Try a different reed (new) of the same strength.
2. Try a harder reed (increase by one-half strength increments).
3. Try a better quality reed.

Have several reeds of some combination of harder and better quality available for the student to try. Compare old sound (using the old reed) with the new sound. Chances are that you will hear the difference, and your student will hear and feel the difference (see "The Single Reed" later in this chapter).

Mouthpiece

Playing on a reed and mouthpiece that are compatible will improve tone quality. Changing to a better quality mouthpiece will do the same. A more open mouthpiece tip calls for a softer reed. A more closed tip calls for a harder reed. Concerning reed and mouthpiece choices, consult with a trusted private teacher (see "The Mouthpiece and Ligature" later in this chapter).

Listening

By listening to artist performers, teachers and students develop opinions about clarinet tone. These opinions can lead to preferences that result in concepts of tone, toward which teachers may lead students and toward which students may aspire (see Table 7.1).

Vibrato

Vibrato is not viewed as a standard technique for classical clarinet in the United States, though it is used judiciously by some players. Clarinet vibrato finds greater acceptance outside the United States. Vibrato is used in jazz clarinet playing.

CLARINET TONGUING

Pre-tonguing Activity, Contact Point, and Vowel Shape

During initial embouchure development, "HIH" (a breath attack) is used to begin sustained tones. A ballpark embouchure combined with a fast air stream should result in a sustained, *forte*, unwavering tone that is relatively in tune, that is, the student produces at or near F-sharp concert on the small piece and transfers this *feel* to the fully assembled clarinet.

The basic articulation involves touching the tip of the tongue to the tip of the reed. The tip of the tongue refers to a location on top and a very little bit back from the actual tip of the tongue. The contact point for the tongue is the tip of the reed. This tip refers to a point just a bit below the actual tip of the reed. Real tonguing resembles saying "TIH." Notice that the vowel in "TIH" creates an arched shaped to the tongue, which is an important aspect of the embouchure.

Teaching Tonguing: Two Alternatives

Traditional Approach to Teaching Tonguing

The traditional approach to teaching tonguing is holistic, to use terminology from psychology. Tonguing is kept intact; it is not broken into its component parts. Modeling by the teacher, with voice and instrument, is integrated with the following steps.

1. Off the instrument, students say "TIH" using their speaking voices.

2. Off the instrument, students form a "cooling soup" aperture in the lips and legato tongue a series of "TIH"s on a continuous stream of air.

3. With your thumbnail, show students the ideal contact point on the reed.

4. On the instrument, students finger a mid-range note, form an embouchure, position the tongue on the tip of the reed, press against the reed with the tongue, and initiate the start of a tone as if saying "TIH." Sustain.

5. On the instrument, students do a series of four "TIH"s, tip of tongue to tip of reed. They tongue a continuous airstream.

Backward Approach to Teaching Tonguing

The traditional approach works for many students. It doesn't work for others who are unable to coordinate air stream, embouchure, and tongue. They fail to put it all together at once. Or they unknowingly articulate from the throat (glottal tonguing). The *Backward Approach* teaches tonguing by starting with something that we know students can do successfully, that is, start a tone with a pre-tonguing technique (a breath attack), and progressing into unknown tonguing territory. Keep in mind that the approach in this book is one that begins with tone production as an isolated element. Tone is not integrated with tonguing. Tonguing is introduced *after* a ballpark accurate embouchure and tone are achieved. Read each step below and compare to the notation in Figure 3.18.

1. As shown in Figure 3.18, student plays a mid-range note using the pre-tonguing articulation to initiate tone, sustains for 2 beats, and on beat 3 stops the tone by simply stopping the air stream. Repeat as necessary in order to allow student to *find beat 3*.

2. Student plays, sustains for 2 beats, and on beat 3 *stops* the tone by touching the tip of the tongue to the tip of the reed (HIH—T). With a fingernail, show the student the ideal contact point on the reed. Repeat this process several times in order to allow the student to *find the spot where the tongue goes*.

3. Student repeats Step 2 but when the tongue touches the reed, it touches for only an instant. It is immediately pulled away (imagine the reed being hot!) while the air stream keeps going (HIH—TIH—). Extend this process by tonguing successive quarter notes in legato tongue fashion (HIH—TIH—TIH—TIH).

4. Start the tone with the tongue in traditional manner (TIH—).

FIGURE 3.18 Backward Approach to Teaching Tonguing

Step 3 reiterated. Work hard to get students to legato tongue here. They should keep the air moving while tonguing. They will want to treat each note as a separate entity rather than a part of a series of notes that should be played as a line of music. Some will want to breathe after every note. Some will want to re-set their embouchure after every note. Don't let these faults creep in now; they are hard to correct later.

Assessment and Tonguing

I considered calling this section Addressing Problems in Tonguing, but it's actually about something bigger and more far reaching in your development as a music teacher. We'll call it assessment. Don't confuse this form of assessment with making up, giving, and grading tests. Assessment as I intend it here is one thing that good teachers do that makes them good.

Simply, assessment is collecting information. When I'm about to leave my office to walk across campus, I look outside my window to determine whether I should take an umbrella. I assess with my eyes. At my desk, my back is turned to the window, so frequently I hear thunder or rain before I see the visible effects. I assess with my ears. Assessment is something that people do all the time in order to get along in life. In the music room and rehearsal hall, effective teachers are keen observers, taking in information, some obvious and some very subtle, in order to make wise moment-to-moment decisions about what to do. This recurring cycle of collect–decide–act is fundamental to the structured teaching/learning setting. The teacher's skills of observation and assessment are greatly enhanced when she knows what to look for and listen for relative to tonguing.

Things the Teacher Can See

1. Is the jaw moving? Jaw movement is caused by large tongue movements. Confine movement to the front of the tongue—as if saying "d-d-d-d" at a fairly rapid pace. Articulate with little outward sign of movement, like a ventriloquist. To fix excessive jaw movement, the teacher must slow the student down, isolate the problem, and do some detailed work. The exercise in Figure 3.19 should be played on an easy-to-produce note. Use a legato tongue (do not stop the air between notes). Ask yourself: Is the tongue shaped as if saying "IH"? On contact, is the tip of the tongue touching the tip of the reed? Is the tongue moving only slightly away from the contact point? Is the jaw still?

FIGURE 3.19 Isolate Tongue Movement

2. Glottal tonguing. Be on the lookout for glottal tonguing (starting the sound in the throat), which can been seen and heard. Some beginners will unknowingly "tongue" from the throat. They think that they are tonguing correctly, not realizing their error.

Things the Teacher Can Hear

1. No tongue at all, a sort of huffing or puffing.

2. A "THU"-like sound. If the articulation sounds like "THU," the tongue is not pressing firmly enough against the teeth just prior to the release of the air.

3. Lack of coordination between tongue and fingers in fast passages or involving certain awkward note pairs regardless of tempo. The student must slow down! Isolate the specific problem (e.g., a two-note sequence) and slow the tempo enough for errorless performance across successive trials. Increase the tempo in small increments while maintaining errorless performance. Coordination problems can be fixed also by starting at a very slow tempo, playing each note short, fingering each note just a bit *before* tonguing it, and continuing this process while increasing the tempo in small increments. At a certain tempo, it becomes impossible to finger *before* tonguing, so at this point the practice procedure has reached its limit.

THE CLARINET MECHANISM

Brief History

Johann Denner invented the clarinet in 1690. The clarinet's predecessor was an instrument called the chalumeau, which played only in the chalumeau register (see "Range and Registers" below). Denner added the register key, which raised the notes of the chalumeau by a 12th. The Mannheim orchestra popularized the clarinet as an orchestral instrument. It had two clarinet players in 1758. Mozart wrote his clarinet concerto in 1791. The present-day fingering system, developed by flutist Theobald Boehm, was applied to the clarinet by Hyacinthe Klose and Louis-August Buffet about 1850. This is the Klose who wrote the standard clarinet method book, and the Buffet whose clarinet by the same name remains perhaps the best-known professional model instrument. Believe it or not, until about 1850 the clarinet was played with the reed located on top of the mouthpiece!

The role of the clarinet as a primary instrument in ragtime and jazz at the turn of the 20th century should be acknowledged in any historical account of the instrument. The clarinet remained a mainstay in jazz instrumentation until about 1945. In jazz style, the clarinet is typically played with vibrato. Big-name jazz clarinetists include Sidney Bechet, Benny Goodman, Artie Shaw, and Woody Herman.

Family, Transposition, and Clef

Soprano Clarinet in E-flat

1. Intonation is a greater problem here than on the soprano clarinet in B-flat.

2. Sounds up a minor 3rd.

Soprano Clarinet in B-flat

1. This is what people know as "the clarinet." This is the beginning instrument of the clarinet family.

2. Sounds down a major 2nd.

Clarinet in A

1. Common in orchestral writing. Use the same mouthpiece and reed for matched B-flat and A clarinets. Matched means the same make and model.
2. Sounds down a minor 3rd.

Alto Clarinet

1. Can be done without except in clarinet choir literature and a few band solo parts (e.g., works by Dello Joio); needs good player to make sound welcome.
2. Has neck and pronounced bell.
3. Support with neck strap.
4. Sounds down a major 6th.

Bass Clarinet

1. Has neck and pronounced bell.
2. Support with neck strap or peg.
3. The mouthpiece enters the mouth at a slightly upward angle.
4. Fingerings in the high register involve the half-hole technique.
5. Sounds down a major 9th.
6. Try tenor saxophone reeds on bass clarinet for better upper register response.

Note well. There are three important differences in tone production between soprano clarinet and bass clarinet. Compared to soprano clarinet playing:

1. The bass clarinet player should take in more mouthpiece.
2. The bass clarinet embouchure is more relaxed—some say more like the saxophone embouchure—than the soprano clarinet embouchure.
3. For bass clarinet, use a softer reed (perhaps not exceeding medium).

Contra-alto Clarinet in E-flat

1. Created to allow for an octave lower complement to the alto clarinet.
2. Sounds down an octave and a major 6th.

Contra-bass Clarinet in B-flat

1. Sounds down two octaves and a major 2nd.
2. Don't underestimate the value to overall band sonority of a contra-bass clarinet played well. In doubling the bass clarinet, especially an octave lower, it strengthens the harmonic foundation of the music and adds richness to the tone.

Note well. The parts for every instrument in the clarinet family are written in treble clef. The player of the larger instruments reads in treble clef while playing instruments that *sound down* into the tenor and bass ranges.

Instrument Manufacturing

Clarinets have a cylindrical bore and are made of grenadilla wood, rosewood, or synthetic material (plastic). Synthetic instruments are intended as student models. These can be very acceptable and certainly durable instruments.

Be aware of distinctions between professional and student line models. Most manufacturers produce both; in other words, one name (e.g., Leblanc) most often comprises several different models of clarinet and types of clarinet (e.g., E-flat soprano clarinet, bass clarinet). Student model instruments start at roughly $400.00. Professional instruments range from roughly $4000.00 to $7000.00 and up.

Buffet makes what is likely the most well-known professional quality clarinet. The following lists of instrument manufacturers are not exhaustive:

1. Professional model instruments are made by manufacturers Buffet, Leblanc, Selmer, Yamaha, and others.
2. Student model instruments are made by manufacturers Amati, Buffet, Jupiter, Olds, Selmer Leblanc, Yamaha, and others.

Range and Registers

1. All instruments in the family have the same theoretical range; however, the larger instruments do not respond well in the upper register (see Figure 3.20).
2. The range of professional-level bass clarinets extends to low E-flat on some models and low C on others.
3. Unlike flute, saxophone, oboe, and bassoon, the lowest notes of the clarinet require no extra effort to produce. They speak readily even at the *pp* dynamic level.
4. The clarinet range is divided into four registers as shown in Figure 3.20. The notes in each register are linked by some common characteristic (fingering, tone quality). The tone quality in the throat register is noted for its stuffiness.
5. *Crossing the break* occurs between throat and clarion registers, either ascending or descending, when moving between notes requiring few fingers to notes requiring many fingers or vice versa.

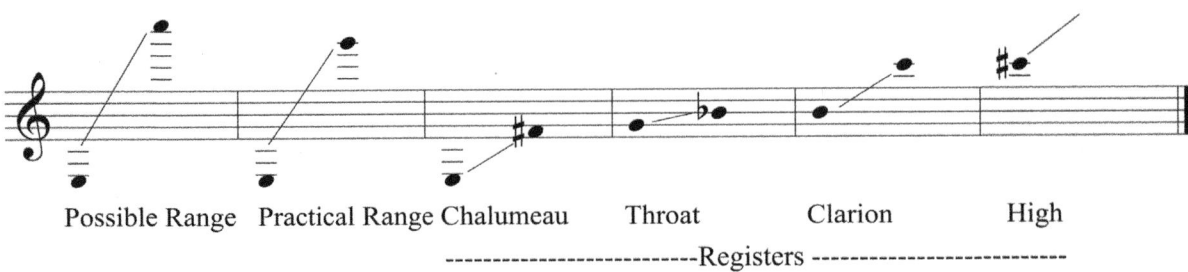

FIGURE 3.20 Clarinet Range and Register

Fingering Issues

Throat Tones and Right Hand Down

The notes in the throat tone register shown in Figure 3.21 are "short-tube" notes, meaning that their basic fingerings, which call for few or no fingers, primarily engage only a short length of the full tubing of the instrument. These notes tend to be deficient in tone quality (stuffy) and pitch (sharp). The right-hand portion of the fingering for the clarion register notes and their enharmonic equivalents shown in Figure 3.22 can be kept down while playing any of the throat tones.

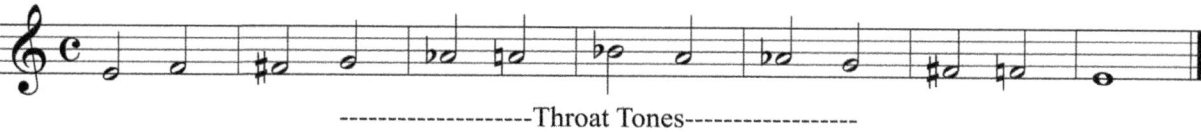

FIGURE 3.21 Throat Tones

FIGURE 3.22 Right-Hand Fingers in the Right-Hand-Down Technique

Right hand down is an intermediate and above technique that benefits the throat tones in three ways. It improves tone quality, lowers the pitch, and makes for less finger movement and consequently a more fluid finger technique when moving from throat to clarion register and vice versa. Figure 3.23 shows how to mark right hand down in a clarinet part. In the figure, the right-hand fingers for third space C are depressed one note early, during throat tone G. In measure 2, the right hand remains down during the throat tones A and G (see dotted line) because it has to be down for the regular fingering of C on beat 3. By fingering the passage as described, the finger movement has been reduced and the throat tones are likely to sound better and more in tune.

FIGURE 3.23 Marking a Right-Hand-Down Passage

Register Key 12th

The clarinet's left thumb manipulates two keys—a ring key and the register key. The register key has the look of an octave key, but because it changes pitch by a 12th, not an octave, it is properly called a register key. Figure 3.24 shows some of the clarinet's 12th relationships. For example, playing middle C, then depressing the register key produces a clarion register G.

FIGURE 3.24 The Use of the Register Key to Produce 12ths

In the Figure 3.24, the Rs and Ls refer to right pinky and left pinky fingerings that depress the four spatula keys on the instrument's right side and the three spatula keys on the left side, pictured in Figure 3.25. "Tucked" is my description of the location of the right pinky F-sharp (tucked in close to the last open hole). "Under" describes the location of the left pinky F under the other spatulas. "Outside" describes the location of the left pinky F-sharp to the outside of the instrument. And "Inside" describes the location of the left pinky E to the inside of the instrument.

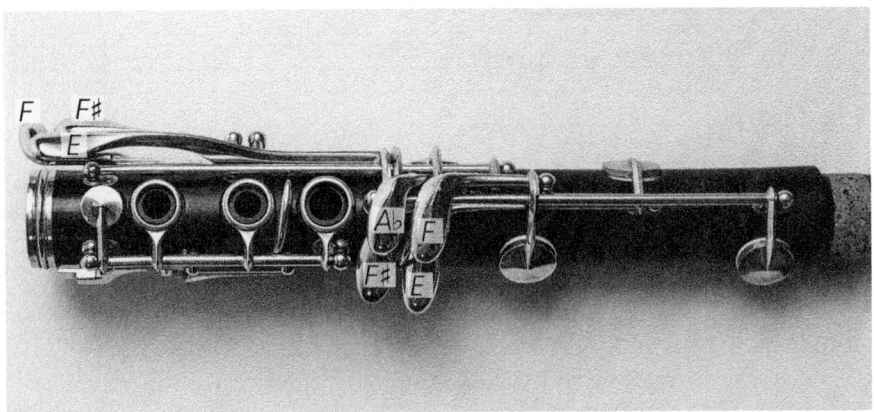

FIGURE 3.25 Labeled Pinky Keys on the Lower Joint
(Produced by Paige Jarreau at Paige's Photos)

Crossing the Break: Teaching It

The terminology "crossing the break" is typically used when moving from throat to clarion register and vice versa (few fingers to many fingers or vice versa). To teach it systematically in a way that sets up the student to succeed as much as possible, consider the following task analysis. A thoughtful, unhurried, and planned approach to introducing and developing the ability to cross the break fluidly is ultimately faster, more thorough, and less frustrating than having no approach.

1. Don't tell the student that it is difficult. With some practice, it's not.
2. Make sure that the student is relatively secure in playing in the chalumeau register.
3. Make sure that the student is relatively secure in playing in the clarion register.
4. Student slurs first space F-sharp to throat tone A and back by rolling the index finger to and from the A key. This motion is a key to crossing the break successfully.
5. Cross the break starting with C to A, descending and slurred. Do until secure. A descending cross of the break is easier than ascending.
6. Repeat step 5 pointing out that all fingers of the right hand can remain down during the A. This minimizes finger movement.
7. Cross the break by going from A to C as follows: a) tongue A, b) stop the tone, c) move fingers to C, d) tongue C. Repeat this deliberate process.
8. Point out that all fingers of the right hand can be placed in the C position during the A. In other words, prepare C with the right hand down on A. This minimizes finger movement.
9. Slur A to C. Keep fingers close to the keys. Move the fingers with conviction all at once. Stress the importance of blowing *through* the finger change. Keep blowing even though the C may not respond immediately.

Cross-Fingerings

Cross-fingering is woodwind terminology that refers to the use of left and right pinky fingers in alternation on successive notes. The clarinetist looks to avoid using successive right pinkies or successive left pinkies because same-pinky combinations make fluid finger technique difficult and slurring impossible in most instances. The knowledgeable player identifies what we will call the *red flag notes* in his part, creates a fingering plan that avoids same-pinky combinations, and marks the part with Ls (left pinky) and Rs (right pinky) to serve as reminders.

The procedure for identifying and marking cross-fingerings is outlined below and illustrated in Figure 3.26. It is important that you thoroughly understand and can apply numbers 1 through 3.

1. Number 1. These notes and their enharmonic equivalents are the red flag notes. Identify them in the clarinet part.
2. Number 2. These red flag notes and enharmonic equivalents can be fingered in one way only—as marked in Figure 3.26. All other red flag notes can be fingered in two ways: R or L.
3. Number 3. a) Mark an R or L over all *one fingering-only* notes. b) From each of these notes, as much as possible, label backwards (right to left), alternating between Rs and Ls for all red flag notes. When you *must* work forward (left to right), this is okay. Label only red flag notes!

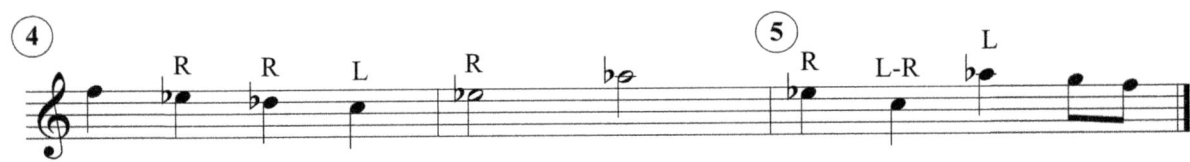

FIGURE 3.26 Cross-Fingerings: How to Figure Them Out

4. Number 4. If you cannot avoid successive same-pinkies, sliding in a downward finger direction is preferable to sliding upward (see E-flat to D-flat in Figure 3.26). Notice also that F has no finger marking because it is not a red flag note.

5. Number 5. A slide can sometimes be avoided by changing from L–R or R–L during the duration of a note. This technique is called organ fingering.

The excerpts in Figure 3.27 are intended to increase understanding of and skill in playing a few cross-fingerings. Excerpt 1a provides experience with left F and right A-flat. In the fingering chart at the end of the chapter, find the appropriate F and A-flat keys. Practice 1a, then play 1b.

Excerpts 2a and 2b focus on left C and right E-flat. You'll find these fingerings to be identical to 1a and 1b except for the addition of the register key. Of interest is the fact that the C to E-flat is often the first cross-fingering young clarinetists are challenged by. In 2b mark the left C and right E-flat.

Excerpts 3a and 3b target right B, left C-sharp, right D-sharp, and left B. The D-sharp is the same as the E-flat in Excerpt 2.

FIGURE 3.27 Cross-Fingering Examples

Some Trill Fingerings

The trill fingerings in Figures 3.28a and 3.28b involve something other than the normal fingerings for the two notes. The grey key(s) is the one that should be trilled. More comprehensive collections of trill fingerings are available online.

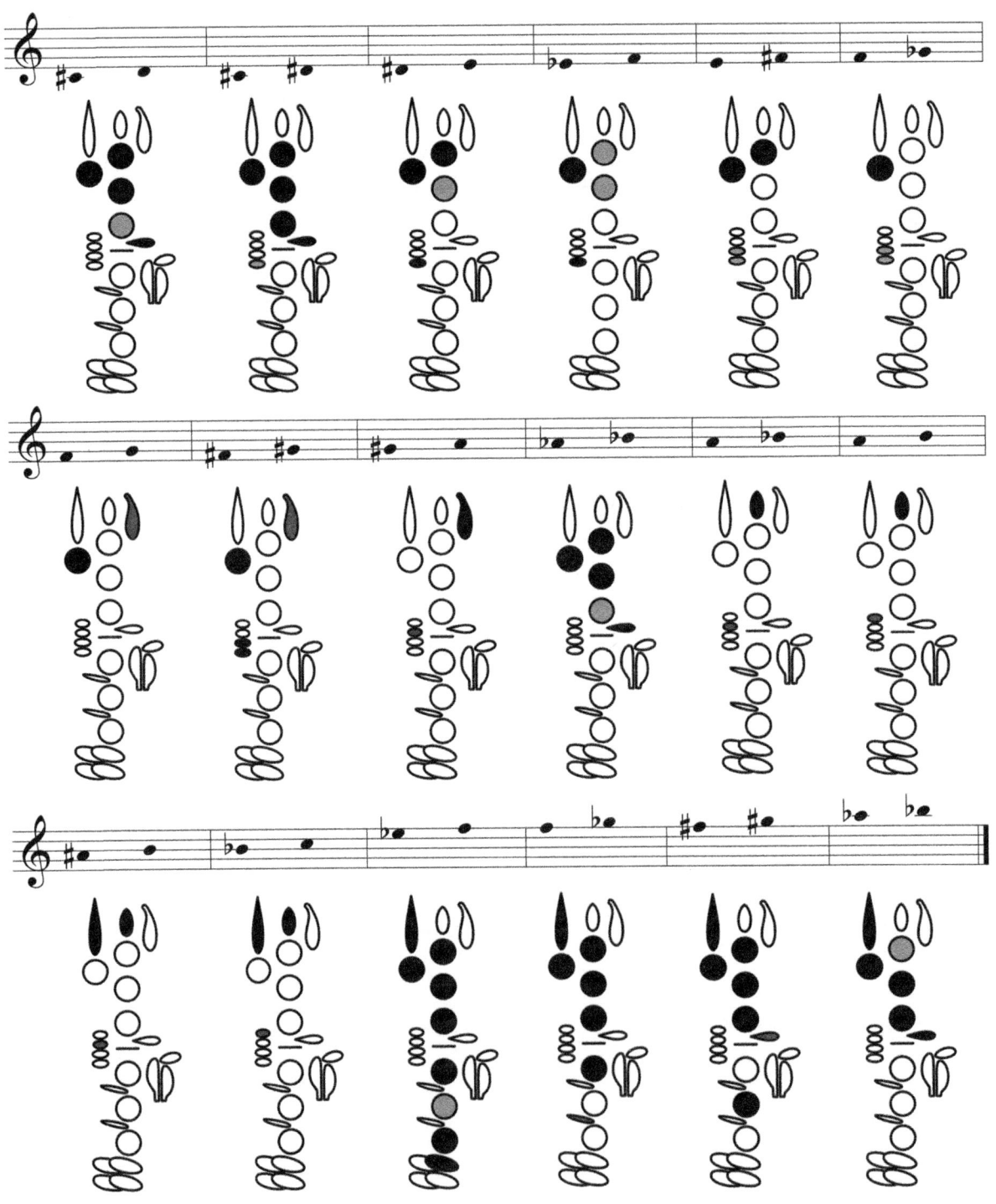

FIGURE 3.28A Clarinet Trill Fingerings page 1

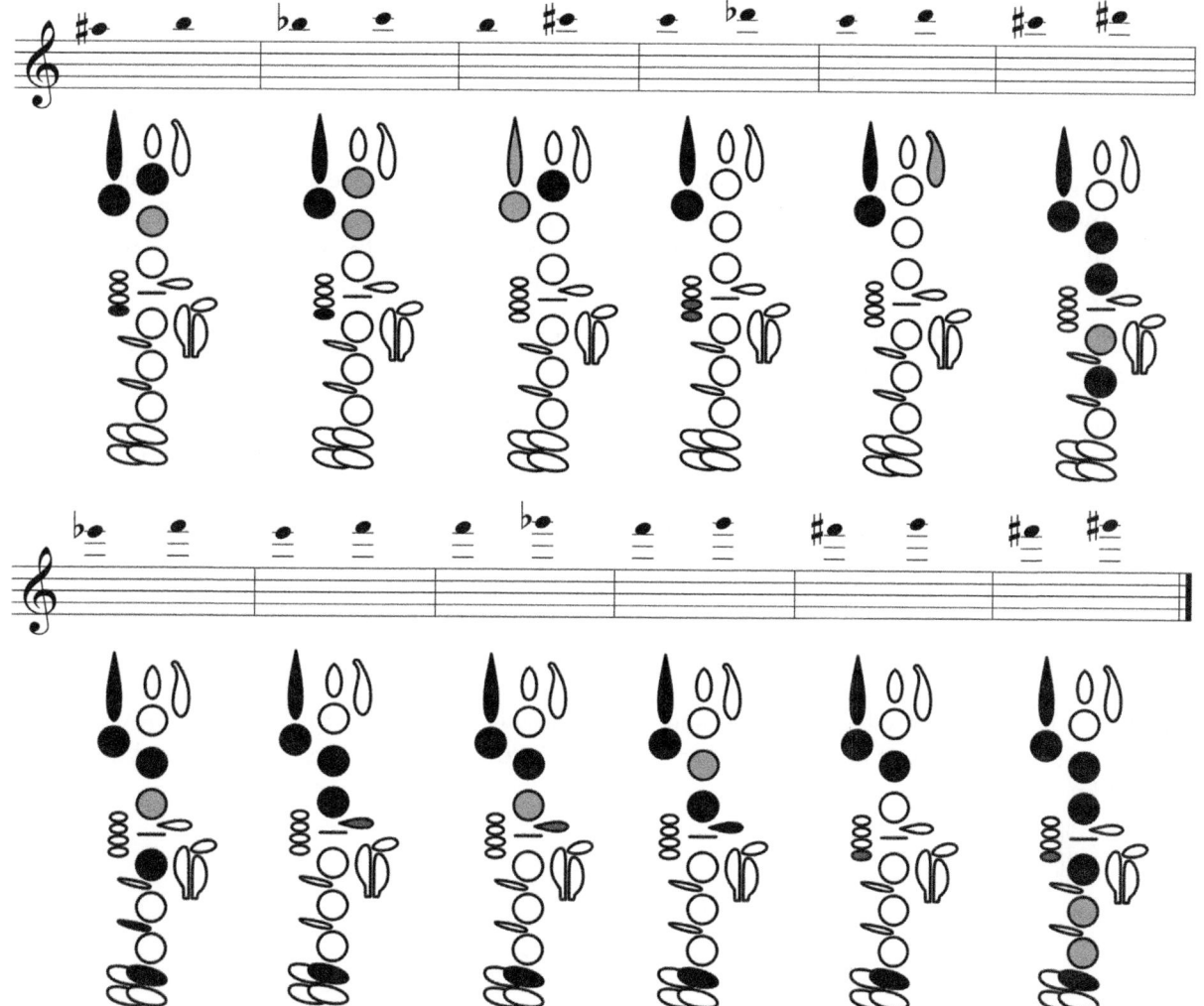

FIGURE 3.28B Clarinet Trill Fingerings page 2

Tuning and Intonation

Basic Information

1. The clarinet is designed to play in tune (A 440) when the barrel is pulled from the upper joint about 1/8 inch (3mm).
2. Tuning the embouchure. Achieve F-sharp concert on the mouthpiece and barrel or concert C on the mouthpiece alone. The clarinetist plays in the *upper middle* of the pitch range of the small piece (small piece or mouthpiece). The saxophonist plays in the *middle* of pitch range of the small piece (mouthpiece). This is an important difference between the two embouchures.
3. In tuning the instrument, insist that your students play at the *forte* dynamic level. This provides an accurate indication of where the instrument sits pitch-wise.
4. Most tuning adjustments are made by pushing or pulling the barrel. It must be remembered, however, that barrel adjustments have more effect on the pitch of short-fingered notes (e.g., the throat tones) than long-fingered notes (e.g., third space C). If the barrel is pulled excessively in order to play third space C in tune, the throat tones and other short-fingered notes will be flat. Read on.
5. Because adjustments at one adjustment place (e.g., the barrel) affect the pitch of certain notes more or less so than others, a thorough and more reliable tuning of the clarinet entails a three-step process (three tuning notes and three adjustment places).

Notated in Figure 3.29 are the standard band and orchestra tuning notes for clarinet, followed by the three-step tuning process. It is important that you learn the three-step process (the notes and the register affected by each).

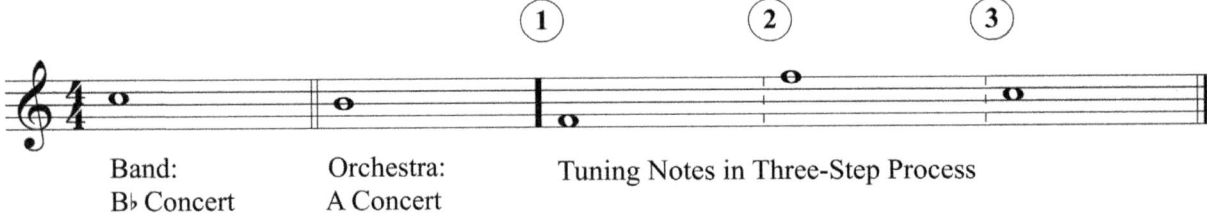

FIGURE 3.29 Clarinet Tuning Notes

Pitch Tendencies

Every wind instrument has pitch tendencies; certain notes, because of the design of the instrument, tend to be sharp, flat, or unstable (sharp and flat). By knowing the pitch tendencies of the clarinet, the effective music teacher is able to predict what might happen with regard to pitch before it actually happens in the lesson or rehearsal. One's job in rehearsal is to listen and discern whether student performance is consistent with the tendencies. If it is, he must know what to do to solve the pitch problems.

Flat Tendency

1. Cold temperature.
2. Loud volume (including *crescendo*).
3. Soft reed.
4. Angle of clarinet to face too great (or head down).

Solutions for Flatness

One of the following combined with a discerning ear will remedy flatness.

1. Lip up. This refers to one or more of the following: Firm the lips; adjust voicing toward "EE."
2. Play softer.
3. Open tone holes that are not open in the regular fingering. The range of E to C in the clarion register can be raised by depressing the low A-flat key.

Sharp Tendency

1. Low register.
2. Soft volume (including *decrescendo*).
3. Hard reed.
4. Throat tones—they are not only sharp but also stuffy in tone quality.

Solutions for Sharpness

One of the following combined with a discerning ear will remedy flatness.

1. Lip down. This refers to one or more of the following: Drop the jaw, loosen the embouchure, open the throat. The verticalness of the embouchure must be emphasized. Techniques: Adjust voicing toward "OH" or "AH"; play as if trying to stifle a yawn; ask student to *play flatter*.
2. Play louder.
3. Close tone holes in addition to those called for in the regular fingering. For the throat tones, put the right hand down (including pinky). The range of low A to C (chalumeau register) tends to be sharp at soft dynamic levels. To flatten, add the low F key or the low E key.
4. Use alternate fingerings. For throat tone B-flat, the alternate fingering (A plus the second right side key from the top) produces a tone quality that is clearer and easier to lip. This is a very useful alternate fingering in the clarinet literature.

Tuning and Intonation Summary

- Assembly
  - Start with the barrel pulled 1/8 inch (3mm).
- Tuning the embouchure
  - Small piece should sound big, resonant, and at F-sharp concert.
- Tuning notes (orchestra/band)
  - Play with best embouchure and at *f* dynamic level.
  - Three-step tuning process to tune throat register apart from the clarion and chalumeau registers.
- Pitch tendencies
  - Temperature: Cold = flat.
  - Register: Low = sharp; throat tones = sharp and stuffy.
  - Volume: Soft = sharp; loud = flat.
  - Reed: Soft = flat; hard = sharp.
  - Bad notes (most notorious): Throat tone B-flat.
- Solutions
  - Lipping.
  - Volume adjustment (e.g., play louder to lower pitch in low register).
  - Alternate fingerings (right hand down for throat tones; A plus the 2nd-from-the-top right side key to produce a clearer and more stable throat tone B-flat).

The Single Reed

Reed Characteristics

1. Reeds are made from cane, not bamboo. The climate of the Mediterranean coast of France is well suited for growing good quality cane, as are locations in Spain and California.

2. Single reeds come in different strengths (labeled 1–5—softer to harder; or labeled soft, medium soft, medium, medium hard, hard). The actual feel of a Number 3 reed will vary among Number 3 reeds of the same brand, among Number 3 reeds of different brands, and depending on the facing and tip opening of the mouthpiece. This is true of reeds of all strengths.

3. Start beginners on a Number 2 or 2.5 cane reed. It is likely that mid-first year through second year players will be comfortable with 2.5 reeds. Beyond the second year, changes in reed strength should occur as needed in half-strength increments. Check for the need to increase strength by gauging student performance on the small piece and in clarion register work; for example, "Embouchure Checkpoint No. 5" (see page 71–2). If all embouchure factors look good and the small piece pitch is a half-step flat, a harder reed might fix the problem. If on the ascending C major scale of Checkpoint 5 the tone cuts out around A above the staff, try a harder reed.

4. The Legere synthetic (plastic) reed has a good reputation among some professional players. The tone is very good. One reed lasts a long time (www.legere.com/home.htm).

5. The goal in reed strength is not to *progress* to a number 5 reed. One does not progress by increasing reed strength. The goal is to find a reed make and strength that in combination with type of mouthpiece provides the proper resistance for the embouchure, leading to the desired tone and response. The reed's strength must be compatible with the facing length and tip opening of the mouthpiece. The more closed the mouthpiece tip, the harder the reed should be. The more open the mouthpiece tip, the softer the reed should be.

6. To understand the text that follows, you will need to be familiar with certain parts of the single reed. They are illustrated in Figure 3.30 and explained as follows:

    a. The tip (Letter A) is the area of the reed that extends back from the actual tip about 1/8 inch (3mm). It should have a thumbnail shape and be uniform in thickness. The tip is the thinnest part of the reed. Its thinness allows it to vibrate freely and to initiate vibration down the rest of the cut portion of the reed.

    b. The sides (Letter B) extend down to the halfway point of the cut. The sides are thin. They are vibrators.

    c. The heart (Letter C) is centrally located in the cut portion of the reed. The heart is darker in color than the tip and sides. The tip and sides are vibrating areas. The heart is a resistance area. Somewhere in the production process (cutting, scraping, sanding), there is an optimal balance in thickness between vibrating and resistance areas.

    d. The cut (or vamp; Letter D) is the portion of the reed that has been cut, scraped, sanded. You will want to purchase French cut reeds. German cut reeds are made for a special-sized German mouthpiece.

    e. The unscraped bark (Letter E).

    f. The table. The flat-surfaced back of the reed (not pictured). For optimal reed performance, it should be flat. Advanced clarinetists *polish* the table in order to detect unevenness. They slide the table back and forth on the non-abrasive side of a piece of sandpaper. The sliding makes the parts of the table that contact the paper shiny. Parts that remain dull are not contacting the paper; they are low spots. Sanding (just a few strokes) is necessary to even out the low spots.

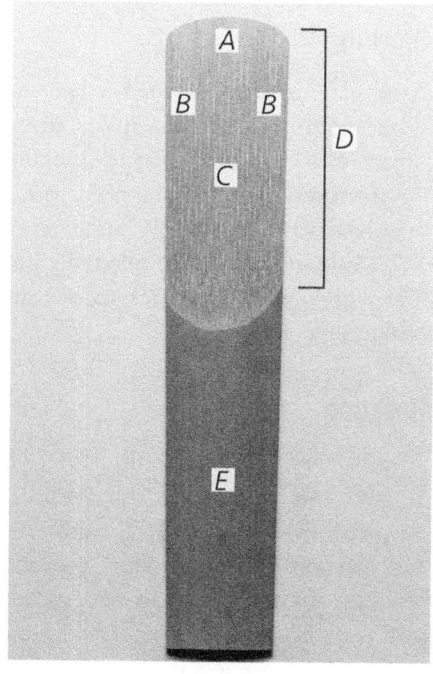

FIGURE 3.30 The Single Reed Labeled (Produced by Paige Jarreau at Paige's Photos)

It is tempting for music teachers who are not woodwind majors to assume that "I can't possibly have much to offer my students about reeds. There is so much to know, including how to make and adjust them, I couldn't possibly learn all that."

It is not necessary to "learn all that" to be an effective teacher of woodwinds. It is, however, reasonable to expect the non-woodwind major music teacher to be familiar with and use basic information about reeds. Take for example the "Wetting the Reed," "Storing," and "Rotating" sections below. A teacher uses this information in one or both of two ways: By teaching it to young clarinet and saxophone players or by observing the "reed behaviors" of his single reed players, noting what they do and don't do, and then leading them to do what is suggested. If you use this information in your teaching, you will be pleasantly surprised at how much you have to offer your students about reeds.

Wetting the Reed

The reed must be wet in order to respond optimally. There are a number of soaking tips that can make clarinet life easier.

1. In instrument assembly, the first step is to soak the reed. It should be soaking while the rest of the instrument is being dealt with.
2. A plastic film case or prescription pill bottle works well as a water-tight container. Water should be changed on a sensible schedule.
3. Soak *all* of the reed for 2–3 minutes in water—tip to butt, front side, and table side.
4. Soaking in tap water rather than saliva will prolong the life of a reed.
5. A warped (wavy) reed tip can be fixed by soaking it longer, or by pressing, with the thumb, the tip of the wet reed flat against the table of the mouthpiece. Warping, which occurs on the back of the reed (also the table), is less visible to the eye. If the reed rocks side to side when laid on a flat surface, the back has warped into a convex shape. Warping often happens as a result of uneven drying between playings (see "Storing" below).
6. During long periods of no play in rehearsal or performance, blowing warm air through the reed and instrument will stop the reed from drying out.

Storing

After playing, remove the reed (avoid handling at the tip) from the mouthpiece. Wipe off excess moisture with the thumb and the index finger. Place the flat back of the reed (the table) against the flat surface of a multi-reed case, plastic container, or cardboard container. Though it is impractical in the school environment, placing the reed *with table up* on a surface in open air is ideal. This allows the reed to dry evenly before storage. When a reed dries evenly across its surface, warping is minimized.

Multi-reed cases are relatively inexpensive and can be found at music stores and in woodwind catalogs. They are generally easier to use and safer for the reed than the one-reed clear plastic or cardboard containers.

Rotating

Ideally, reed players should have two or more reeds that work effectively and that are used in a rotation. If two reeds, there is the Monday–Wednesday–Friday–Sunday reed and the Tuesday–Thursday–Saturday–Monday reed. The constant use of only one reed will wear it out quickly. Because no two reeds will play and feel exactly alike, rotating reeds makes the embouchure (and the player) more flexible. Rotating teaches discrimination in that students are exposed to differences in response, intonation, general feel, and tone quality. The player will learn to tolerate a wider range of reeds—from those that "feel perfect" to those that are less than perfect but still very playable. The change to a new reed by students who play one reed until it dies can be traumatic. These students are not able to tolerate the different feel of the new reed. Finally, rotating ensures that reeds are removed from the mouthpiece on a regular basis.

By rotating, your reed players are never caught "with their pants down"—with no good alternative when the only reed they have been using is damaged and becomes unplayable.

Evaluating Quality

All reeds, both single and double, are evaluated on five criteria: 1) Response, 2) pitch, 3) stability, 4) dynamic range, and 5) tone quality. On single reed instruments, it is not the reed alone, but the mouthpiece and reed relationship that creates these performance characteristics.

1. Response is vibration. Above all else, a reed and mouthpiece must respond immediately to the air and tongue.
2. The pitch level of the clarinet and saxophone is in part dependent on the pitch level that has been built into the reed. A hard reed (hard for the player and/or hard for the type of mouthpiece) will play sharp. A soft reed will play flat. Generally, if response is good, pitch level will also be good.
3. A reed and mouthpiece combination is stable (or balanced) when the resistance they produce as the player blows is comfortable.
4. The ideal reed and mouthpiece relationship allows controlled playing at both *forte* and *piano* levels with relative ease.
5. Tone quality will vary from player to player along a range of bright to dark, and is related to player characteristics (embouchure, air stream, tonal concept), reed attributes, and mouthpiece attributes. Tone quality as it relates to reed selection doesn't much matter unless the reed responds, is in tune, and is stable.

The Needs of Novice Players

Novice reed players should play softer reeds that have good response, pitch, and stability. These qualities allow the embouchure to develop properly. In other words, bad habits are not promoted, as they would be if response, pitch, or stability were deficient. These same reeds, however, may be deficient in tone quality (they may sound bright and thin, not dark and rich). The music teacher must realize that this compromise is a necessary evil of the life of a novice reed player. As the embouchure strengthens, so too can reed strength, which makes available more options in terms of dynamic range and tone quality.

Notice that the recommendation is for use of "softer reeds that have good response, pitch, and stability." These reeds are not necessarily the same as "soft reeds." A number 1 reed is soft, but it has been suggested above that beginners not start on reeds softer than number 2. Beginners need reeds that are on the softer end of the soft to hard continuum, but not so soft that they are not relatively stable.

Finding and Buying Single Reeds

There are many manufacturers of single reeds, which can be purchased at music stores and via woodwind catalogs. Cost and quality vary widely. Refer to catalogs that list woodwind products to learn more about reed selection and specifications. One catalog lists close to 25 clarinet reed brands. One manufacturer includes several levels of quality with prices ranging from $25 to $33 for a box of 10 reeds (2015 figures). Saxophone reeds are a bit more expensive, and come in classical and jazz styles.

Don't expect to buy one reed of a desired strength and to be happy with the way it plays and sounds. Buy a box of reeds in order to find several that work well now, several that will work with adjustment, and several that should be either saved to try again later or discarded.

Visual Characteristics of a Reed

If you have the option of choosing a reed from among a number of reeds, consider the following:

1. Cane should be gold, not green or spotted.
2. Examine the cut of the reed by holding it to a light. Back lighting reveals the nature and quality of the cut. The lighter the color the thinner the cane. Lighter color areas promote vibration. Darker color areas provide resistance (i.e., something for the player to blow against and something to withstand the pressure of the lips and air stream). Are the lighter and darker colorations uniform across the reed? In other words, does the left side look identical to the right side? If not, the workmanship may be faulty. The reed will not vibrate the same on the left side as it does on the right side. Advanced clarinetists use fine sandpaper or reed rush to adjust reeds that are not uniform in thickness.
3. Back lighting reveals another indicator of cane quality. Are the grains or fibers of the reed straight and parallel? Do they extend into the tip, and are they evenly distributed over the entire tip and heart areas?

Two publications provide much practical information on clarinet reeds. They are *The Reed Guide* by George T. Kirck (published by the author) and *Clarinetist's Compendium* by Daniel Bonade (published by Leblanc).

Sterilization

Sometimes the only way to know what the student is experiencing or feeling in terms of a note response problem or reed quality/strength issue is for the teacher to play the student's equipment. It is both good practice and good public relations for the teacher to sterilize the mouthpiece and reed in question both before and after using it. A pump spray product called *Sterisol Germicide* is advertised to sanitize mouthpieces and reeds without causing damage to materials or finish.

What Students Need to Know and Do about Reeds

In a discussion about single reeds, let's begin with an *end* in mind. What do we want our high school single reed players to "look like" in terms of what they know about and do with reeds? Let's decide this *end* now before instruction begins. Let's be detailed and clear-headed about what needs to be taught at the beginning through intermediate levels of clarinet study to ultimately have students who look like we want them to look as high school musicians. We want our high school single reed students to do the following habitually.

1. In preparing to play, high school students will *wet the entire reed*—all of it!—using water or saliva. It would seem that by high school everyone would know to wet the reed before playing. What is not so well known is the importance of wetting all of it, which implies that the reed should be taken off of the mouthpiece during wetting.

2. When finished playing, high school students will a) *remove the reed from the mouthpiece*, b) *with thumb and finger wipe excess moisture from the reed*, and c) *store with table of reed against a flat surface*. Alternatively if there is time and opportunity, wipe off excess moisture, then lay reed table side up, and allow to air dry. This will prevent or minimize warping. You'd be surprised—well, maybe not—at how frequently this *end* is not performed by high school clarinetists.

3. High school students will *recognize and fix a warped reed*. Warping is caused by the constant wet, then dry, then wet, then dry, etc. condition of the reed. With a thumb, press the wavy tip of a wet reed flat against the table of the mouthpiece to fix warping.

4. High school students may be taught to *rotate reeds*. For example, they might have five reeds in a rotation and use a different reed at each daily rehearsal. Label each reed in pencil on the back according to day of the week.

5. High school students may be taught to *close the pores of a new reed*. Try this. Wet a new reed, then blow through the butt end. Water bubbles will likely appear on the vamp. This indicates that pores are open. Closing them prevents the reed from becoming water logged. It can also make a hard reed more responsive. To close pores, lay the table of the wet reed on a flat surface. Pressing firmly, slide your index finger from back to tip of cut. Pick up your finger, return to the back of the reed, and repeat the process. Do this on the entire width of the cut. Make up to 25 passes. Do this for the first several days that you use this reed until the bubbles no longer appear.

6. High school students will *recognize softness and hardness in a reed*. A reed that is too soft will speak easily in mid-register, but sound reedy or bright, and be prone to close at the tip and/or be flat when playing upper register notes. A reed that is too hard will be hard to blow, sound rough (without core to the tone), and play sharp.

7. High school students will know *to raise the reed slightly on the mouthpiece* to make a reed feel harder and *lower the reed slightly on the mouthpiece* to make a reed feel softer.

If you want your high school students to know and do these things, when should they be introduced and taught? Which should be introduced, taught, and established as habits in the first year of study? Answer: Perhaps all of them. Which ones should be dealt with first, from the earliest days of study? Answer: Numbers 1 and 2. The others should come later.

You might think that there isn't much to teach in number 1 (wetting the reed) and number 2 (storing the reed). What more does a teacher do other than to tell students to wet all of the reed and remove, wipe, and store properly at the end of play? An effective teacher will both tell and show her students how to do these things. The effective teacher will also know that the initial tell and show is not really teaching. The initial tell and show is what a teacher does to introduce something new to students. The effective teacher knows that for students to truly understand and do the things that need to be done habitually, the teacher will need to *think for* the students for quite some time before they will begin to think and act for themselves—which in effect will be to think like the teacher. The effective teacher will remind beginners every day for a while to wet the reed. The teacher will monitor this. Are students wetting the entire reed? Is wetting the reed the first thing they do in instrument assembly? For the teacher, the lesson starts not when the first note is played but when the cases are opened for assembly and the reed gets wet. Each of the first several lessons (more if necessary) should start the same way, with the teacher structuring, as if for the first time, the wetting of reeds. Likewise, the teacher will need to remember to allow time for and structure the end-of-lesson things—removing the reed, wiping off moisture, storing flat—many times before these acts become habits for students.

Recognizing and fixing warping, rotating, closing pores, and recognizing reed strength need not and should not be introduced early in the first year. Warping can be dealt with as it occurs, with one student's warping problem being used as a teaching example for all. Rotating need not be considered until the second half of the first year. Closing the pores of a new reed can wait. Reeds will work with open pores, so again, avoid the distraction early on. Reed strength differences make one reed feel different than another. Students naturally experience this as they play on different reeds.

The Mouthpiece and Ligature

Mouthpiece Facts

1. Mouthpieces are made of machined rod-rubber (a hard rubber) or glass or metal or plastic. Machine rod-rubber is the most common mouthpiece material.

2. Four parts of the mouthpiece are labeled in Figure 3.31.

    a. The end rail (Letter A) is the edge of the mouthpiece at the tip. It should be smooth. Dropping a mouthpiece can result in a chipped end rail, which will not allow the mouthpiece to function properly.

    b. The tone chamber (Letter B) is the part that is inside the opening of the mouthpiece. Its shape varies among mouthpiece brands.

    c. The table (Letter C) is the flat surface on which rests the table of the reed.

    d. The bore (Letter D) connects with the bore of the barrel.

    e. The facing. The part of the mouthpiece that curves away from the reed. The facing has length and curvature, both of which vary from one make of mouthpiece to another. Length and curve determine the size of the tip opening. A larger tip opening requires a stronger embouchure because there is more distance for the reed to cover in order for it to make contact with the mouthpiece during vibration.

3. A more open tip opening requires a softer reed. A more closed tip opening requires a harder reed.

4. The facing of a mouthpiece can warp. In fact, mouthpieces can come from the factory warped. A warped mouthpiece can be avoided by tightening the ligature screws so that they are snug rather than as tight as possible and by taking the reed off between playings. A warped mouthpiece may squeak frequently. To check for warping, insert a piece of paper between reed and mouthpiece. At the point at which the paper can go no farther (because reed and mouthpiece meet), the paper should be straight across the reed. If not, this is a sign that the mouthpiece is warped.

5. Wash the mouthpiece in lukewarm, not hot water, which can cause warping. Avoid soaps. Remove condensation by

FIGURE 3.31 The Mouthpiece Labeled
(Produced by Paige Jarreau at Paige's Photos)

using a finger to guide the swab in to wipe the tone chamber and by rolling the swab in order to get inside the bore. Pulling a swab through, over time, can damage the mouthpiece.

6. Mouthpiece patch or cushion. Occasionally, a student will complain about discomfort at the point where the teeth rest on the mouthpiece. A mouthpiece cushion will get rid of this discomfort. It can be purchased for about $5.00. It attaches to the back of the mouthpiece.

Mouthpieces for the soprano clarinet in B-flat come in different sizes and shapes. (This is true also of mouthpieces for all instruments of the clarinet and saxophone families.) More precisely, they come in different bore and tip opening sizes, different tone chamber shapes, and different facing and table lengths. As you might expect then, response, intonation, stability, dynamics, and tone quality vary from one mouthpiece to the next. Over 30 different makes of mouthpiece are listed for soprano clarinet in B-flat alone in one woodwind catalog. Cost varies from $15.00 to over $200.00 for clarinet and to over $300.00 for alto saxophone.

A beginning model clarinet or saxophone comes with what is called a stock mouthpiece. Stock means it came with the instrument. Implied is that this mouthpiece is not of good quality, though it is sufficient for the needs of a beginning level player. After a year or two, it is wise to encourage students and their parents to purchase a *step-up* mouthpiece in order to take advantage of the potential for enhanced response, intonation, dynamics, and tone quality. In some cases, school music teachers arrange with local music store dealers to include a better quality mouthpiece rather than the stock mouthpiece with rental instruments. In other instances, one make of mouthpiece is purchased with school funds so that every clarinet or saxophone player in the band is using the same step-up mouthpiece. The thinking is that if everyone uses the same make of mouthpiece, tone quality will tend to be more uniform across students than it would be if students were given no direction in mouthpiece selection.

It is wise for the music teacher to discuss mouthpiece preference with trusted private teachers, and to decide based on these discussions what make of mouthpiece to promote for student use. The Vandoren 5RV Lyre mouthpiece is considered a good clarinet mouthpiece for student use, though there are other good student mouthpieces. For alto saxophone, the Yamaha 4C mouthpiece is a good step up from stock. The Selmer S80 C★ (C-star) mouthpiece is of good quality for school use. C-star refers to the shape of the facing. The suitability of a mouthpiece is always dependent on finding a good match of a reed for the specific mouthpiece. For example, Vandoren brand mouthpieces are designed to match with Vandoren reeds. Trial and error is the best way to match mouthpiece with reed.

In some woodwind catalogs, you will notice the inclusion of specifications for some mouthpieces. It is wise to opt for medium facing and medium tip opening. Medium is best for most students. Companies that sell instruments and instrument parts have return/trial policies. In one case, the customer can return a mouthpiece after a three-day trial period for refund or exchange.

Ligature Facts

How the reed is held onto the mouthpiece can affect how the reed vibrates. Stock ligatures tend to squeeze at the edges of the reed, preventing full vibration. Better quality ligatures make contact with the reed at points that do not inhibit vibration.

There are many makes and types of ligature listed in woodwind catalogs. Ligatures are made of metal or fabric. Some have two screws; others have one. They can cost between $20.00 and $50.00. The Bonade ligature is metal and has two screws. The Rovner ligature is made of a fabric and has one screw.

They are available in regular and inverted styles. On regular ligatures the screw(s) is located on the player side of the mouthpiece. On the inverted style, the screw(s) is located on the far side of the mouthpiece in relation to the player. Do not allow students to use one as the other. To determine which is which, remember that the screw head(s) should be situated to the right as the player looks at the clarinet in playing position.

STUDY QUESTIONS

1. The target pitch on the small piece of the clarinet is . . .
2. There are two types of ligature. Explain.
3. Explain "goal posts" in clarinet small piece assembly.
4. Explain scribe line in clarinet small piece assembly.
5. Complete or answer the following about clarinet embouchure characteristics.
    a. The reasons for pulling the lower lip *against* the lower teeth are . . .
    b. Lower lip contacts reed where?
    c. Upper teeth contact what?
    d. Lips and cheeks do what?
    e. Jaw does what?
6. Why is the shape of the oral cavity included in the air stream category for clarinet embouchure and air stream? Explain fully.
7. Re-write each item under "What to Look for in Clarinet Embouchure" in abbreviated form—as you might use them tomorrow as a teacher. Use just enough words to remind you of what to look for. For example, the word "head" might be enough to jog your memory for erect head.
8. Demonstrate on your clarinet, what to do when a note will not speak.
9. There is one peculiarity about assembling the lower and upper joints of the clarinet. What is it?
10. What happens first in clarinet disassembly?
11. What does "2 o'clock" mean in clarinet hand position. Why is it important?
12. In clarinet hand position, to what does "no lean" refer?
13. The typical beginning band method book for clarinet does not make use of the notes of the right hand for a very long time. This can lead to bad habits. How can these be avoided?
14. When you practice the clarinet, are you thinking and doing the details listed under "What to Look for in Embouchure" so that you are better able to use this information in your observational role as teacher?
15. In playing the clarinet, have you checked your small piece pitch?

16. In the clarinet embouchure teaching strategies section, the six ideas listed under "For Firm Lips, Lips and Cheeks against Teeth, and Jaw Down" are very strong. Try each of them for yourself.
17. Provide two strategies for dealing with puffed cheeks in clarinet playing.
18. Before tonguing is introduced, clarinet players should use what consonant/vowel to start tone? Why?
19. List the three major differences between playing the bass clarinet and playing the B-flat soprano clarinet.
20. What brand name is likely the most well-known professional quality clarinet?
21. On a staff, write the ranges and names of the four registers of the clarinet.
22. Describe the typical sound of the throat tones. How can this be countered?
23. In the throat tone register, the side key alternate fingering for B-flat is very useful, even in easy-level band literature. Make sure you try this fingering. Learn it.
24. What is "tuning the embouchure" in clarinet study?
25. Demonstrate on your clarinet the three-step tuning process. Explain the range of notes affected by pushing or pulling at a) barrel, b) mid-section, and c) bell.
26. Indicate clarinet pitch tendencies for the following conditions:
    a. Low register.
    b. Throat tone register.
    c. Soft volume.
    d. Soft reed.
27. Beginners should start on what strength reed?
28. True or false:
    a. The tip and sides of a reed are vibrating areas.
    b. The heart is a resistance area.
29. The table of the reed is found where? Its surface should be . . .
30. How is a warped reed fixed?
31. After removing the reed from the mouthpiece, how should the reed be stored?
32. What is reed rotation? What are its benefits to the player?
33. How does a band or orchestra director obtain reeds? Or is this simply the responsibility of the students?
34. What are the sound characteristics of a reed that is too soft?
35. How should a mouthpiece by washed?
36. Describe the mouthpiece patch and its usefulness.

PERFORMANCE TESTING OF UNIVERSITY STUDENTS ON SECONDARY INSTRUMENTS

A rubric is an evaluative tool. The rubric that follows makes clear the expectations of the university student playing the clarinet as he or she approaches the end of an intensive three to four weeks of study. Students may use the criteria to prepare for performance testing and to self-evaluate. Teachers may use the criteria to structure feedback.

1.	Assembled and disassembled (incl. swabbing) the instrument properly		Yes	No
2.	Formed a characteristic embouchure:			
	a.	Optimal amount of lower lip over the lower teeth	Yes	No
	b.	Optimal amount of mouthpiece in the mouth	Yes	No
	c.	Smooth and firm lower lip as platform for reed	Yes	No
	d.	Teeth on top of mouthpiece	Yes	No
	e.	Lips and cheeks against teeth	Yes	No
	f.	Jaw down	Yes	No
3.	Breathed through corners of the mouth, leaving the lower lip and upper teeth contacts in place		Yes	No
	Demonstrated phrasal breathing		Yes	No
4.	Sustained a *ff* and unwavering small piece pitch		Yes	No
	Pitched at F-sharp concert or under it by less than a half step		Yes	No
5.	Achieved a resonant and unwavering tone on the instrument		Yes	No
6.	Maintained correct hand position:			
	a.	Right thumbprint to body; side to thumb rest, centered between tip and knuckle	Yes	No
	b.	C formation of right-hand thumb and index finger	Yes	No
	c.	Left thumb at 2 o'clock	Yes	No
	d.	Fingers curved	Yes	No
	e.	Fingerprints over the center of the keys	Yes	No
	f.	Fingers held close to the keys	Yes	No
7.	Recalled and played primary fingerings from low E to high C		Yes	No
8.	Slurred to high B or C without the tone cutting out		Yes	No

9.	Recalled and played selected alternate fingerings	Yes	No
10.	Tongued unmarked notes and first notes of slurs	Yes	No
	Consecutive notes were legato tongued unless marked otherwise	Yes	No
	Kept embouchure still while tonguing	Yes	No
11.	Achieved clean register key 12th slurs	Yes	No
12.	Play expressively by varying volume and tempo as indicated or dictated by the notes	Yes	No
13.	Performance showed evidence of sufficient practice	Yes	No

CLARINET FINGERING CHART

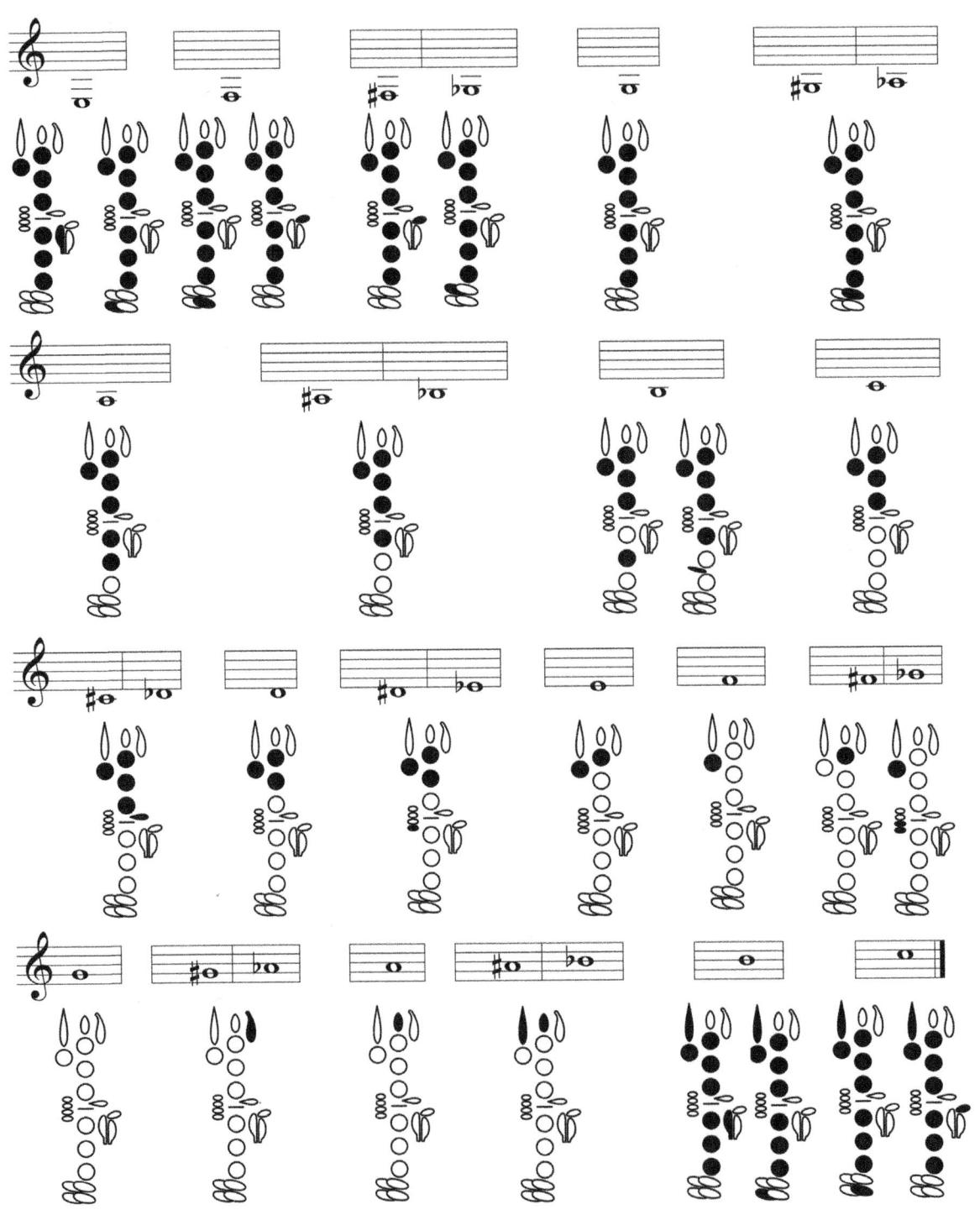

FIGURE 3.32A Clarinet Fingerings page 1

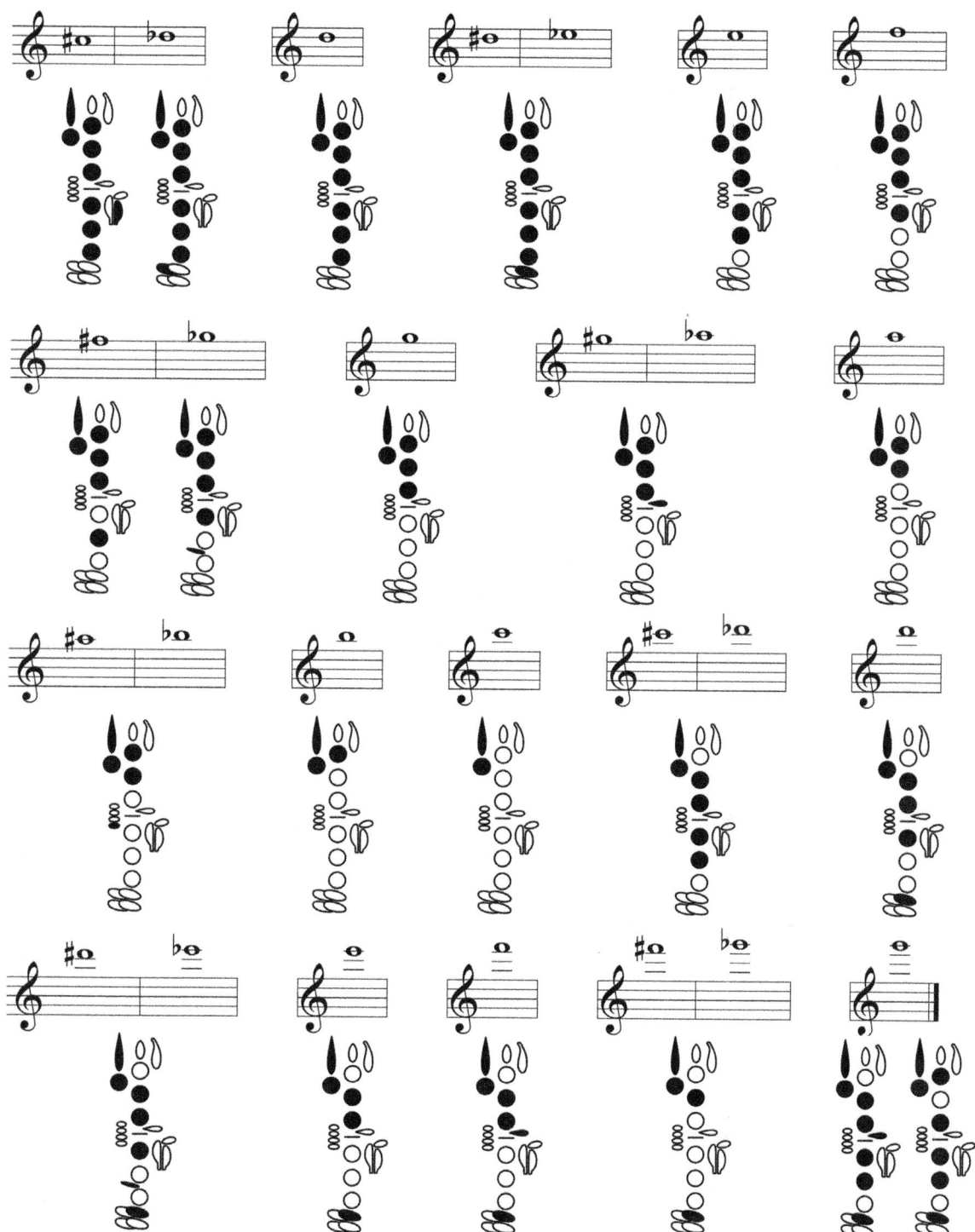

FIGURE 3.32B Clarinet Fingerings page 2

CHAPTER 4

Saxophone

SAXOPHONE TONE AND EARLY STAGE EMBOUCHURE

Your first order of business as a student is assembling the small piece and as a teacher teaching assembly of the small piece. Assembly of the saxophone small piece is more complicated and time-consuming than that for the other woodwind instruments.

Small Piece

Ideally, the small piece of the saxophone is the assembled mouthpiece, reed, and ligature. The mouthpiece alone provides the most accurate information about embouchure quality. When embouchure pressures and air stream are correct, the mouthpiece pitch will sound a concert A. Frequently, novice players will squeeze too hard on the reed and mouthpiece causing the pitch to be sharp to the A. Or they will put too little mouthpiece into the mouth, making the small piece pitch hard to produce. Using the A as a reference, these embouchure faults can be detected and corrected. If small piece work is not done, embouchure problems can go undetected.

At the beginning stage of saxophone instruction, however, playing on the mouthpiece alone can be problematic. It is not easy for someone who has never played a wind instrument to produce an acceptable tone on such a short tube. The assembled mouthpiece and neck form a longer tube. During the first lessons, have beginners form a basic embouchure using the combined mouthpiece and neck. The pitch of this longer piece is not reliable as an embouchure-quality checkpoint because pitch depends in part on how far the mouthpiece is pushed onto the neck. Assuming the mouthpiece is located appropriately on the neck, the pitch should be roughly A-flat concert. Later, when students are more at ease with making an embouchure and blowing through the instrument, have them play on the mouthpiece alone to gauge the nature of embouchure pressures.

Embouchure: Early Stage

Small Piece Assembly and Disassembly

Assembly of the mouthpiece and neck is nearly identical to that for the clarinet small piece. It is presented below in lesson plan format complete with objective and step-by-step procedures. Assuming a group setting, several lessons may be necessary to thoroughly guide students through assembly of the small piece, initial embouchure formation, first sounds, and disassembly of the small piece.

Objective: By the end of the lesson, students will have assembled and disassembled the mouthpiece, neck, and reed.

Before class: Teacher soaks reeds and applies cork grease to necks that need it.

Procedures:

1. Teacher provides a reed to each student, *all* of which has been soaked in water. While holding the reed at its side, student places the tip end in the mouth, flat side on the tongue.

2. Cases are laid on the floor with students kneeling alongside. *Note*: It is sometimes easiest for many young people to place the case on the floor and sit or kneel beside it. For the following, I will assume chairs are being used.

3. Before students open cases, teacher checks to see that instrument cases are situated with the correct side up.

4. Assembly of small piece

    a. Remove mouthpiece, ligature, and neck from case. Leave mouthpiece cap in the case. Close case. Place case to the side of the chair.

    b. Remove ligature from mouthpiece by loosening the screws three to four turns. In other words, the mouthpiece should be naked. Place the ligature on the instrument case.

    c. Grasp the neck in the left hand as if it were a pistol. The thumb should hold the key closed. Assemble the mouthpiece and neck by simultaneously pushing and turning in short back and forth arcs. The mouthpiece should cover approximately three-quarters of the cork. Precise placement is determined by tuning to a pitch standard, which is not necessary now. Align the opening in the mouthpiece with the brace on the underside of the neck. *Note*: If possible, the teacher should apply cork grease *prior to* the lesson. If dealt with during the lesson, this can be a big time waster.

    d. Take the reed out of the mouth. While holding it on the side with tip-end up, place the flat side against the opening of the mouthpiece. Line up reed with mouthpiece (at the tip, on the sides, and at the bottom). Tip of reed should be even with the end of the mouthpiece. *Note*: The reed need not be aligned perfectly at this stage; we will take a more detailed look at alignment in step g below. While holding the neck in the palm of one hand, keep the reed in place with the thumb of that same hand.

    e. Inspect the ligature. The end with the larger circumference is the bottom. With the screws facing you, fit the larger circumference end over the mouthpiece. Guide the ligature down toward the stock end of the reed.

    Note 1: Pay attention to what you are doing here. As shown on the clarinet in Figure 4.1, steady your hand

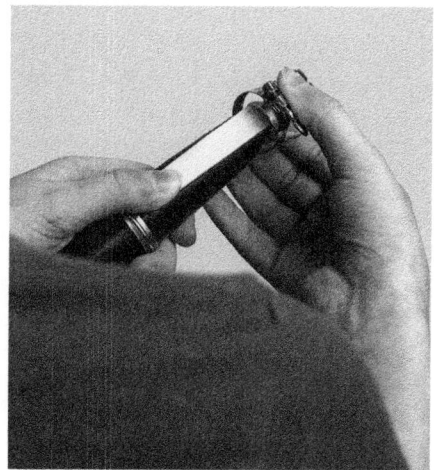

FIGURE 4.1 Steadied Hand with Ligature
(Produced by Paige Jarreau at Paige's Photos)

104 TEACHING THE INSTRUMENTS

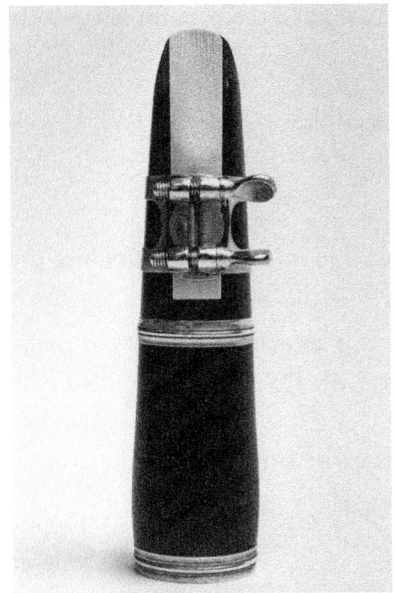

FIGURE 4.2 Correctly Positioned Screw Heads

(Produced by Paige Jarreau at Paige's Photos)

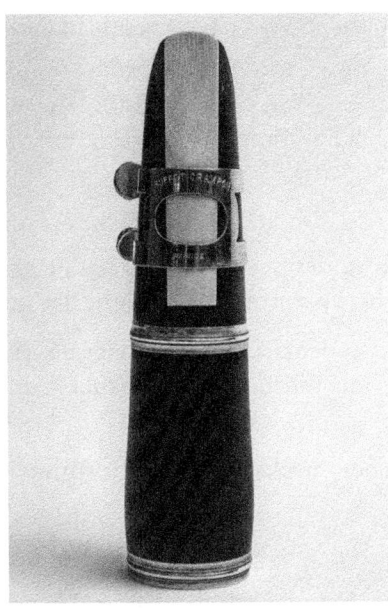

FIGURE 4.3 Incorrectly Positioned Screw Heads

(Produced by Paige Jarreau at Paige's Photos)

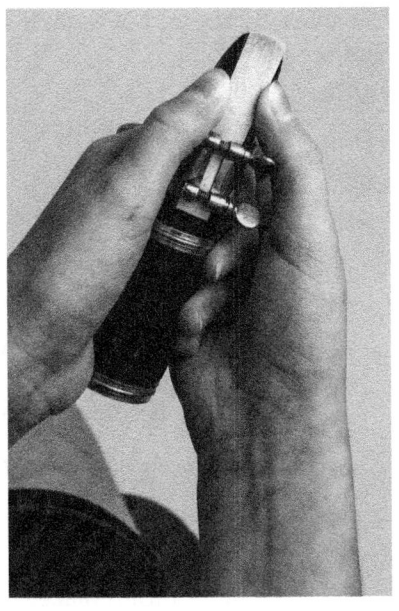

FIGURE 4.4 "Goal Posts" in Reed Position Adjustment

(Produced by Paige Jarreau at Paige's Photos)

by touching one side of the ligature against the back of the mouthpiece, then fitting the ligature over the reed. If the ligature makes contact with the tip of the reed, perhaps because of an unsteady hand, the reed is likely to be damaged.

Note 2: Ligatures are available in regular and inverted styles. On regular ligatures the screw(s) is located on the player side of the mouthpiece. On the inverted style, the screw(s) is located on the far side of the mouthpiece in relation to the player. To determine which is which, remember that the screw head(s) should be situated to the right as the player looks at the saxophone small piece in playing position. Do not allow students to use one style of ligature as the other. In Figure 4.2 the screw heads, shown on a clarinet, are positioned correctly. In Figure 4.3, they are positioned incorrectly.

f. Pull the ligature down so that it is slightly below the top scribe line on the mouthpiece. If the mouthpiece has no scribe line, the ligature should be low enough that there is no part of it protruding above the angle on the back of the mouthpiece.

g. Cradle the small piece in your palms, establishing your thumbs as *goal posts*. Use the thumbs to further align the reed with the mouthpiece at the tip, sides, and bottom. In Figure 4.4, notice the thumbs as goal posts.

h. Tighten the screws until snug. They are snug enough if you cannot pull the ligature off when trying to do so.

5. Check reed alignment and ligature position on each mouthpiece.

6. Initial embouchure work (not developed here).

7. Disassembly of small piece.
   a. Open the instrument case on the floor.
   b. Loosen the ligature screws three to four turns.
   c. While holding the bottom end of reed in place with thumb, carefully remove the ligature. Place it on your lap.
   d. Remove reed. Hold on side.
   e. Using thumb and index finger, wipe off excess moisture.
   f. Place flat side of reed against flat surface of reed guard, plastic container, or cardboard container. Place in instrument case.
   g. Disassemble mouthpiece and neck using back and forth motions. Place neck in case.
   h. Re-assemble ligature on mouthpiece for storage. Cover mouthpiece with cap. Place in case.

Follow this plan daily with the teacher leading and controlling until habit formation begins to develop. Monitor individuals. Gradually give responsibility to students to do independently, but remain observant.

Note: You have noticed that swabbing has not been covered. This is intentional for several reasons: Time constraints, mental capacity (the above is enough new information for now), and limited attention spans (swabbing at this point would distract or take away from a focus of attention on *what's most important now*). There will be a time and place for swabbing—after instrument assembly and disassembly, after initial embouchure work, and after introduction of hand position.

Characteristics of Embouchure and Air Stream

Embouchure

1. Some pink of the lower lip covers the teeth.
2. The fulcrum (the point at which the mouthpiece begins its curve away from the reed) contacts the lower lip.
3. Teeth rest on top of mouthpiece.
4. Mouth in the shape of "OO," as such bringing the corners in and the jaw somewhat down.

Air Stream

1. Blow straight ahead.
2. Blow fast air.
3. While blowing, maintain the open, round feeling of the whistle-like "OO" shape.

Teaching Embouchure

Given the sameness of mouthpiece between saxophone and clarinet, it is tempting to compare the embouchures. The saxophone requires a more relaxed, less firm embouchure than does the clarinet.

More precisely, the lower lip of the saxophone embouchure provides a cushion for the reed; the clarinet lower lip provides a firm platform. The saxophone lower lip should be wrinkled, as it is when one whistles. The middle of the lower lip of the clarinet should be flat (not wrinkled) and firm. To view this saxophone/clarinet difference from another perspective, consider that the clarinet small piece should sound in the *upper middle* of its pitch range. If the lower lip functions as a firm platform on which the reed rests, the upper middle of the pitch range can be achieved. The saxophone small piece, in contrast, should sound in the *middle* of its pitch range. A cushion-like lower lip coupled with jaw down is conducive to achieving the middle of the pitch range. The saxophone embouchure is a round shape. Pressures are equally distributed around the entire reed and mouthpiece.

Another difference between saxophone and clarinet embouchure involves the amount of lower lip over the lower teeth. Generally, saxophonists play with *slightly* more lower lip over the teeth than do clarinetists.

Early saxophone embouchure work should involve the mouthpiece and neck only. In working with a group of beginning saxophonists trying to make first sounds, the teacher's approach might consist of the following sequence of instruction.

Sequence for Making First Sounds in Group Instruction

This sequence of instruction with a group of beginning saxophone players is divided into several chunks of activity, each of which should be approached with careful consideration by both teacher and students. While reading the text, be aware of what is quoted material and what is not quoted.

First Chunk

- Teacher demonstrates a thumb and fingertips hold of the small piece. Students imitate. In Figure 3.1 (see page 52), a small piece hold is demonstrated.

Second Chunk

- Without instrument, teacher to students: "Sit tall, head erect." Students do.

- Without instrument, teacher to students: "Open mouth slightly. Put some lower lip over your lower teeth." Teacher demonstrates. Students imitate. Repeat several times. Check individuals. *Note*: Ultimately, the reed will rest on the active "pink" of the lower lip, so putting so much lip over the teeth such that all of the "pink" is tucked inside the mouth should be avoided. Puckered lips should also be avoided.

Don't be in a hurry to move on to the next step. Take some deliberate time with the second chunk across several class meetings. Build habit strength in sitting tall with erect head. See how students develop by having multi-class experiences with a controlled amount of lip over the teeth.

Third Chunk

- With the nail of your index finger, show how much reed should be in the mouth. The fingernail shows the point on the reed (the fulcrum) that makes contact with the lower lip. Teacher to students: "Place your fingernail on this part of your reed, the fulcrum. This is the part of your reed that rests on your lower lip. Notice how much reed goes inside your mouth."

- With mouthpiece and neck, teacher to students: "Sit tall. Open your mouth. Lip over teeth. Place the reed at fulcrum on top of the lip." Teacher demonstrates. Students imitate. Repeat this sequence several times: 1) Sit tall, 2) open mouth, 3) lip over teeth, 4) place reed at fulcrum. Check individuals for amount of reed in mouth. This is a good time to have students consider the angle of small piece to face. There should be a slightly upward angle from the instrument's neck to the player's face.

- Teacher to students: "Teeth on top." Close the mouth only enough to allow the upper teeth to contact the top of the mouthpiece. Have students do this without closing their lips around the mouthpiece. At this point, you should be able to see the teeth making contact—a stabilizing contact, not a biting contact.

- On the teacher's deliberately paced command, rehearse: 1) Sit tall, 2) open mouth, 3) lip over teeth, 4) place reed at fulcrum, 5) teeth on top. Check individuals.

It goes without saying that without a mirror I cannot *see* how much reed I have in my mouth with the instrument in my mouth. Using the side view of reed and mouthpiece to find the fulcrum provides a visualization of imagined mouthpiece placement on the lower lip. The students know what the goal is. And, importantly, finding the fulcrum provides a way to make a "mountain" out of something that is often overlooked in beginning saxophone—how much reed goes in the mouth. As their teacher, help them with the part they cannot see by making individual contacts and by providing mirrors. Peers can help each other in finding the optimal amount of mouthpiece in the mouth. There is a tendency to put too little in the mouth.

Notice in the third chunk the choice of the word *place*. *Place* the fulcrum on the lip. *Place* rather than start at the tip of the reed and *push in*. Pushing or sliding the reed against the lower lip drags lip with it. Too much lip over the teeth dampens tone quality and can cause squeaking.

Fourth Chunk

- Teacher demonstrates for students. 1) Sit tall, 2) open mouth, 3) lip over teeth, 4) place the reed, 5) teeth on top, 6) close the lips in a "circle" around the reed and mouthpiece. Say "OO" as you close, creating a whistle-like look and feel. Avoid raising the jaw. Step 6 is new. Have students do the steps on the teacher's deliberately paced command. Repeat. Check individuals.

- Teacher to students: "Blow fast air straight ahead!" Teacher demonstrates. Students sustain a first sound.

FIGURE 4.5 Front View of Embouchure (Middle School Musician)

(Produced by Paige Jarreau at Paige's Photos)

In Figures 4.5 and 4.6, notice these embouchure characteristics: Erect head, slightly upward angle of instrument neck to face, amount of mouthpiece in the mouth, lips making a "circle" around the reed and mouthpiece, and jaw down. Notice also in the front view that you can see some pink of the lower lip, giving some indication of how much lower lip is over the teeth. There is lip over the teeth but not so much that some pink does not show on the outside. This 7th grader makes an excellent sound.

The ultimate goal with mouthpiece and neck work is for students to produce an A-flat concert (A on the mouthpiece alone) at *forte* dynamic and with resonant tone. A-flat concert on mouthpiece and neck is a sign that the embouchure—the parts of it that can be seen by the teacher *and* the parts of it that are inside the mouth—is either correct or well on its way to being correct.

Initial Embouchure Work: A Closer Look

Notice that the first sounds sequence above makes no reference to the jaw down characteristic of embouchure. There is good reason for this. When I prepare to introduce embouchure, I ask myself, "What can I accomplish with a group of beginning saxophone players in the time available? What is a reasonable expectation on my part? Over the next several weeks, I will be happy if my students are *in the ballpark* in terms of embouchure. Ballpark accuracy leaves the teacher in position to refine embouchure and air stream.

With these questions and desires as a backdrop, I make decisions about how to proceed based on *what is necessary now*. The issues that are pertinent now are: a) holding the small piece a certain way; b) sitting tall with head erect (the length of the neck strap is key); c) getting lower lip over the teeth but paying attention to how much lip is over teeth; d) placing the reed at the fulcrum on the lip; e) resting the teeth on top, f) closing the lips in a circle shape; g) angling the neck properly; and h) blowing fast air. For 11- and 12-year-old students, these are do-able things. And this is enough challenge for the first several lessons. After several lessons dominated by me leading students through this embouchure sequence, students should be well on the way toward doing these things on their own—habitually—without reminder from me. I do not want to have beginning saxophone players who in October play with the head bowed, or with too little mouthpiece in the mouth, or without teeth on top of the mouthpiece, or with a weak air stream. Students need opportunities to do these things many times correctly *in my presence* in order that October be reserved for fine-tuning embouchures.

Please note that if a student's lips reach forward away from the teeth or the jaw is pressing upward into the reed in an exaggerated way, immediate attention is warranted (see "Embouchure Teaching Strategies" below).

Back to the jaw down embouchure characteristic. Though not directly introduced to students to this point, I am aware of its importance. I'm noticing who among my students naturally gravitates to a jaw that is down. About these students, I'm saying to myself "Cool!"

For those students who are not natural on this issue, I'm thinking about how and when to address it. Letters a through h in the above paragraph, if done correctly, are somewhat conducive to jaw down. So providing ample experience in and good feedback about a–h is critical. But in the class setting, embouchure flaws are inevitable in some students. Ideally, the time to deal with major embouchure flaws is between ample experience with a–h and the introduction of tonguing.

FIGURE 4.6 Side View of Embouchure
(Produced by Paige Jarreau at Paige's Photos)

Potential for Success in Saxophone Study

Probably the best indicator of whether a student is suited for saxophone study is his ability to get in the right ballpark concerning small piece work. This can reveal itself in an instrument selection experience involving a 3-minute, one-on-one session with a teacher. Is the student able to sustain a tone while keeping the head erect, while keeping the teeth on top of the mouthpiece, while avoiding puffing the cheeks, and without pressing the jaw upward in exaggerated fashion? If the answer is no to some or all of these points, there is a chance that saxophone is not a wise choice for this student. This being said, it is also possible for this student, with the help of a good teacher, to overcome these deficiencies. A student with a strong desire to play an instrument can often overcome initial difficulties. The question is: "Can this happen before the student loses interest and before the deficiencies take root and become hard to change?"

Students with disabilities (physical, cognitive, emotional, sensory) should be given a more comprehensive evaluation than that described above concerning potential for success. The music teacher should consult with the student's team of teachers/counselors, as well as his parents, to develop a full knowledge of the student's capabilities.

Teaching/Learning Sequence: Small Piece Practice

As your students are working toward a ballpark-accurate small piece tone, practice of desired behaviors can be organized in a process that I call the teaching/learning sequence. Note the sequence for mouthpiece and neck work.

1. Sit tall.
2. Head erect.
3. Small piece to you.
4. Lower lip.
5. Fulcrum.
6. Teeth on top.
7. Circle.
8. Angle.
9. Fast air.

The sequence presented in Figure 4.7 is an abbreviated form or skeleton of a step-by-step process of what to do *before* making a tone on the small piece. The substance of each step has already been established by you in the minds of the students. It is at this point that students need only brief reminders of what comes next in the sequence. Students know based on teacher instruction and guided experiences what *sit tall* and *head erect* mean. They know that *small piece to you* means to bring the small piece to the head rather than bowing the head to meet the small piece. They know that *lower lip* refers to putting some of it over the lower teeth. *Fulcrum* is a reminder to place it on the lower lip. *Teeth on top* is a reminder to place teeth on top of the mouthpiece. *Circle* is about lip/mouth shape (a whistle-like OO), and *angle* refers to the slightly upward angle of the neck to the student's mouth.

This instructional sequence is a checklist of what one thinks about and does in preparing to make a tone on the mouthpiece and neck. At the beginning level, a student who repeatedly fails to do one or more of the steps in this sequence is not unsuccessful because he is incapable of doing the behaviors. He fails to do them because his brain does not tell him what to do. The teaching/learning sequence represents a proactive approach to teaching and learning in that it organizes student thought and action up-front—from the beginning. If properly rehearsed, it promotes good habits before bad ones have a chance to take hold.

110 TEACHING THE INSTRUMENTS

In effect, the sequence breaks down into individual steps what an accomplished saxophonist would do all at once—as one big action. We must rehearse the parts at a deliberate pace, and eventually hasten the pace such that nine separate steps begin to meld together and become one big action. This idea can be promoted by rehearsing the sequence rhythmically. Each step is chanted by you in 4-beat durations during which students respond accordingly.

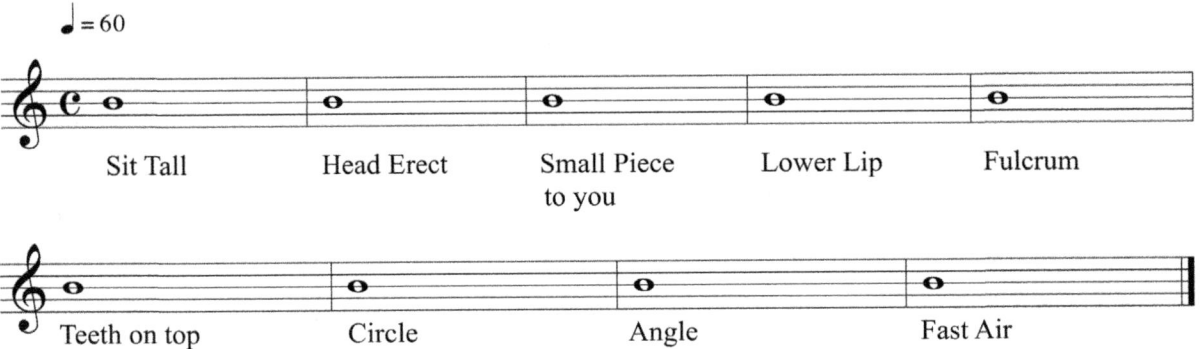

FIGURE 4.7 Teaching/Learning Sequence: Small Piece Practice

At appropriate times, the pace from step to step can be accelerated by chanting in 2-beat durations, then 1-beat durations at roughly quarter note equals 60. With enough in-class repetition, most students will memorize this sequence seemingly without trying. To ensure that everyone memorizes and habitually does this sequence, the effective teacher will consider testing students on it.

Performance Testing

The performance test shown in Table 4.1 is no more than the "Small Piece Teaching/Learning Sequence" arranged in test format. Set up a video recorder in a practice room. Students, one at a time, unobtrusively leave class in a pre-arranged order to take the test. Each student enters the practice room, sits in a chair in view of the recorder (which is recording continuously), and demonstrates the small piece sequence. When finished, the student unobtrusively returns to class as the next student, waiting outside the practice room, enters the test room. At a later, convenient time, you view the recording, complete the test form, and assign grades.

All students are able to sit tall one time when asked. The goal, though, is for them to sit tall *every time* when playing the saxophone—without having been asked! All students can put enough mouthpiece in the mouth one time when reminded. The goal is to get them to do it every time—and to remind themselves! Teaching/learning sequencing and performance testing are tools that promote doing things the same way each time, doing things as a matter of habit, and attending to the details.

As you lead students through the embouchure-building sequence, consider for number 9 first asking them to not try to get a sound. Blow lightly while simply maintaining the "circle" mouth/lip formation. Give them some time to get acclimated to maintaining this circle shape while blowing, but with no intent to get a sound. The point of this strategy is to pre-empt what often happens, which is students will do *anything* to produce a sound, even if it means destroying embouchure structure to get it.

TABLE 4.1 Performance Test: Saxophone Embouchure (mouthpiece and neck)

Name:		
Date:		
	Yes	No
1. You sat tall.		
2. Your head was erect.		
3. You brought the small piece to your erect head.		
4. You put some lower lip over your teeth.		
5. You placed the fulcrum on the lower lip.		
6. You rested your teeth on top of the mouthpiece.		
7. You made a circle with the lips around the reed and mouthpiece.		
8. You made a slightly upward angle—instrument neck to face.		
9. You blew a fast air stream while sustaining the pitch.		
10. Your small piece pitch was concert A-flat.		
Grade:		

Note: 10-point test; -1 if order is incorrect. 9–10 Yes = A (Proficient), 8 Yes = B (Developing), 6-7 Yes = C (Novice)

Notes to teacher:

- For this test, situate the recorder, as much as possible, so that you are able to view a close-up of the student's head from an oblique angle (part frontal and part side view).

- As you can see on the grading scale, the student must do all or nearly all steps correctly in order to receive an A or B grade. The expectations are high because students were provided many opportunities to perform the sequence (and hence the test) in class or lessons.

Recall from earlier in this chapter that the one very good gauge of embouchure quality is the pitch that the student gets on the saxophone mouthpiece alone. If embouchure pressures are correct, reed/mouthpiece combination compatible, and reed strength appropriate, the mouthpiece-alone pitch will be concert A. The longer mouthpiece and neck has been used up to this point because it is easier for the student to blow and handle. On this longer piece, you're looking for an approximate concert A-flat. After an initial period of acclimation on this longer piece, have students use the mouthpiece alone as the *official* saxophone small piece.

Ideally, students would not be introduced to the assembled instrument until embouchure work on the small piece had resulted in most students achieving a reliable ballpark embouchure and air stream. Instrument assembly, instrument care, and hand position are explained here now, although there is more to be dealt with concerning embouchure development. Small piece work should continue because of its potential to help teach embouchure and provide much information about embouchure quality.

SAXOPHONE ASSEMBLY, DISASSEMBLY, AND BASIC CARE

Assembly Sequence

1. Lay the closed case on the floor to the side of the student's chair. Check that the case is situated correct side up. Usually the lid is narrower than the bottom of the case. Oftentimes, latches open up, not down. Open the case.

2. Put the neck strap around the neck. Do not adjust its length now.

3. Complete assembly of the neck and mouthpiece are described above in "Embouchure: Early Stage." Get in the habit of adjoining the *naked* mouthpiece (no reed or ligature) to the neck before affixing the reed. It is difficult for young saxophone players to adjoin the mouthpiece to the neck when the reed is already in place.

4. Remove the body of the saxophone from the case by grasping at the bell and lifting it out. Remove the end plug, which protects the octave key lever. Put the end plug in the case.

5. Holding the body in an upright position, rest the curve of the bell on the chair between the legs. Support the body by grasping with the left hand in its normal playing position. Closing keys while maneuvering instrument parts will never harm the instrument. Or grasp with the left hand high on the body—very near the opening to the bore. With the right hand, grasp the neck (with mouthpiece adjoined) with hand on top and mouthpiece facing back—in the general direction of your body. The octave key should stayed closed. *Note*: Small children may need to lay the instrument's body on its side on their laps. A right-hander would lay the upright instrument down to the right. Assemble the neck and mouthpiece as explained above.

6. With small back and forth turns, slide the neck into the body until it will not go further. The body of the saxophone may be further steadied with light pressure by the inner thighs. *Note*: If the neck does not slide into the body easily, check to see that the tension screw has been loosened. If the neck does not slide easily, the tenon may be dirty. Wipe it and the receiver area with a cloth.

7. Align the brace on the neck with the connecting lever (a bridging device) on the body. Tighten the tension screw.

8. Attach the instrument to the neck strap. Allow the instrument to hang from the neck either in front or to the right side of the player's body. Either is acceptable. Positioning the instrument to the side is the traditional way. In the frontal position, the instrument should hang, not rest on the chair. The bottom of the instrument must be free of obstruction in order that it is angled correctly (to create a slightly upward angle of the instrument's neck to the player's mouth). This necessitates that the player sit forward on the chair.

9. Adjust the length of the neck strap. With the player seated in an upright position and with head held erect, the mouthpiece should make contact at approximately the lower lip. The goal in playing position is to have the mouthpiece positioned rather firmly against the upper teeth, not laying on the lower lip. In order to adjust the length of the strap, there must be no pressure on the strap. So with the strap attached, rest the instrument on a thigh and pull the clasp such that the strap becomes shorter, thus raising the instrument.

10. If playing in the traditional manner (to the side), turn the mouthpiece in order that the head remains erect while playing.

Disassembly and Swabbing

1. Unhook the neck strap. Place the upright instrument on the chair between the legs. Loosen the tension screw at the top of the body a few turns. Remove the neck with the mouthpiece and reed attached.

2. Lay the body on its side on your lap.

3. Open the instrument case.

4. Loosen the ligature screws three or four turns. Remove the ligature carefully while holding the base of the reed in place with the thumb. Place the ligature on your lap.

5. Remove the reed (avoid handling at the tip). Wipe off excess moisture with thumb and index finger. Place the flat back of the reed (called the table) against the flat surface of a reed guard, plastic container, or cardboard container. Or place the reed with table up on a surface in open air. This allows the reed to dry well before storage.

6. Disassemble mouthpiece and neck. Wipe the inside of the mouthpiece with the swab by using a finger to guide the swab in wiping the tone chamber and by rolling the swab in order to get inside the bore of the mouthpiece. When swabbing is complete, place the ligature on the mouthpiece, the cap over the mouthpiece, and store in the case. Pulling the swab through the mouthpiece frequently can damage the mouthpiece.

7. Swab the neck with a pull-through silk saxophone swab. Swab the body with a pull-through silk swab (same as above) by inserting the weight in the bell.

8. Grasp the bell, insert the end plug, and return the body to the case.

Care

In the first weeks of saxophone study, knowledge of the following instrument care issues by teacher and students is sufficient. Additional information about care is provided below in Chapter 7 (see "Foundations of Assembly and Disassembly" and "Foundations of Instrument Care").

1. If the instrument must be laid down on a chair, do so with keys up.

2. Treat the instrument gently even when it is in its case. A dropped case with instrument inside can damage the instrument.

3. Watch that students get in the habit of removing the reed from the mouthpiece after lessons and rehearsals in order to swab the mouthpiece. Otherwise, the mouthpiece will become very dirty. It can be washed with lukewarm water. Hot water will cause warping. Avoid soaps on rubber mouthpieces.

SAXOPHONE HAND POSITION

Left Hand

1. Sit forward in the chair.
2. The left thumb contacts the thumb rest at a *2 o'clock* angle.
3. The corner of the left thumb extends above the thumb rest just enough to overlap the bottom edge of the octave key. The octave key will be depressed by rocking the thumb, not by sliding it.
4. The left thumb and index finger form a C-shape (see Figure 4.8).
5. The left-hand fingers point in a slight downward angle.
6. The left pinky hovers just above the G-sharp key.

FIGURE 4.8 Shape of Left Hand in Instrument Hold
(Produced by Paige Jarreau at Paige's Photos)

Right Hand

7. The right thumbprint contacts the body of the instrument under the thumb rest. The side of the thumb contacts the thumb rest about halfway between the first knuckle and the tip. With the instrument attached to neck strap, push forward with the bottom thumb to move the mouthpiece toward the mouth.
8. The right thumb and index finger form a backward C (from the player's perspective). The index finger should not lean into and help support the instrument.
9. The right-hand fingers point straight across the instrument.
10. The right pinky hovers just above the low E-flat key.
11. Fingers are slightly curved.
12. Fingerprints close or hover above the center of the key pearls. Allow the instrument to hang from the neck either in front or to the right side of the player's body. Either is acceptable. Positioning the instrument to the side is the traditional way. In the frontal position, the instrument should hang, not rest on the chair. The bottom of the instrument must be free of obstruction in order that it is angled correctly (to create a slightly upward angle of the instrument's neck to the player's mouth.) This necessitates that the player sit forward on the chair. The weight of the instrument should be on the neck; there should be minimal upward pressure from the thumb in holding the instrument.

With proper neck strap adjustment, the mouthpiece should be brought to the player's mouth rather than the player bowing the head to meet the mouthpiece. On the saxophone, this is achieved in large part by pushing slightly forward with the bottom thumb, which moves the mouthpiece toward the player.

SAXOPHONE TONE DEVELOPMENT

What to Look for in Saxophone Embouchure

1. Is the head erect?

2. Is there enough mouthpiece in the mouth? There should appear to be more mouthpiece in the mouth than is the case for clarinet players. The saxophone mouthpiece is bigger than the clarinet mouthpiece. The bigger the mouthpiece, the more goes in the mouth. Apply this knowledge to the larger saxophones (tenor and baritone).

3. Do the mouthpiece and neck approach the mouth at a slightly upward angle?

4. Does the lower lip provide a cushion for the reed?

5. Are the teeth on top? You must check for this often during the early stages.

6. Is the mouth in a circle shape? Is the jaw down?

7. Are bottom and top teeth aligned?

For most students, these steps involve actions that are do-able. They become hard, however, when we try to get students to do them as corrections to bad habits. In other words, once a student gets comfortable playing with the head down, it is difficult to play with the head erect. Once one gets used to playing without teeth on top, playing with the teeth on top is not so easy. So work hard to get students to do things the right way early and often, so that bad habits don't develop. What students need in order to succeed with this sequence is frequent correct repetition of it.

Number 6 (mouth in a circle; jaw down) is somewhat more difficult to attain if in fact it does not come naturally to a student. The lips should form a circle (as if saying "OO"), leading to pressures being equally distributed around the reed and mouthpiece. A smile embouchure should be avoided. Jaw down is characteristic of all wind instrument embouchures. You want the saxophone reed to be supported by the lower lip, not the jaw pushing upward.

The side view of Figure 4.9 shows a number of desirable embouchure characteristics: Erect head, sufficient amount of mouthpiece in the mouth, a slight upward angle (instrument neck to face), lips making a circle around the reed and mouthpiece, and jaw down. This 11th grader makes an excellent sound.

FIGURE 4.9 Side View of Embouchure (High School Musician)
(Produced by Paige Jarreau at Paige's Photos)

Figure 4.10 shows a negative example. The chin is bunched up; the jaw is oriented in an upward, not downward, direction. Too much skin is making contact with the reed. There appears to be too much lower lip in the mouth. And notice that the ligature has been assembled incorrectly; the screw heads should not protrude to the player's left.

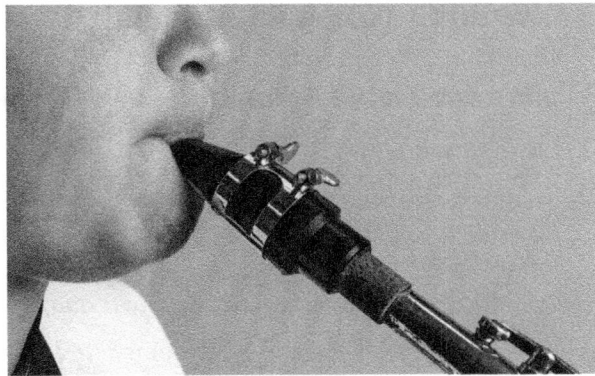

FIGURE 4.10 Negative Embouchure Example
(Produced by Paige Jarreau at Paige's Photos)

What to Listen for in Saxophone Embouchure

1. Volume. Is the student blowing fast air? From the beginning, encourage your students to blow big!—to make a big sound—to play *ff* always. You want the tone to be free and vibrant, which it won't be if the student is not blowing with an aggressive air stream. But look out—the sax is easily overblown.

2. Concert A. Is the student producing a concert A (or close to it) on the mouthpiece alone? This is both an embouchure-teaching and embouchure-evaluating tool. Learn this technique well.

3. The pitch sounds an octave too high or as a harmonic. This is caused by an embouchure that is too tight, which is often caused by a jaw that is not down. It instead bunches up in the direction of the reed. Another way of viewing this problem is that the lower lip/jaw is pushing into the reed too much.

4. Small sound or flat pitch. Both can result from not enough mouthpiece in the mouth, too much lower jaw pressure, too slow a speed of air. It is not uncommon for a teacher to ask a student to put a bit more mouthpiece in the mouth and for the student's tone quality to improve and volume increase.

5. Strident tone—a honk or a blast. This can be caused by having too much mouthpiece in the mouth, puffed cheeks, a lower lip that is turned out, or too little lip firmness around reed and mouthpiece.

What to Feel for in Saxophone Embouchure

Teeth on top. Grasp the neck near the cork while the student plays and move it side to side. If it feels mushy, the upper teeth are not making contact with the mouthpiece.

What to Do When a Note Will Not Speak

When a note will not speak or speaks with difficulty, it is helpful for the teacher to have an organized plan of attack designed to diagnose the problem.

1. Have the student sustain an easily obtained note with good tone quality. Now slur toward the problem note diatonically. For example, if low D will not speak, start on second space G (if in fact this is an easily obtained note) and add one finger at a time down to low D—slurred). The best low register is produced by taking in less reed and squeezing a bit more around the reed and mouthpiece. Keep the firmness used in making the mouthpiece alone A. A less desirable fix for low register response is a more relaxed embouchure as the notes descend toward D and beyond. Once

the student experiences the embouchure feel for low D, try starting on that note, first without tongue (as if saying "HOO"), then with tongue.

2. Try the instrument yourself. Is the reed worn, chipped, warped, misaligned, too soft, too hard? Is the mouthpiece chipped? Is there a leaky pad? Suspect a leaky pad if all else seems okay, and a note squawks frequently or sounds fuzzy when it does speak.

Sometimes the only way to know what the student is experiencing or feeling in terms of a note response problem or reed quality/strength issue is for the teacher to play the student's equipment. It is both good practice and good public relations for the teacher to sterilize the mouthpiece and reed in question both before and after using it. A pump spray product called *Sterisol Germicide* is advertised to sanitize mouthpieces and reeds without causing damage to materials or finish.

Embouchure Teaching Strategies

For Embouchure in General

The combination of correct embouchure pressures, a fast air stream, and an appropriate strength reed should result in:

- concert A on the mouthpiece alone (alto sax)
- concert A-flat on the mouthpiece and neck (alto sax)
- concert G on the tenor sax mouthpiece
- concert E-flat or D on the baritone sax mouthpiece.

If the pitch is sharp to the standard, it is likely due to a pinched, tight embouchure or an incorrect amount of mouthpiece in the mouth. The pitch is not likely to be flat on the saxophone mouthpiece. By contrast, young clarinet players tend to be flat on the small piece. Essentially, mouthpiece-alone work constitutes *tuning the embouchure*. The goal is for students to memorize the *feel* of the embouchure when A is being produced, then reproduce this feel when playing the fully assembled saxophone. How much correct repetition of a sustained mouthpiece pitch do you think is necessary to memorize the feel and then transfer it to the assembled instrument? Answer: A lot! Work toward concert A on the mouthpiece and then transfer this feel to the saxophone from the beginning and for as long as it takes.

To Achieve the Correct Amount of Mouthpiece in the Mouth

1. Realize the tendency to put too little in the mouth.
2. Fulcrum on lower lip.
3. Intentionally have the student put too little mouthpiece in the mouth and experience the resultant weak, anemic tone (or squeak) as being something to avoid.

To Check for Teeth on Top

While the student is sustaining a pitch, grasp the neck near the cork and move it side to side. If teeth are not making contact, it will feel mushy.

To Create Proper Lip and Jaw Formation

1. Form the lips into a firm whistle formation, drop the jaw, and maintain.

2. Have the student, while sustaining a pitch, try to push the upper lip down toward the mouthpiece. This will automatically lower the chin.

3. Teacher circles his thumb and middle finger around the lower forearm of student. In this manner, he simulates proper lip pressure, too much lip pressure, and not enough lip pressure.

4. Open the mouth about one inch (2.5cm), move the jaw forward so that the bottom teeth and top teeth are parallel. Put bottom lip over bottom teeth, place reed on lip, close in a circle shape. The jaw forward aspect of this approach orients the jaw in a forward rather than upward (as in biting) direction.

5. Instead of approaching the embouchure by placing the reed on the lower lip first, as is typical, open the mouth and place the mouthpiece against the upper teeth first. Then put some lower lip of the bottom teeth. Then close the mouth from bottom up. Focus student attention on avoiding an upward thrust of the lower jaw into the reed.

6. "OO" as an inner mouth shape is a reasonable point of departure for the beginner; however, for optimal tone quality, the inner mouth shape of an accomplished saxophone player changes across the range of the instrument, that is, from "OO" in the low to mid-registers to "IH" in the area just above the staff (G–A to palm key notes) to "EE" in the altissimo register.

To Eliminate Puffed Cheeks

Have the student play a tone with puffed cheeks. As he sustains it, have him retract the cheeks. In other words, fix the problem by doing the problem, then during the sustain, retract the cheeks.

Vibrato

When for Vibrato?

Vibrato can be introduced late in the middle school years, though there should be no hurry to do so. Without question, vibrato should not be introduced before a student has had ample time to develop a well-supported and stable straight tone. One school of thought says to leave the teaching of vibrato to the private teacher. The students who study privately will tend to be ahead of the others in terms of tonal development, finger technique, and tongue technique. These students will likely occupy the top chairs. When vibrato is most advantageous—that is, during solo work—these students will be in a position to use it.

Teaching Vibrato

The most common form of saxophone vibrato is jaw vibrato. It can be introduced as follows:

1. Use the syllables ("AH-EE" or "VAH-VAH"); say distinctly and at a deliberate pace, then increase speed emphasizing fluidity and blending of syllables.

2. At a fast pace, the jaw should influence pitch only; do not move the tongue with the jaw; the tongue should be relaxed.

3. Play a 3rd line B at a comfortable dynamic and sustain; try to bend the pitch by using the syllables; do it slowly and rhythmically at first—exaggerate the movement and the effect on the pitch (see "Teaching Vibrato" in Chapter 2).

4. Try to blend the up and down movement of the jaw; minimize movement; exaggerate less.

5. The pitch should bend below the in-tune pitch level, not above. Work vibrato into simple tunes.

Listen to accomplished performers and imitate their vibrato (its speed and amplitude).

Other Important Factors in Saxophone Tone Development

Reeds

Some unknowing students play on reeds that are too soft or too hard. Soft reeds will produce a bright or thin tone. They will not respond readily in the upper register (B–C and into the palm key notes), making clean tonguing difficult. They will tend to play flat. Hard reeds will sound rough, unrefined, and sharp.

Take aside a student whose sound indicates a soft reed and do one or more of the following:

1. Try a different reed (new), same strength.

2. Try a harder reed (increase strength in one-half increments).

3. Try a better quality reed (e.g., change from LaVoz to Vandoren, or from the standard to premium Mitchell Lurie reed).

Have several reeds of some combination of heavier and better quality available for the student to try. Compare old sound (using the old reed) with the new sound. Chances are that you will hear the difference, and your student will hear and feel the difference.

Mouthpiece

Playing on a reed and mouthpiece that are compatible will improve tone quality. Changing to a better quality mouthpiece will do the same. Mouthpieces with a larger rather than smaller tone chamber produce darker tone. Concerning reed and mouthpiece choices, consult with a trusted private teacher.

Listening

By listening to artist performers, teachers and students develop opinions about saxophone tone. These opinions can lead to preferences that result in concepts of tone toward which teachers may lead students and toward which students may aspire (see "Building Concept of Tone" for notable saxophonists in Chapter 7, page 229).

SAXOPHONE TONGUING

Pre-tonguing Activity, Contact Point, and Vowel Shape

During initial embouchure development, "HOO" (a breath attack) is used to begin sustained tones. A ballpark embouchure combined with a fast air stream should result in a sustained, *forte*, unwavering tone that is relatively in tune, that is, the student produces at or near A-flat concert on the mouthpiece and neck and transfers this *feel* to the fully assembled saxophone.

The basic articulation involves touching the tip of the tongue to the tip of the reed. The tip of the tongue refers to a location on top and a very little bit back from the actual tip of the tongue. This tip refers to a point just a bit below the actual tip of the reed. Real tonguing resembles saying "TOO." Notice that the vowels in "TOO" promote a round feel and sense to the saxophone embouchure.

Teaching Tonguing: Two Alternatives

Traditional Approach to Teaching Tonguing

The traditional approach to teaching tonguing is holistic, to use terminology from psychology. Tonguing is kept intact; it is not broken into its component parts. Modeling by the teacher, with voice and instrument, is integrated with the following steps.

1. Off the instrument, students say "TOO" (or some appropriate variant) using their speaking voices.
2. Off the instrument, students form a "cooling soup" aperture in the lips and legato tongue a series of "TOO"s on a continuous stream of air.
3. With your thumbnail, show students the ideal contact point on the reed.
4. On the instrument, students finger a mid-range note, form an embouchure, position the tongue on the tip of the reed, press against reed with tongue, and initiate the start of a tone as if saying "TOO." Sustain.
5. On the instrument, students do a series of four "TOO"s, tip of tongue to tip of reed. They tongue a continuous airstream.

Backward Approach to Teaching Tonguing

The traditional approach works for many students. It doesn't for others who are unable to coordinate air stream, embouchure, and tongue. They can't put it all together at once. Or they unknowingly articulate from the throat (glottal tonguing). The *Backward Approach* teaches tonguing by starting with something that we know students can do successfully, that is, start a tone with a pre-tonguing technique (a breath attack), and progressing into unknown tonguing territory. Keep in mind that the approach in this book is one that begins with tone production as an isolated element. Tone is not integrated with tonguing. Tonguing is introduced *after* a ballpark accurate embouchure and tone are achieved. Read each step below and compare to the notation in Figure 4.11.

1. As shown in Figure 4.11, student plays a mid-range note using the pre-tonguing articulation to initiate tone, sustains for 2 beats, and on beat 3 stops the tone by simply stopping the air stream. Repeat as necessary in order to allow student to *find beat 3*.

2. Student plays, sustains for 2 beats, and on beat 3 *stops* the tone by touching the tip of the tongue to the tip of the reed (HOO—T). With a fingernail, show the student the ideal contact point on the reed. Repeat this process several times in order to allow the student to *find the spot where the tongue goes.*

3. Student repeats Step 2 but when the tongue touches the reed, it touches for only an instant. It is immediately pulled away (imagine the reed being hot!) while the air stream keeps going (HOO—TOO—). Extend this process by tonguing successive quarter notes in legato tongue fashion (HOO—TOO—TOO—TOO).

4. Start the tone with the tongue in traditional manner (TOO—).

Step 3 reiterated. Work hard to get students to legato tongue here. They should keep the air moving while tonguing. They will want to treat each note as a separate entity rather than a part of a series of notes that should be played as a line of music. Some will want to breathe after every note. Some will want to re-set their embouchure after every note. Don't let these faults creep in now; they are hard to correct later.

FIGURE 4.11 Backward Approach to Teaching Tonguing

Assessment and Tonguing

I considered calling this section Addressing Problems in Tonguing, but it's actually about something bigger and more far reaching in your development as a music teacher. We'll call it assessment. Don't confuse this form of assessment with making up, giving, and grading tests. Assessment as I intend it here is one thing that good teachers do that makes them good.

Simply, assessment is collecting information. When I'm about to leave my office to walk across campus, I look outside my window to determine whether I should take an umbrella. I assess with my eyes. At my desk, my back is turned to the window, so frequently I hear thunder or rain before I see the visible effects. I assess with my ears. Assessment is something that people do all the time in order to get along in life. In the music room and rehearsal hall, effective teachers are keen observers, taking in information, some obvious and some very subtle, in order to make wise moment-to-moment decisions about what to do. This recurring cycle of collect–decide–act is fundamental to the structured teaching/learning setting. The teacher's skills of observation and assessment are greatly enhanced when she knows what to look for and listen for relative to tonguing.

Things the Teacher Can See

1. Is the jaw moving? Jaw movement is caused by large tongue movements. Confine movement to the front of the tongue—as if saying "d-d-d-d" at a fairly rapid pace. Articulate with little outward sign of movement, like a ventriloquist. To fix excessive jaw movement, the teacher must slow the student down, isolate the problem, and do some detailed work. For the exercise in Figure 4.12, use an easy-to-produce note. Use a legato tongue (do not stop the air between notes). Ask yourself or your student: Is the tongue shaped as if saying "OO." On contact, is the tip of the tongue touching the tip of the reed? Is the tongue moving only slightly away from the contact point? Is the jaw still?

FIGURE 4.12 Isolate Tongue Movement

2. Glottal tonguing. Be on the lookout for glottal tonguing (starting the sound in the throat), which can been seen and heard. Some beginners will unknowingly "tongue" from the throat. They think that they are tonguing correctly, not realizing their error.

Things the Teacher Can Hear

1. No tongue at all, a sort of huffing or puffing.
2. A "THU"-like sound. If the articulation sounds like "THU," the tongue is not pressing firmly enough against the teeth just prior to the release of the air.
3. Lack of coordination between tongue and fingers in fast passages or involving certain awkward note pairs regardless of tempo. The student must slow down! Isolate the specific problem (e.g., a two-note sequence) and slow the tempo enough for errorless performance across successive trials. Increase the tempo in small increments while maintaining errorless performance. Coordination problems can be fixed also by starting at a very slow tempo, playing each note short, fingering each successive note just a bit *before* tonguing it, and continuing this process while increasing the tempo in small increments. At a certain tempo, it becomes impossible to finger *before* tonguing, so at this point the practice procedure has reached its limit.

THE SAXOPHONE MECHANISM

Brief History

Adolphe Sax confronted the imperfections of various woodwind and brass instruments by inventing the saxophone in roughly 1840. In effect, the first saxophone, a bass instrument, was a combination of existing instruments—it had a metal body like that of a bass ophicleide, a mouthpiece and reed like that of a bass clarinet, and keys, not valves. The development of the saxophone is not to be confused with the sax horn, a family of valved brass instruments also invented by Sax.

The saxophone is a prominent member of concert bands, wind ensembles, and various jazz mediums. The saxophone quartet literature is quite extensive. The instrument is infrequently called for in the orchestral literature. Exceptions are Bizet's *L'Arlesienne*, Milhaud's *La Creation du monde*, Gershwin's *Rhapsody in Blue*, and Ravel's *Bolero*.

Soloist Rudy Wiedoft (1893–1940) is recognized by some as the father of saxophone playing in the United States. Notable classical players of the 20th century include Frenchman Marcel Mule (1901–2001) and Americans Sigurd Rascher, Cecil Leeson, and Larry Teal. Later in the century, Jean-Marie Londeix, Fred Hemke, Eugene Rousseau, and Donald Sinta were major players. Notable jazz players include Lester Young, Coleman Hawkins, Charlie Parker, Cannonball Adderly, John Coltrane, Phil Woods, Bill Evans, and Branford Marsalis.

Family, Transposition, and Clef

Sopranino in E-flat

- Sounds up a minor 3rd (same as soprano clarinet in E-flat).

Soprano in B-flat

- Comes in two shapes. Most frequently it is built in a straight line and is held like a clarinet. The older style shape has the curve of an alto saxophone. It is of course smaller than the alto.
- Sounds down a major 2nd.

Alto in E-flat

- This is the beginning instrument of the saxophone family.
- Sounds down a major 6th (same as alto clarinet).

Tenor in B-flat

- Sounds down an octave plus a whole step (major 9th). Transposition is the same as that for bass clarinet.
- As a test for the embouchure, the mouthpiece alone pitch should be at or very near concert G.
- Because the mouthpiece is bigger, take more into the mouth than for alto saxophone.
- With more mouthpiece in the mouth, the contact point for the tongue is farther away from the reed's tip than it is for alto sax.

Baritone in E-flat

- Sounds down an octave and a major 6th (same as contrabass clarinet in E-flat).
- As a test for the embouchure, the mouthpiece alone pitch should be at or very near concert D.
- Because the mouthpiece is bigger, take more into the mouth than for alto and tenor saxophone.
- With more mouthpiece in the mouth, the contact point for the tongue is farther away from the reed's tip than it is for alto or tenor.

Bass in B-flat

- Sounds down two octaves and a major 2nd (same as contrabass clarinet in B-flat).

C Melody Saxophone

- Sounds down one octave.
- Looks like a tenor saxophone.
- Is obsolete but occasionally one will show up on a school band inventory.

Note well. The parts for every instrument in the saxophone family are written in the treble clef. The player of the large instruments reads music in treble clef while playing instruments that sound down in the tenor and bass ranges.

Instrument Manufacturing

The saxophone is a member of the woodwind family because its sound source is a wooden reed with a clarinet-like mouthpiece. The body of the instrument is finished with clear lacquer, silver plating, or gold plating.

Be aware of distinctions between professional and student line models. Most manufacturers produce both; in other words, one name (e.g., Selmer) most often comprises several different models of saxophone (student line through professional) and types of saxophone (e.g., alto saxophone, tenor saxophone, baritone saxophone). Generally, student model saxophones are more expensive than student model flutes and clarinets. Saxophones start at roughly $800. Professional model instruments can cost in the range of $6000 to $9000. Selmer makes perhaps the most well-known professional quality saxophone. The following lists of saxophone manufacturers are not exhaustive.

- Professional model instruments are made by manufacturers Selmer Paris, Keilwerth, Yamaha, Yanagisawa, and others
- Student model instruments are made by manufacturers Amati, Jupiter, Olds, Selmer, Vito, Winston, Yamaha, and others.

Range and Registers

1. All instruments in the family have the same theoretical range; however, the larger instruments do not respond with ease in the upper register (see Figure 4.13).
2. The range of the saxophone divides into four registers: the first octave (low B-flat to C-sharp), the second octave (D to C-sharp), a *short* third octave (high D to F or F-sharp), and the altissimo register.
3. The range extends to high F-sharp on some models of alto and tenor saxophone and to low A on some baritone saxophones.
4. Like the oboe and the bassoon, the lowest notes of the range normally require extra effort to produce. The best low register is produced by taking in less reed, compressing it, and keeping the firmness used in making the mouthpiece alone A. A less desirable fix for low register response (low D and below) is a more relaxed embouchure. These notes do not speak with ease at soft dynamic levels.

5. *Crossing the break* is the name for note pairs that involve few fingers to many fingers and vice versa—for example, third space C or C-sharp to fourth line D. Negotiating the break crossing is less of a challenge on saxophone than on clarinet because the saxophone keys are covered (plateau style).
6. The notes in the altissimo register are produced differently from the notes in the other registers. For example, if low B-flat is fingered, manipulations of the tongue (more or less arching of its back—"EE" to "AH" and all points in between) will produce notes in the B-flat harmonic series, the uppermost ones extending into the altissimo register. Altissimo register playing is an advanced technique that has been mastered by many accomplished saxophonists. Mouthpiece design and reed strength must be conducive to playing in this extreme register.

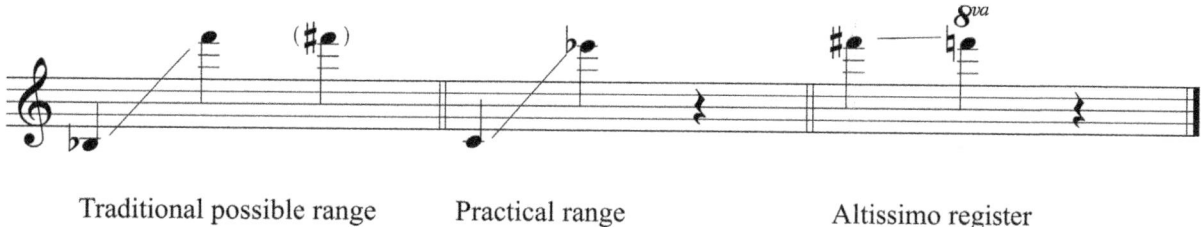

Traditional possible range   Practical range   Altissimo register

FIGURE 4.13 Saxophone Range and Register

Fingering Issues

Right Hand Down

Any single or combination of right-hand fingers can be depressed during the short-tube notes shown in Figure 4.14.

FIGURE 4.14 Short-Tube Notes

This right-hand-down technique has three benefits. It improves tone quality, lowers the pitch of C and C-sharp, and makes for less finger movement and consequently a more fluid technique when crossing the break. Figure 4.15 provides examples. In the first instance of right hand down, two fingers remain down (the right-hand fingers for E). In the second, three fingers remain down (the right-hand fingers for D). As a reminder, the player or teacher might mark the part as shown.

FIGURE 4.15 Right-Hand-Down Technique

Rollers

Unlike the clarinet where consecutive pinkies are avoided by using cross-fingerings, the saxophone has no cross-fingering issues. The use of consecutive pinkies is a viable and necessary finger technique made possible by rollers on right and left pinky keys, which promote sliding between pinky keys.

Articulated G-sharp/A-flat

When G-sharp is interspersed among notes involving the fingers of the right hand, the G-sharp key can remain depressed during the right-hand fingered notes with no ill effects on pitch or tone. In the Figure 4.16 notice how leaving the G-sharp key down eliminates awkward finger movement. Please note that the word *articulated* in this sense makes no reference to the tongue.

FIGURE 4.16 Articulated G-sharp

Alternate Fingerings

Figure 4.17 presents five alternate fingerings that are useful in intermediate and above music for the saxophone. It might be helpful to think of these fingerings as follows: Fork F-sharp, three different B-flats, and side C.

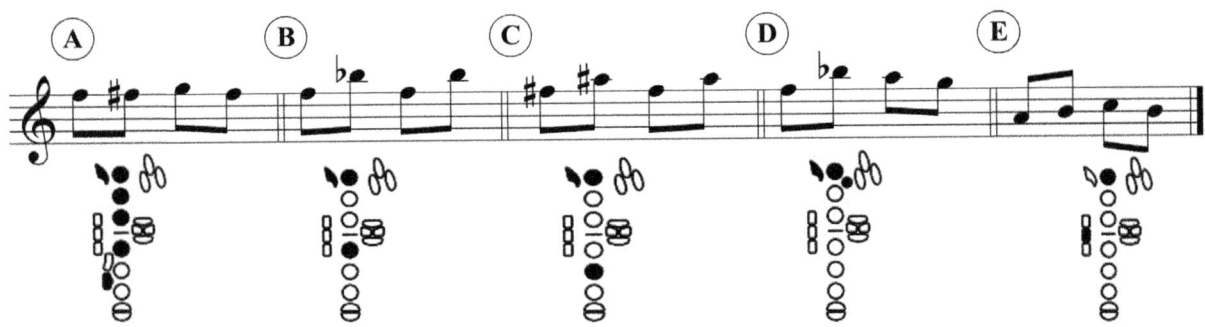

FIGURE 4.17 Alternate Fingerings

    In Letter A, use of alternate F-sharp avoids having to exchange fingers 1 and 2 of the right hand as would be the case with use of regular F-sharp.
    Using the B-flat fingers in Letters B and C makes it possible to avoid the awkward finger movement between F or F-sharp and regular B-flat/A-sharp (1–2–bottom side key).
    For Letter D use bis key B-flat. Depress both the B pearl and the smaller pearl directly under it with the first finger for the entire passage. The key with the smaller pearl is called the bis key. This is a way to finger B-flat using only one finger, somewhat like the thumb B-flat on flute. Use bis key B-flat only if B natural is not in the passage. B natural would require an awkward slide of the first finger off the bis key. Flat keys are good for the bis key (flat keys do not have B naturals unless they occur as accidentals.)

In Letter E, use of the side C fingering avoids an awkward exchange of fingers 1 and 2 as would be the case with regular C.

Palm Key Notes

Most of the palm keys are located under the palm of the left hand, hence the name. The keys are depressed with palm and underside of knuckles, not with the fingerprints of one's fingers. Figure 4.18 shows the notes and the fingerings. Notice how the fingerings are cumulative as they ascend chromatically. Accomplished saxophonists are able to play the palm key notes while keeping the fingers close to the instrument rather than extended away from it.

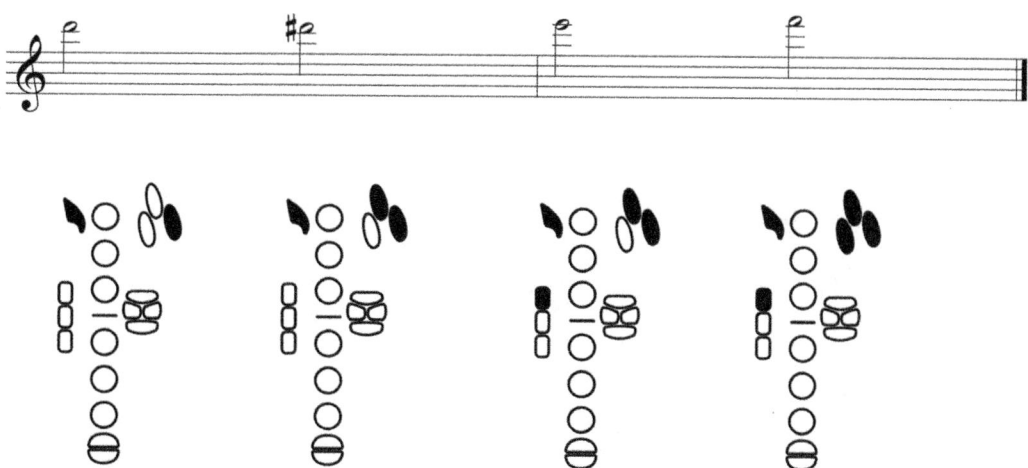

FIGURE 4.18 The Palm Key Notes

Some Trill Fingerings

The trill fingerings in Figure 4.19 involve something other than the normal fingerings for the two notes. The grey key(s) is the one that should be trilled. More comprehensive collections of trill fingerings are available online.

Tuning the Saxophone

Basic Information

1. Tuning the embouchure. Achieve a concert A on the alto mouthpiece alone and a concert G on the tenor mouthpiece alone. The saxophonist plays in the middle of the pitch range of the small piece. The clarinetist plays in the upper middle of the pitch range of the small piece. This is an important distinction.

2. In tuning the instrument, insist that your students play at a *forte* dynamic level. This provides an accurate indication of where the instrument sits pitch-wise.

3. Figure 4.20 shows saxophone tuning notes. The best tuning note for the alto, tenor, and baritone saxophones is written F-sharp (concert A). The standard band tuning note, concert B-flat (written

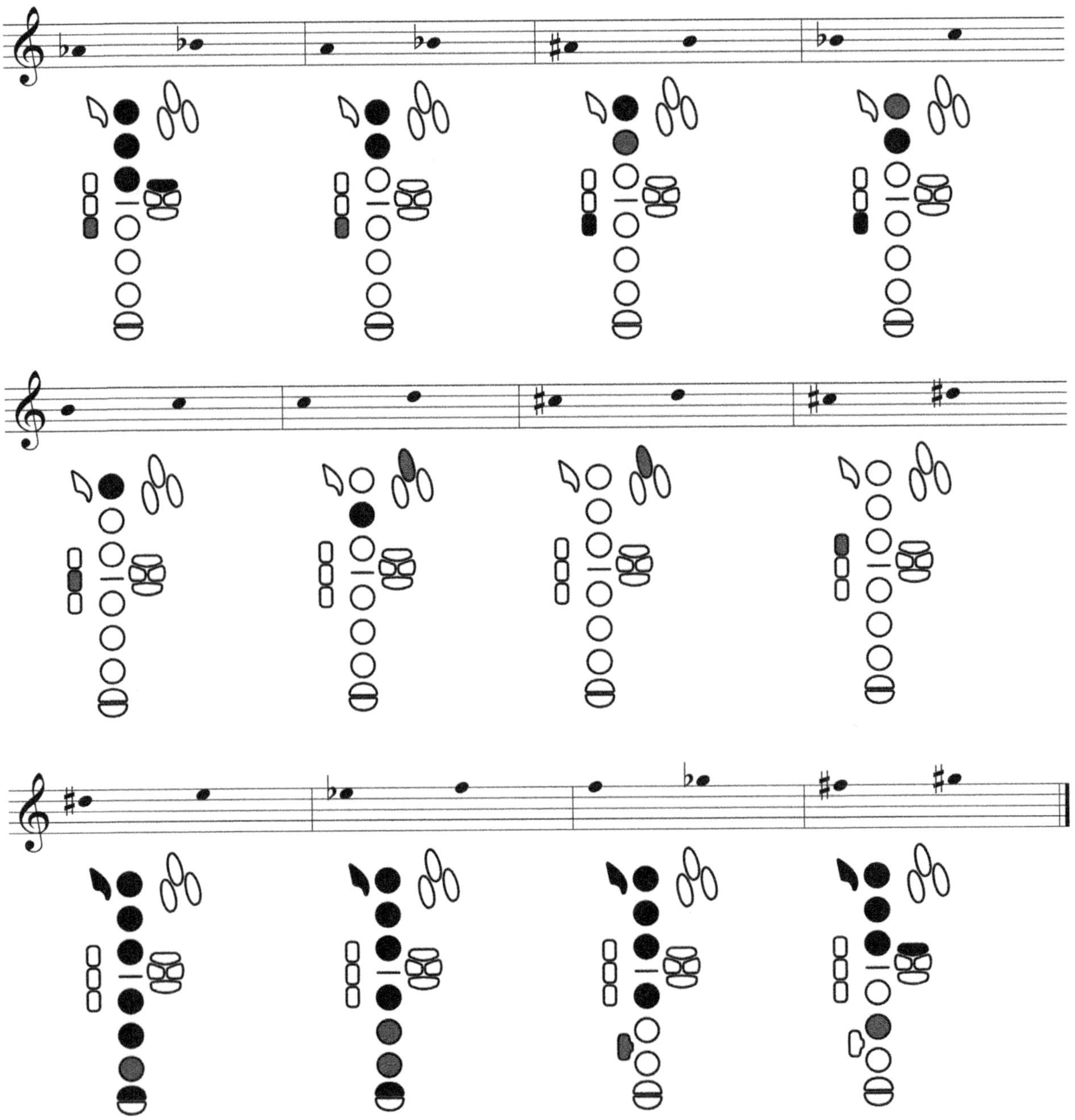

FIGURE 4.19 Trill Fingerings

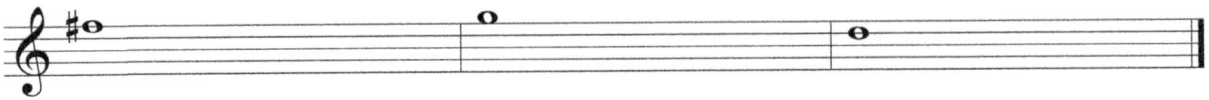

FIGURE 4.20 Saxophone Tuning Notes

G), has a sharp tendency on the saxophone, so it is not ideal for general tuning. Another common band tuning note is concert F. This is a D on the alto sax. D also has a sharp tendency.

4. Tuning adjustments are made by pushing or pulling the mouthpiece. The mouthpiece can be positioned in many different places on the cork of the neck, though there is only one correct location. For novice players in the early stages of embouchure development, use a third line B (concert D) and compare it to a tuner to determine a ballpark placement for the mouthpiece on the neck. Consider putting a pencil mark on the cork as a reference point for future ballpark placement of the mouthpiece.

5. If the mouthpiece is pulled too much, low notes will gurgle.

Pitch Tendencies and Solutions

Every wind instrument has pitch tendencies; certain notes, because of the design of the instrument, tend to be sharp or flat. By knowing the pitch tendencies of the saxophone, the effective music teacher is able to predict what might happen with regard to pitch before it actually happens in the lesson or rehearsal. The conductor's job in rehearsal is to listen and discern whether student performance is consistent with the tendencies. If it is, the conductor must know what to do to solve the pitch problems.

Flat Tendency

1. Cold instrument.
2. Loud volume (including *crescendo*).
3. Soft reed.
4. Short-tube C-sharps (can be sharp or flat).

Solutions for Flatness

One of the following combined with a discerning ear will remedy flatness.

1. Lip up. This refers to one or more of the following: Firm the lips; adjust voicing toward "EE."
2. In a pinch, play softer.
3. Change to a harder reed.
4. For short-tube C-sharps, see "Adding Keys" and Figure 4.21 below.

Sharp Tendency

1. Low register (B-flat to D).
2. The third octave (palm key notes—D to F).
3. Soft volume (including *decrescendo*).
4. Hard reed.
5. 4th line D.
6. Short-tube C-sharps (can be sharp or flat).

Solutions for Sharpness

One of the following combined with a discerning ear will remedy flatness.

1. Lip down. This refers to one or more of the following: Drop the jaw, make the embouchure more round, lower the tongue. The verticalness of the embouchure must be emphasized. Techniques: Adjust voicing toward "OH" or "AH"; play as if trying to stifle a yawn, ask student to play flatter.
2. In a pinch, play louder.
3. On certain notes, add keys, see "Adding Keys" and Figure 4.21 below.

Adding Keys for Pitch Adjustment

For some out-of-tune notes, lipping is not sufficient to remedy flawed pitch. Instead of or in addition to lipping, the pitch of the notes shown in Figure 4.21 can be improved by adding keys. You will notice that in some cases, adding a key opens a tone hole, which raises the pitch. In other cases, adding a key closes a tone hole, which lowers the pitch.

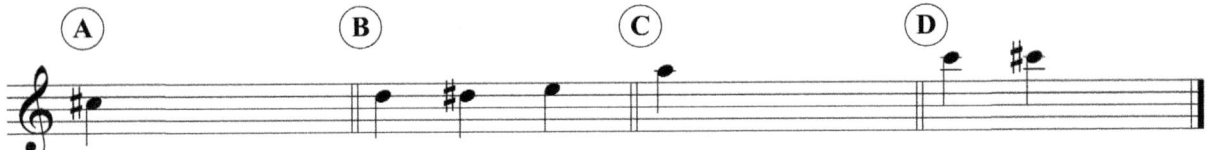

FIGURE 4.21 Adding Keys for Pitch Adjustment

- Letter A. If this short-tube C-sharp is flat, add the side C key. If sharp, add the right hand.
- Letter B. If these notes are sharp, add the low B key. On E, add the low B-flat key.
- Letter C. If this A is sharp, add finger 3 of the right hand.
- Letter D. If these short-tube notes are sharp, add the right hand.

Tuning and Intonation Summary

- Tuning the embouchure
    - Mouthpiece alone should sound a big, resonant A concert (alto saxophone)
    - G concert (tenor saxophone)
    - E-flat or D concert (baritone saxophone)
- Tuning note
    - Play with best embouchure and at *f* dynamic level
    - Top line F-sharp is the best tuning note
    - Push or pull mouthpiece
- Pitch tendencies
    - Temperature: Cold = flat
    - Register: Lowest B-flat to D = sharp; palm key notes = sharp

- Volume: Soft = sharp; loud = flat
- Reed: Soft = flat; hard = sharp
- Bad notes (most notorious): Short-tube C-sharp, 4th line D
- Solutions
    - Lipping
    - Add keys.

The Single Reed

See "The Single Reed," pages 88–94. The information is the same for saxophone.

The Mouthpiece and Ligature

See "The Mouthpiece and Ligature," pages 94–96. Read below for information on the jazz mouthpiece.

Jazz Mouthpiece

Performance practice provides room for the jazz saxophonist to deviate from the sound of a classically trained musician. From one accomplished jazz player to the next, this deviation can range from just a subtle change in tone quality to large variations in sound—large/small, heavy/light, focused/breathy, in-tune/flat—and vibrato—small versus deep fluctuations. The writings and discographies of Jerry Coker are excellent sources in the study of the saxophone's sound in the jazz idiom. The choice of reed and style of mouthpiece have significant effect on tone quality. High school students who are jazz savvy are often aware of the possibilities in tone quality. They will want to purchase mouthpieces that allow them to alter their classical sounds. For example, for rock and fusion styles they will want to sound brighter, shriller, and more metallic—characteristics that coincidentally allow the sound to project better in an ensemble dominated by brass instruments.

There are many brands of mouthpiece that are distinguished by facing, shape of tone chamber, and material, all of which affect tone quality. Round, large chamber mouthpieces produce a darker sound; square chamber mouthpieces produce a more penetrating, reedy sound. Metal mouthpieces are generally brighter sounding than plastic or hard rubber mouthpieces.

Some woodwind catalogs provide mouthpiece facing charts that allow comparison of the dimensions of various mouthpieces. Mouthpieces can be obtained on a trial basis before purchase is necessary.

If the school jazz band consists of intermediate-level students and/or jazz novices, it is recommended that saxophonists play with their classical tone qualities. In fact, well-known classical and jazz clarinetist Eddie Daniels has played jazz on a classical mouthpiece. Challenge students with the literature, its various styles, and in all the ways one challenges them as members of a concert band or orchestra (rhythm reading, phrasing, intonation, finger technique, dynamics). The issue of tonal variety can come later, but perhaps not too much later because to mimic the idiosyncrasies and nuances of Phil Woods's sound (alto sax and clarinet) or Bill Evans's sound (tenor and soprano saxophone) can be both fun and inspiring.

The Saxophone in the Jazz Band

The standard big band instrumentation includes five players in the sax section: 1st and 2nd alto, 1st and 2nd tenor, and baritone. Traditional seating left to right (from the conductor's perspective) across the front of the ensemble is:

Tenor 1—Alto 2—Alto 1—Tenor 2—Baritone

Most of the solo work is in the Tenor 1 part, so it is good to situate this player close to the rhythm section, which is located to the left of the ensemble.

Doubling

It is not uncommon in advanced jazz band literature to have saxophone parts call for doubling, that is, for the part to stipulate saxophone and flute, or saxophone and clarinet, or all three. Professional saxophonists with a jazz specialty are proficient doublers.

If flute or clarinet parts are called for in high school jazz literature, the most expedient approach is to have a flute or clarinet player join the band and cover the part. Alternatively, saxophone players can learn the flute or clarinet. This is a slow process, but educationally sound if there is time for the doubler to develop on these secondary instruments.

Selected Jazz Resources

    Jamey Aebersold Jazz, www.jazzbooks.com

    Christopher Azzara and Richard Grunow. *Developing Musicianship through Improvisation*, GIA Publications.

    Jerry Coker. *How to Listen to Jazz*. All of the many jazz books by Jerry Coker are excellent resources.

    JaZZed: The Jazz Educators Magazine. Publication of Jazz Education Network.

    Richard Lawn. *The Jazz Ensemble Director's Manual*. Barnhouse.

    The *Smithsonian Collection of Classic Jazz* is a five-CD set chronicling in sound the history of jazz. The written material that accompanies the set is excellent.

    The International Association for Jazz Educators (IAJE), as of 2009, is no longer in existence.

Saxophone Quartet

There are two standard quartet instrumentations:

- Common for school: Alto 1, alto 2, tenor, baritone—for example, *Allegro de Concert* by J. B. Singalee.
- French quartet: Soprano, alto, tenor, baritone—for example, *Quartet* by J. Fischer.

STUDY QUESTIONS

1. Talk smart about the real saxophone small piece versus the other saxophone small piece that is more practical for early instruction. Include target pitches.

2. The clarinet small piece and the saxophone mouthpiece each produce a range of pitches. How are the optimal pitches for each explained in terms of the range?

3. What are the differences between the clarinet and saxophone embouchures?

4. Make yourself a cheat sheet that puts in order the steps for making first sounds when teaching a group of saxophone players. Make a list. Don't be wordy. Choose the most important words to jog your memory.
5. Explain the thinking involved in adjusting the length of the saxophone neck strap.
6. When you practice the saxophone, are you thinking and doing the details listed under "What to Look for in Saxophone Embouchure" so that you are better able to use this information in your observational role as teacher?
7. In playing the saxophone, what difficulties have you had in producing an A on the mouthpiece? What solutions have you discovered?
8. How is saxophone vibrato produced? Demonstrate it methodically on your saxophone.
9. In tonguing, to what does "tip of the reed" refer to in saxophone playing?
10. Beginners should start on what strength reed?
11. True or false:
    a. The tip and sides of a reed are resistances areas.
    b. The heart of a reed is a vibrating area.
12. The table of the reed is found where? Its surface should be . . .
13. How is a warped reed fixed?
14. After removing the reed from the mouthpiece, how should the reed be stored?
15. What is reed rotation? What are its benefits to the player?
16. How does a band or orchestra director obtain reeds? Or is this simply the responsibility of the students?
17. What are the sound characteristics of a reed that is too soft?
18. How should a mouthpiece by washed?
19. Describe mouthpiece patch and its usefulness.
20. Who invented the saxophone? When?
21. What brand name is perhaps the most well-known professional quality saxophone?
22. What notes belong to the altissimo register of the saxophone? How is this register produced?
23. Demonstrate the articulated G-sharp fingering technique.
24. Knowledge and skill with multiple F-sharp, B-flat, and C fingerings are useful on the saxophone. Play the "alternate fingerings" explained and notated in the text.
25. Find the palm key notes in a fingering chart and play them in sustained fashion.
26. The best tuning note for all saxophones is . . .

27. Indicate saxophone pitch tendencies for the following conditions:
    a. 4th line D
    b. Short-fingered C-sharps.
28. What does one do physically to "lip down" on the saxophone to correct sharpness?
29. What are the two saxophone quartet instrumentations?
30. Draw a diagram of the traditional saxophone section seating in a jazz band (big band).
31. What saxophone part calls for most of the solo work in a jazz band?
32. What is doubling?

PERFORMANCE TESTING OF UNIVERSITY STUDENTS ON SECONDARY INSTRUMENTS

A rubric is an evaluative tool. The rubric that follows makes clear the expectations of the university student playing secondary saxophone as he or she approaches the end of an intensive three to four weeks of study. Students may use the criteria to prepare for performance testing and to self-evaluate. Teachers may use the criteria to structure feedback.

1.	Assembled and disassembled (incl. swabbing) the instrument properly	Yes	No
2.	Formed a characteristic embouchure:		
	a. Optimal amount of mouthpiece in the mouth	Yes	No
	b. Optimal amount of lower lip over lower teeth	Yes	No
	c. Teeth on top of mouthpiece	Yes	No
	d. Lips and cheeks against teeth	Yes	No
	e. Round look to mouth/jaw formation	Yes	No
	f. Teeth aligned	Yes	No
	g. Jaw down	Yes	No
3.	Breathed through the corners of the mouth	Yes	No
	Breathed according to phrase	Yes	No
4.	Achieved a vibrant and unwavering tone across the range of notes	Yes	No
5.	Maintained correct hand position:		
	a. Curved fingers	Yes	No
	b. Fingerprints centered over the key pearls	Yes	No

	c. Fingers held close to the keys	Yes	No
	d. Left thumb at 2 o'clock	Yes	No
	e. C formation in the thumb and index finger of both hands	Yes	No
6.	Recalled and played primary fingerings from low D to high C	Yes	No
7.	Recalled and played alternate fingerings (articulated G-sharp, alternate F-sharp, C, and B-flat)	Yes	No
8.	Recalled and played at least two of the palm key notes	Yes	No
9.	Tongued unmarked notes and first notes of slurs	Yes	No
	Legato tongue was convincing	Yes	No
	Kept embouchure still while tonguing	Yes	No
10.	Play expressively by varying volume and tempo as indicated or dictated by the notes	Yes	No
11.	Performance showed evidence of sufficient practice	Yes	No

136 TEACHING THE INSTRUMENTS

SAXOPHONE FINGERING CHART

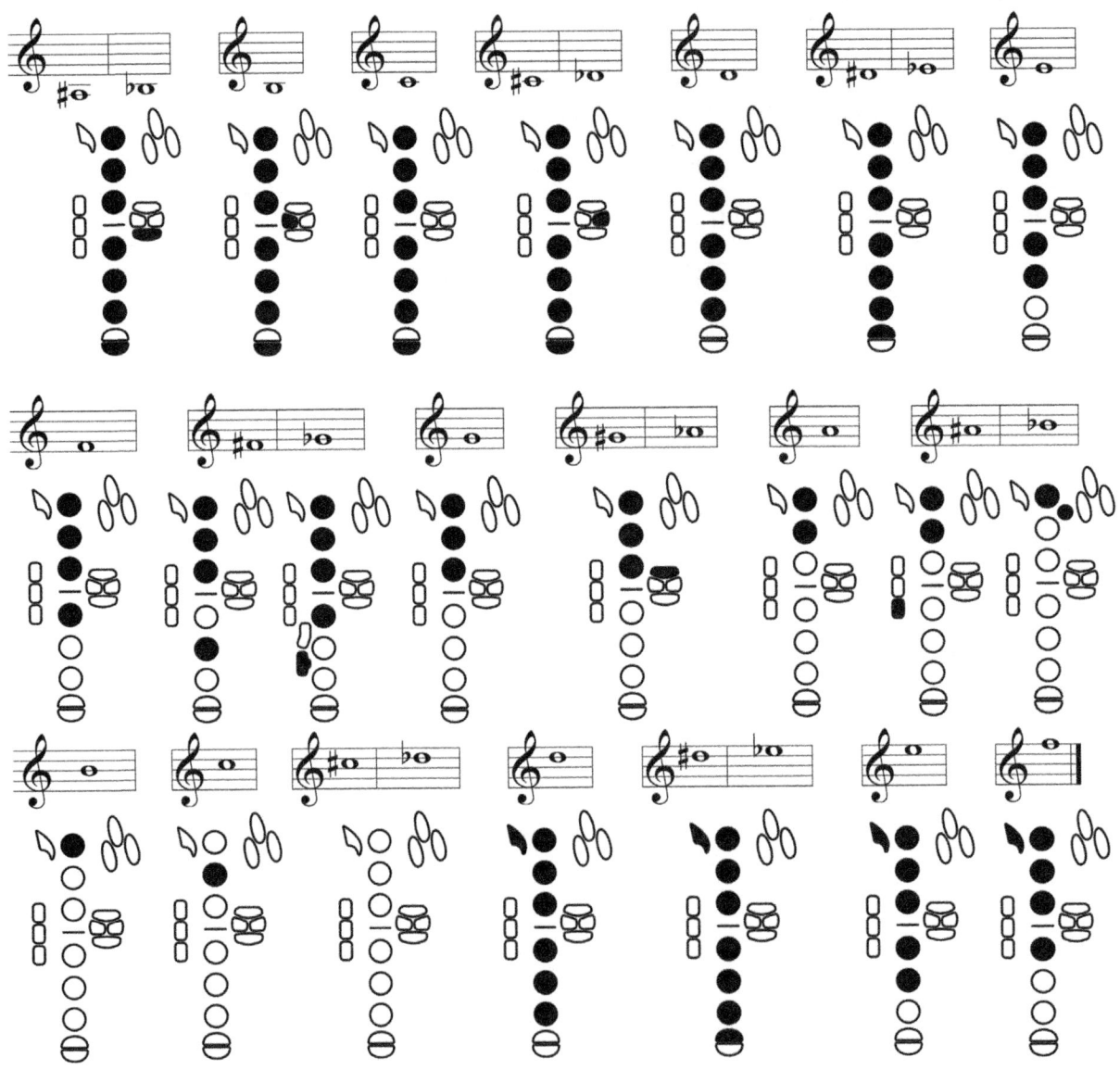

FIGURE 4.22A Saxophone Fingering Chart page 1

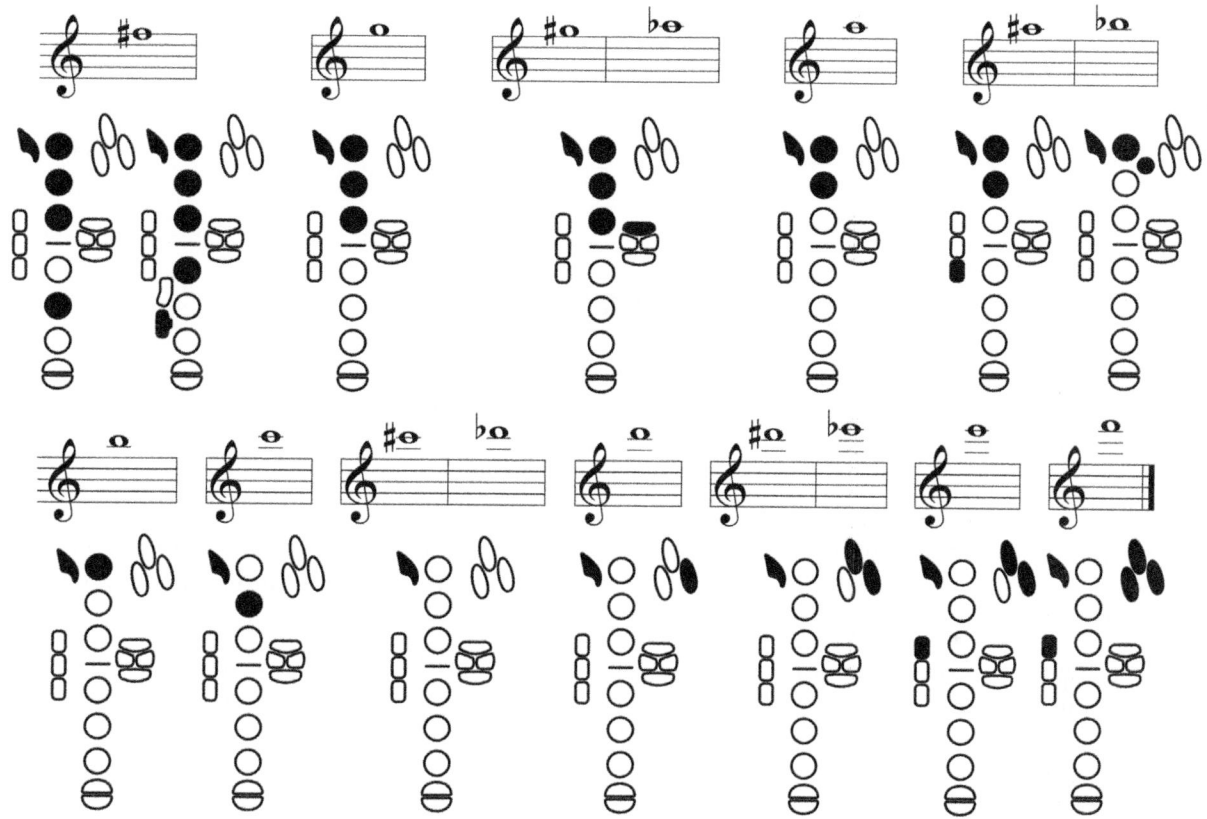

FIGURE 4.22B Saxophone Fingering Chart page 2

CHAPTER 5

Oboe

POTENTIAL FOR SUCCESS IN OBOE STUDY

The chapters for oboe and bassoon, unlike those for flute, clarinet, and saxophone, begin with "Potential for Success" because of inherent differences between the double reed instruments and the standard beginning woodwind instruments. The differences follow.

1. The double reed instruments typically are not considered beginning instruments, though there are exceptions to this common practice. Often, teachers create oboe players out of students who first played another instrument. This switch normally occurs in the second or third year of instrumental study.

2. Usually, school-based oboe students use instruments provided by the school system. There are only so many of these available. They must be distributed intelligently in order to keep to a minimum the number of oboe players who do not make consistent progress. The teacher must be selective in recruiting double reed students.

3. The standard band instrumentation calls for many fewer double reed players than clarinet and flute players. Two oboes and two bassoons will suffice in a band or orchestra. As many as four of each is acceptable. That so few are called for raises the stakes in recruiting double reed students.

4. Oboe players must function effectively in a musical world in which there is one player on a part and where composers of the more advanced band and orchestral literatures assign exposed parts to the oboe.

Clearly, it is important to consider a student's potential for success on oboe *before* approaching him or her about playing the instrument. Recruit bright, motivated students to play oboe. Recruit students who have the potential to function effectively as the only player on the part. Some students thrive on this independence; others do not! Recruit students (and their parents!) who are likely to be receptive to private lessons.

The focus on potential success is not motivated by the fact that the oboe is inherently more difficult to play than the other woodwinds, and therefore requires smarter, more "into it" students. This is a common misconception, though smart and into it are always good. Actually, the embouchure of the oboe is less complicated than that of the flute or clarinet. Except for the fact that traditional beginning band method books force compromises on how the oboe is approached in the first year, early fingering challenges need not be more complex than those of the flute, clarinet, and saxophone.

So why the misconception that the oboe is so difficult to play? In fact, many students struggle mightily with the oboe not because of the challenges the instrument itself presents, but because of poor quality and hard-to-make-work reeds. If the reed is appropriate for the student, the oboe is not more difficult to play than the flute and clarinet.

Recruiting is a full-time, continuous activity. It does not stop when students select or have been selected to play the oboe. Pay attention to double reed players. Be their advocate. Find a private teacher who is willing and able to make and adjust reeds. Absent a private teacher, find a source for good reeds. Realize the importance of a properly soaked reed. Know what an appropriate-sized reed opening looks like. Learn how to crow a reed, what to listen for in a crow, and what this tells you about what to expect in your student's performance. Learn how to detect a leak in a reed. Make sure the instruments you provide are in good playing shape.

Students who are successful flute, clarinet, or saxophone beginners, if they are willing to switch instruments, can become good oboe players. The fingerings for oboe are quite similar to those for flute and saxophone. One difference students will notice is that the keys of the oboe are spread farther apart than on the single reed instruments and flute.

To summarize, students who are most likely to succeed on the oboe are a) bright, b) motivated, c) capable of being musically independent, and d) willing to take private lessons. But, as a teacher, be careful. If you hold out for this package of traits in one person (the perfect prospect!), you may have no oboe players. So be appropriately flexible in your thinking.

OBOE TONE AND EARLY STAGE EMBOUCHURE

The oboe embouchure is not complicated. It is a double lip embouchure; that is, some lip covers lower and upper teeth. Like the saxophone embouchure, the mouth and lips are rounded, as if saying "OO" or "OH," with lip pressures evenly distributed around the reed. Other important considerations are amount of reed in the mouth, amount of lip over teeth, and direction of air stream.

Small Piece

The small piece of the oboe is the reed alone. No assembly required. The reed should be wet up to the string. Soak for about 3 minutes. In instrument assembly, soak the reed first. This is the only woodwind small piece that does not facilitate embouchure development, other than to allow first blowing experiences without involving instrument hold.

Teaching Embouchure

In the school setting, the most efficient way to introduce the oboe to one or two beginners is to separate them from the large group of beginning instrumentalists. Perhaps several individual meetings can be arranged during or outside the school day in order that students get a good start on the instrument before being included in the large group setting.

Sequence of Instruction for Making First Sounds (Reed Alone)

1. Teacher to student: "Open your mouth. Stick out your tongue. Catch the reed with your tongue. Draw the reed onto your lower lip with the halfway point of the cane portion contacting the lip."

2. With reed resting on the lower lip, teacher to student: "Watch my lips as I say 'OH.' Now you make an 'OH' shape around the reed allowing your lips to close around it."

3. The reed should be held at a 35° angle to the face (with head held erect).

4. Teacher to student: "Blow fast air straight ahead. Keep the round feeling of 'OH' as you blow."

Assuming the reed is appropriate, embouchure pressures neither too firm nor too loose, the air speed fast enough, and the right amount of reed in the mouth (half of the cane part of the reed remains outside of the mouth—between the lips and the top of the string), a C should result. Other concerns include the amount of lip over the teeth (the teacher should be able to see some lip outside of the mouth) and the nature of the jaw. As with all wind instruments, the jaw ultimately should be down. It is a component of the even distribution of lip pressures around the reed and a presumed product of the 'OH' shape of the lips and jaw.

OBOE ASSEMBLY, DISASSEMBLY, AND BASIC CARE

Assembly Sequence

1. Lay the closed case on a flat surface (the student's lap; the floor if the lap is too small). Check that the case is situated right side up.

2. Open case. Remove water container if stored in the case. Remove the reed from its case. Place the water container on the floor behind a front leg of the chair, safely out of the line of traffic and your own feet. Soak the reed (not including the string) for about 3 minutes.

    To save time, soak the reed first while the rest of the instrument is being assembled. A plastic film case or prescription pill bottle works well as a water-tight container. Water should be changed on a sensible schedule.

    During soaking, the reed forms into its playing shape after having lost some of that shape by drying. Soaking will cause the tip opening to get larger. If a reed is left in water for a prolonged period, the tip opening will become very large, perhaps to the point of making the reed temporarily unplayable. If this happens, coax the wet tip opening shut by closing it between the thumb and index finger.

    If the reed has a tip opening that tends to close somewhat during playing, soak the reed for a longer period of time. The longer the soaking, the more open the tip.

3. Remove the bell and lower joint from the case. The lower joint has a cluster of two, three, or four keys that stick out. This cluster of keys should be facing up. Place the side of the lower joint that has no keys in the palm of the left hand, with palm facing you. Grasp the joint near the *up* end by wrapping thumb and fingers around in a manner that closes several keys. Grasp the bell in the right hand. If the bell has a key, close it with the thumb. This is important because it raises a bridge key. Join the bell and the lower joint by making small back and forth motions. During this time, look at the bridge keys. The goal is to align them.

4. Remove the upper joint from the case. Situate the tenon cork end facing down. Place the one-keyed side of the upper joint in the palm of the left hand. Wrap the thumb and fingers 2, 3, and pinky around the joint in a manner that closes several keys. Keep the index finger raised in order to avoid applying pressure to the side octave key, which sticks out and will bend easily. With the right hand, grasp the already assembled part between the lower joint and bell. Face the keys of both joints toward you, then turn them slightly away from you so that you can see the near side, not both sides, of the bridge key mechanism. Insert upper joint into lower joint. Use small back and forth turns to assemble. Watching the near side bridge key mechanism, align the bridge keys on the side in view.

5. Remove the reed from the water container. Hold it at the top end of the cork between the thumb and the first two fingers. Carefully shake or sip the excess water off and out of it. With the oboe placed vertically on a thigh or between the legs on the chair and while grasping the oboe near the top, slide the cork end of the reed into the opening on the top of the instrument until it stops. There is a ledge that will stop it. The reed should be turned so that it aligns with the thumb rest or octave key. If the reed does not slide smoothly and easily into the opening, apply cork grease.

Disassembly and Swabbing

In disassembly, take care of the reed first. Get it off the instrument and safely into its case. Take the instrument apart in reverse order of assembly.

1. Grasp the reed firmly at the top of the cork. Turn and pull it out. Remove saliva by sipping at the tip end and blowing through the cork end. Place in a reed case. Three-reed cases are inexpensive. Unlike the clear plastic cylinder-type containers, a three-reed case allows air in so that reeds will dry during storage, and the open nature of the case does not promote damage to the reed tip.

    If the cylinder-type container is the only choice, the teacher should make one or two air holes in it to allow the reed to dry during storage. Otherwise, mildew will develop. Additionally, the student should be made aware of how easy it is to damage the tip of the reed when placing it in this type of container. As the tip of the reed is brought to the mouth of the container, anchor a finger or fingers on the container to steady the hand and thus guide the tip through the opening in a controlled manner.

2. If using a pull-through swab, pull it through the assembled instrument from bell to upper joint. Wipe tenon receivers dry as you disassemble each joint.

3. Grasp the upper joint and lower joint/bell as described in Step 4 under "Assembly Sequence." While looking at the bridge keys closest to your body, make small back and forth turns to separate upper and lower joints.

4. If using a swab not intended to be pulled through the upper joint, insert the weight at the tenon cork end. Pull it until it gets snug, then pull it out from the tenon joint end. Return the upper joint to the case.

5. Swab the lower joint and bell while they are assembled. Insert the weight into the bell and pull the swab through.

6. Grasp the lower joint and bell as described in Step 3 under "Assembly Sequence." While looking at the bridge keys, make small back and forth turns to separate lower joint and bell. Return them to the case.

7. Spread the swab out over the instrument inside the case. Balling it up and storing it in a case compartment does not allow it to dry.

Care

"Traveling (walking) with" instrument, laying the instrument down, handling it while in its case, and the effects of temperature are care issues of practical concern. They are covered here. Additional information on instrument care is provided in Chapter 7 (see "Foundations of Asssembly and Disassembly" on page 236 and "Foundations of Instrument Care" on page 237).

1. "Traveling with" (walking with) the instrument. Oboe reeds stick out. Anything that sticks out is susceptible to damage. When walking with the instrument, the reed should not be in the instrument. It should be in a case or in the player's mouth.

2. Laying the instrument down. Take the reed out and place it on the music stand, preferably in a reed case. Separate upper and lower joint and lay these two pieces with keys up on a chair. Do not stand the instrument vertically on its bell.

3. Instrument in case. Treat the instrument gently even when it is in its case. A dropped case with instrument inside can damage the instrument.

4. Extreme temperatures and cracking. In extremes of temperature, wood will crack. Do not place or store woodwind instruments in prolonged hot or cold (on a heater or in a car in freezing weather). If an oboe gets extremely cold, warm it up gradually by cradling it in hands and against the body. Don't be too quick to blow hot air (98.6°) into the bore.

OBOE POSTURE, HANDS, AND HOLDING

Right Hand

1. The right thumbprint contacts the body of the instrument under the thumb rest. The side of the thumb contacts the thumb rest halfway between the first knuckle and the tip.

2. The right thumb and index finger form an imperfect backward C shape. As shown in Figure 5.1, the fingers approach the instrument at a near 45° downward angle. More than likely, this will be the natural angle formed by simply bringing the hand/arm to the instrument. The side of the index finger should not contact the instrument.

Left Hand

3. The left thumb should contact the wood of the instrument just under the octave key. For second octave notes, it will depress the octave key. The left thumb should not dangle. It should be angled at 2 o'clock (neither horizontal nor vertical to the oboe).

4. As shown in Figure 5.1, the fingers approach the instrument at a near 45° downward angle. This angle allows the left index finger to lean into the second (or side) octave key when necessary.

Both Hands

1. Fingers should be slightly curved (including finger 3 and the adjacent pinky) and relaxed, not straight and tense.
2. Fingerprints contact the center of the keys.
3. All fingers should be situated above the instrument.

What to Look for in Hand Position

1. Is the head erect? The air stream should be directed forward, not downward.
2. Is the instrument held at a 35° angle?
3. Is the thumb positioned properly under the thumb rest?
4. Do the right thumb and index finger form an imperfect backward C with no side key contact by the index finger?
5. Are the fingers angled downward (approximately 45°)?
6. Are the fingers curved?

OBOE TONE DEVELOPMENT

4 Beats On/4 Beats Off

FIGURE 5.1 Oboe Hand Position
(Produced by Paige Jarreau at Paige's Photos)

In order to provide students with many early opportunities to form a suitable embouchure, the notes in Figure 5.2 played on the assembled instrument work well. Ideally, this is done as a rote exercise. The teacher, on her oboe, plays what is notated. During the rests the students, by listening and watching, imitate. The students have no music. The fingerings are simple, and the 4 beats on/4 beats off pattern provides equal play and rest. Initially, the tongue need not be used to start the tone; simply start the air as if saying "HO."

In measure 15 of Figure 5.2, notice the C. C is a note that provides the teacher with important information about the amount of reed in the mouth. If the C is strident in tone and sharp in pitch, there is likely too much reed in the mouth. Have the student take in less reed and play always with this lesser amount of reed in mouth.

First note experiences can be expanded to include the slurred half notes and quarter notes, shown in Figure 5.3. This is best done as a rote exercise. Without losing a beat, the student imitates the teacher's model. Without losing a beat, the teacher re-enters with the next measure. In order to keep the focus on embouchure and air stream, the tongue need not be used.

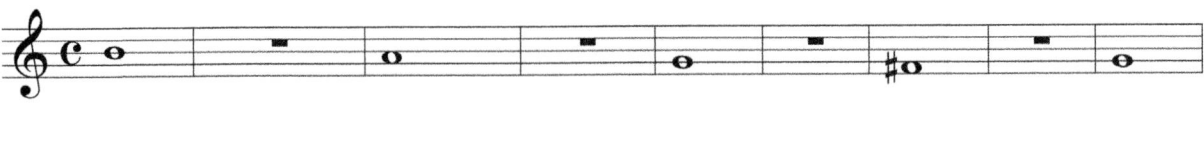

FIGURE 5.2 First Notes: Call and Response

FIGURE 5.3 First Notes: Disguised Long Tones

This can be done with the teacher singing while fingering a phantom oboe. But there is no better teaching scenario than the teacher demonstrating proper posture and instrument hold and characteristic breathing, embouchure, and tone while the student watches and listens.

Figure 5.4 presents an extended experience in rote practice of posture, breath, embouchure, tone, and first fingerings. The teacher plays what is notated. Students respond with same during the two-measure rests. As an early experience in oboe playing, slur all. Allow the focus to be on embouchure strengthening and development, not tonguing.

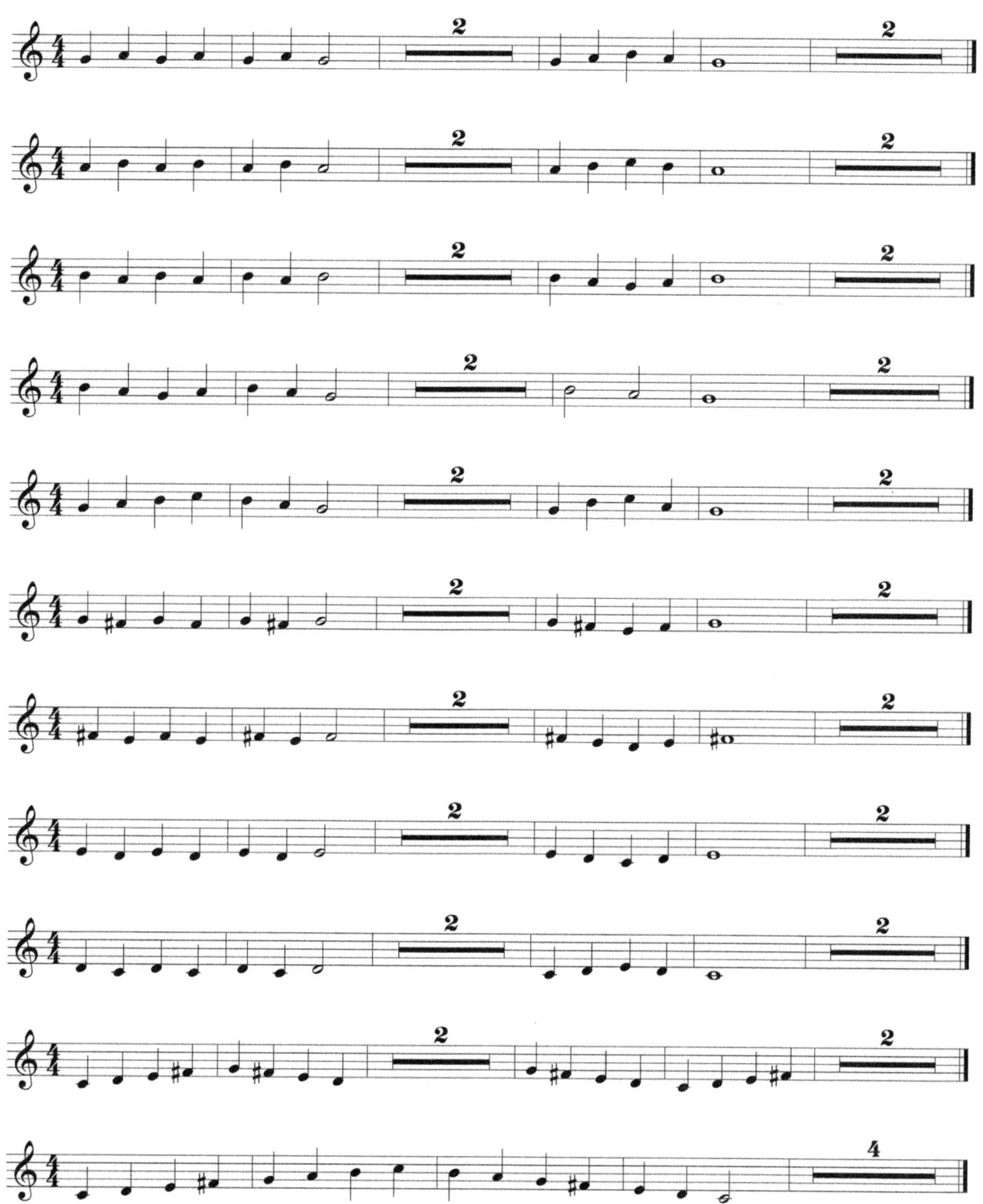

FIGURE 5.4 Rote Study for Oboe

Characteristics of Oboe Embouchure

Notice the following characteristics in Figures 5.5 and 5.6.

1. Roughly half of the cane portion of the reed is in the mouth. The natural tendency is to put too much reed in the mouth.

2. The mouth and lips are rounded as if saying an exaggerated and sustained "OH." When blowing, lip pressures are evenly distributed around the reed.

3. An exaggerated "OH" places lip over both teeth. Notice in Figures 5.5 and 5.6 that some lip is visible outside the embouchure. Lip contact with the reed does not extend to the change of color between lip and skin.

4. An exaggerated "OH" situates the jaw downward.

5. The head is held erect, allowing a fast air stream to point *straight ahead* against the reed, not *into* the opening of the reed.

6. The instrument is held at a 35° angle to the player's body.

FIGURE 5.5 Front View of Embouchure
(Produced by Paige Jarreau at Paige's Photos)

FIGURE 5.6 Side View of Embouchure
(Produced by Paige Jarreau at Paige's Photos)

Many oboe beginners are converts from other woodwind instruments. As a teacher, it is wise to think in terms of embouchure tendencies the novice oboist may have from having played another instrument. Urge former clarinet players to play with a more relaxed grip on the oboe reed. This tendency to be too firm on the oboe is less an issue for the converted saxophone player whose embouchure should have been oboe-like on the sax.

Breathing

When the student's tone has developed to the point of playing the above first notes and first note sequences with a tone that is *forte* and unwavering, he is ready to begin the habit of taking a preparatory breath on beat 4. Breathing should be in tempo, shoulder-less, and as if saying a backwards "HO." "HO" forces the breathing action to take place abdominally rather than in the chest. To take a breath on the oboe, the mouth opens with the reed resting on the lower lip. Maintain this lower lip contact point while inhaling.

What to Look for in Oboe Embouchure

1. Amount of reed in the mouth. Is there some distance between the lips and the winding on the reed? The tendency is to put too much reed in the mouth.
2. Mouth shape. Are the lips rounded in the shape of "OH"? Is the jaw down?
3. Lip over teeth. Does a little lip show outside the embouchure?
4. Head. Is the head erect? Is the air stream directed straight ahead?
5. Angle. Is the instrument held at a 35° angle to the player's body?

What to Listen for in Oboe Embouchure

1. Volume. Is the student blowing a fast air stream?
2. Pitch. Is third line B (first finger only) relatively in tune? Check with tuner or piano.
3. Pitch. Third space C is strident and sharp. There is likely too much reed in the mouth.
4. Pitch. Pitch is flat, shaky. There may not be enough reed in the mouth.
5. Pitch. Pitch is flat, especially in the top end of the second octave. The reed is likely too soft (too much cane has been removed from the heart). The reed does not provide enough resistance for the pitch to stay up.
6. Volume. The volume is loud, harsh, uncontrolled. The reed tip opening may be too open, forcing the student to blow extremely hard to get the reed to vibrate.
7. Volume. Volume is small, soft, sharp. The reed tip may be too closed. Student cannot push enough air through the small opening to produce a big tone. Or the lips may be exerting too much pressure on the reed thus closing the tip.

Embouchure Teaching Strategies

To Achieve Lip Pucker, Round Feel, and Pressures Evenly Distributed

- Whistle, then drop the jaw while maintaining the whistle formation.
- Say an exaggerated "OH" and hold this shape.
- As if stifling a yawn.
- Have the student, while sustaining a pitch, try to push the upper lip down toward the reed. This should automatically lower the jaw.

To Promote Less Reed in the Mouth

- "Put only enough reed in the mouth that you are able to tongue it."
- Play middle of the staff B to C. If it is a "wide" half step, put less reed in the mouth. Compare wide half step to in-tune half step.

Intentional Deviations from Normal Embouchure

In oboe performance, intonation deficiencies often must be corrected by lipping, that is, deviating from the normal embouchure. A note that is sharp in pitch can be brought down by one or some combination of the following: Relax the grip of the lips, lower the jaw, voice in the direction of "OH" or "AH," or bow the head (as a last resort). These actions constitute lipping down. A note that is flat in pitch can be raised by one or some combination of the following: Firming the grip of the lips around the reed while keeping the jaw down or voicing in the direction of "EE." This is called lipping up.

In the beginning stage of study, the pitch of novice woodwind players tends to sag (go flat) at the ends of last notes of phrases, last notes of pieces, and notes before rests. This sagging is particularly noticeable on the oboe and bassoon. Many novice double reed players hear this sagging effect and find it offensive (as they should!). Many soon discover that they can avoid the sagging pitch by stopping the note with the tongue—an undesirable circumstance at the end of a phrase or melody. Pitch sag happens because the air stream slows *without* an accompanying firming of the embouchure. The pitch lowers with a slower air stream; it raises with a firmer lip grip around the reed. The goal is to find the ideal combination of slower air and increased lip grip to prevent end-of-phrase pitch sag.

On the double reed instruments, the pitch may be flat in *piano* passages or go flat as one plays a *decrescendo* unless the slower air stream is compensated for by firmer lip pressure evenly distributed around the reed. Likewise, in order to allow more air into the tip opening for *forte* or *crescendo*, the embouchure pressures must be relaxed at the same time that air speed is increased.

Finally, playing in the extreme low or high register of the oboe necessitates deviation from normal embouchure. Playing on anything but a perfect reed, for the low register (roughly low B-flat through E-flat) the embouchure must be open and less firm than in the mid- and upper registers. For the register beginning at high E (above the staff) and above, a more than normal amount of reed should be placed in the mouth (toward the string), and the lips should be firmer than in lower registers. The jaw should stay down while the lips firm.

Vibrato

Vibrato is applied as a standard technique to both enhance and project tone on the flute, oboe, bassoon, and saxophone. A so-called diaphragmatic vibrato is commonly used on oboe. It is more probable that the abdominal muscles, not the diaphragm, are the active agents in this type of vibrato. Say an accented "Hah!"

When for Vibrato?

Vibrato can be introduced late in the middle school years, though there should be no hurry to do so. Without question, vibrato should not be introduced before a student has had ample time to develop a well-supported and stable straight tone. One approach is to leave vibrato instruction to the private teacher. The students who study privately will tend to be ahead of the others in terms of tonal development, finger technique, and tongue technique. These students will likely occupy the top chairs. When vibrato is most advantageous—that is, during solo work—these students will be in a position to use it.

Teaching Vibrato

1. Say "Hah!" Repeat slowly to experience the initial "source" and feel of a vibrato. Then remove the vocalization, that is, "Hah" expels air, not vocal tone. Repeat.

2. Repeat "Hah" without vocalization but with a "cooling soup" embouchure. Hold your hand in front of your mouth, take a big breath, and slowly pulse the air with repeated "Hah"s so that you feel it on your hand.

3. Do the same thing into the oboe on an easy to produce note (e.g., B). Start with slow, large, rhythmic pulsations as represented in Figure 2.15 (see page 36). As you learn to control the evenness of the pulsations, increase speed of pulsation as shown.

4. Gradually across practice sessions and multiple lessons, increase the speed of the pulses. Resist the urge to pulsate fast too soon. Concentrate on a controlled, rhythmic pulsing. Avoid the fast shake of a bleating goat.

5. Apply the above pulse rhythms to a simple tune of whole, half, and quarter notes done at a slow pace; for example, "Hot Cross Buns." Continue making the pulses rhythmic, even mechanical sounding.

6. Once this becomes a more natural act, refine by rounding the "edges" of the pulses. Work for a more fluid, less abrupt, vibrato. This often happens as a result of a practice technique involving 4, 5, 6, and 7 pulses per beat at quarter note equals 60.

Provide the opportunity for young oboists to hear good vibrato through live and recorded performances. For a good demonstration of a process involved in teaching vibrato, see the James Galway master class on vibrato at www.youtube.com/watch?v=u0yCw9xm0E4.

OBOE TONGUING

Pre-tonguing Activity, Contact Point, and Vowel Shape

During initial embouchure development, "HOH" is used to articulate. A ballpark embouchure combined with a fast air stream should result in a sustained, *forte*, unwavering tone that is relatively in tune (check third line B with a sound source).

The basic articulation involves touching the tip of the tongue to the tip of the bottom blade of the reed, as if saying "DOH" or "TOH." The 35° angle of the instrument to the body positions the reed such that the tip of the tongue, with a small upward movement, makes contact with the tip of the reed.

Teaching Tonguing

To introduce, develop, and assess tonguing on the oboe, the approaches presented in the flute, clarinet, and saxophone chapters are fully applicable, of course with appropriate adaptations to oboe. Please see the "Tonguing" section of any of those chapters.

THE OBOE MECHANISM

Brief History

From the 15th and 16th century shawm came the hautboy (oot-bwa), the immediate predecessor of the oboe. The hautboy, translated *high wood*, was a key-less or nearly key-less instrument used from the first half of the 17th century until the early 19th century when it was replaced by the *keyed* oboe. Between 1810 and 1900, the oboe was transformed into the present-day instrument. Interestingly, the late 1800s introduction of vibrato as a performance technique is linked to the development of the oboe. Vibrato was a means by which oboists could compete in terms of resonance and carrying power with the other instruments of the large orchestra.

To view the above dates in perspective relative to two well-known composers, Bach (1685–1750) wrote prominent obbligato solos for the hautboy in many of his cantatas. These are now of course played on the oboe. Mozart composed the innovative Oboe Quartet in F for oboe and strings in 1781. A large hautboy section was a principal element of the military band until replaced by clarinets circa 1750. Imagine the pre-1750 sound of the military band!

Oft-recorded Swiss soloist Heinz Holliger brought positive attention to the oboe in the mid-20th century. Frenchman Marcel Tabuteau (1887–1966), long-time member of the Philadelphia Orchestra, is known as the father of the American school of oboe playing. His approach changed the concept of tone from the brighter, lighter French sound to a darker, richer American sound. He accomplished this by lengthening the scrape on the reed (from short scrape to long scrape). His ideas with regard to oboe performance and pedagogy are much respected by all accomplished and informed woodwind players.

Major solo works have been composed by Saint Saëns, Jacob, Vaughan Williams, Richard Strauss, Hindemith, Poulenc, and Britten. Noted oboe performers include John Mack, Harold Gomberg, Robert Bloom, John de Lancie, Alex Klein, Joseph Robinson, and Richard Woodhams.

Family and Transposition

Oboe

- A non-transposing instrument.

English Horn

- Sounds down a perfect 5th. If the part calls for an English horn and you do not have the instrument, important passages can be covered on the oboe, range permitting, by reading the English horn part down a perfect 5th.
- Essentially a big oboe—nearly the same fingerings and range as the oboe.
- Has no low B-flat.
- Bell shaped as a bulb.
- From second octave G to the top of the range, pitch is not as stable and the instrument does not respond as well as oboe.
- Can be played with or without a neck strap.
- Has a bocal. Bocals are usually numbered as 1, 2, or 3—number 1, the shortest; number 3, the longest. A number 2 bocal is preferred. Most instruments come with two bocals of different length.

Oboe d'Amore in A

- Translated—*oboe of love*.
- Sounds down a minor 3rd (like the clarinet in A).
- Dark, sweet tone.
- Bulbous shape of bell.
- Favored instrument during the Baroque period.

Bass Oboe

- A C instrument that sounds down one octave.
- Also called baritone oboe.

Instrument Manufacturing

The current fingering system of the oboe is based on the acoustic principles of Theobald Boehm. This fingering system was developed in France during the mid to late 19th century and is called the conservatory system. Full conservatory system means that the instrument comes with a low B-flat key, fork F resonance keys, a left F key, and several trill keys, some or all of which do not come with the simplified conservatory system. The full conservatory system is more expensive and appropriate for advanced level players.

152 TEACHING THE INSTRUMENTS

Oboes have a conical bore. They are made of grenadilla wood (a very hard wood) or a synthetic material (various plastics). Synthetic instruments are intended for student use. These can be very acceptable and certainly durable instruments.

Be aware of distinctions between professional and student line models. Most manufacturers produce both; in other words, one name (e.g., Fox) comprises several different models of oboe (student line through professional), and in the case of Fox produces both oboes and English horns. Better quality instruments have an *even scale*, meaning the player will have to do less rather than more lipping to play in tune. Better quality instruments have an even tone quality, meaning that tone is uniform across registers and from note to note. The most well-known professional model oboe is made by Loree. New instrument costs range from approximately $800 for a student line oboe to $5000 or more for a professional model oboe. The following lists of oboe manufacturers are not exhaustive.

- Professional model instruments are made by manufacturers Loree, Laubin, Fox, Prestini, Buffet, Selmer, Yamaha, and others.
- Student model instruments are made by manufacturers Buffet, Jupiter, Olds, Larilee, Fox, Selmer, Yamaha, and others.

Range and Its Divisions

Figure 5.7 provides the range of the full conservatory system oboe and its three octave divisions.

First Octave   Second Octave   Third Octave

FIGURE 5.7 Oboe Range and Octaves

Like the flute, saxophone, and bassoon, the lowest notes of the oboe require extra effort to produce. The embouchure must be more open (or less firm) than in mid- and upper registers. In addition, the nature of the reed scrape and size of the tip opening affect low register response. It is a challenge for even accomplished oboists to play at *piano* dynamic levels and articulate with finesse in the low register of the instrument.

Fingering Issues

Half-Hole and Octave Key Notes

In Figure 5.8 Letter A, the notes and their enharmonic equivalents require use of the half-hole. The half-hole acts like an octave key; it raises the pitch one octave. The notes in Letter A sound in the correct octave when the first finger slides down from its normal position, keeping the key depressed but exposing or opening the hole in the middle of the key. This is called the half-hole technique. When the half-hole is used, the top thumb remains on the wood of the instrument beneath the back octave key.

In Figure 5.8 Letter B, the notes require the use of the back octave key, and in Letter C the side octave key. The back octave key may or may not be depressed during side octave key notes.

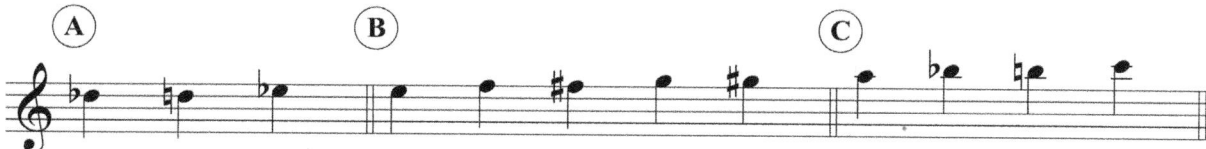

FIGURE 5.8 Half-Hole and Octave Key Notes

Three Fingerings for F: Primary, Fork, and Left

It is important that both teacher and student understand when to use which of three fingerings for F, because wrong choices in fingering cause problems in intonation and finger technique. The following information pertains to first space (no octave key) and top line F (with octave key), not high F.

Figure 5.9 presents the fingerings for primary F (the main F fingering), fork F, and left F. Determine which to use according to the F rule:

The F Rule: Use fork F or left F when F is preceded or followed by D-flat, D, E-flat, or low C.

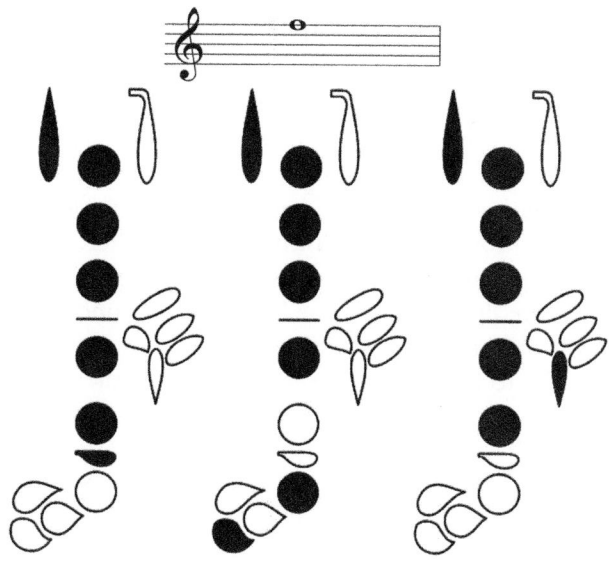

Primary F should be used in every case except when the F Rule applies. Primary F is an uncomplicated fingering, its tone quality is consistent with most other notes on the instrument, and its pitch is stable and without sharp or flat tendencies.

In Figure 5.10, notice the application of the F Rule in the note groupings. The X reminds students to use fork F. Fork F allows note pairs to be negotiated without having to slide fingers from one key to another. However, the pitch of fork F is unstable and the tone quality inferior to the overall tone quality of the instrument. Accomplished oboe players, where possible, avoid fork F by using left F (see Figure 5.11). The pitch of left F is stable and the tone quality consistent with the rest of the instrument. To remind students to use left F, an L is marked above the note.

FIGURE 5.9
Regular F, Fork F, and Left F Fingerings

FIGURE 5.10 Fork F in Context

FIGURE 5.11 Left F in Context

FIGURE 5.12 F Fingerings in Context

Figure 5.12 shows various F fingerings in real music contexts. Remember that in terms of finger technique, fork F and left F accomplish the same thing—the avoidance of finger sliding. In terms of pitch and tone, left F is always a better choice. In Example A, either fork F or left F works because a D precedes an F (see the F Rule above). Left F, however, is the best option for three reasons—pitch, tone, and finger technique. Moving from left F to E is very easy; if fork F were used, it is awkward. In Example B, different F fingerings are used in close proximity. Use of primary F on beat 3 is consistent with the idea of using it always when it *can* be used. In Example C, left F is the best option because F is sustained. The use of fork F would create a sustained tone/intonation problem.

Ideally, novice oboe students would first learn the primary F fingering because it is an easy fingering (derived from E, a half step below) of characteristic tone and secure pitch. Primary F is used in the C and F major scales because in these scales Fs are not preceded or followed by D, E-flat, D-flat, or low C. Ideally, students would have many experiences with primary F before being introduced to the more awkward fork F. One must use fork F (or left F) in the B-flat and E-flat major scales.

In beginning band method books, however, fork F is the first F to be introduced. Most beginning books are dominated by the key of B-flat concert, because it is a convenient key for clarinets, trumpets, and trombones. Not so for oboes and bassoons players, who must play in a key that is not "friendly." In order to keep the oboes in unison with the flutes and an octave away from the clarinet and trumpet,

FIGURE 5.13 Oboe in Beginning Band Method Books

fork F is a too early necessity. Figure 5.13 illustrates how well the first fingerings for clarinet lie. Each successive note involves lifting one finger. In contrast, the flute player crosses the break (C to D) and deals with the first finger-up and -down challenge. Even more challenging, the oboe player crosses the break (C to D), uses the half-hole technique, and negotiates an initially awkward E-flat to fork F.

Because of this early focus on fork F, students become accustomed to it to the point of using it disadvantageously later on. It is not uncommon to find middle school and high school oboe players using fork F on the F major scale (where it is not necessary) or during sustained Fs in their band music. This should be corrected.

Left E-flat

It is important that both teacher and student understand when to use which of two fingerings for E-flat, because wrong choices in fingering cause problems in finger technique. The following information pertains to first line and 4th space E-flat, not high E-flat.

Figure 5.14 presents the fingerings for primary E-flat (the main fingering) and left E-flat. Determine which to use according to the E-flat rule:

E-flat Rule: Use left E-flat when E-flat is preceded or followed by D-flat and low C.

Primary E-flat should be used in every case except when the E-flat Rule applies. There are no tone quality or pitch differences between primary E-flat and left E-flat. Left E-flat is advantageous as a cross-fingering—for example, the right pinky of D-flat "crossing to" the left pinky of left E-flat, as shown in Figure 5.15.

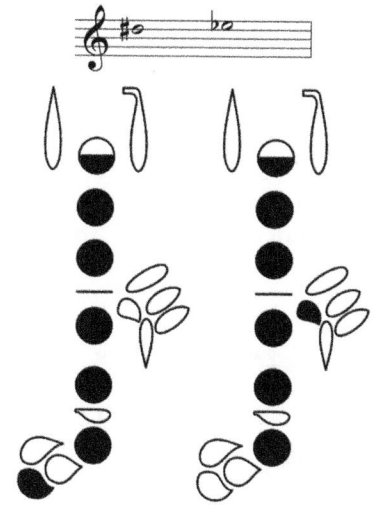

FIGURE 5.14
Right E-flat and Left E-flat Fingerings

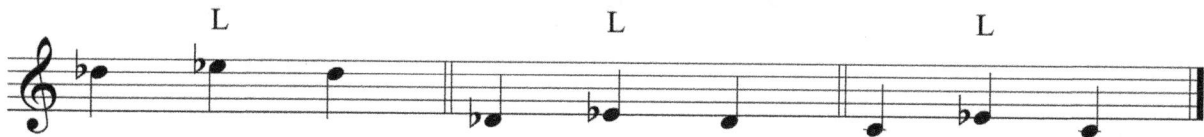

FIGURE 5.15 Left E-flat in Context

By using left E-flat as stated in the rule, one avoids having to slide a pinky finger from one key to another. Left E-flat is introduced with the key of A-flat major. In the scale in Figure 5.16, the D-flat preceding the E-flat forces one to use left E-flat. The F that follows can only be played with the fork fingering because the left pinky (needed for the better sounding and in tune left F) is occupied on the preceding E-flat.

FIGURE 5.16 The A-flat Major Scale

Articulated G-sharp/A-flat

When G-sharp is interspersed among notes involving the fingers of the right hand, the G-sharp key can remain depressed during the right-hand notes with no ill effects on pitch or tone. In Figure 5.17 notice how leaving the G-sharp key down throughout eliminates awkward finger movement.

FIGURE 5.17 Articulated G-sharp/A-flat

Some Trill Fingerings

Many trills on woodwind instruments are performed by using the primary fingerings of the notes involved. For some trills, however, primary fingerings don't work. Special trill keys and trill fingerings exist to make trills possible that otherwise would be awkward. The collection in Figure 5.18 is not exhaustive. Refer to the Internet for more comprehensive trill collections. Many of the low octave trill fingerings not included in Figure 5.18 are the same as their one-octave-higher counterparts, of course minus the half hole or octave key.

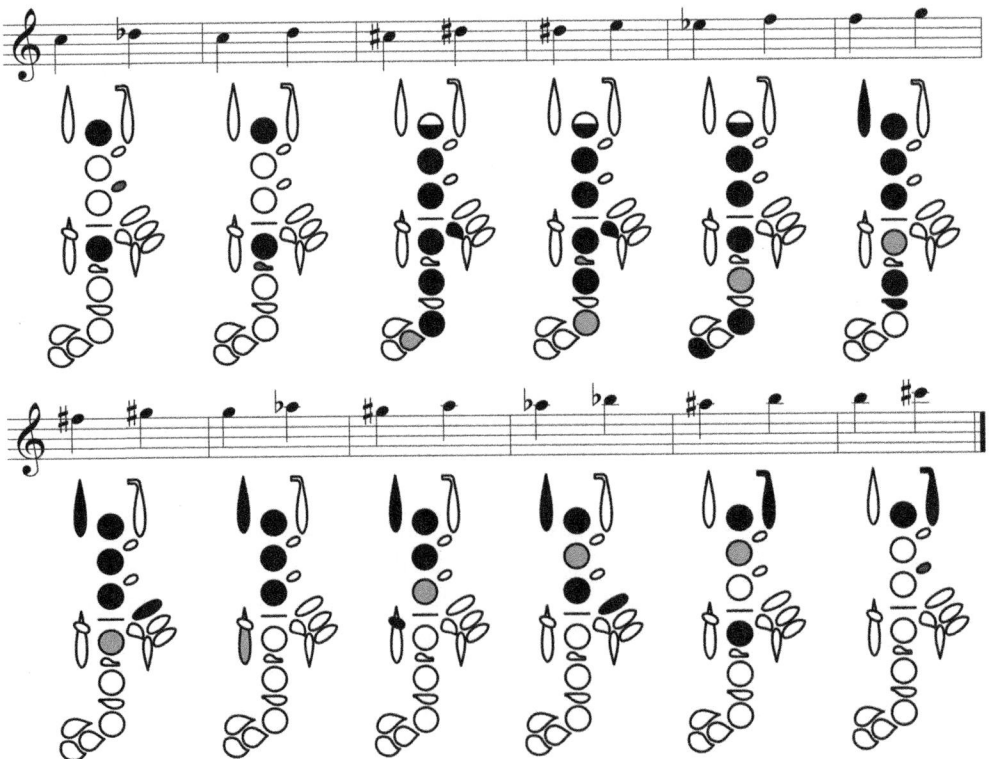

For A-sharp to B, slide 1st finger across to depress spatula key also.

FIGURE 5.18 Oboe Trill Fingerings

Tuning and Intonation

Tuning Notes

Figure 5.19 shows oboe tuning notes—the orchestra A, the traditional band B-flat and F. These should be given while the oboist views a tuner.

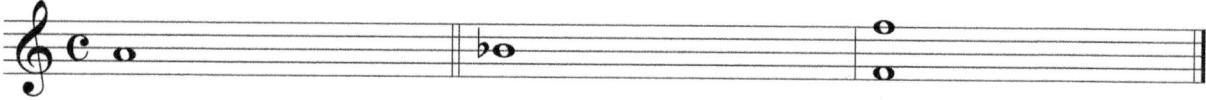

FIGURE 5.19 Oboe Tuning Notes

A discussion of the pitch tendencies of the oboe can be organized into five primary areas: a) reed condition, b) amount of reed in the mouth, c) embouchure flaws, d) register, and e) individual notes.

Reed Condition: The Crow

The overall pitch level of the oboe is determined by the reed. A reed is in tune when it crows a C. A reed crow is produced by intentionally putting too much reed in the mouth (lips touching the top of the string) and blowing an unfocused stream of air. A quasi embouchure is used, not the formal oboe embouchure—the lips simply seal around the string. By having no lip on cane, the reed vibrates as it naturally vibrates, unencumbered by lip pressure. This gives teacher and student a picture of the reed's baseline condition or quality, especially regarding pitch and response.

In an ideal crow, the reed responds readily with a C at a soft dynamic. As you increase the volume, the crow should add a C an octave higher. If one must blow very hard to make a crow, the sound on the instrument will be difficult to control and impossible to play at soft dynamics.

A crow with only a single pitch means that the reed is not vibrating enough or the tip is too closed. The sound on the instrument will be weak (lacking projection), and the low register will be difficult to produce. To remedy, more cane should be removed or the tip opened.

If the reed crows a C-sharp, it will play sharp on the instrument. If the reed crows under C—for example, B—it will play flat on the instrument. A capable oboe player with a good ear will be forced to manipulate the flawed reed with the lips in order to bend the pitch up or down to compensate. Lipping of any kind is tiring on the embouchure. In time, the oboe player who plays on reeds that are flat will lip up until it becomes the norm for the embouchure. This is called biting, and it has a deleterious effect on tone.

These reed deficiencies cannot be compensated for by pushing or pulling. Unlike the flute, clarinet, and saxophone, for which tuning includes changing the length of the instrument by pushing or pulling various joints, the oboe is designed to play best when the reed is pushed in all or nearly all the way. It should be pulled no more than 1/8 inch (3mm). Beyond this, the instrument will not respond optimally.

Oboists who make their own reeds use the crow frequently during the final stages of reed making. The crow provides information they need in order to know what to do next in the reed-making process. If the reed crows sharp to C, there is too much cane on it. Some cane must be scraped away with a knife. If the reed crows flat, too much cane has been taken out. Cane cannot be put back on, so the only alternative is to raise the pitch by shortening the reed. In this case, a small sliver of tip is cut from the reed.

The effective music teacher, despite a lack of reed-making skills, can help reduce or even prevent much of the frustration that is incorrectly assumed to be an unavoidable *right of passage* in oboe life. The teacher who crows a reed and understands the information provided by the crow knows what can be expected of the oboe player. If the reed crows octave Cs, the student can be expected to play reasonably in tune with good control of tone and response. The more the crow departs from C in either direction, the more difficult it will be for the student to play in tune. The only remedy to a reed with a flawed crow is to have it adjusted by a skilled reed maker, or change reeds.

Amount of Reed in the Mouth

Be aware of the tendency for novice and inexperienced students to put too much reed in the mouth. This will cause the pitch to be sharp, and especially strident on third space C. If a note or a passage is slightly sharp, sometimes it can be fixed by asking the student to put a bit less reed in the mouth.

Embouchure Flaws: The Pros and Cons

As with all wind instruments, lip/jaw pressures that are too tight will cause sharpness; too loose, flatness. However, these very *flaws* are used to remedy pitch problems. A sharp note can be lipped down by loosening or relaxing the lips. A flat note can be lipped up by firming the lips around the reed.

Pitch Tendencies: Register

The low register (from low D down) tends to be flat in pitch, like the flute. It is more of a problem in solo literature than in large ensemble music, because large ensemble composers tend not to write much for oboe below D.

Pitch Tendencies: Individual Notes

- Cs are sharp and strident if too much reed is in the mouth.
- Fork Fs are unstable in pitch and tone quality. Lipping is often necessary. Use of the E-flat key in this fingering is either/or. Try fork F with and without the E-flat key to determine best pitch and tone quality.
- E (especially fourth space E) is sharp. Lipping is necessary.
- F-sharp (especially top line F-sharp) is unstable. Some lipping is necessary.

In preparation for rehearsal, a thorough analysis of a musical score includes consideration of the pitch tendencies of the oboe. By knowing pitch tendencies, the effective music teacher is able to predict what might happen with regard to pitch before it happens in the lesson or rehearsal. One's job in rehearsal is to listen and discern whether student performance is consistent with the tendencies. If it is, the teacher must know what to do to solve the problem.

Tuning and Intonation Summary

- Is the reed in tune?
  - Reed should crow a Cs in octaves and respond at soft and loud dynamics

- Tuning notes (orchestra, band)
    - Play with best embouchure and at a *f* dynamic level
    - Reed can be pulled 1/8 inch (3mm); that's it!
- Pitch tendencies
    - Register (lowest B-flat to D = flat)
    - Reed (soft = flat; hard = sharp)
    - Bad notes (most notorious: fork F)
- Solutions
    - Reed condition
    - Less reed in mouth to lower pitch (is there a half step between B and C?)
    - Lipping.

Oboe Reeds

It is tempting for music teachers who are not woodwind majors to assume that "I can't possibly have much to offer my students about reeds. There is so much to know, including how to make and adjust them, I couldn't possibly learn all that."

It is not necessary to *learn all that* to be an effective teacher of woodwinds. It is, however, reasonable to expect the non-oboist music teacher to be familiar with and use basic information about reeds. Take for example the information included under the first four categories that follow (wetting, crowing, storing, and rotating). A teacher uses this information by teaching it to beginning oboe players or by observing the behaviors of experienced players, noting what they do and don't do, then leading them to do what is suggested. If you use this information in your teaching, you will be pleasantly surprised at "how much you have to offer your students about reeds."

In the university woodwind class, do what is necessary to acquire a good oboe reed for yourself. Study its feel and appearance. At the completion of the course, save the reed for future reference.

Wetting

Reeds must be wet in order to respond optimally. There are a number of soaking tips that if followed make oboe life easier:

1. Soak the reed for roughly 3 minutes in water, up to but not including the string. If the string gets wet, it may lose its tight wrap.
2. Warm water works faster than cold water.
3. Soaking in tap water rather than saliva will prolong the life of a reed.
4. During long periods of no play in rehearsal or performance, blowing warm air through the reed and instrument will keep the reed from drying out.

Use of a water-tight container (prescription pill container, small cylinder bottle) that can be stored in an oboe case cover is an optimal condition. Usually there is not enough room in the oboe case itself to include a water container. Minus a water container, get the reed wet with a "splash" of tap water and allow the water to remain on and inside the reed as you set it aside during instrument assembly. During this time the reed is "soaking."

Crowing

An oboe reed should crow octave Cs. The reed is soft when there is little or no high pitch in the crow. On the instrument, a soft reed will sound thin and reedy. The overall pitch level will be flat. The reed is too hard when there is little or no low pitch in the crow, and when the crow is difficult to produce without blowing very hard. On the instrument, a hard reed will sound rough or unrefined. The low register will be slow to respond. Soft playing will be difficult or impossible. Hardness can be corrected by scraping cane away with a knife. A more complete description of the reed crow can be found above in the section "Tuning and Intonation."

Storing

Place reeds carefully in cases that allow them to dry completely between playings. Reeds that do not dry will develop mildew. Cases designed to hold three reeds allow drying, and can be purchased for $7–$10. They are preferable to plastic cylinder-type containers that do not allow air in for drying. If plastic containers are used, make one or two holes in the sides to allow for drying. Otherwise, mildew will develop on the reed. Students should be aware that it is easy to ruin a reed by bumping its tip when placing it in a plastic tube. As the reed tip is brought to the mouth of the container, anchor a finger or fingers on the container in order to steady the hand. Then guide the tip through the opening in a controlled manner.

Rotating

Ideally the oboe player should have at least two reeds that work effectively and that are used in a rotation—the Monday–Wednesday–Friday–Sunday reed and the Tuesday–Thursday–Saturday–Monday reed. The constant use of one reed will wear it out quickly.

Because no two reeds play or feel exactly alike, rotating reeds makes the player (and the embouchure) more flexible. The player will learn to tolerate a wider range of reeds—from those that feel perfect to those that are less than perfect, but still playable.

Evaluating Quality

An oboe reed is evaluated on five criteria: Response, pitch, stability, dynamic range, and tone quality.

1. Response is vibration. Above all else, a reed must respond immediately to the air and tongue.
2. The pitch level of the oboe is based almost entirely on the pitch level that has been built into the reed. The oboe is not designed to have joints pulled for tuning. The reed can be pulled only 1/8 inch (3mm).
3. A reed is stable when octave As can be produced with little or no change in embouchure on the upper A.
4. The ideal reed allows controlled playing at both *f* and *p* levels with relative ease.
5. Tone quality will vary from player to player along a range of bright to dark, and is related to both player characteristics (embouchure, air stream, tonal concept) and reed attributes. Tone quality doesn't much matter unless the reed responds, is in tune, is stable, and allows extremes of dynamic range.

The Reed Needs of Novice Players

Novice oboe players should play softer (rather than harder) reeds that have good response, pitch, and stability. These qualities allow the embouchure to develop properly. In other words, bad habits are not promoted, as they would be if response, pitch, or stability were deficient. These same reeds, however, may be deficient in dynamic range (they may play loud easily, but not soft) and tone quality (somewhat bright and thin, not dark and rich). The music teacher must realize that these compromises are a necessary evil of the life of a novice oboe player. As the embouchure strengthens, so too can reed strength, which makes available more options in terms of dynamic range and tone quality.

More so than the other woodwind instruments, a student's early success on the oboe depends on the condition of the reed. The number 2 reeds used by beginning clarinet and saxophone students will vary slightly in tone quality and the ease with which they blow. These small variations among reeds generally do not hinder the progress of single reed players. Tone quality and ease of blowing, however, among commercially made oboe reeds vary greatly. It is not unusual for a perfectly fine-looking oboe reed to be completely unplayable for a novice oboe student or to be playable in a way that promotes improper embouchure habits (e.g., biting).

Store-Bought Reeds

Commercial reeds can be purchased at music stores and by mail order. They come in different strengths (soft, medium soft, medium, medium hard, hard). A reed at the softer end of the scale will respond (vibrate) with less effort (less embouchure strength) and produce a brighter, thinner tone than will a harder reed. A harder reed produces a darker, less reedy tone.

The quality of store-bought reeds varies widely. Many are scraped with an eye to easy response (soft to a fault) so that when purchased, the reed will *work*. However, easy response or softness is not conducive to a dark, rich tone. A dark, rich tone comes from a reed that has more cane left on it "in the right places." Often this reed will not *work* well when purchased because it just isn't finished. It requires more scraping. It may be inconvenient but this reed, when adjusted, has the potential to be a good one.

Other store-bought reeds are simply not well constructed. They may be too long, too open or too closed at the tip, not well sealed on the sides, or scraped in a style that is not conducive to a dark, rich tone.

Visual Characteristics of a Reed

If you have the option of choosing a reed from a selection of reeds, choose as follows:

1. Cane should be gold, not green.
2. Cane should have a tight grain.
3. Look at the tip opening. Avoid a tip opening that is too big. It will open bigger when wet. Avoid a tip opening that is completely closed. It may not open enough when wet.
4. Avoid a reed whose sides do not meet for their entire length. The sides may not close when wet.
5. Avoid a short (French) style of scrape. A short scrape reed looks like its name implies. The scrape (that which has been cut with a knife) is short, meaning about half of the wood part of the reed is scraped. The other half has not been scraped; the bark remains. A tone of a short scrape reed is

brighter, more lazer-beam like than that of the other style of scrape—the long scrape. The scraped portion of the long scrape reed extends farther back, almost to the string. This allows the vibrations of the reed to travel unobstructed farther into the back of the reed, promoting greater depth and darkness in the tone.

6. A well-made reed will not need a wire.

7. When looking at the reed with and without backlighting, one blade should look like the other. Further, the scrape of the left half and right half of each blade should look alike. In other words, the scrape of the reed should be very close to symmetrical. If not, the workmanship may be faulty.

The best test of a reed is the crow, though this is implausible when choosing from a music store selection of reeds. Another revealing test involves plugging the tube end of the wet reed and blowing through the tip. If the reed leaks on its sides, you will feel and hear it.

Reed Parts

The names and functions of the parts of the oboe reed are situated here near the end of the "Oboe Reeds" section to show the reader how much practical and helpful information there is to know about reeds, even *without* knowing the names of the parts. This is not meant to imply that knowing the names of reed parts is unimportant. It is meant to point out that if one were to create a rating scale for oboe reed information ranging from least to most useful (to the teacher and student), wetting, storing, crowing, rotating, evaluating, and purchasing would have priority status over naming the reed parts.

1. The tube (or staple) is made of metal that is covered with cork on one end (see Letter F of Figure 5.20). Figure 5.21 is a non-labeled version of the reed in Figure 5.20.

2. The blades are the two pieces of cane that when held together by string on a tube create the *double* in double reed.

3. The winding is the thread used to hold the blades on the tube (see Letter E of Figure 5.20).

4. The cut is the portion of the reed that has been cut or scraped. There are two basic cuts of oboe reed. In the French cut (or short scrape), the bark is not scraped from the bottom half of the blades. In the long scrape, used predominantly in the United States and shown in Figure 5.20, cane is scraped down the back of the blades almost to the winding.

5. The tip is the area of the reed that extends back from the actual tip in the shape of a thumb nail or roof top (see Letter A in Figure 5.20). The tip is the thinnest part of the reed. Its function is to allow the reed to vibrate freely and to initiate vibration down the rest of the scraped portion of the reed.

6. The heart (or hump) is located south of the tip, and through backlighting will appear darker than the tip (see Letter B in Figure 5.20). Whereas the tip promotes vibration, the heart is a resistance area. Somewhere in the production (scraping) process there is an optimal balance in thickness between vibrating and resisting areas. If too much cane is removed from the heart, the reed will be unstable. If too little cane is removed from the heart, the reed will be unresponsive.

7. The spine is a heavier ribbon of cane that runs down the center of each blade (see Letter C in Figure 5.20). The spine is a resistance area.

8. The sides refer to the left and right halves of each blade. On the long style scrape the sides have cane scraped out almost to the winding (see the two Letter Ds in Figure 5.20).

9. The rails are the unscraped edges of cane that extend down the sides of the each blade. The combination of heart, spine, and rails constitute the support structure of a well-made reed.

Basic Reed Troubleshooting

Tip Opening

A wet reed whose tip tends to close can be coaxed open by squeezing gently with thumb and index finger from the sides and thus opening the tip. This same reed tip can be coaxed open by soaking it longer or soaking it in warm rather than cold water. A wet reed whose tip tends to be too open can be coaxed shut by closing it and holding it closed for 30 seconds or so. These generally are temporary fixes.

FIGURE 5.20
Labeled Oboe Reed
(Produced by Paige Jarreau at Paige's Photos)

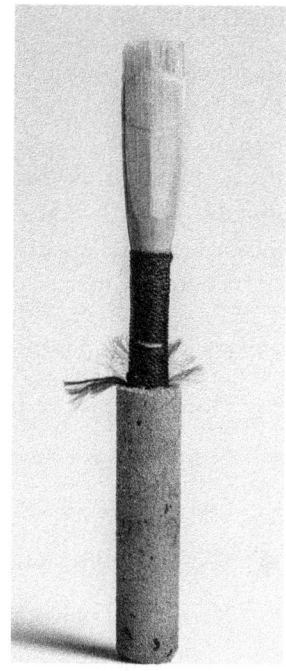

FIGURE 5.21
Unlabeled Oboe Reed
(Produced by Paige Jarreau at Paige's Photos)

Sharp Pitch

A reed that is sharp can be pulled about 1/8 inch (3mm). Cane can be removed to lower pitch.

Leak in Reed

A leak in the sides of a reed can be stopped by wrapping fish skin around the reed. Refer to a double reed catalog for fish skin.

Getting Extra Life Out of an Old Reed

As a last resort, some extra life can be coaxed out of an old, dying reed by inserting paper between the blades of a wet reed. Close the reed tip onto the paper and pull the paper out. This will remove some but not all of the build-up on the inside of the reed. This build-up is a part of all reeds and is one reason that good reeds are good. Removing all of it will change the reed drastically. Removing some of it will change the reed less drastically. It may make it feel more open and play with better response and pitch. Use this technique only as a last resort in an attempt to temporarily revive an aging reed.

The band or orchestra director need not have reed-making skill to guide and work effectively with oboe students. One must, however, compensate for lack of reed-making skill by securing a good private teacher (one who makes reeds!), or otherwise finding a good reed-making source. Be ready to help students and parents who do not have the benefit of good private instruction with the purchase of reeds, soaking, storing, drying, rotating, and detecting reed deterioration.

Reed Sources

Refer to catalogs that list woodwind products to learn more about reed selection and specifications. One catalog lists close to 15 reed brands. Prices per reed for student quality reeds range from $6.00 to roughly $15.00. The Meason oboe reed is a decent commercially made reed that sells for about $7.00. Plastic or fibercane reeds are not recommended because they are typically inferior in tone quality and unstable in pitch. The catalogs of companies that specialize in the double reed instruments and accessories sell professional quality reeds for prices ranging from $12.00 to $24.00 per reed.

There are many commercial manufacturers of oboe reeds. The following list is not exhaustive.

- Charles Double Reed Co., www.charlesmusic.com
- Hodge Products, Inc., hodgeproductsinc.com
- North Texas Oboe Reeds and Cane, www.oboereedstore.com
- Oboe Cane and Reeds by Stuart Dunkel, www.stuart-dunkel.com
- Weber Reeds, www.webreeds.com
- Kerry Willingham, www.reedmaker.com
- Mark Chudnow Woodwinds, www.mcwoboe.com
- Woodwind & Brasswind, www.wwbr.com
- Artist Series oboe reed

David Weber is the author of two resources on oboe reed making: *The Reed Maker's Manual* and *The Reed Maker's Video*. Another excellent source on reed making is *The Oboe Reed Book* by Jay Light.

A good reed source can often be found locally, and if so, this is preferable to the above sources. Contact a private teacher or university oboe major who is an accomplished reed maker (not all are) to inquire about reeds and reed adjustment.

INITIAL PLAYING MATERIAL

Functional initial performance experiences for university students learning to play secondary flute, clarinet, and saxophone in class settings can be found in any number of beginning band method books. The concert B-flat key orientation of these method books, however, is not conducive to good initial performance experiences for oboe. This is explained above under "Fingering Issues" and illustrated in Figure 5.13.

For this reason, I provide in Figures 5.22, 5.23, 5.24, 5.25, and 5.26 five sets of playing material intended to introduce and orient the university student to secondary oboe. Consider also several oboe-specific beginning method books, among them the *Rubank Elementary Method for Oboe* and the *Gekeler Method for Oboe*.

Set 1 exercises focus on the left hand and tongue. Set 2 exercises focus on the right hand and the various F fingerings. Set 3 exercises extend into the second octave and use of the half hole and octave key. Set 4 introduces the chromatic notes of the left hand. Set 5 does the same in the right hand.

FIGURE 5.22 Oboe Left-Hand Exercises

FIGURE 5.23 Oboe Right-Hand Exercises

FIGURE 5.24 Oboe Second Octave Exercises

FIGURE 5.25 Oboe Left-Hand Chromatics

FIGURE 5.26 Oboe Right-Hand Chromatics

STUDY QUESTIONS

1. In terms of students selecting and teachers assigning students to play the oboe, there are four differences between oboe playing and flute, clarinet, and alto sax playing that should be considered. In very few words summarize these.

2. Summarize the desired traits in one who is a good candidate for oboe study.

3. That the oboe is inherently harder than flute, clarinet, and saxophone is a misconception. Why is this a misconception?

4. Make a list of characteristics for oboe embouchure from the "Early Stage Embouchure" section of the text.

5. What part of the oboe reed should be soaked? For how long? When in the assembly process?

6. There is one peculiarity in oboe assembly involved in holding the upper joint. What is it?

7. How far should the oboe reed cork go into the upper joint?

8. Oboe reeds should be able to "breathe" in storage. Explain.

9. In oboe hand position, the top hand thumb should not . . .

10. Describe finger angle in relationship to the oboe.

11. Does your reed crow a C in octaves when you blow at an *mf* level?

12. On the assembled instrument, what does a sharp, strident 3rd space C indicate about oboe embouchure?

13. Complete the following relative to oboe embouchure characteristics.

    a. Roughly half of the cane portion of the reed should . . .
    b. Describe mouth and lip shape.
    c. Describe lip contact with the reed.
    d. The head is held . . .
    e. The jaw is . . .

14. What do oboes players actually do physically when they "lip down"?

15. Is oboe vibrato produced the same as flute vibrato? Explain.

16. In tonguing, to what does "tip of the reed" refer to in oboe study?

17. Who is considered the father of the American school of oboe playing? More important, why is this so?

18. Transposition. The English horn sounds . . .

19. The most well-known professional model oboe is made by . . .

20. On a staff, write from low to high each note in: a) the half hole range, b) the first octave key range, and c) the second octave key range.

21. There are three fingerings for F on the oboe. Explain.

22. In the A-flat scale, an alternate E-flat fingering (left E-flat) is used. Explain.

23. On the trill fingering chart, find and play the 3rd space C to D trill.

24. Tuning the oboe is about two things: a) reed crow and b) proper embouchure. It is not about pushing and pulling reed or instrument joints. The ideal reed crow produces what sound under what conditions? Demonstrate on your reed.

25. Indicate pitch tendencies for the following:

    a. Short fingered Cs
    b. Fork F
    c. 4th space E.

26. How can you as teacher help your students find good oboe reeds?

27. Explain reed troubleshooting concerning oboe tip opening.

PERFORMANCE TESTING OF UNIVERSITY STUDENTS ON SECONDARY INSTRUMENTS

A rubric is an evaluative tool. The rubric that follows makes clear the expectations of the university student playing secondary oboe as he or she approaches the end of an intensive three to four weeks of study. Students may use the criteria to prepare for performance testing and to self-evaluate. Teachers may use the criteria to structure feedback.

1.	Reed:		
	a. Crowed the reed properly	Yes	No
	b. Crow was pitched at or very near C	Yes	No
2.	Instrument situated correctly in relation to the body:		
	a. Head was erect	Yes	No
	b. Oboe at 35° to body	Yes	No
3.	Formed a characteristic embouchure:		
	a. Mouth in the round shape of "OH"	Yes	No
	b. Only enough reed in mouth to tongue	Yes	No
4.	Breathing:		

	a.	In taking a breath, the lower lip stayed in contact with reed	Yes	No
	b.	Breathed according to phrase	Yes	No
5.	Tone:			
	a.	Achieved a characteristic basic tone—*forte*, freely vibrating, and unwavering	Yes	No
	b.	Played in tune 90% of the time	Yes	No
6.	Fingers:			
	a.	Maintained correct hand position	Yes	No
	b.	Recalled and played primary fingerings in the range of low C to B-flat above the staff	Yes	No
	c.	Recalled and played alternate fingerings (Fs and E-flats)	Yes	No
	d.	Technique was well practiced	Yes	No
7.	Articulation:			
	a.	Tongued and slurred as marked	Yes	No
	b.	Legato tongued in convincing fashion	Yes	No
8.	Expressive Performance:			
	a.	Varied dynamic and tempo as appropriate for expressive effect	Yes	No

OBOE FINGERING CHART

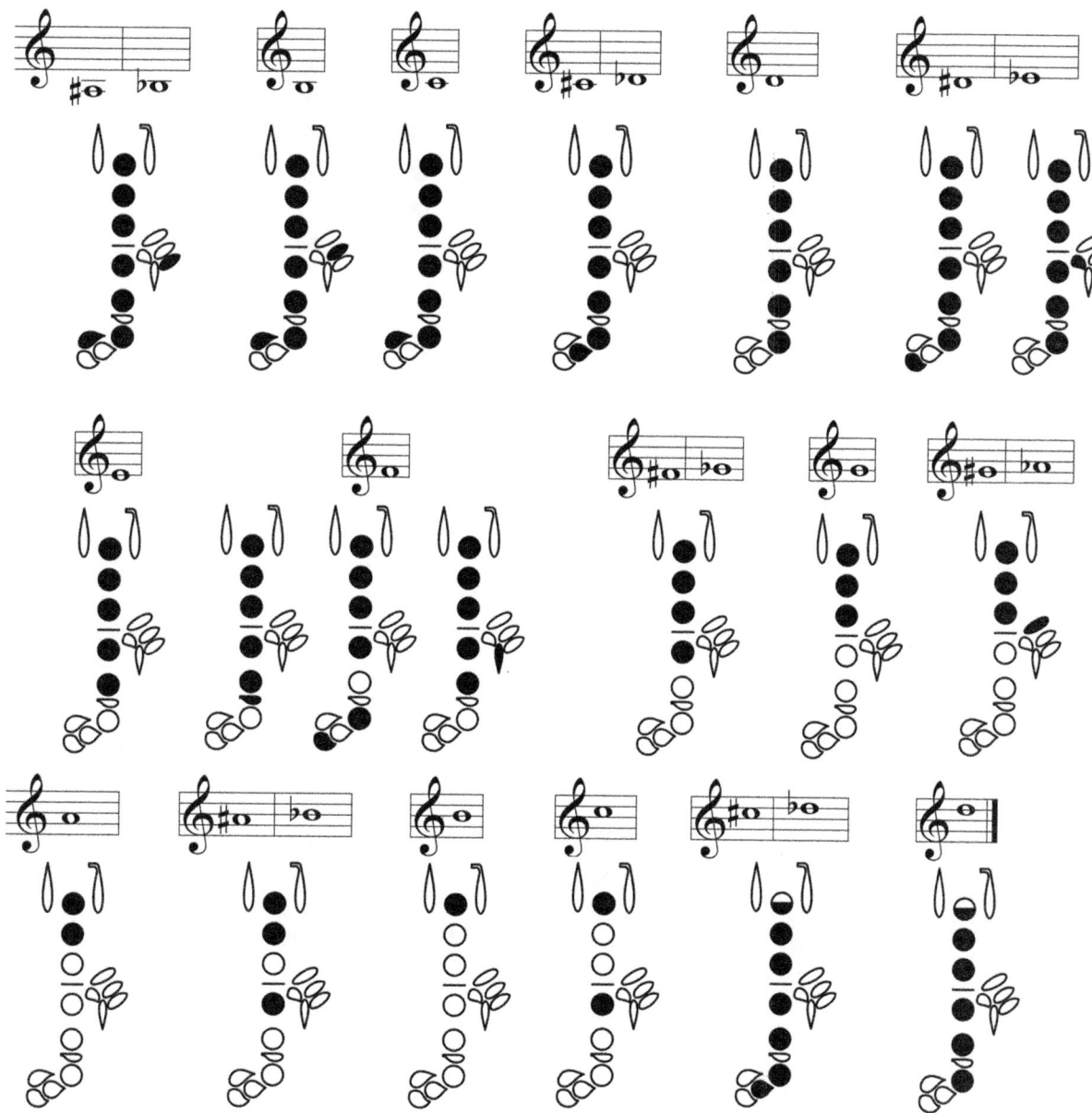

FIGURE 5.27A Oboe Fingering Chart page 1

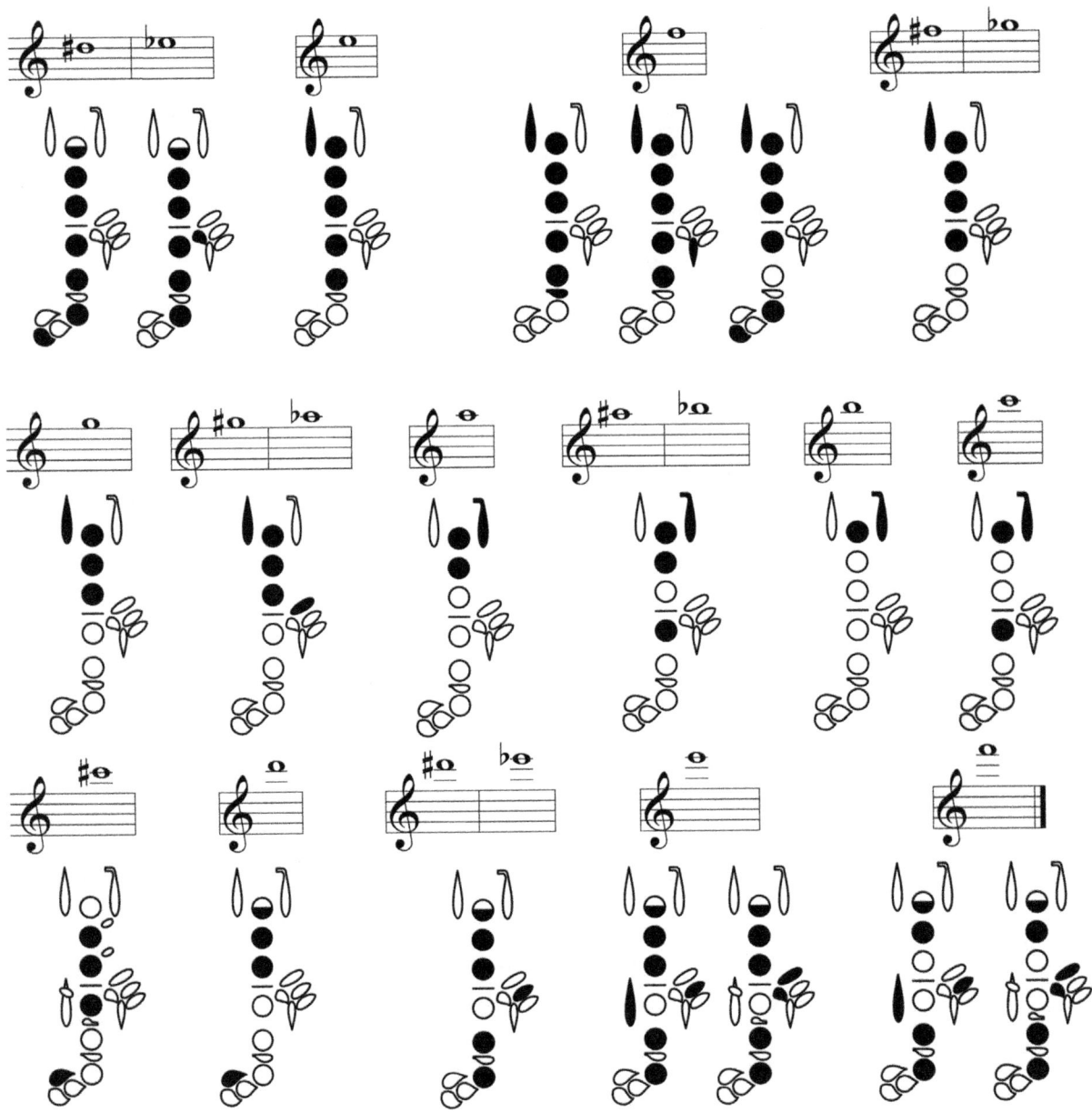

FIGURE 5.27B Oboe Fingering Chart page 2

CHAPTER 6

Bassoon

POTENTIAL FOR SUCCESS IN BASSOON STUDY

The chapters for bassoon and oboe, unlike those for flute, clarinet and saxophone, begin with "Potential for Success" because of inherent differences between the double reed instruments and the standard beginning woodwind instruments. The differences follow.

1. The double reed instruments typically are not considered beginning instruments, though there are exceptions to this common practice. Often, teachers create bassoon players out of students who first played another instrument. This switch normally occurs in the second or third year of instrument study.

2. Usually, school-based bassoon students use instruments provided by the school system. There are only so many of these available. They must be distributed intelligently in order to keep to a minimum the number of bassoon players who do not make consistent progress. The teacher must be selective in recruiting double reed students.

3. The standard band instrumentation calls for many fewer double reed players than clarinet and flute players. Two oboes and two bassoons will suffice in a band or orchestra. As many as four of each is acceptable. That so few are called for raises the stakes in recruiting double reed students.

4. Bassoon players must function effectively in a musical world in which there is one player on a part and where composers of the more advanced band and orchestral literatures assign exposed parts to the bassoon.

It is important, therefore, to consider a student's potential for success in bassoon study before approaching him or her about playing the instrument. Recruit bright, motivated students to play bassoon. Recruit students who have the potential to function effectively as the only player on the part. Some students thrive on this independence; others do not! Recruit students who have studied piano seriously for several years; the ability to read bass clef is a tremendous asset for the novice bassoonist. Recruit students (and their parents!) who are likely to be receptive to private lessons.

This focus on potential success is not motivated by the fact that the bassoon is inherently more difficult to play than the other woodwinds, and therefore requires smarter, more "into it" students. This is a common misconception, though smart and into it are always good. Actually, the embouchures of the oboe and bassoon are less complicated than those of the flute and clarinet. Except for the fact that traditional beginning band method books force compromises on how the double reeds are approached in the first year, early fingering challenges need not be more complex than those of the flute, clarinet, and saxophone.

So why the perception that the double reed instruments are so difficult to play? In fact, many students struggle mightily with bassoon not because of the challenges the instrument itself presents, but because of poor quality and hard-to-make-work reeds. If the reed is appropriate for the student, the bassoon is not more difficult to play than flute and clarinet.

Recruiting is a full-time, continuous activity. It does not stop when students select or have been selected to play the bassoon. Pay attention to double reed players. Be their advocate. Find a private teacher who is willing and able to make and adjust reeds. Absent a private teacher, find a source for good reeds. Realize the importance of a properly soaked reed. Learn how to crow a reed, and what to listen for in a crow. Know what an appropriate-sized tip opening looks like. Make sure the instruments you provide are in good playing condition.

Students who are successful flute, clarinet, or saxophone beginners, if they are willing to switch instruments, can become good bassoon players. The most common physical deterrent to success on the bassoon is small hands. The hands must be big enough and the fingers and thumb long enough.

To summarize, students who are most likely to succeed on the bassoon are a) bright, b) motivated, c) large enough with long enough hands and fingers, d) capable of being musically independent, e) able to read bass clef, and f) willing to take private lessons. But, as a teacher, be careful. If you hold out for this package of traits in one person (the perfect prospect!), you may have no bassoon players. So be appropriately flexible in your thinking.

BASSOON TONE AND EARLY STAGE EMBOUCHURE

The bassoon embouchure is not complicated. It is a double lip embouchure; that is, some lip covers lower and upper teeth. Like the saxophone embouchure, the mouth and lips are rounded, as if saying "OH" or "AH," with lip pressures evenly distributed around the reed. Other important considerations are amount of reed in the mouth and amount of lip over teeth.

Small Piece

The small piece of the bassoon is the assembled reed and bocal. Before involving the student in small piece work, it is wise for the teacher to check the condition of the reed as follows. Soak the entire bassoon reed for about 3 minutes. Grasp it at the winding (at the ball of thread or in the wire area) and shake off excess water. Through the winding end, blow out the remaining water.

Crow the reed by intentionally putting too much reed in the mouth (lips touching the first wire) and blowing an unfocused stream of air into it. Use no formal bassoon embouchure—the lips simply seal around the reed. This allows the teacher to assess the reed's baseline condition, especially regarding ease of response.

Using moderate air speed, the bassoon reed should crow what sounds like a multi-pitched, loose rattle. A loose rattle crow is desirable. If one must blow very hard to get a response or if only one pitch results or if a squawk occurs, the reed may be faulty. Blowing extra hard to get a response means that the reed is too hard (has too much cane on it) or its tip is too open. A single pitch can result from a too closed tip opening or by placing too little reed in the mouth. A squawk occurs when the reed is too soft (too much cane has been taken off in certain areas) or when it becomes soft through use.

Find a bocal in the bassoon case (usually one or two bocals are secured beneath the long joints). It you have a choice, use the bocal with a number 2 etched into its body. With the cork end of the bocal pointing down, place the reed firmly on the bocal so that the length of tip opening extends horizontally, not vertically. Assembled reed and bocal constitute the small piece of the bassoon.

Teaching Embouchure

In the school setting, the most efficient way to introduce the bassoon to a student is to separate him/her from the large group of instrumentalists. Individual meetings can be arranged during or outside the school day in order that the student gets a good start on the instrument before being included in the large group setting.

Sequence of Instruction for Making First Sounds (Small Piece)

Characteristic bassoon tone is a function of embouchure and air stream. The two work together in tone production. Use the small piece (reed and bocal) to introduce embouchure.

- *Embouchure*. As shown in Figure 6.1, use the reed and bocal only.
    1. Grasping the bocal near the curve, bring the bocal to the face while keeping the head erect. Stick out your tongue. "Catch" the reed with the tongue, and in so doing, guide it into your mouth.
    2. Put some lower lip over the teeth.
    3. Take in reed *almost to the first wire*.
    4. Keeping the lips close to the teeth, make a circle with the lips as they close around the reed. Allow the circle shape (think "OH" or "AH") to put upper lip over the teeth.
    5. Create a slightly upward angle of the bocal as it approaches the mouth.
- *Air stream*
    1. Blow straight ahead.
    2. Blow fast air.
    3. While blowing, maintain an open, round look and feel.

FIGURE 6.1 Front View of Embouchure
(Produced by Paige Jarreau at Paige's Photos)

Figures 6.1 and 6.2 show the embouchure from front and side views. Notice the erect head, the round and open nature of the embouchure, the amount of lip over the teeth, and the slightly upward angle of the bocal's approach to the mouth. Figure 6.2 provides a great view of amount of reed in the mouth. While the amount of reed varies somewhat among accomplished bassoonists with the precise amount being determined by quality of sound and response, it is perhaps wise to get novice bassoonists to think "more rather than less" reed in the mouth. This counters the tendency to take in too little reed.

The small piece of the bassoon serves as a tool to help teach embouchure and diagnose embouchure-related problems. Using a characteristic embouchure (or one that is ballpark accurate), a reed with a loose rattle crow, and a fast air stream, the student should produce the pitch C, or very near it on the small piece. If the reed is suitable, but the pitch sharp, the mouth is too closed or too tight around the reed. Open the mouth more in order to match C. If the reed is suitable, but the pitch flat, the embouchure is likely too open, the lips not firm enough, or the air stream too slow.

FIGURE 6.2 Side View of Embouchure
(Produced by Paige Jarreau at Paige's Photos)

Diagnosing Small Piece Pitch and Tone Quality

Pitch and tone quality on both the small piece and the fully assembled instrument are affected by five factors: a) direction of air, b) speed of air, c) amount of reed in the mouth, d) embouchure shape and firmness, and e) reed condition. When diagnosing the pitch and tone quality produced by a novice bassoon player on the reed and bocal alone, ask yourself:

1. Is the head erect? Does the bocal approach the mouth at a slightly upward angle? (*Direction of air*)
2. Is the air speed fast enough? (*Speed of air*)
3. Is there too little or too much reed in the mouth? (*Amount in mouth*)
4. Does the embouchure appear to be round? Is it too firm or not firm enough? (*Embouchure firmness*)
5. Does the reed crow a loose rattle? Is the reed tip too open or too closed? (*Reed condition*)

Small Piece Practice

In working with a novice bassoon student, a call and response pattern (4 beats on/4 beats off) between teacher and student works well in structuring small piece experiences focusing on embouchure and air stream. Instruct the student to *memorize the feel* when the embouchure and air stream produce the C pitch and desired resonant tone. Focus attention on the round nature of the mouth, fast air stream, the amount of reed in the mouth (nearly to the first wire), and the slightly upward angle of the bocal into the mouth.

More so than the other woodwind instruments, a student's early success on the bassoon or the oboe depends on the condition of the reed. Tone quality and ease of blowing vary a lot among commercially made bassoon reeds. It is not unusual for a perfectly fine-looking bassoon reed to be unplayable for a novice student or to be playable in a way that promotes improper embouchure habits (e.g., biting).

There are certain qualities that the informed music teacher looks for, listens for, and, by playing it, feels for in a bassoon reed to determine its appropriateness for the beginning student. These qualities are presented below in the "Bassoon Reeds" section (see "Crowing the Reed," "Evaluating Quality," and "The Visual Characteristics of a Reed").

BASSOON ASSEMBLY, DISASSEMBLY, AND BASIC CARE

Assembly Sequence

Because of the size of the bassoon and its unique playing position relative to the player's body, it helpful initially to think of assembly as a sequence involving assembly, holding, and hand position. Viewed this way, teaching bassoon assembly requires more time than is the case for the other woodwind instruments. In the university woodwind class, first-day assembly and disassembly may take most of one 50-minute class.

1. Lay the closed case on the floor to the left side of your chair. Check that the case is situated right side up.
2. Open case. You will see what is pictured in Figure 6.3. Letter A is the boot joint. Letter B the tenor joint. Letter C the bass joint. Letter D the bell. Letter E the bocal. Letter F the hand rest. Typically, the bocal is secured and stored under the instrument. Not pictured is the seat strap.

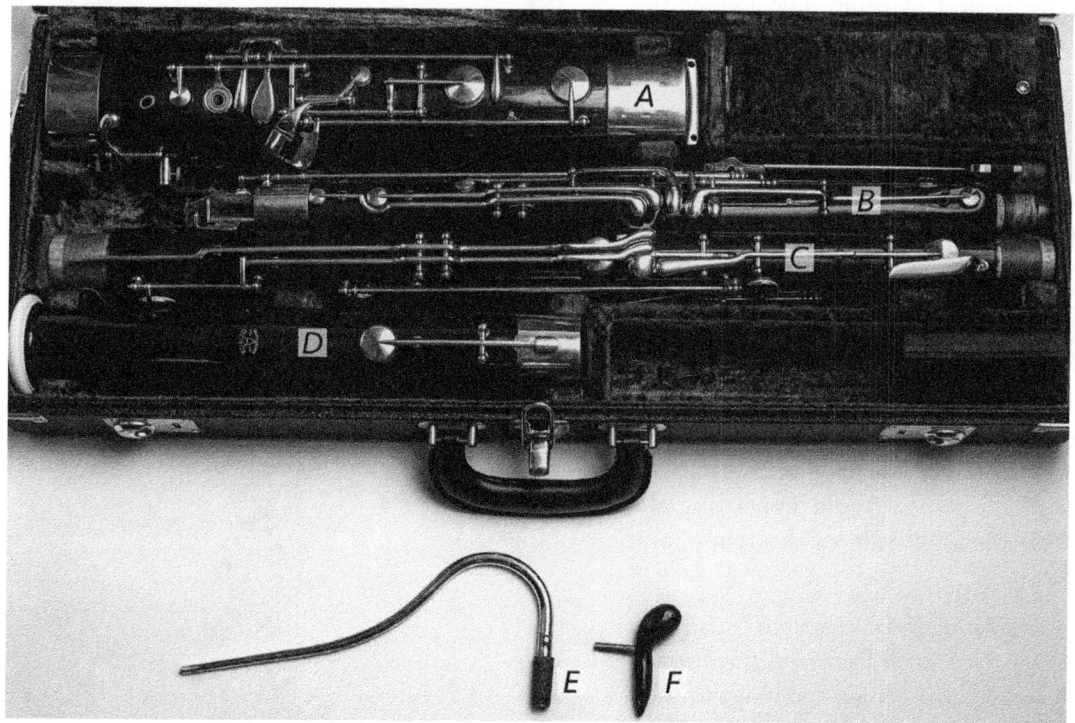

FIGURE 6.3 Parts of the Bassoon
(Produced by Paige Jarreau at Paige's Photos)

Remove water container if stored in the case. Remove reed from its case. Place the water container on the floor behind a front leg of the chair, out of the line of traffic and your own feet. Soak all of the reed for about 3 minutes.

To save time, soak the reed first, while the rest of the instrument is being assembled. A plastic film case or prescription pill bottle works well as a water-tight container. Water should be changed on a sensible schedule.

During soaking, the reed forms into its playing shape after having lost some of that shape by drying. Soaking will cause the tip opening to get larger. If a reed is left in water for a prolonged period, the tip opening will become very large, perhaps to the point of making the reed temporarily unplayable. If this happens, coax the wet tip opening shut by closing it between the thumb and index finger.

If the reed has a tip opening that tends to close somewhat during playing, soak the reed for a longer period of time. The longer the soaking, the more open the tip.

3. Stand up and situate the seat strap across the chair, 2 inches (5cm) from the front. The hooked end should dangle from the right side of the chair as you sit on it. *Note*: Don't attach the bassoon yet (see Figure 6.4).

FIGURE 6.4 Seat Strap at Front Edge
(Produced by Paige Jarreau at Paige's Photos)

4. Sit down. As shown in Figure 6.5, place the boot joint on the floor in front of you with the small hole to the right.

5. With the right hand, hold the boot joint at its top. With the left hand, hold the tenor joint near its top—concave side making contact with the palm of the hand. Avoid contacting the long rod on the right side of the tenor joint (see Figure 6.6).

6. Insert the tenor joint into boot joint (small hole on the right). Use small back and forth turns. Watch the bridge key. Align the tenor joint to form concentric circles (concave body of tenor joint concentric with large opening on boot joint).

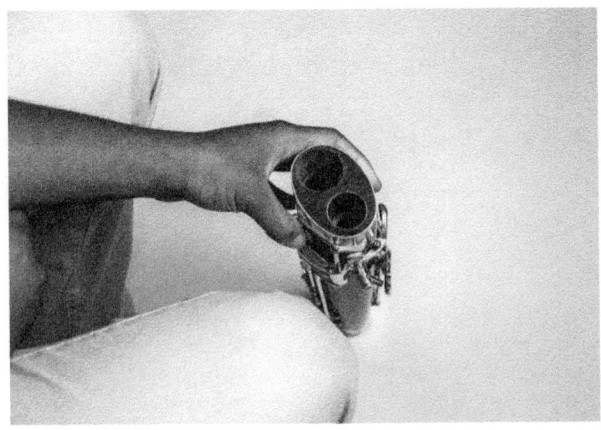

FIGURE 6.5 Small Hole to the Right in Assembly
(Produced by Paige Jarreau at Paige's Photos)

FIGURE 6.6 Tenor Joint to Boot Joint
(Produced by Paige Jarreau at Paige's Photos)

FIGURE 6.7 Bass Joint to Boot Joint
(Produced by Paige Jarreau at Paige's Photos)

7. With the left hand, grasp the bass joint at its top (at the larger end). The part with no keys will fit along side the concave portion of the tenor joint. With the right hand, continue to hold the boot joint at the top (see Figure 6.7).

8. With small back and forth turns, insert the bass joint into the boot joint. A lock mechanism located near the top of the tenor joint may need to be attended to during insertion of the bass joint into

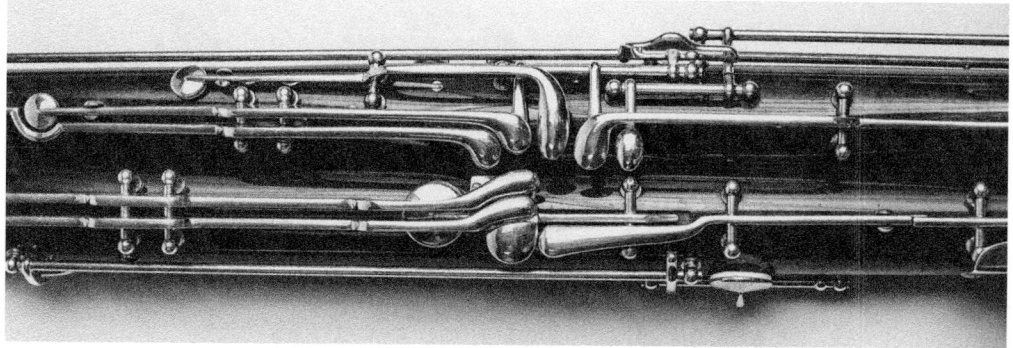

FIGURE 6.8 Thumb Keys Alignment
(Produced by Paige Jarreau at Paige's Photos)

the boot joint. This lock holds the tenor and bass joints together. If there is no lock mechanism, the bass joint should be aligned such that the left thumb keys are arranged in a quasi-circle quite near each other (as shown in Figure 6.8).

Figure 6.9 shows the top of the tenor joint and an unlocked lock mechanism. Figure 6.10 shows a locked mechanism, the lock bar having been lowered into the receiver.

9. Holding the bell such that its key is closed (thus raising the bridge portion of the key), attach bell to bass joint. Align the bridge keys.

10. Attach the hand rest (also called the crutch) to its female receiver on the boot joint. It may be situated in whatever way is most comfortable for the hand.

11. Remove the bocal from the case.

12. With the bassoon in a vertical position in front of you, grasp the bocal at the curve (see Figure 6.11) and with small back and forth turns, insert it into the tenor joint. Align the whisper key with the bocal vent hole. Never grasp the bocal at the reed end.

13. Attach the seat strap to the bottom of the boot joint. The weight of the bassoon rests on the strap.

14. With your torso leaning slightly forward, your head erect, and the bassoon bell tilted somewhat forward and to your left, the end of the bocal should touch your bottom lip. Raise and lower the bassoon by lifting your heals, thus raising your hamstrings, and sliding the seat strap to the left or right respectively.

Figures 6.12 and 6.13 show the instrument hold from front and side views. In the front view, notice the across-the-body orientation of the bassoon enabling the player to read music from a stand directly in front. In the side view, notice the seat strap placement near the edge of the chair and the bell-tipped-forward orientation of the instrument. With the bell tipped forward the bocal approaches the mouth

FIGURE 6.9 Unlocked Mechanism
(Produced by Paige Jarreau at Paige's Photos)

FIGURE 6.10 Locked Mechanism
(Produced by Paige Jarreau at Paige's Photos)

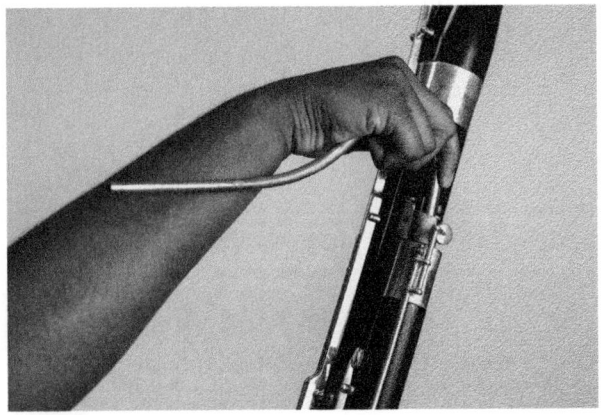

FIGURE 6.11 How to Grasp the Bocal
(Produced by Paige Jarreau at Paige's Photos)

FIGURE 6.12 Front View of Instrument Hold
(Produced by Paige Jarreau at Paige's Photos)

FIGURE 6.13 Side View of Instrument Hold
(Produced by Paige Jarreau at Paige's Photos)

correctly at a slightly upward angle. Notice too that if the player were to lean back in the chair, the bell angle and bocal angles would be compromised.

15. Holding the wet reed at the ball or in the wire area, push it onto the bocal until it stops and feels like the union is secure. Use small back and forth turns.

There are a number of important points to emphasize and expand on in bassoon assembly.

1. Wet all of the reed.
2. During soaking, the reed forms itself into playing shape after having lost some of that shape by drying. Soaking will cause the tip opening to get larger. If a reed is left in water for a prolonged period, the tip opening will become very large, perhaps to the point of making the reed temporarily unplayable. If this happens, coax the tip opening shut by closing it, while wet, between the thumb and index finger. If the reed has a tip opening that tends to close somewhat during playing, soak the reed for a longer period of time. If the reed has a tip opening that tends to be too open, do not over-soak it.

3. Assembly can be made easier if the tenor and bass joints are inserted together as one unit into the boot joint. This will work only if the tenon corks are properly fitted and well greased.

4. Do not underestimate the importance of positioning the seat strap 2 inches (5cm) from the front of the chair. Young students tend to be sloppy with this detail. Be observant of the body size and shape to make adjustments as needed. Some angling of the strap on the chair may be necessary.

5. Use of the hand rest is optional, depending on size of the hand and comfort provided. Note that its height can be adjusted somewhat. The hand rest provides a home base for the hand—something to rest against. Its use also makes it easier for the right thumb to dangle properly above the pancake key. A small hand, however, may struggle to reach the tone holes, making hand rest use unwise. Without hand rest in early study, the thumb needs to anchor against the rod or metal plate near the pancake key.

6. When handling the bocal for any reason, "grasp the bocal at the curve" should be the young bassoonist's mantra. Otherwise, the thin metal will bend and kink. When walking or "traveling" with the bassoon, advise students to remove the bocal in order to avoid damage from bumping it (see "Traveling with Instrument" in the "Care" section on page 237).

7. If the tenor or bass joint fit too easily into the boot joint, the boot joint may fall off. The thickness of the tenon corks can be increased by wrapping them with waxed dental floss.

8. Be aware that a neck strap is used when the bassoon is played while standing. The hook for the strap is located on the top of the boot joint. When seated, a seat strap must be used. The instrument cannot be played properly without a seat strap. If there is no seat strap in the case, one can be purchased or made quite simply by cutting the buckle off of an old belt, inserting a length of coat hanger through a belt hole, and using pliers to bend the wire into the shape of a hook.

Disassembly and Swabbing

Proper swabbing is a more complicated process for the bassoon than it is for the other woodwinds. Ordinarily, a bassoon should have two swabs in the case—one for the tenor joint and one with a chain cord for the boot joint. Most bassoonists use a tenor joint swab that can be pulled through. For the boot joint, a combination of rotating and shaking the boot joint coaxes the long chain cord around the curve. Pull-through swabs are sleek and generally made of silk. Insert swabs from large end to small end of joints.

School-owned bassoons, especially older models, come with brush-like wool swabs or a cleaning rod with cloth like that of the flute. Avoid the brush-like swabs because the wool wears off through use and gets caught up in the bore of the instrument. Also with wear, bare metal from the swab may scratch the bore. The cleaning rod is cumbersome compared to the pull-through swab.

Every month or so a bocal swab should be used to swab the bocal. It is wise for the school band/orchestra director to purchase a bocal swab for the school. This swab should be considered basic in terms of bassoon maintenance. Use it in the cleaning of bocals during yearly inventory checks.

Disassemble the instrument in reverse order of assembly.

1. Remove the reed from the bocal. Remove saliva by sipping at the tip end or blowing through the wrapped end. Place in a reed case that allows the reed to dry between playings. Four-, five-, and six-reed cases are available commercially (see Figure 6.14). Rectangular *Sucrets* or *Altoids* mints

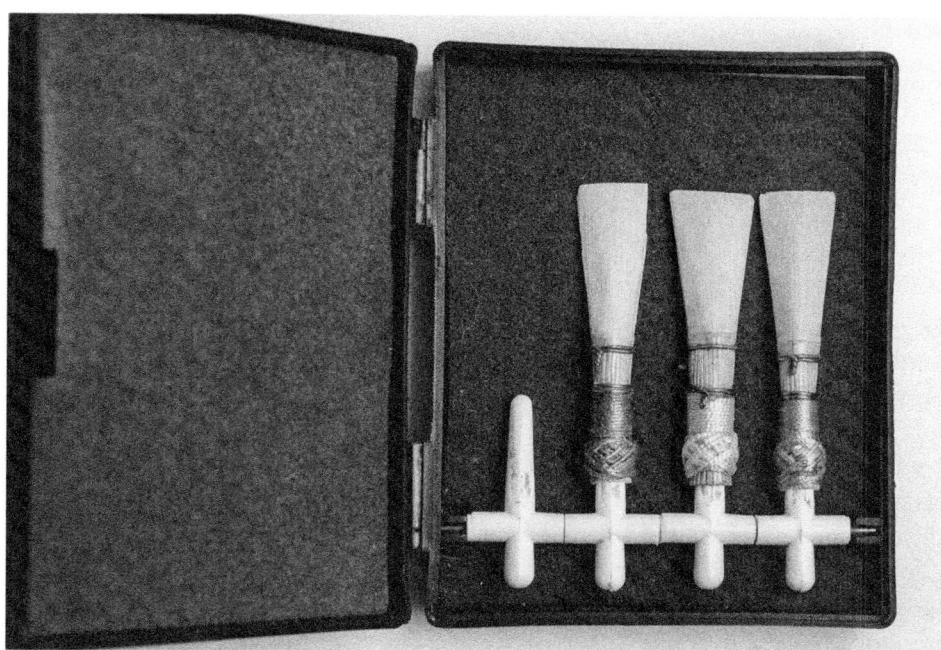

FIGURE 6.14
Reed Case

(Produced by Paige Jarreau at Paige's Photos)

containers are good alternatives. Plastic versions of these do not rust as metal is prone to do. Create a bed of tissue paper on the floor of the container. Secure the reeds with tissue paper on top.

If the clear plastic cylinder-type container is the only choice for reed storage, the teacher should make two air holes in it to allow the reed to dry during storage. Otherwise, mildew will develop. Additionally, the student should be made aware of how easy it is to damage the tip of the reed when placing it in this type of container. As the reed tip is brought to the mouth of the container, anchor a finger or fingers on the container to steady the hand. Then guide the tip through the opening in a controlled manner.

2. Unhook the bassoon from the seat strap. Position the instrument vertically in front of you with the boot joint resting on the floor.

3. Grasping the bocal at the curve, remove it with small back and forth turns. Tap the cork end of bocal on the thigh to encourage water to come out. Plugging the whisper key vent with thumb or finger, blow a fast stream of air through the cork end to remove excess moisture.

4. Open the bassoon case on the floor to your left. Return the bocal to the case.

5. Grasping at the top of the long joint and bottom of the bell, remove the bell. Return it to the case. No need to swab.

6. Disengage the lock mechanism on the tenor joint. Grasping at the top of the boot joint and the top of the bass joint, remove the bass joint. Return it to the case. No need to swab.

7. Grasping at the top of the boot joint and the top of tenor joint, remove and swab the tenor joint. Return it to case.

    As an alternative to returning bass and tenor joints to the case separately, it may be helpful to re-assemble them *before* returning them to the case as a single unit.

8. Remove the hand rest.

9. Turn the boot joint over and empty any moisture that has collected. Swab the boot joint. Return it to case.

    Spread or open the swab as much as possible before storing it in its compartment in the case. Balling it up does not allow it to dry.

Care

"Traveling with" (walking with) instrument, laying the instrument down, handling it while in its case, and the effects of temperature are care issues of practical concern. Additional information on instrument care is provided in the section "Foundations of Instrument Care."

1. Traveling (walking) with the instrument. Any time a bassoonist walks with the assembled bassoon (e.g., from warm-up room to audition room or concert hall), the reed should be removed and placed in the mouth, the bocal removed and dangled in the bell of the instrument, and the seat strap held so that it does not drag on the floor. Keep in mind that the reed and bocal stick out. If bumped, they damage easily. Therefore, insist that your bassoonists travel properly with the bassoon. To reiterate, traveling with the bassoon entails the following: Reed in mouth, bocal in bell, and no-drag seat strap.

2. Laying the instrument down. If you must lay the instrument down, take the reed off and bocal out. Put them in a safe place. Lay the instrument down on a chair or instrument case with the many-keyed side facing up. An alternative is to prop the bassoon up vertically in a corner of a room. For this, you need a carpeted floor to prevent slippage. In a crowded rehearsal room, if you must leave the instrument unattended, disassemble all instrument parts.

3. Instrument in case. Treat the instrument gently even when it is in its case. A dropped case with the instrument inside can damage the instrument.

4. Extreme temperatures and cracking. In extremes of temperature, wood will crack. Do not place or store woodwind instruments in prolonged hot or cold (on a heater or in a car in freezing weather). If a bassoon gets extremely cold, warm it up gradually by cradling instrument joints in your hands and against your body. Don't be too quick to blow hot air (98.6°) into the bore.

BASSOON POSTURE, HANDS, AND HOLDING

Left hand

1. Thumb depresses whisper key, labeled F in Figure 6.15.

2. Fingers are slightly curved except for the ring finger, which may need to be straight to reach its tone hole.

3. Lean the bassoon against the nearly full length of the index finger. Figure 6.16 shows a close-up of this lean and of a straight ring finger.

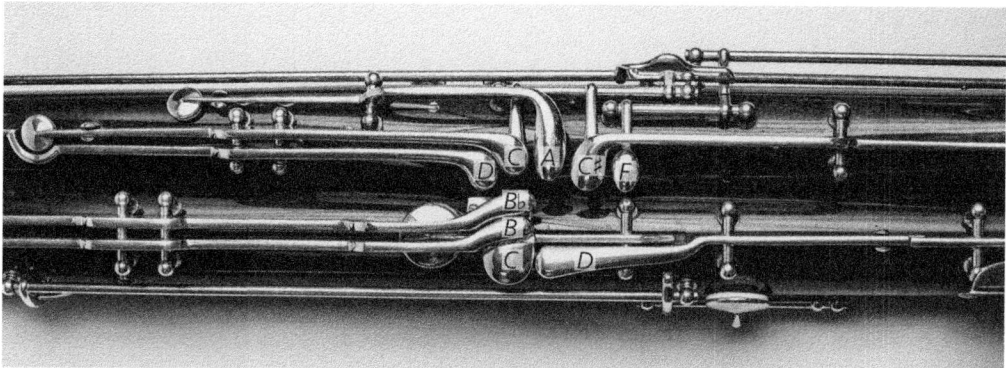

FIGURE 6.15 Left-Hand Thumb Keys Labeled
(Produced by Paige Jarreau at Paige's Photos)

4. The half-hole technique involves the index finger, which either covers the tone hole completely or rocks or slides downward to expose approximately half of the hole. It helps to think of the index finger tensing to open the hole (half hole) and relaxing to close or cover the hole.

5. Up to nine thumb keys necessitate that the thumb vary from:

   - a normal curved position (when playing whisper key notes) to

   - a flat position in order to depress multiple keys at once (e.g., the C-sharp and D keys in Figure 6.15) to

   - a knuckle contact point in order to rock between adjacent keys (the C to B keys in Figure 6.15).

Right hand

1. Use of the hand rest is optional. Students with large hands and/or long fingers often prefer to use the hand rest. Students with smaller hands/shorter fingers may not be able to use it. Figure 6.17 shows the screw mechanism (above or to the right of the E key) into which the hand rest fits.

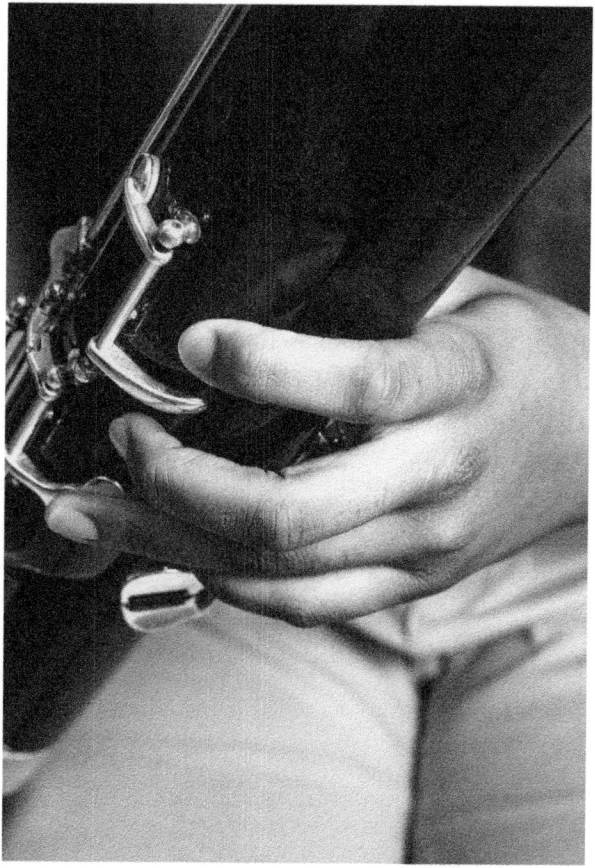

FIGURE 6.16 Lean of Instrument against Index Finger
(Produced by Paige Jarreau at Paige's Photos)

188 TEACHING THE INSTRUMENTS

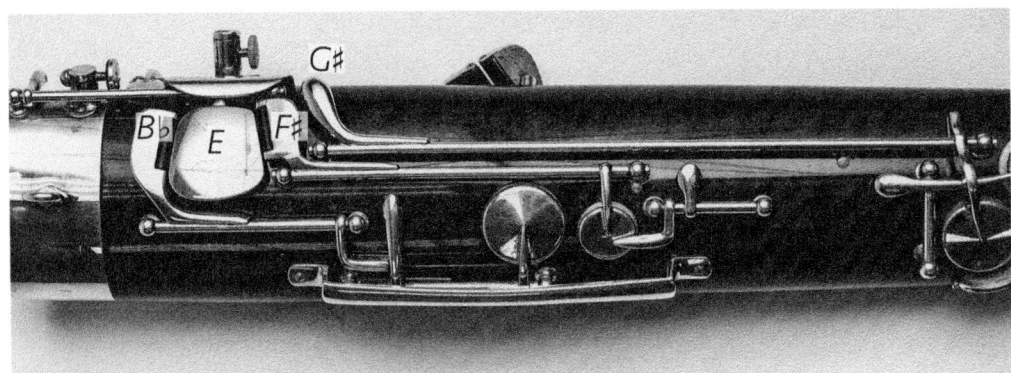

FIGURE 6.17 Boot Joint Thumb Keys Labeled
(Produced by Paige Jarreau at Paige's Photos)

2. The thumb hovers above the pancake key (the E key) or, if no hand rest, novice players will benefit by anchoring the thumb against the plate or rod next to the pancake key. In Figure 6.17, notice the anchor plate for thumb next to the E key.

3. Fingers are slightly curved.

4. Depending on length of fingers, the ring finger may need to be straight to reach its tone hole.

Two Angles

Bassoon playing position is often misunderstood by novices. Two angles must be established and maintained.

1. The bassoon should cross the body at a diagonal such that the player looks naturally straight ahead (to the right of the instrument) to see the music stand. Assess by viewing player from the front.

2. The bell of the bassoon should tip forward, leaning against the index finger, so that the bocal enters the mouth at a slightly upward angle. Assess by viewing player from the side.

What to Look for in Bassoon Hand Position and Holding

1. Is the seat strap 2 inches (5cm) back from the front edge of the chair?

2. Is the instrument positioned diagonally across the body so that the student views the music stand straight ahead (with the bell to his left)?

3. Is the bell tipped forward?

4. Does the left index finger make constant contact with the instrument?

5. Does the upper torso lean forward slightly?

6. Does the bocal approach the face at a slightly upward angle? Is the head erect? Does the length of the seat strap allow the head to be erect?

7. Is the left thumb depressing the whisper key?

8. Is the right thumb anchored against the plate or rod? If the hand rest is used, is the right thumb dangling above the pancake key?

BASSOON TONE DEVELOPMENT

The embouchure information below is consistent with, though more detailed than, that found previously under "Early Stage Embouchure." Following the complexities of instrument assembly, hand position, and holding, which serve as distractions in early embouchure work, it is wise to return to a focus on embouchure, now with the fully assembled bassoon.

4 Beats On/4 Beats Off

In order to provide students with many early opportunities to form a suitable embouchure, the notes in Figure 6.18 played on the assembled instrument work well. Ideally, this is done as a rote exercise. The teacher, on her bassoon, plays what is notated. During the rests, the students, by listening and watching their teacher, imitate. The students have no music. The fingerings are simple, and the 4 beats on/4 beats off pattern provides equal play and rest. Initially, the tongue need not be used to start the tone; simply start the air as if saying "HO."

Assuming the reed has a good crow, the first E in Figure 6.18 provides the teacher with important information about embouchure pressure. If the E comes out as a pretty good E (a leading tone to F), this is a good sign. However, if the E comes out flat (as an E-flat), it is likely that the embouchure is too loose.

FIGURE 6.18 First Notes: Call and Response

First note experiences can be expanded to include the slurred half notes and quarter notes, shown in Figure 6.19. As in the above exercise, this is best done as a rote exercise. Without losing a beat, the student imitates the teacher's model. Without losing a beat, the teacher re-enters with the next measure. In order to keep the focus on embouchure and air stream, the tongue need not be used.

This can be done with the teacher singing while fingering a phantom bassoon. But there is no better teaching scenario than the teacher demonstrating proper posture and instrument hold and characteristic breathing, embouchure, and tone while the student watches and listens.

190 TEACHING THE INSTRUMENTS

FIGURE 6.19 First Notes: Disguised Long Tones

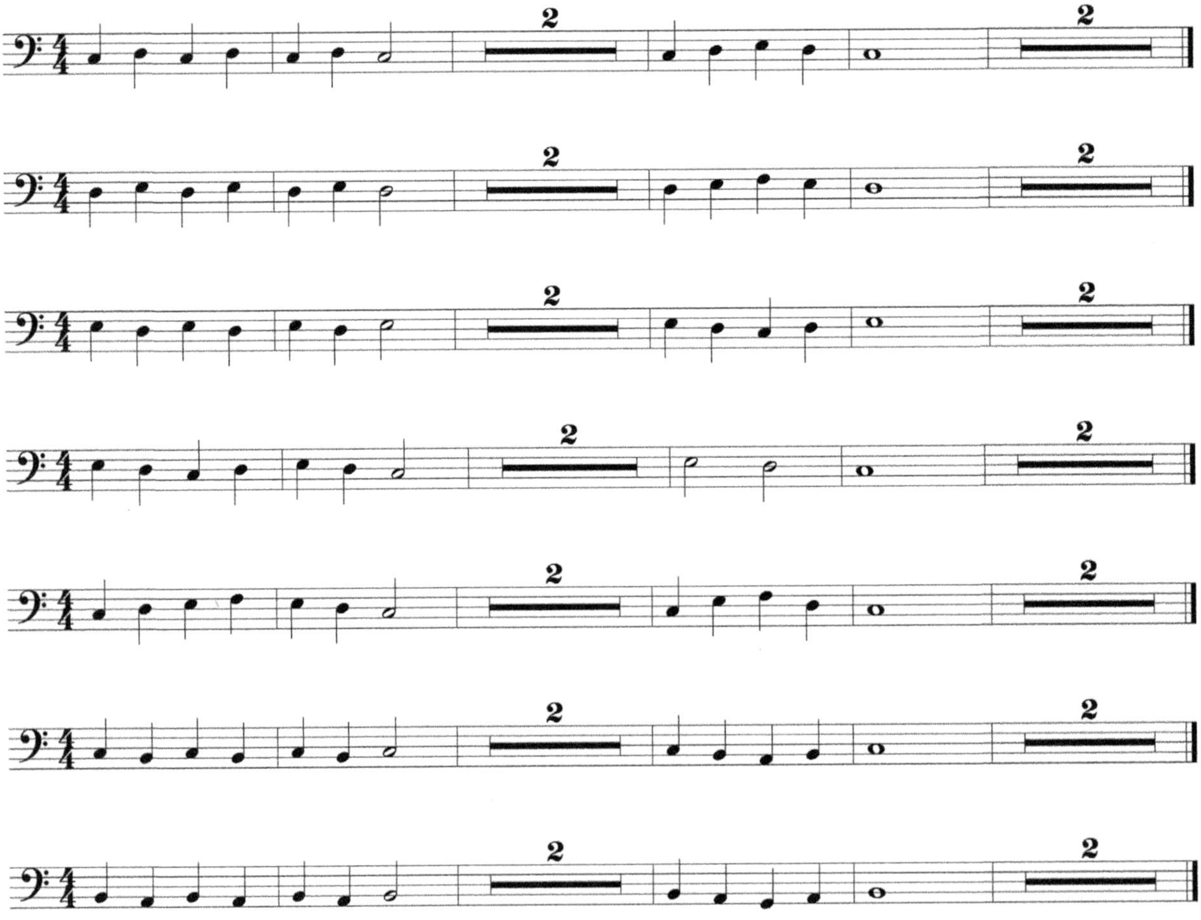

FIGURE 6.20 Rote Study for Bassoon

FIGURE 6.20 Continued

Figure 6.20 presents an extended experience in rote practice of posture, breath, embouchure, tone, and first fingerings. The teacher plays what is notated. Students respond with same during the two-measure rests. As an early experience in bassoon playing, slur all. Allow the focus to be on embouchure strengthening and development, not tonguing.

Characteristics of the Bassoon Embouchure

1. Corners of lips are drawn toward the reed. An exaggerated "OH" draws the lip corners in. Saying the word "HOW" and applying it to the embouchure will do the same. Some bassoonists think in terms of having lip pressures equally distributed around the reed. Others prefer to focus on the pressure of the top and bottom lip as that which controls pitch and tone, while pressure of the lip corners simply prevents air from leaking out the sides of the embouchure.

2. There is neither too much nor too little lip over the teeth. Lip contact with the reed approaches but does not reach the lip/skin color change. There is a point on the lips where they are in a position of strength (lip grip of the reed) with only moderate support from the teeth. This is a good place to be. Too much lip the over the teeth is a place where the lips are weak and the teeth become too involved in gripping the reed.

   Form the lips into a whistle. While maintaining this shape, drop the jaw. Now lay the reed on the lip, and close the top lip. This is another way to approach bassoon embouchure, one that avoids putting too much or too little lip over the teeth.

3. The jaw is down; the chin is normal—not bunched up toward the reed. As with all wind instruments, the jaw ultimately should be down. An exaggerated "OH" shape of the mouth and jaw is conducive to jaw down, though the challenge for some novices is maintaining the "OH" shape while gripping the reed and blowing an air stream.

   Ultimately, failure to get the jaw down and avoid an upward push of the jaw (biting) will cause the tone to be thin, the pitch sharp, and low register response difficult. Dropping the jaw will both open the tone, thus allowing greater resonance, and lower the pitch. Helpful techniques include:

"Say an exaggerated 'OH'," "Drop your jaw to the floor," "Make a long face," or "Create the feel and look of a stifled yawn." Biting or its less common opposite (too little lip pressure around the reed) can be detected aurally by returning to the small piece. If the pitch is above C, the student is likely biting (the jaw must be dropped and/or lip pressures reduced). If the pitch is below C, lip pressures likely need to be increased. Of course, the reliability of small piece work is dependent on the reed being suitable (neither too hard nor too soft).

The "action place" is the center of the lower lip—its contact point with the reed. If the jaw and lip are exerting too much pressure on the reed, pull the center of the lip down and/or turn it out slightly (less lip over teeth).

Another checkpoint for biting involves having the student play second space C-sharp, a note which is typically sharp. Have the student drop the jaw to match this C-sharp to a tuner. Memorize this feel and adopt it as the normal embouchure.

To develop a sense for more or less lip pressure around the reed, the teacher can make a circle with his/her thumb and finger around the student's lower forearm. By increasing and decreasing thumb/finger pressure, the teacher demonstrates too much lip pressure, not enough lip pressure, and the pressure change that is necessary to correct either.

4. Slightly upward angle of the bocal to the face. The slightly upward angle of the bocal to the face is a function of the bell being tipped forward and, for some students, the upper torso having a small amount of forward lean.

5. Optional. Create an overbite. The top lip contacts the reed nearly to the first wire. The bassoon can be played well with either embouchure—overbite or lips opposite each other. The overbite embouchure, in theory, lessens the effects of unintended biting because the lips are not opposite each other—they are offset. If the lips are opposite each other, a little biting (either the result of a faulty embouchure or simply getting tired) will close the reed and as a result raise the pitch and stifle resonance. If the lips are offset, it is harder to close the reed by biting.

Many bassoon beginners are converts from other woodwind instruments. As a teacher, it is wise to think in terms of embouchure tendencies the novice bassoon player may have from having played another instrument. Urge former clarinetists to play with a more relaxed embouchure on bassoon. The tendency to be too firm on bassoon is less of an issue for the converted saxophone player.

Breathing

When the student's tone has developed to the point of playing the above first note sequences with a tone that is sustained, *forte*, and unwavering, they are ready to begin the habit of taking a preparatory breath on beat 4. Breathing should be in tempo, shoulder-less, and as if saying a backwards "HOE." "HOE" opens the mouth and forces the breathing action to take place abdominally rather than in the chest. To take a breath on the bassoon, the jaw drops while the reed maintains contact with the upper lip. Watch for and do not allow breathing through the nose.

What to Look for in Bassoon Embouchure

1. Head. Is the head erect? Is the air stream directed straight ahead?
2. Amount of reed in the mouth. Is the top lip almost touching the first wire? The tendency is to put too little reed in the mouth.

3. Angle of bocal. Does the bocal approach the mouth at a slightly upward angle?
4. Lip. Can I see some lip outside the embouchure?
5. Mouth shape. Are the lips rounded in the shape of "OH"? Is the jaw down?

What to Listen for in Bassoon Embouchure

1. Volume. Is the student blowing a fast air stream?
2. Pitch. Is the small piece pitch a C?
3. Pitch. Is the interval between F and E (in the staff) a half step? This is an important checkpoint for the bassoon embouchure. The E should sound a half step down from F. If instead it sounds an approximate whole step down, lip pressure around the reed is too loose or the reed is too soft. The student should blow fast air and make a slightly more firm circle around the reed.
4. Tone is small and thin. The embouchure is too tight. The reed tip is too closed.
5. Tone is loud, harsh, uncontrolled. The reed tip opening may be too large, forcing the student to blow extremely hard to get any sound to come out.
6. Tone is small, soft. The reed tip may be too closed. Student cannot push enough air through the small opening to produce a big tone.

Embouchure Teaching Strategies

To Achieve Round, Open Feel with Pressures Evenly Distributed

- Lip shape, mouth formation. As if sipping on a thick milkshake through a straw, then lower the jaw as if saying "OH."
- Make a whistle formation, then drop the jaw while maintaining the whistle formation.
- Say an exaggerated "OH" or "HOW" and hold this shape.
- As if stifling a yawn.
- Lower the back of the tongue.
- Have the student, while sustaining a pitch, try to pull the *upper lip* down toward the reed. This will automatically lower the jaw.

To Promote Enough Reed in the Mouth

- "Upper lip almost touches the first wire."

To Protect the Reed from Damage

- "Catch the reed with your tongue."

Intentional Deviations from Normal Embouchure

In bassoon performance, intonation deficiencies often must be corrected by lipping, that is, deviating from the normal embouchure. A note that is sharp in pitch can be brought down by doing one or some combination of the following: Relax the grip of the lips, lower the jaw, voice (change the inner mouth shape) in the direction of a more exaggerated "OH" or "AH." All of these are aspects of lipping down. A note that is flat in pitch can be raised by doing the following: Firm the grip of the lips around the reed while keeping the jaw down, voice in the direction of EE. These are aspects of lipping up.

In the beginning stage of study, the pitch of novice woodwind players tends to sag (go flat) at the ends of last notes of phrases, last notes of pieces, and notes before rests. This sagging is particularly noticeable on the oboe and bassoon. Many novice double reed players hear this sagging effect and find it offensive (as they should!). Many soon discover that they can avoid the sagging pitch by stopping the note with the tongue—an undesirable circumstance at the end of a phrase or melody. Pitch sag happens because the air stream slows *without* an accompanying firming of the embouchure. The pitch lowers with a slower air stream; it raises with a firmer lip grip around the reed. The goal is to find the ideal combination of slower air and increased lip grip to prevent end-of-phrase pitch sag.

The performance of certain dynamics necessitates deviation from normal embouchure. On the double reed instruments, the pitch may be flat in *piano* passages or go flat as one decrescendos unless the slower air stream is countered by slightly firmer lip pressure evenly distributed around the reed. Likewise, in order to allow more air into the tip opening for *forte* or *crescendo*, the embouchure pressures must be relaxed at the same time that air speed is increased.

Finally, playing in the extreme low or high register of the bassoon necessitates deviation from normal embouchure. In order for the low register (roughly low B-flat ascending a fifth through F) to speak, the embouchure must be open and less firm than in the mid- and upper registers. In order to counter the flat tendency of the register beginning at D above the staff and above, the lips should be firmer than in lower registers, the air stream fast, and perhaps a bit more reed taken into the mouth. The jaw should stay down while the lips firm.

Vibrato

Vibrato is applied as a standard technique to both enhance and project tone on the flute, oboe, bassoon, and saxophone. A so-called diaphragmatic vibrato is commonly used on bassoon. It is more probable that the abdominal muscles, not the diaphragm, are the active agents in this type of vibrato. Say an accented "Hah!"

When for Vibrato?

Vibrato can be introduced late in the middle school years, though there should be no hurry to do so. Without question, vibrato should not be introduced before a student has had ample time to develop a well-supported and stable straight tone. One approach is to leave vibrato instruction to the private teacher. The students who study privately will tend to be ahead of the others in terms of tonal development, finger technique, and tongue technique. These students will likely occupy the top chairs. When vibrato is most advantageous—that is, during solo work—these students will be in a position to use it.

Teaching Vibrato

1. Say "Hah!" Repeat slowly to experience the initial "source" and feel of a vibrato. Then remove the vocalization, that is, "Hah" expels air, not vocal tone. Repeat.

2. Repeat "Hah" without vocalization but with a "cooling soup" embouchure. Hold your hand in front of your mouth, take a big breath, and slowly pulse the air with repeated "Hah"s so that you feel it on your hand.

3. Do the same thing into the bassoon on an easy to produce note (e.g., whisper key F or second space C). Start with slow, large, rhythmic pulsations as represented in Figure 2.15 (see page 36). As you learn to control the evenness of the pulsations, increase speed of pulsation as shown.

4. Gradually across practice sessions and multiple lessons, increase the speed of the pulses. Resist the urge to pulsate fast too soon. Concentrate on a controlled, rhythmic pulsing. Avoid the fast shake of a bleating goat.

5. Apply the above pulse rhythms to a simple tune of whole, half, and quarter notes done at a slow pace—for example, "Hot Cross Buns." Continue making the pulses rhythmic, even mechanical sounding.

6. Once this becomes a more natural act, refine by rounding the "edges" of the pulses. Work for a more fluid, less abrupt, vibrato. This often happens as a result of a practice technique involving 4, 5, 6, and 7 pulses per beat at quarter note equals 60.

Provide the opportunity for young bassoonists to hear good vibrato through live and recorded performances. For a good demonstration of a process involved in teaching vibrato, see the James Galway master class on vibrato at www.youtube.com/watch?v=u0yCw9xm0E4.

BASSOON TONGUING

Pre-tonguing Activity, Contact Point, and Vowel Shape

During initial embouchure development, "HO" (a breath attack) is used to begin sustained tones. A ballpark embouchure combined with a fast air stream should result in a sustained, *forte*, unwavering tone that is relatively in tune, that is, the student produces at or near a C on the reed and bocal and transfers this feel to the fully assembled bassoon.

The basic articulation involves touching the tip of the tongue to the tip of the bottom blade of the reed. The tip of the tongue refers to a location on top and slightly back from the actual tip of the tongue. Real tonguing resembles saying "TOE." The slightly upward angle of the bocal as it approaches the face positions the reed such that the tip of the tongue, with a small upward movement, makes contact with the tip of the reed. For the same reason, the slightly upward angle characteristic is true also of the alto, bass, and contrabass clarinet mouthpieces and the alto, tenor, and baritone sax mouthpiece. Notice that the vowel in "TOE" promotes a round feel and sense to the bassoon embouchure.

Teaching Tonguing

To introduce, develop, and assess tonguing on the bassoon, the approaches presented in the flute, clarinet, and saxophone chapters are fully applicable, of course with appropriate adaptations to bassoon. Please see the "Tonguing" section of any of those chapters.

THE BASSOON MECHANISM

Brief History

The predecessor of the bassoon was the dulcian, a one-piece instrument that was used through the beginning of the 18th century. The first bassoon appeared in the first half of the 17th century (it was specified in a composition by Schutz in 1629). This new *jointed* instrument had four joints and a greater range than the dulcian. It also featured the doubling back of the bore. The present-day German system bassoon was developed by Carl Almenraeder and J. A. Heckel in the mid-1800s.

To position this information in perspective relative to two well-known composers, Vivaldi (1678–1741) wrote more concertos for bassoon (at least 37) than he did for any other instrument except violin. The Mozart bassoon concerto, written in 1774, is perhaps the most significant work in the bassoon repertory.

Family, Transposition, and Clefs

The bassoon family consists of the bassoon and contrabassoon. The bassoon is a non-transposing instrument. The contrabassoon sounds down one octave. Parts are written in the bass, tenor, and treble clefs.

Fingering Systems

Two different fingering systems are in use in Europe—the German and the French systems. The German (or Heckel) system is used in the United States. The Heckel factory in Germany was established in 1831. The French system bassoon has a smaller bore and thinner tone quality than the German system instrument.

Interesting aside. In the 1930s there were two New York orchestras, the Symphony and the Philharmonic. Walter Damrosch, conductor of the New York Symphony believed that string players should be Russian or Polish Jews, brass players German, and woodwind players French. Therefore, French bassoons were used in his orchestra. However, the New York Philharmonic bassoonists played on German Heckel instruments. Over time and with the influence of Simon Kovar, bassoonist and teacher, the German sound and carrying power became preferred, and the Heckel and its fingering system were generally adopted in the United States. At Juilliard, there were teachers for both systems for a time.

Instrument Manufacturing

Be aware of distinctions between professional and student line models. Most manufacturers produce both; in other words, one name (e.g., Fox) comprises several different models of bassoon, student line through professional, and in the case of Fox produces both bassoons and contrabassoons. Better quality instruments will have an "even scale," meaning that the player will have to do less rather than more lipping to play a scale in tune. Better quality instruments will have an even tone quality, meaning that the tone quality of certain registers or certain notes will be less rather than more different from adjacent registers or notes.

Bassoons are made of maple or a synthetic material (e.g., polypropylene). Synthetic instruments are intended for student use. These can be very acceptable and certainly durable instruments. Wood instruments are finished with brown, black, or mahogany (brownish red) stain, none of which has an effect on playing quality.

The standard bassoon has 22 keys and four rollers. Useful extra keys or features are a high D key, an A-flat to B-flat trill key on the boot joint, extra rollers, and a whisper key lock mechanism. The most well-known professional model instrument is made by Heckel. New instrument costs range from approximately $2100 for a student line bassoon to $20,000 and more for the best professional instruments. The following lists of bassoon manufacturers are not exhaustive.

- Professional model instruments are made by manufacturers Heckel, Fox, Moosman, Puchner, Schreiber, and others.
- Student model instruments are made by manufacturers Amati, Schreiber, Olds, Selmer, Linton, Fox (Renard), and others.

The Bocal

The bocal may be the most important part of the bassoon. A good bocal on a mediocre instrument can make the instrument sound quite good. Problems with pitch, tone, response, or projection may diminish when a better quality bocal is used.

Bocals are numbered according to length (00, 0, 1, 2, 3, 4 in order of increasing length). Numbering systems are not consistent across manufacturers. Inquire about what number corresponds with A = 440 (the Schreiber number 3 bocal, for example). Letters stamped into the bocal surface refer to various characteristics, such as bore dimensions and wall thickness. Enlist the help of a professional bassoonist when dealing with bocal diagnosis and purchase. The best bocals by Heckel are cost prohibitive ($600 and up). The Fox CVX bore bocal is a good quality bocal, costing about $250.

The whisper key vent (hole) on the bocal can become clogged over time. To check for this, fill the bocal with warm water, plug the cork end with the thumb, and over a sink blow through the bocal, forcing the water out of the whisper key hole. If no water comes out, the hole is plugged and must be cleared carefully with a needle. Do this gently or the opening can be damaged.

Range and Its Divisions

The range of the bassoon spans three and a half octaves. Figure 6.21 shows the possible range in the bass clef and again with the highest note represented in the tenor clef. The F to D range is an appropriate

FIGURE 6.21 Bassoon Range

goal for a serious first-year student. The B-flat to F range should be expected of an average high school student.

Like the flute, saxophone, and oboe, the lowest notes of the bassoon require extra effort to produce. The embouchure must be open and less firm than in mid- and upper registers. In addition, the nature of the reed scrape and size of the tip opening affect instrument response. It is a challenge for even accomplished bassoonists to play at *piano* dynamic levels and articulate with finesse in the low register of the instrument.

Fingering Issues

Whisper Key

The whisper key (in Figure 6.17 above, the F key) is not an octave key or register key. The upper register of the bassoon is achieved not by depressing the whisper key. The upper register is achieved not with the help of an octave key, but primarily by firming the embouchure and increasing air speed. By *not depressing* the whisper key, the bocal vent (hole) remains open, thus allowing the upper register to speak. The low register on the bassoon is achieved by *depressing* the whisper key, which closes the bocal vent. In short, the bocal vent is open for high notes (left thumb is up) and closed for low notes (left thumb is down).

In contrast, on the saxophone and oboe, the upper register is achieved by depressing the octave key, which opens a hole. On the clarinet, the upper register is achieved by depressing a register key, which opens a hole and raises the pitch a 12th.

The pancake key (in Figure 6.15 above, the E key), used to produce low notes, also closes the bocal vent. There is no need to depress the whisper key (left thumb) when the pancake key is depressed by the right thumb. The whisper key is sometimes neglected by beginners. Police their use of it. In Figure 6.22, the low B-flat to E range requires use of the pancake key, which closes the bocal vent. The F to G-sharp range requires use of the whisper key (left thumb), which closes the bocal vent.

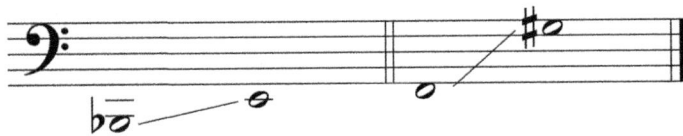

FIGURE 6.22 Whisper Key Range

Half-Hole

The notes in Figure 6.23 sound in the correct octave when the first finger slides down (or rocks) from its normal position, thus opening part of the hole. The half-hole acts like an octave key; it raises the pitch one octave. If you get a growl on half-hole notes, this is a sign that the hole is not uncovered enough or is uncovered too much. It is important to note that the thumb depresses the whisper key for these three notes. A common mistake made by novice bassoonists is to raise the thumb during half-hole notes.

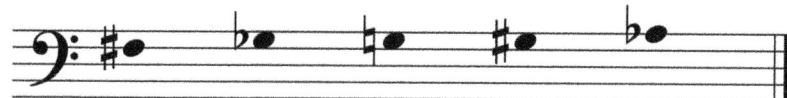

FIGURE 6.23 Half-Hole Notes

Left Thumb

Up to nine left thumb keys, shown in Figure 6.24, necessitate that the thumb vary from a normal curved position when playing most whisper key notes (F in Figure) to a flat position in order to depress multiple keys (e.g., for second space C-sharp) to a knuckle contact point in order to rock between adjacent keys (low C to B).

The second space C-sharp, notated in Figure 6.25 is an unusual fingering. It requires that three thumb keys be depressed at once. Depress both the whisper key and the adjacent C-sharp key. Then flatten the thumb to depress the low D key, contacting it near the base of the thumb. The fingering for C-sharp *above* the staff involves just two thumb keys—the C-sharp key and the low D key. In ascending from C to C-sharp (measure 2), position the thumb high on the whisper key for C. Then rock or "lean" the thumb into the bottom of the C-sharp key while flattening the thumb to reach the D key. In descending from C-sharp to D, rock the thumb back to the whisper key.

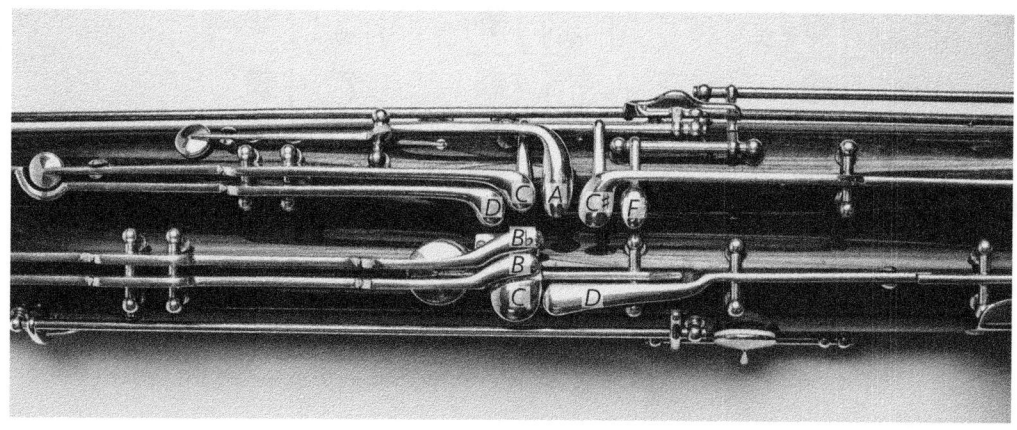

FIGURE 6.24 Left-Hand Thumb Keys Labeled
(Produced by Paige Jarreau at Paige's Photos)

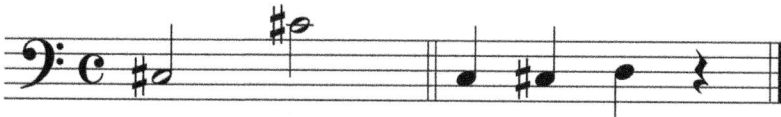

FIGURE 6.25 C-sharps

Right Thumb or Pinky?

The use of the right thumb or pinky on bassoon is similar in concept to cross-fingerings on clarinet and oboe. There are two fingerings each for F-sharp and G-sharp (low and middle registers) on the bassoon. As shown in the fingering charts of Figure 6.26, one fingering involves the right thumb, the other involves the right pinky finger. The objective is to avoid using consecutive pinky fingers or consecutive thumbs.

When a note preceding or following F-sharp or G-sharp involves the right thumb, use the pinky fingering for F-sharp and G-sharp. In the E major scale of Figure 6.26, the first F-sharp follows an E, which involves the right thumb. So for F-sharp use the right pinky fingering, as pictured. Following the same logic, use the right thumb for G-sharp. In the second octave of the scale, Figure 6.26 shows the option of using a thumb/pinky (T/P) progression or the reverse.

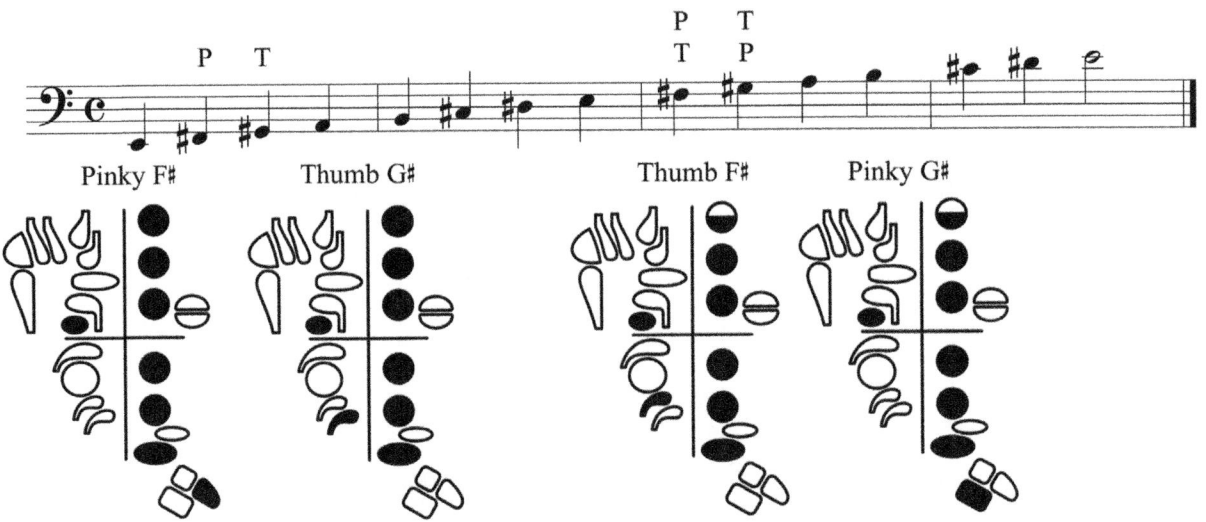

FIGURE 6.26 Thumb or Pinky?

Flick Key Technique

One of the imperfections of the bassoon mechanism is its reluctance to allow a clean slur involving wide intervals ending on the notes shown in Figure 6.27. For example, try slurring from low A to top line A by simply raising the whisper key. Frequently, the slurred-to note responds slowly or in the wrong octave or as a squawk. Flicking a key will allow a clean slur. Here's how it works. In coordination with the note change, slide the thumb from whisper up to the flick key (indicated below the staff in Figure 6.27) and then immediately off the key. This technique is typically thought of as an intermediate level challenge, but it becomes a necessity at whatever point the music calls for it.

Figure 6.24 shows the A, C, and D keys that serve as flick keys for the notes in Figure 6.27. The one-measure excerpts in Figure 6.28, the first two of which are not uncommon in middle school band music, are best performed with the flick key technique. Flick the A key simultaneously with the onset of the second note in each measure. In the first two measures, the thumb slides deftly from whisper key to the flick key, for an instant opening the tone hole, then immediately off.

Flick the high: A key-------------------C key--------------------C or D key

FIGURE 6.27 Flick Key Notes

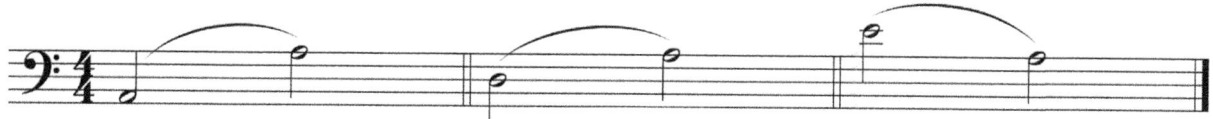

FIGURE 6.28 Flick Key Passages

Alternate Fingerings for E-flat

The E-flat in Figure 6.29 is often difficult to control using the standard T–1–3 fingering. To stabilize it, add the thumb B-flat key or the right second finger *or* both as shown in Figure 6.29. These alternate fingerings are referred to as *long* or *resonance* fingerings for E-flat.

Tenor Clef

Upper intermediate and advanced solo literature, Grades V and VI band literature, and the standard orchestral literature will on occasion require the bassoonist to read the tenor clef. It is used in high register playing in order to reduce the number of ledger lines that would be necessary if the bass clef were used. In Figure 6.30, notice the ledger lines in this comparison of bass and tenor clef unison note sequences. Private bassoon instruction at the intermediate level and beyond should include experience in reading the tenor clef. One source for tenor clef reading is *Introducing the Tenor Clef for Trombone (Bassoon)* by Reginald Fink.

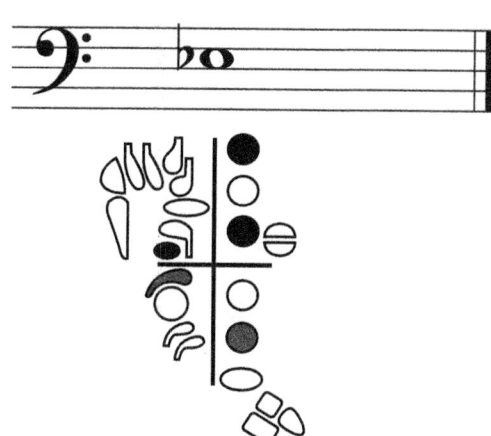

FIGURE 6.29 Alternate Fingerings for E-flat

FIGURE 6.30 Tenor Clef

Some Trill Fingerings

Many trills on woodwind instruments are performed by using the primary fingerings of the notes involved. For some trills, however, primary fingerings don't allow facile trilling. Special trill keys and trill fingerings exist to make trills possible that otherwise would be awkward or impossible. The collection in Figures 6.31a and 6.31b is not exhaustive. Refer to the Internet for more comprehensive trill fingering collections.

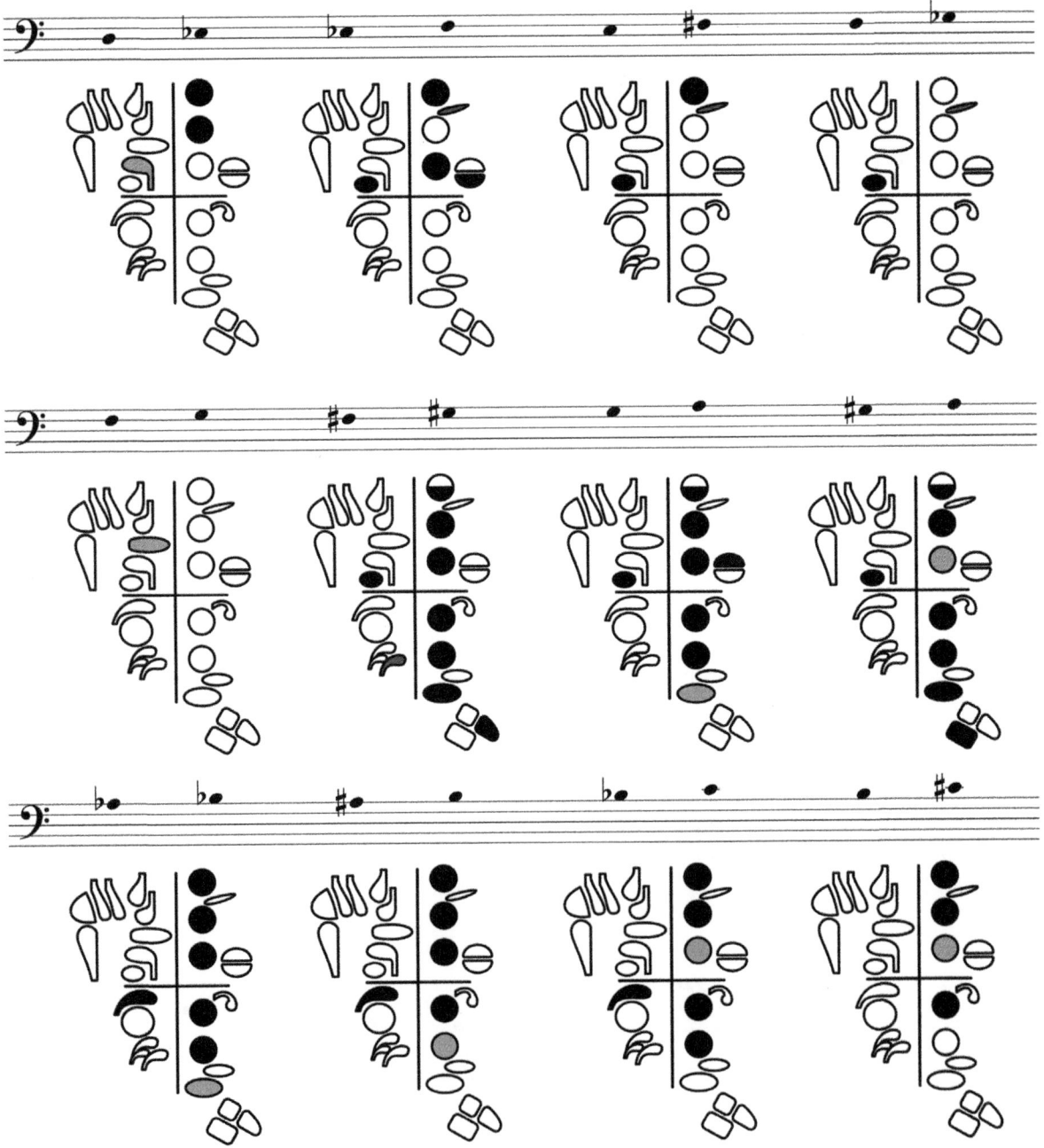

FIGURE 6.31A Bassoon Trill Fingerings page 1

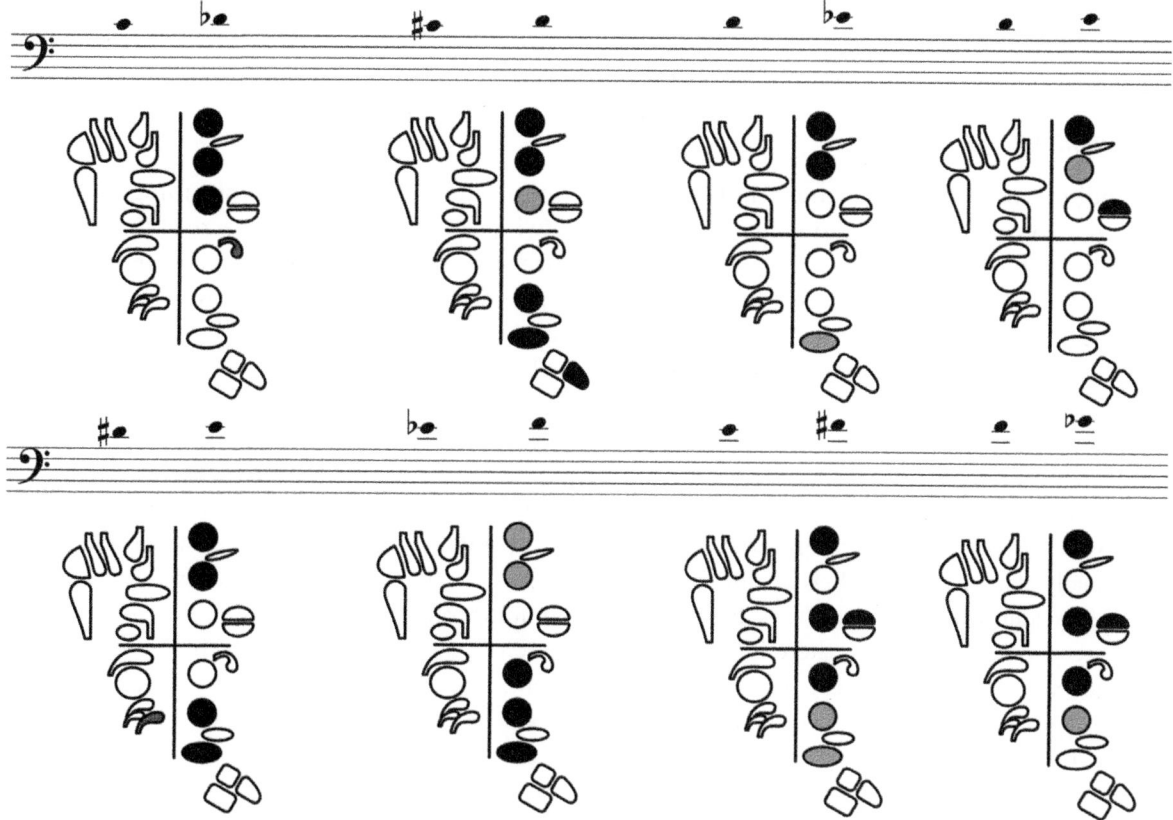

FIGURE 6.31B Bassoon Trill Fingerings page 2

Tuning and Intonation

Tuning Notes

Figure 6.32 shows bassoon tuning notes—the orchestra A and the traditional band B-flat. Unlike the flute, clarinet, and saxophone, where pushing and pulling instrument parts is a standard way of adjusting pitch, the intonation of the bassoon is "built into" the reed. The reed must crow a loose

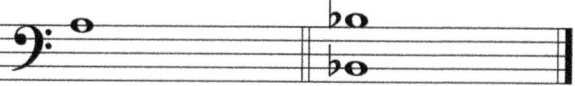

FIGURE 6.32 Bassoon Tuning Notes

rattle in order for the instrument to be in the A = 440 ballpark. There is very little room at the bocal to push and pull. There is some room to pull the bass joint at the boot intersection that helps lower the pitch of a naturally sharp low register. So the orchestra and band "tuning" notes serve as little more than "checks" for tuning. If out of tune, the likely source in need of attention is the reed.

Recall that bocals are made in slightly differing lengths. Use a bocal whose length corresponds to A 440. For sharpness, it is logical to think that the bocal should be pulled, watching of course that the whisper key vent remains covered by the whisper key. But in fact, pulling more than 1/4 inch (6mm) may actually cause more intonation problems.

A discussion of intonation as it pertains to the bassoon can be organized into six primary areas: a) reed condition, b) amount of reed in the mouth, c) embouchure flaws, d) instrument register, e) individual notes, and f) the bocal.

Reed Condition: The Crow

The condition of the reed has much influence on bassoon pitch level, among other things. One way to discern reed condition is to crow the reed. A reed crow is produced by putting the reed in the mouth, with both lips to the first wire, and blowing an unfocused stream of air into it. A quasi-embouchure is used, not the formal bassoon embouchure. The lips simply seal around the reed. Blow at a *mf* dynamic level. The objective is to test the reed's capacity to vibrate naturally, unencumbered by lip pressure. This allows the teacher and student access to the reed's baseline condition or quality. Bassoonists who make their own reeds use the crow frequently during the final stages of reed making. The crow provides information they need in order to know what to do next in the reed-making process.

A bassoon reed should crow a loose rattle or several pitches, both low and high at once. The reed is soft when there is little or no high pitch in the crow. On the instrument, a soft reed will sound reedy in the low register. The upper register will be difficult to produce. The overall pitch level will be flat. An unusually flat third space E is an indication that the reed may be too soft. Minor softness can be corrected by adjusting the wires (see "Basic Reed Troubleshooting" below).

The reed is too hard when there is little or no low pitch in the crow, and when the crow is difficult to produce without blowing very hard. On the instrument, a hard reed will sound rough or unrefined. The low register will be slow to respond. Soft playing will be difficult or impossible. Hardness can be corrected by some combination of scraping, sanding, and wire adjustment.

The effective music teacher, despite lack of reed-making skill, can reduce or even prevent much of the frustration that is incorrectly assumed to be an unavoidable right of passage in bassoon life. The teacher who crows a reed and understands the information provided by the crow knows what can be expected of the bassoon player. If the crow is a loose rattle, the student can be expected to play reasonably in tune with good control of tone and response. The more the crow departs from the loose rattle, the more difficult it will be for the student to play in tune. He or she will have to fight the reed by making embouchure changes to make it work.

Amount of Reed in the Mouth

Be aware of the tendency of novice students to put too little reed in the mouth. This will cause the pitch to be flat. Too much reed in the mouth, a much less common occurrence, will cause the tone to be some combination of strident, rough, and honky. Response will be difficult to control.

Embouchure Flaws

As with all wind instruments, lip/jaw pressures that are too tight will cause sharpness; too loose, flatness. However, these embouchure *flaws* are used to remedy pitch problems. A sharp note can be lipped down by loosening or relaxing the lips. A flat note can be lipped up by firming the lips around the reed.

If the reed is appropriate, the small piece (reed and bocal) pitch should be C. Lip pressures can be gauged and the embouchure *tuned* using this C target. If the lips are too tight (biting), the pitch will be sharp to C. If too loose, the pitch will be flat to C.

Register

In preparation for rehearsal, a thorough analysis of a musical score includes consideration of the pitch tendencies of the bassoon. By knowing pitch tendencies, the effective music teacher is able to predict what might happen with regard to pitch in the lesson or rehearsal. One's job in rehearsal is to listen and discern whether student performance is consistent with the tendencies. If it is, the teacher must know what to do to solve the problem.

The bassoon's low register (lowest B-flat up to bottom line G) tends to be sharp. One must get in the habit of lipping down (dropping the jaw, relaxing lip pressures, lowering the back of the tongue) in this register. The bass joint or bell or both may be pulled to compensate for low register sharpness. For extreme sharpness, take less reed into the mouth.

The upper register (D above the staff up to F) tends to be flat. Firm the lips slightly and blow a faster air stream. In extreme cases, take more reed into the mouth, even touching the first wire in the highest part of the playing range.

Individual Notes

The half-hole notes in the staff tend to be sharp. One must get in the habit of lipping down or relaxing lip pressures for these notes. On half-hole G, many bassoonists add the low E-flat key (top left pinky) or the pancake key (right thumb) to enhance tone quality and bring the pitch down. In addition, it is beneficial to open more rather than less of the half hole when playing G. G will tend to squawk if the half hole is not open enough or if the half hole opens late in the sequence of fingerings.

Third space E-flat is a notoriously unstable note. Depending on instrument, bocal, and reed, this E-flat can be sharp, flat, or just wild. Lipping is necessary, but the problem is difficult to remedy. As detailed in Figure 6.29, use a long fingering for E-flat.

Bocal

If the reed is slightly flat, but otherwise good, change to a shorter bocal. If the reed is slightly sharp, but otherwise good, change to a longer bocal. The bocal can be the cause of intonation problems. When E and F in the staff are consistently flat, when middle G is more than normally sharp, or when E-flat in the staff is more than normally unstable or sharp, the bocal may be the problem. Try another bocal and test these notes.

Certain notes will be sharp in pitch when the instrument leaks, that is, when a pad or pads is not sealing completely.

Tuning and Intonation Summary

- Is the reed in tune?
    - Reed should crow a loose rattle
- Tuning the embouchure
    - If the reed is right, reed and bocal pitch should be C
- Tuning notes (orchestra, band)
    - Play with best embouchure and at *f* dynamic level
    - Bocal cannot be pulled beyond whisper key coverage of vent hole
    - Bocal can be source of intonation problems. Try another

- Pitch tendencies
    - Register (low = sharp; mid-upper—D to F = flat)
    - Reed (soft = flat; hard = sharp)
    - Bad notes (most notorious: half-hole notes = sharp; third space E-flat = unstable)
- Solutions
    - Reed
    - Is there enough reed in the mouth?
    - Pull the bass joint, bell, or both to compensate for low register sharpness
    - Lip a lot! Lip down for the low register and the hole notes
    - Special fingerings: To half-hole G, add the top pinky key in the left hand; to unstable E-flat, add some combination of thumb B-flat or right second finger.

Bassoon Reeds

It is tempting for music teachers who are not woodwind majors to assume that "I can't possibly have much to offer my students about reeds. There is so much to know, including how to make and adjust them, I couldn't possibly learn all that."

It is not necessary to *learn all that* to be an effective teacher of woodwinds. It is, however, reasonable to expect the non-bassoonist music teacher to be familiar with and use basic information about reeds. Take for example any of the wetting, crowing, storing, and rotating information below. A teacher uses this information in one or both of two ways: By teaching it to beginning bassoon players or by observing the behaviors of experienced players, noting what they do and don't do, then leading them to do what is suggested. If you use this information in your teaching, you will be pleasantly surprised at "how much you have to offer your students about reeds."

In the university woodwind class, do what is necessary to acquire a good bassoon reed for yourself. Study its feel and appearance. At the completion of the course, save it for future reference.

Wetting the Reed

The reed must be wet in order to respond optimally. There are a number of soaking tips that can make bassoon life easier:

1. In instrument assembly, the first step is to soak the reed. It should be soaking while the rest of the instrument is being dealt with.
2. Soak *all* of the reed for roughly 3 minutes in water.
3. Warm water works faster than cold water.
4. Soaking in tap water rather than saliva will prolong the life of a reed.
5. During long periods of no play in rehearsal or performance, blowing warm air through the reed and instrument will keep the reed from drying out.

Use of a water-tight container (prescription pill container, small cylinder bottle) that can be stored in a bassoon case cover is an optimal condition. Minus a water container, get the reed wet with a "splash" of tap water and allow the water to remain on and inside the reed as you set it aside during instrument assembly. During this time the reed is "soaking."

Crowing the Reed

A bassoon reed should crow a loose rattle or several pitches, both low and high (but more low) at once. The reed is soft when there is little or no high pitch in the crow. On the instrument, a soft reed will sound reedy in the low register. The upper register will be difficult to produce. The overall pitch level will be flat. An unusually flat third space E is an indication that the reed may be too soft. Create a vacuum by plugging the end of the reed and sucking the air out of the reed. If the reed holds a vacuum for more than a second, it is too soft. Minor softness can be corrected by adjusting the wires. See below.

The reed is too hard when there is little or no low pitch in the crow, and when the crow is difficult to produce without blowing very hard. On the instrument, a hard reed will sound rough or unrefined. The low register will be slow to respond. Soft playing will be difficult or impossible. Hardness can be corrected by some combination of scraping, sanding, and wire adjustment. A more complete description of the reed crow can be found above in the section "Tuning and Intonation."

Storing

Place reeds carefully in cases that allow them to dry completely between playings. Reeds that do not dry will develop mildew. Four-, five-, and six-reed cases are available commercially for $10–15 (see Figure 6.14 above). Rectangular *Sucrets* or *Altoids* mints containers are good alternatives. Plastic versions of these do not rust as metal is prone to do. Create a bed of tissue paper on the floor of the container. Secure the reeds with tissue paper on top. Cases designed to hold three or four reeds allow drying and can be purchased for $10–15.

If the clear plastic cylinder-type container is the only choice for storage, the teacher should make two air holes in it to allow the reed to dry during storage. Otherwise, mildew will develop. Students should be made aware of how easy it is to damage the tip of the reed when placing it in this type of container. As the reed tip is brought to the mouth of the container, anchor a finger or fingers on the container in order to steady the hand. Then guide the tip through the opening in a controlled manner.

Rotating

Ideally the bassoon player should have at least two reeds that work effectively and that are used in a rotation—a Monday–Wednesday–Friday–Sunday reed and a Tuesday–Thursday–Saturday–Monday reed. The constant use of one reed will wear it out quickly. Because no two reeds will play or feel exactly alike, rotating reeds makes the player (and the embouchure) more flexible. The player will learn to tolerate a wider range of reeds—from those that feel perfect to those that are less than perfect, but still playable. The change to a new reed by students who play one reed until it dies is traumatic. These students are not able to tolerate the different feel of the new reed.

Evaluating Quality

All reeds, both single and double, are evaluated on five criteria: Response, pitch, stability, dynamic range, and tone quality.

1. Response is vibration. Above all else, a reed must respond immediately to the air and tongue.
2. The pitch level of the bassoon is in large part dependent on the pitch level that has been built into the reed. Often, if reed response is good, pitch level will also be good.

3. A reed is stable when certain notes (e.g., E-flat, E, F, and C-sharp in the staff) are not flat in pitch when sustained.

4. The ideal reed allows controlled playing at both *f* and *p* levels with relative ease.

5. Tone quality will vary from player to player along a range of bright to dark, and is related both to player characteristics (embouchure, air stream, tonal concept) and reed attributes. Tone quality as it relates to reed building doesn't much matter unless the reed responds, is in tune, and is stable.

Reed Parts

The names and functions of the parts of the bassoon reed are situated here near the end of the "Bassoon Reeds" section to show the reader how much practical and helpful information there is to know about reeds, even *without* knowing the names of the parts. This is not meant to imply that knowing the names of reed parts is unimportant. It is meant to point out that if one were to create a rating scale for bassoon reed information ranging from least to most useful (to the teacher and student), wetting, storing, crowing, rotating, evaluating, and purchasing would have priority status over naming the reed parts. Nevertheless, Figure 6.33 shows the following:

- The cut. This is the portion of the cane from tip almost to the first wire, which has been scraped by a machine or reed maker. You see symmetry in the cut. The reed maker has tried to scrape cane evenly across the left and right halves of each blade. Through backlighting, one should be able to see this symmetry and also that one blade looks like the other blade, signs of good craftsmanship.

- The tip. The area above Letter A is the tip. The tip must be scraped thin enough to allow vibrations to begin and travel down the reed.

- The back. The area at and below Letter B is the back of the reed. Cane is scraped here in order to allow vibrations to travel down into the reed. Only somewhat visible in Figure 6.33 is the fact that the center of the reed, the vertical line extending beneath Letters A and B, has been left heavier with cane in order to provide a spine-like and stabilizing structure to the reed. To either side of this center, the sides of the reed are scraped somewhat thinner.

- The wires. Letter C is the first wire. Letter D is the second wire. And there is a third wire underneath the winding (Letter E).

- The tube. Letter F designates the tube end of the reed, which joins the bocal.

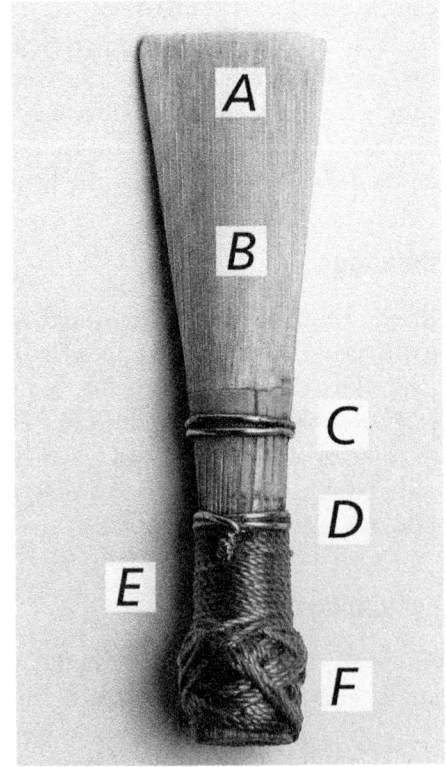

FIGURE 6.33 Bassoon Reed Parts
(Produced by Paige Jarreau at Paige's Photos)

The Needs of Novice Players

Novice bassoon players should play softer reeds that have good response, pitch, and stability. These qualities allow the embouchure to develop properly. In other words, bad habits are not promoted, as they would be if response, pitch, or stability were deficient. These same reeds, however, may be deficient in dynamic range (they may play loud easily, but not soft, or soft easily, but not loud) and tone quality (they may sound bright and thin, not dark and rich). The music teacher must realize that these compromises are a necessary evil of the life of a novice bassoon player. As the embouchure strengthens, so too can reed strength, which makes available more options in terms of dynamic range and tone quality.

Store-Bought Reeds

Commercial reeds can be purchased at music stores and by mail order. They come in different strengths (labeled soft, medium soft, medium, medium hard, hard). A reed at the softer end of the scale will respond (vibrate) with less effort (less embouchure strength) and produce a brighter, thinner tone than will a harder reed. A harder reed produces a darker, less reedy tone.

The quality of store-bought reeds varies widely. Many are too hard, that is, too much cane has been left on. Students struggle to make them work, and tire quickly. Tone is harsh, pitch is sharp, and response difficult. These are not necessarily bad reeds; they just aren't finished. Cane must be removed and the wires adjusted (for tip opening).

Visual Characteristics of a Reed

If you have the option of choosing a reed from a selection of reeds, choose as follows.

1. Cane should be gold, not green or spotted.

2. Cane should have a tight grain.

3. The tip should open about 1/16 inch (1.5mm) at its widest point. The tip opening can be adjusted by manipulating with pliers one or both of the first two wires. (A third wire is located under the winding.) (See "Reed Basic Troubleshooting" below for information on how to adjust the size of the tip opening.)

4. The tip opening should be symmetrical. Figure 6.34 shows a tip opening that is symmetrical and about 1/16 inch (1.5mm) at its widest.

5. When looking at the reed with and without backlighting, one blade should look like the other. Further, the left half of one blade should look like the right half of the same blade. In other words, the scraping and sanding of cane from the blades should result in a symmetrical or nearly symmetrical look. If not, the workmanship is faulty.

FIGURE 6.34 Bassoon Reed Tip Opening
(Produced by Paige Jarreau at Paige's Photos)

Reed Sources

Refer to catalogs that feature woodwind products to learn more about reed selection and specifications. One catalog lists 14 reed brands. Prices per reed range from $7.00 to roughly $22.00. Reeds come in student and professional quality grades. The Meason bassoon reed is a decent commercially made student reed that sells for about $7.00. Plastic or fibercane reeds are not recommended because they are typically unstable.

There are many commercial bassoon reed sources. The list, which follows, is not exhaustive.

- Charles Double Reed Co., www.charlesmusic.com
- Hodge Products, Inc., www.annhodge.com
- Forrests: The Double Reed Specialists, www.forestsmusic.com
- Frederic H. Weiner, Inc., www.weinermusic.com
- The Woodwind & Brasswind, www.wwbw.com.

If a good reed source can often be found locally, this is preferable to the above sources. Contact a private teacher or university bassoon major who is an accomplished reed maker (not all are) to inquire about reeds and reed adjustment.

Two publications provide much practical information on bassoon reeds. They are *Teacher's Guide to the Bassoon* by Homer Pence (published by Selmer) and *Bassoon Reed Making* by Mark Popkin and Loren Glickman (published by The Instrumentalist).

Basic Reed Troubleshooting

Tip Opening Adjustment

There is one reed adjustment that can be made by the teacher who has limited or no reed-making skill. It involves the tip opening, and requires only a pair of needle nose pliers. Visually, the tip opening should be about 1/16 inch (1.5mm) at its widest point. However, a more precise gauge of whether the tip opening is appropriate is the response of the reed when played.

Indicators that the tip opening may be too closed are a thin, reedy tone, flat pitch level, and difficult upper register response. Open the tip opening by squeezing the sides of the first wire with pliers. In Figure 6.33, the first wire is the top wire. An indicator that the tip opening may be too open is difficult response—the reed is hard to make vibrate. Close the tip opening by squeezing at the top and bottom of the first wire. When working with pliers, the reed must be wet. Look at the tip opening while squeezing. Make only small adjustments before trying the reed on the instrument. When you see any movement of the blades at all, stop and test it by playing.

The inexpensive pamphlet *Teacher's Guide to the Bassoon* by Homer Pence (published by Selmer) is an excellent source for more complete information on wire adjustment.

Leak in Reed

A leak in the reed is easy to diagnose and relatively easy to repair, though repair is probably beyond the scope of the teacher without reed-making skill. If while playing the student gets a swish-like, airy quality to the tone, the reed may be leaking out one side. To test for a reed leak, plug the end of the reed with a finger and blow into the reed. Soaking the reed longer may fix the problem. If not, have the student play with the reed turned one way, then the other way on the bocal. Sometimes you hear the leak with the reed turned one way, but not the other. A final fix involves tightening the wires and re-testing, a process not suggested for the non reed-maker.

Leak at Juncture of Reed and Bocal

A swish-like, airy tone quality could also result from a leak at the juncture of reed and bocal. To test for this, plug the cork end of the bocal along with the whisper key hole. Blow into the reed. If air leaks out of the junction of reed and bocal, a reed-maker would ream the tube end of the reed with tool called a reamer. The reamer will take cane out of the tube, allowing the reed to fit farther onto the bocal. Reeds that leak as they join the bocal indicate that the tube is not perfectly round. The reamer will allow the removal of a small amount of cane to correct.

Getting Extra Life out of an Old Reed

As a last resort, extra life can be coaxed out of an old, dying reed by inserting paper between the blades of a wet reed. Close the reed tip onto the paper and pull the paper out. This will remove some but not all of the build-up on the inside of the reed. This build-up is a part of all reeds and is one reason that good reeds are good. Removing all of it will change the reed drastically. Removing some of it (as is the aim with the procedure describe above) will change the reed less drastically. It may make it feel more open and play with better response. Use this technique only as a last resort in an attempt to temporarily revive an old reed.

Another reed-reviving procedure involves lightly scraping off the dead, discolored cane on the outside of the reed.

The band or orchestra director need not have reed-making skill to guide and work effectively with bassoon students. One must, however, compensate for lack of reed-making skill by securing a good private teacher (one who makes reeds!); otherwise finding a good reed-making source, and helping students (and parents) with reed issues (purchase, soaking, storing, drying, rotating, sources, detecting deterioration) become the responsibility of the band or orchestra director.

INITIAL PLAYING MATERIAL

Functional initial performance experiences for university students learning to play secondary flute, clarinet, and saxophone in class settings can be found in any number of beginning band method books. The concert B-flat key orientation of these method books, however, is not conducive to good initial performance experiences for bassoon. The key of B-flat requires use of a somewhat complicated B-flat fingering, an unstable and awkward fingering in third-space E-flat, half-hole G, and crossing the break.

For this reason, I provide in Figures 6.35, 6.36, 6.37, 6.38, and 6.39 five sets of playing exercises intended to introduce and orient the university student in a "friendly" way to secondary bassoon. Consider also the bassoon-specific *Rubank Elementary Method for Bassoon*.

Set 1 exercises focus on the left hand and tongue. Set 2 exercises focus on the right hand. Set 3 exercises extend into the second octave and use of the half hole. Set 4 introduces the chromatic notes of the left hand. Set 5 does the same in the right hand.

FIGURE 6.35 Bassoon Left-Hand Exercises

FIGURE 6.36 Bassoon Right-Hand Exercises

FIGURE 6.37 Bassoon Second Octave Exercises

FIGURE 6.38 Bassoon Left-Hand Chromatics

FIGURE 6.39 Bassoon Right-Hand Chromatics

STUDY QUESTIONS

1. In terms of students selecting and teachers assigning students to play the bassoon, there are four differences between bassoon playing and flute, clarinet, and alto sax playing that should be considered. In a few words, summarize these.

2. Summarize the desired traits in one who is a good candidate for bassoon study.

3. That the bassoon is inherently harder than flute, clarinet, and saxophone is a misconception. Why is this a misconception?

4. Describe the ideal sound of a bassoon reed crow.

5. Under what conditions should the player be able to produce the desired C pitch on the bassoon reed and bocal?

6. How much of the bassoon reed should be soaked?

7. How is the bassoon seat strap situated on the chair?

8. "Small hole to the right" refers to what in bassoon assembly?

9. There is a lock mechanism on most bassoons. Where is it located? What does it do?

10. "Grasp at the curve" refers to what in bassoon assembly?

11. The torso is situated how when playing the bassoon?

12. Demonstrate removal of water from the bocal in disassembly.

13. How and how often should the bassoon bocal be swabbed?

14. In bassoon disassembly, what should happen every time with the boot joint?

15. Demonstrate "traveling with" the bassoon.

16. There is one peculiarity about the top hand index finger in bassoon hand position. What is it?

17. Demonstrate and describe the two angles in holding the bassoon.

18. Make a list of what to look for in bassoon hand position and holding. Use jog-your-memory words only.

19. In the bassoon embouchure, describe:

    a. The amount of reed inside the mouth
    b. The angle of the bocal
    c. The shape of the lips and mouth
    d. The position of the jaw.

20. During a breath, what part of the embouchure remains in contact with the reed?

21. When you practice the bassoon, are you thinking and doing the details listed under "What to Look for in Embouchure" so that you are better able to use this information in your observational role as teacher?

22. When you practice:
    a. Does the reed crow a loose rattle?
    b. Are you blowing a fast air stream?
    c. Do you get a *forte* C when you play the reed and bocal alone?
    d. Is the interval between thumb F and E a half step or a whole step? It not, firm up the lip circle around the reed.

23. Is bassoon vibrato produced the same as flute vibrato? Explain.

24. Before tonguing is introduced bassoon players should use what consonant/vowel to start tone? Why?

25. Bassoon music is written in what clefs?

26. The most well-known profession model bassoon is made by . . .

27. Bocal length. Explain.

28. What is the function of the whisper key on bassoon?

29. Third space E-flat is an unstable note. What can one do to stabilize it? What works best on your bassoon?

30. Demonstrate your reed crow. Is it a loose rattle? If not, is there little or no high pitch? Or little or not low pitch? What does all this mean in terms of what you can expect from your student on this reed?

31. How much bassoon reed should be inside the mouth?

32. Indicate bassoon pitch tendencies for the following conditions:
    a. Low register
    b. D above the staff up to F
    c. Half-hole G.

33. Talk smart about solving the sharp half-hole G.

34. Talk smart about storing the bassoon reed.

35. Reed tip opening is often a source of problems (tone, pitch, response) for bassoon players. It is quite easy to adjust the size of the opening, even for a novice reed adjuster. Explain.

PERFORMANCE TESTING OF UNIVERSITY STUDENTS ON SECONDARY INSTRUMENTS

A rubric is an evaluative tool. The rubric that follows makes clear the expectations of the university student playing secondary bassoon as he or she approaches the end of an intensive three or four weeks of study. Students may use the criteria to prepare for performance testing and to self-evaluate. Teachers may use the criteria to structure feedback.

1. Assembled the instrument properly:

a.	Wet all of the reed	Yes	No
b.	Small hole to the right	Yes	No
c.	Thumb keys make continuous circle	Yes	No
d.	Grasped bocal at the curve	Yes	No

2. Positioned bassoon properly:

a.	Seat strap 2 inches from front of chair	Yes	No
b.	Slight forward lean of upper torso	Yes	No
c.	Head was erect	Yes	No
d.	Two instrument angles were maintained	Yes	No

3. Reed crow:

a.	Crowed the reed with enough reed in mouth	Yes	No
b.	Achieved a loose rattle crow	Yes	No

4. Formed a characteristic embouchure:

a.	Upper lip almost to first wire	Yes	No
b.	Optimal amount of lip over bottom teeth	Yes	No
c.	Jaw down in exaggerated fashion	Yes	No

5. Tone:

a.	Achieved a characteristic basic tone—*forte*, freely vibrating, and unwavering tone	Yes	No
b.	Played in tune 90% of the time	Yes	No
c.	Lipped down half-hole notes to avoid sharp tendency	Yes	No

6.	Breathing:		
	a. In taking a breath, the upper lip stayed in contact with the reed	Yes	No
	b. Breathed according to phrase	Yes	No
7.	Fingers:		
	a. Maintained correct hand position	Yes	No
	b. Recalled and played primary fingerings in the range from low E to E-flat above middle C	Yes	No
	c. Recalled and played the long fingering for E-flat	Yes	No
	d. Recalled and played alternate fingerings for F-sharp and G-sharp	Yes	No
8.	Articulation:		
	a. Tongued and slurred as marked in the music	Yes	No
	b. Legato tongued convincingly	Yes	No
9.	Expressive performance:		
	a. Varied dynamic and tempo as appropriate for expressive effect	Yes	No

BASSOON FINGERING CHART

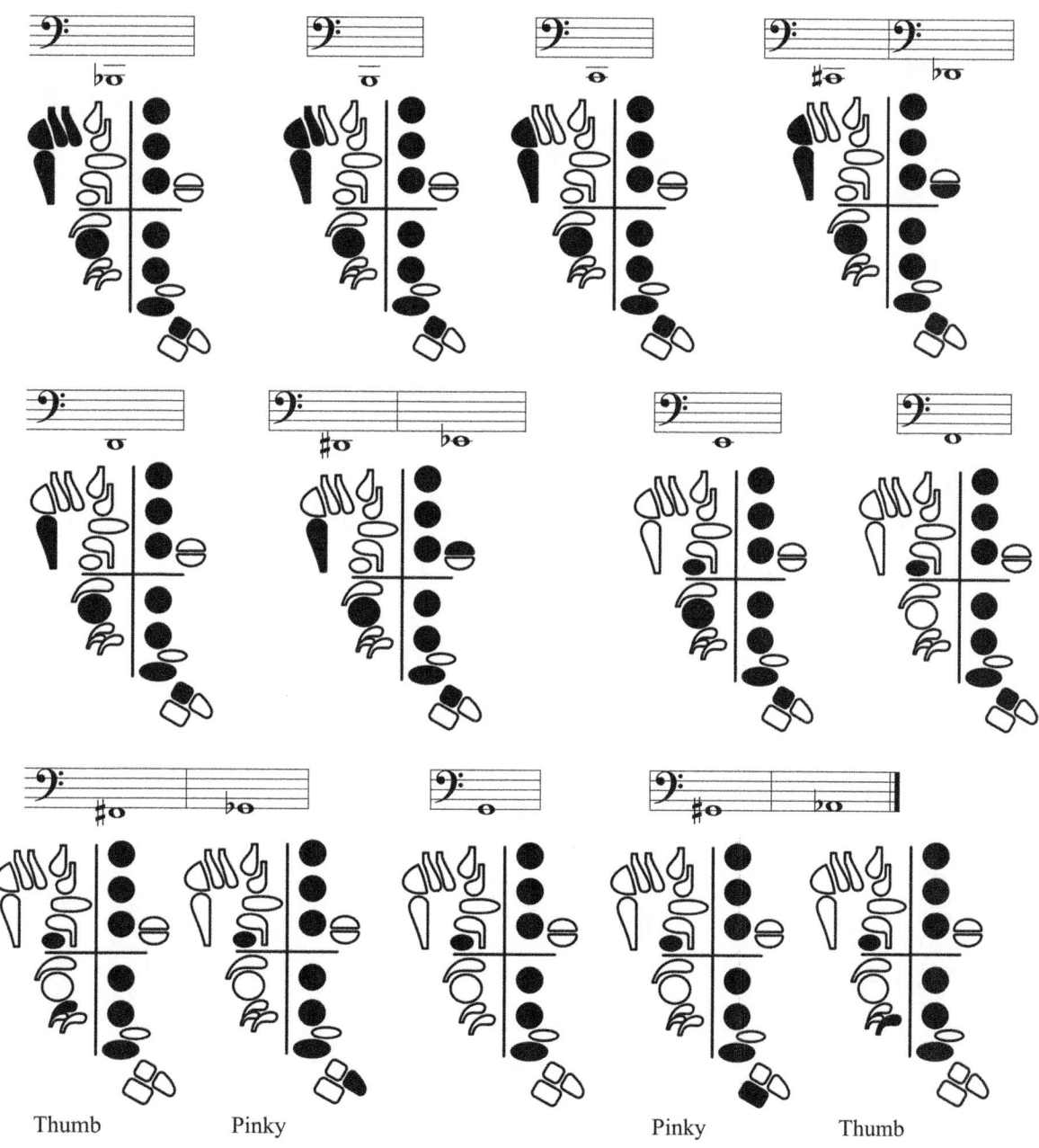

FIGURE 6.40A Bassoon Fingering Chart page 1

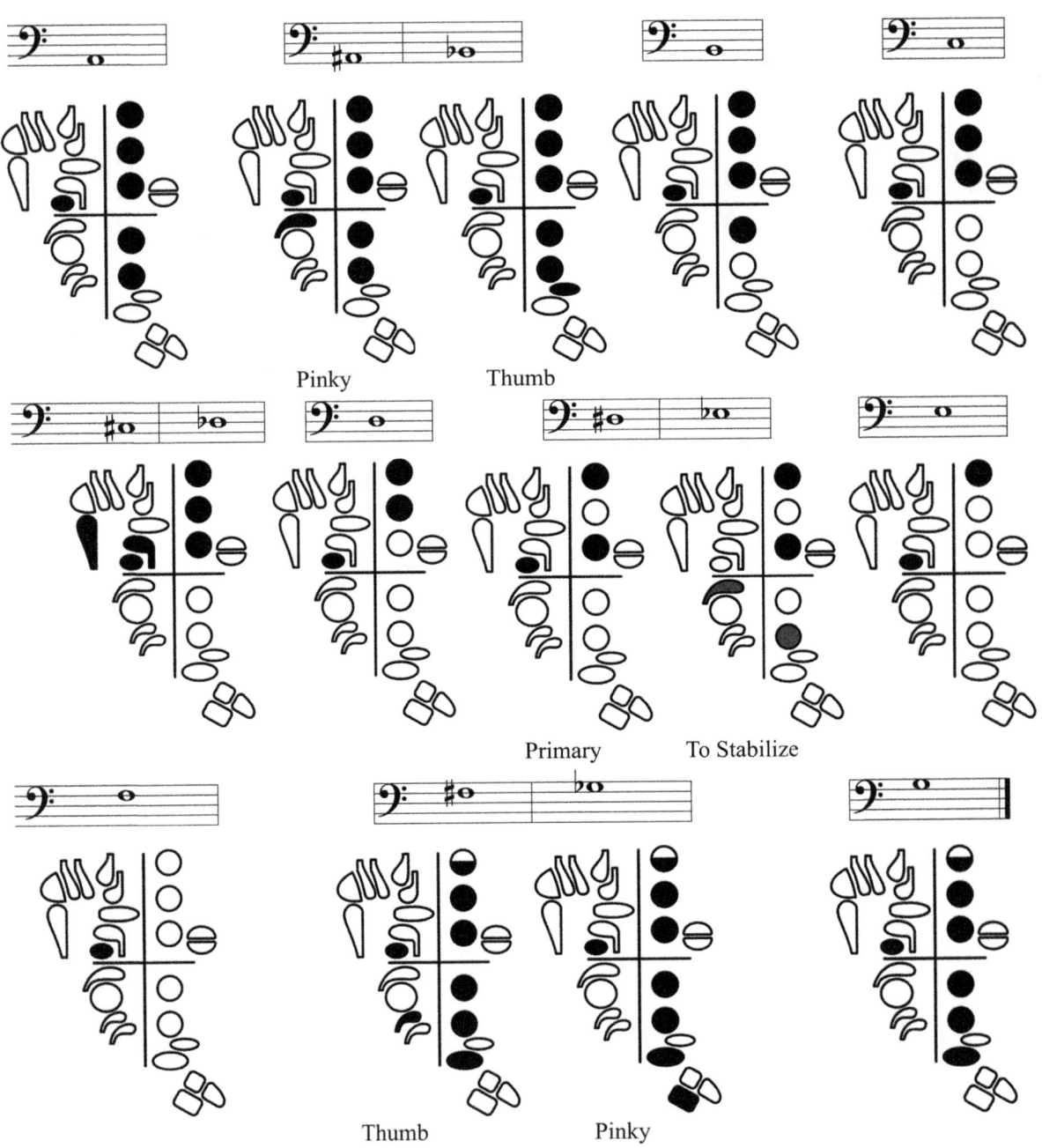

FIGURE 6.40B Bassoon Fingering Chart page 2

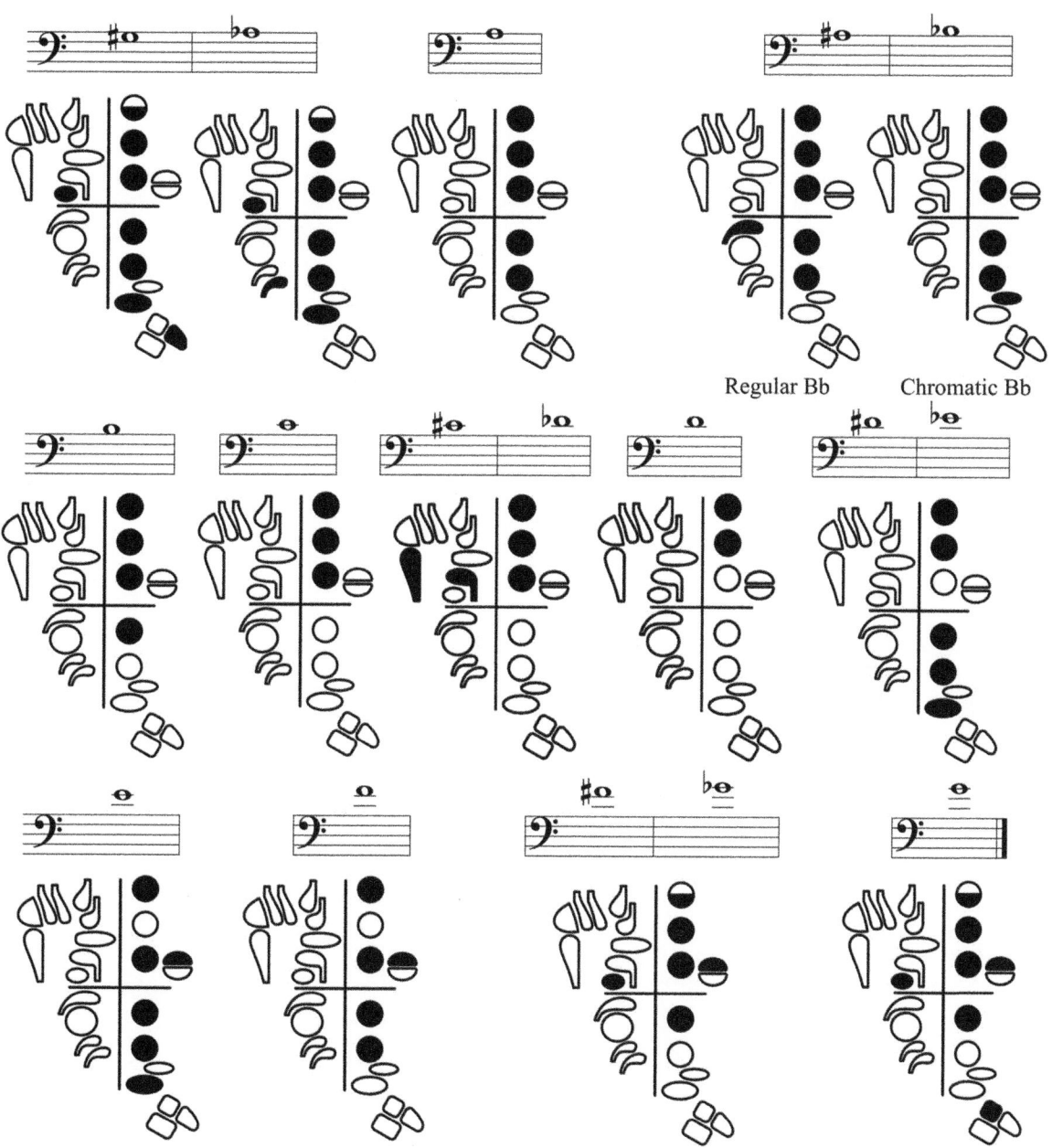

FIGURE 6.40C Bassoon Fingering Chart page 3

PART 3

Thinking Foundationally
about the Woodwinds and Woodwind Teaching

CHAPTER 7

Using Foundations for Perspective

FOUNDATIONS OF TONE QUALITY

It is important that you approach tone quality and its development guided by foundational anchors.

Embouchure as First and Primary Concern

In learning to play a wind instrument (and in teaching an instrument), the first major challenge is embouchure. Embouchure is so critical to achieving characteristic tone that it should be your primary concern throughout course work on the secondary wind instruments. Your thought process in approaching an instrument should not be, "Put instrument in mouth. Play." Instead, discipline yourself to conjure a mental checklist of embouchure characteristics that need to be set prior to producing a tone and maintained during tone production. Then, judge your sound. Does it sound like you know a clarinet should sound? If you're teaching novices, help them become discriminating about tone quality. Working to build habit strength in embouchure formation *while* producing tone begins with detailed attention to setting the embouchure *prior to* producing tone.

Oral Cavity

The nature of the oral cavity, sometimes referred to as voicing, plays an important role in shaping the air stream and thus facilitating air speed that is compatible with characteristic tone. The downward orientation of the jaw and the rounded oral cavity of woodwind embouchures are critical in creating a facial structure that, with habit strength, prevents muscles from collapsing and applying unnecessary lip/teeth pressure to the reed. This facial structure also prevents too much skin from contacting the reed—contact that limits vibration and resonance. The shape of the tongue in woodwind study ranges from a high or arched "shhh" or "ih" for clarinet and altissimo register saxophone to a low, flat tongued "ahhh" (as in stifled yawn) for bassoon. For all instruments, there should be the sense that the throat is open.

Embouchure Flexibility

The basic embouchure is one that the performer makes consistently, as a matter of habit. The accomplished performer maintains the basic embouchure as much as possible, but makes small adjustments to it (e.g., more or less lip firmness or openness) to compensate for variations in reed strength, mouthpiece dimensions, and issues of range, articulation, intonation, and dynamics. There is flexibility built into the basic.

Embouchure and Air Stream as One

Achieving characteristic tone begins with a concern for embouchure and air stream. The two work as one in tone production.

Fast Air

During the first weeks of study, focus student attention on blowing a fast air stream—fast enough to produce an acceptable tone, fast enough to feel the clarinet or saxophone push back at you. Keep in mind that on the flute, unlike the clarinet and saxophone, a fast air stream is more than just blowing fast. Fast air just flies out of a flute aperture that is too large, making it impossible to sustain tone. A small aperture is necessary. Techniques dedicated to developing a small aperture can be found in the flute chapter.

Breathing

An often overlooked element of teaching is its timing. The approach to early tone production instruction in this book does not stress breathing (inhalation) in a formal way until well after embouchure and air stream have been introduced. No doubt, breathing is an important aspect of instrumental performance. It is intentionally left out of early instruction in order to avoid complicating the teaching of embouchure formation. In producing their first sounds, most students will use the air that naturally resides in their bodies. Others should be asked to "take a breath" or "take a bigger breath."

Over time, teach students about correct breathing. In a good breath, the chest is high (this happens naturally when you sit tall with the head erect). The stomach, sides, and back—yes, the back—expand. Inhale through the nose; you will naturally fill the lungs from bottom up. Transfer this sensation to mouth breathing. Physically, correct breathing for playing an instrument is very much the same as the natural breathing we do in ordinary living. Two differences, however, are that instrumentalists must inhale quickly (in rhythm, often in one or less than one beat) and exhale in a controlled manner.

Preparatory Breath

When students are able to do "4 beats on/4 beats off" as described in this text, they are ready to begin the habit of taking a preparatory breath. This is a good time to address breathing as being: a) in tempo, b) not wrong, and c) with attention to embouchure contact points. Not wrong means don't allow students to breathe high, with chest expansion. If the natural way is to breathe abdominally, no instruction is necessary. If the natural way is high and chesty, give instruction about how to change that to the belly. In taking the breath, maintain lower lip contact with the head joint and oboe reed; lower lip and upper teeth contact for the clarinet and saxophone ("breathe through the corners"); and upper lip contact for the bassoon ("breathe from below"). Nose breathing should be avoided, except as a pedagogical technique to show how natural and easy it is to inhale abdominally.

No Rush to Tongue

In the development of embouchure and air stream, there should be no rush to introduce tonguing. Structure an extended period during which students primarily sustain tone. Long tone melodies are slurred melodies—no articulation necessary. After the embouchure and the air stream are well within the "ballpark," add the tongue, but continue to sustain (legato tongue).

Reed Strength and Tip Opening

Optimal strength of reed and size of tip opening create a sensation that, as the player pushes (blows), the instrument pushes back in a way that feels balanced or comfortable.

Building Concept of Tone

By listening to artist performers, you and your students develop opinions about tone. These opinions can lead to preferences that result in concepts of tone, toward which you may lead students and toward which students may aspire. The lists of notable classical performers in Table 7.1 is far from exhaustive, but provides starting points for models for use in tonal concept-building.

TABLE 7.1 Artist Performers as Models of Tone Quality

Flute	*Oboe*	*Clarinet*	*Saxophone*	*Bassoon*
Marcel Moyse 1889–1984	Marcel Tabuteau 1887–1966	Daniel Bonade 1896–1976	Marcel Mule 1901–2001	Simon Kovar 1890–1970
Julius Baker 1915–2000	Robert Bloom 1908–94	Robert Marcellus 1928–96	Larry Teal 1905–89	Sol Schoenbach 1915–99
Jean Pierre Rampal 1922–2000	Harold Gomberg 1916–85	Elsa Ludwig-Verdehr	Sigurd Rascher 1907–2001	Bernard Garfield
James Galway	John Mack 1927–2006	Ricardo Morales	Jean-Marie Londeix	David McGill
Ransom Wilson	Joseph Robinson	Sabine Meyer	Eugene Rousseau	Kim Walker
Jeanne Baxtresser	Alex Klein	David Shifrin	Fred Hemke	Milan Turkovic

FOUNDATIONS OF TEACHING

Component Parts and Their Organization

Your ability to separate wholes (e.g., embouchure) into do-able component parts (aspects of embouchure) and to organize or order sensibly the experiences students have with the parts is a key to student learning.

A teaching/learning sequence can be applied in various teaching situations, but in this book it applies mainly to embouchure instruction. The embouchure is separated into component parts, some of which are easily do-able, others of which are do-able with practice. The parts are ordered or sequenced logically. With the teacher's guidance, students practice doing each part separately; then they practice maintaining previous parts while adding subsequent parts. It is a cumulative process, and this is where the challenge lies. For example, the young flute player must have some lower lip hanging over the embouchure hole *while* making a small aperture *while* maintaining a parallel relationship between line of lips and line of flute and *while* blowing an airstream across the hole. The teaching/learning sequence removes the complexities at the start and gives young people the chance to ease into the embouchure-as-a-whole through this additive process.

The Small Piece: Its Usefulness

Most of the woodwind instruments, and arguably all five (oboe included), have small pieces (head joint, clarinet mouthpiece and barrel, saxophone mouthpiece, reed and bocal) that facilitate embouchure development. The small pieces are useful because they are easy to handle, avoid the distraction and complications of the assembled instrument, and provide the knowledgeable and observant teacher with information about quality of embouchure, air stream, and articulation. Even after the assembled instrument has been introduced, use of the small piece should continue as necessary to further embouchure development and as a check for maintenance of desirable qualities.

Creating Magic in and around Small Piece Practice

In the first weeks of study, make a mountain out of small piece practice. Be in no hurry to get to the assembled instrument. Use the small piece teaching tool to its fullest potential until everyone can rather consistently produce requisite ballpark sounds. The approach will combine group work with many brief individual contacts.

But—there's a problem to be solved. How do we sustain small piece practice over multiple class periods without it becoming a drag and without "me having to do a lot of sitting and waiting while my teacher works with my flute friends?" This question runs into another question: How can we tap into and take advantage of the natural excitement students bring to these early instrument experiences? How can we keep it magical? Think magical versus mundane. Which do we want? On a continuum with magical and mundane at the poles, how much can we teachers ensure that we "live" mostly on the magical side? So it's the first days with instruments. Your plan is to get the reeds wet, the small pieces assembled, a first embouchure created, and a sound made. Nothing wrong with that plan. Important stuff. Sounds efficient, but pretty cut and dried. Let's not stymie the excitement. How can we ride that wave and extend it much longer into the future?

Consider this. First day with instruments. Students seated in chairs or on the floor. On your cue, clarinet players open their cases. Without touching, what do they see? What do they notice? Wait for someone to share something. The teacher in a riveting voice: "How interesting! I noticed that too." To the class: "What else do you notice?" Have the non-clarinet players gather round and notice too about the clarinet. Someone says: "There are five pieces." Someone else notices the round thingies—the keys—some are open and some are covered. As a teacher, guide and extend their noticing. Your goal is to make this special thing inside the case even more special by getting students to realize that there is more there than they know. The teacher: "Carefully take out one of the big pieces. Put it on your lap. What happens when you press down on a key? . . . Try another key. . . . Did you notice that when you press down and let go, the keys return to their starting position? Why is that?" Someone notices that by pressing one key, another key goes down too. As a teacher, run with that idea. Improvise. You're trying to create specialness, awe, excitement, magic with the instrument. "Let your neighbor hold the clarinet piece." And so on.

Repeat the process with flute players and saxophone players with others gathered around. The teacher: "How heavy is the piece you're holding? Does your instrument or case have a smell? I like the smell of mine. Look how big the saxophone is—most of it in one piece! Compare instruments. Can you find writing on it? Why are these called woodwinds? Two of them are not made of wood." Play some of "Take Five" done by the Dave Brubeck Quartet.

Now imagine small piece practice—a not so vanilla small piece practice. After you've made an impression by showing them how to soak a reed and how to protect while handling, would it be a mess if students were to figure out a best way to attach the reed to the mouthpiece? Maybe it would be. How about this? You get them to watch you while you attach the reed to the mouthpiece while saying nothing. No talk, no explaining. They need to pay attention because they will do it themselves next. Perhaps in pairs—one doing the work, the other "helping out." Then switch roles.

Having introduced embouchure and blowing on the small piece, imagine creating a class in which students "share" 4-second small piece tones. Extend the "what did you notice" question to this sound experience. Describe the sound you heard. Listen again. Why does Mary sound different from Michael? Who's sound is higher, softer, rougher? Your goal is to expose young people to way more in sound than they would know to pay attention to without your lead.

Small piece activities include setting the pre-blowing embouchure characteristics, sustaining sound, matching teacher-provided and student-provided pitch, increasing speed in finding optimal placement of the small piece, manipulating direction of air stream (flute). Of course, as students are practicing small piece activities, it's appropriate to spend time emphasizing steady pulse, singing and sizzling rhythm patterns in simple and compound time, doing breathing exercises, having students name notes, and practicing assembling and disassembling the instrument.

Relationship between Small Piece Tone and Instrument Tone

If a student produces a weak small piece tone, he will produce a weak tone on the assembled instrument. And this bad tone will be complicated by future challenges—holding the instrument, reading and fingering notes, counting rhythms, and soon after, having to use the tongue! Quality small piece practice will reap big rewards and minimize what could be long-term frustration when the first notes are played on the assembled instrument. Three important considerations arise for the teacher:

1. In the early stages, should students be sent home with the small piece only—leaving the rest of the instrument in school—in order to promote practice on the small piece alone? Answer: Maybe.

2. If small piece performance is so important, should it be tested? Answer: Probably.

3. Students joined the band to play an instrument, not a small piece. How long can they be kept from the assembled instrument before they get antsy? Answer: Not long if you don't know what you're doing; longer if you know what you're doing.

So the teacher must be knowledgeable and well-planned concerning small piece experiences. In the early stages, the teacher must work "like a dog" to lead students to produce ballpark or better tones and to make small piece practice interesting.

Embouchure One-on-One

Depending on several factors—size of class, make-up of class, age of students, length of lesson, and number of lessons per week—you might prefer to introduce embouchure on an individual basis rather than to the group. Introducing embouchure one-on-one has one very attractive feature—in the beginning the teacher places and holds the small piece for the student while the student blows. This allows the knowledgeable teacher to lead the student to acceptable first sounds more quickly than would be the case in a strict group approach.

Working from Student to Student

If introducing embouchure on an individual basis, be aware that you will need to work quickly and progress from one student to the next at a fairly steady pace. Once you have visited each child, repeat the embouchure-forming steps for the entire group to do together. Have them sustain the small piece sound for 4 moderately paced beats. Without removing the small pieces from their mouths, have them repeat the 4-beat tone. Monitor their performance. As you do so, ask yourself, "How much repetition of this 4-beat tone do my students need now, such that they begin to form correct embouchure habit strength?"

Positive Habit Strength

Positive habit strength develops through correct repetition. How will you structure your teaching so that correct repetitions dominate incorrect repetitions in student performance, both during the lesson/class/rehearsal and during independent student practice? Remember you have the power to foster correct repetitions in your students. You also have the power to foster *incorrect* repetitions in your students.

Teacher Demonstration

Teacher demonstration is a key element in the development of embouchure, air stream, and tonal concept. Have your own small pieces and instruments in hand in order to demonstrate. Don't underestimate the power of demonstration as a teaching tool. You will find that students respond better to your words combined with your model than to your words alone. The teaching, many times, is in the demonstration, not in the words.

But—practice your model. A bad or uncertain or nervous model has negative consequences.

Early Rote Approach

During the pre-method book period, much of the approach should be rote based. The teacher models; students imitate. The model both in look and in sound is a great teaching tool.

Continuous Development of Your Secondary Instrument Performance Skills

Develop your performance skills on secondary instruments to a level beyond that of your beginning students. You begin this process in the secondary instrument class. The best among you will see to it that learning and skill development relative to the secondary instruments continue *after* the class and into your teaching careers.

Notes that Reveal

Certain notes on the assembled instrument provide better first and early experiences than others because they "demand" that students do more things right than wrong; otherwise, the notes simply do not work (no response or a squeak). These notes when used as a basis for early tone production reveal more to the teacher (and the student) about how the student is doing than do notes that require minimal effort and attention to detail. To illustrate, chalumeau register G on the clarinet (thumb and six fingers), a long tube note, is a revealing early experience note around which to structure numerous playing opportunities with novice clarinetists. At a minimum, the learner must form a decent embouchure, produce a reasonably fast air stream, sit correctly, and use adequate hand position or else G will not speak. In contrast, thumb and 1 E, a short-tube note, is an easy note to make sound—so easy that flawed embouchure and air stream and posture and hand position will likely not prevent the E from speaking. Can you see how early emphasis on E and other short-tube notes could give false impressions of competence? There is value in getting clarinetists to play into the chalumeau register sooner rather than later.

Skill Habits and Thought Habits

The goal in teaching and learning is the formation of positive habits of two related kinds—skill habits and thought habits. The likelihood of positive habit formation is affected consequentially by what you have students do, how you organize their thinking, and the extent to which you are consistent in your approach. Positive habits, whether they happen or not, are about you the teacher (see teaching/learning sequences in the flute, clarinet and saxophone chapters).

Ballpark Accuracy

In the early stage of instrument study, some students respond to group instruction, not surprisingly, in inexact and imprecise ways. Your immediate goal should be to guide them through the inexactness and imprecision toward ballpark accuracy with the embouchure and air stream. Being in the right ballpark means that student response is not perfect but it is close enough to accurate in performing any given step in a sequence to move forward on subsequent steps of the sequence. Ballpark accuracy is a point from which the student will be able to proceed to near-complete or complete accuracy at a later time. Another way to view ballpark accuracy is that the student is at a point where he is not building difficult-to-repair negative habit strength.

The Individual Student is the Priority

Though many of you will teach small and large groups of beginners, the individual must be your first priority. You must find ways to get to individuals within the group setting or else your quest for positive habit formation will be curtailed. Get to individuals without compromising the group experience. Get to the group without compromising the individual experience.

Individual Student Contacts

Some students will achieve ballpark accuracy easily. Other students will have difficulty. At some point following initial group instruction, the effective teacher makes numerous individual contacts spread across days. The teacher moves fluidly and skillfully from group to individual instruction because the need for individual attention in embouchure development is great. When attending to an individual, the teacher does what he can to get the student in the right ballpark, but is conscious of the time other students sit idly. Brief individual encounters across multiple lessons are preferable to one long individual encounter during which others must sit idly. I like to refer to these brief individual contacts as "10-second lessons." A teacher can hear four individuals play two measures of music, giving each this proverbial 10-second lesson, and return to the tutti ensemble in roughly 2 minutes.

Fine Discriminations and Judgments

You must make increasingly finer discriminations and judgments with your eyes and ears about student performance. So, too, students must make discriminations and judgments about the sounds they produce and the sensations they feel. How will you structure your teaching so that students are engaged in an ongoing way in their own progress?

You as Master Assessor

The effective teacher is a keen observer of how individual students react to instruction. Students need repeated opportunities *in your presence* to do what you tell and show them to do and to think as you direct them to think. Teachers also need these repeated opportunities in order to observe and evaluate the responses of individuals. What happens when you say, "Pull your lower lip against your teeth?" Who does it correctly the first time? Who needs more tries? Who misinterprets your intentions and ends up with a whole lot of, or too little, lower lip in the mouth? The teacher must notice in order to chart a course of action for correcting the problem.

Keys to the teacher's success are his knowledge of the embouchure characteristics, organization of this information for presentation to students, ability to demonstrate, and powers of observation, which determine feedback and necessary intervention. It is often assumed that a teacher must accumulate substantial teaching experience before he can become a keen observer and a master assessor of student performance. Experience is a wonderful thing, but novice teachers are in a position to set themselves up to be competent observers. It starts with doing well in woodwind techniques class. It requires thinking and planning. Think about what observation means. As instrumental music teachers, we observe with our eyes and with our ears. See "What to Look For" and "What to Listen For" sections throughout this book.

Beyond Ballpark Accuracy

There comes a time after the introduction of new information or a new skill when ballpark accuracy is not good enough. This is the period during which the teacher's goal is to move students toward near-complete or complete accuracy. In watching an effective teacher manage the combination of group and individual instruction, one sees a teacher who is hustling, even "stealing time" (brief visits with a child before or after class or during a break) in order to reach individuals. If it sounds like hard work, it is very hard work!

4 Beats On/4 Beats Off

As students become more at ease and proficient with the embouchure, proceed to "4 beats on/4 beats off." Students place the small piece and blow fast air producing a tone for 4 beats followed by 4 beats of rest, and they do this repeatedly, but thoughtfully, under your guidance. The nature and quality of your guidance determines the extent of their thoughtfulness. Read that sentence again. It's important. At some point, have them remove the small piece from the mouth, re-place it, sustain pitch for 4 beats, then repeat the process. Removal of the small piece between tones challenges students to find optimal placement—to find it on their own and, in time, to find it quickly.

Fired up for Refining

Arguably, many teachers are good at introducing new information or a new skill (e.g., embouchure), but many fewer seem able to refine student responses beyond the introductory stage. In fact, many teachers come to class quite fired up about "teaching" something new, but their enthusiasm and teaching skill wane when what is needed is more than introductory in nature. By following the step-by-step procedures suggested for making first sounds, the teacher has merely *introduced* embouchure and air stream. To introduce students to embouchure—to provide first-day experiences in embouchure—is not to teach embouchure. The introduction is simply the first in a series of similar experiences over time that combined with much detailed observation and feedback may result in the teacher having taught and the student having learned a characteristic embouchure.

Performance Testing

If it is important to you that your students sit with good posture, hold the head joint (and ultimately the flute) correctly, and make a characteristic tone—and you want these objectives to be important to your students—you will consider testing them on various performance elements. Students tend to think that what gets tested is important. Testing puts the onus on the individual student to perform at some competent level. What is the likelihood that a well-thought-out program of testing might compel each student to act more responsibly while making them increasingly aware of their contribution to the ensemble? A few sample performance tests are included in the instrument chapters.

Individual testing can be administered using video. Set up a video recorder in a practice room. Students, one at a time, unobtrusively leave class in a pre-arranged order to take the test. Each student enters the practice room, sits in a chair in view of the video recorder (which is running continuously), and demonstrates the head joint teaching/learning sequence. When finished, the student unobtrusively returns to class/rehearsal as the next student, waiting outside the practice room, enters the test room. At a later, convenient time, the teacher views the recording, completes a test form, and assigns grades.

FOUNDATIONS OF ASSEMBLY AND DISASSEMBLY

Naming the Parts: No Big Deal

At a time in a child's musical life when time, attention, and effort should be focused on learning how to play the instrument, the teacher need not make a big deal about or spend undue time with the names of instrument parts. If the teacher simply *uses* the correct terminology and provides opportunities for students, individually, to use correct terminology during the normal course of instruction, students will tend to learn the correct words without trying. When doing head joint work, the teacher will inevitably say *head joint* many times. When teaching and observing instrument assembly, the teacher will probably say *body*, *foot joint*, and *keys* many times.

How to Make Assembly and Disassembly Easy and Safe for the Instrument

Assembly is easier and safer for the instrument when there is no need for rough handling by the assembler. Flute joints fit together easily when they are clean, as long as they are not out of round. Wipe both surfaces with a soft cloth. Instruments with cork tenon joints require cork grease for ease of assembly. When teaching assembly, the teacher should apply it prior to the class if possible. If dealt with during the lesson, it can be a big time waster. If dealing with new instruments, the corks may seem thick. With cork grease and normal wear from use, they will settle into a good fit. If the teacher fails to address the tenon cork issue or deals with it as an after-thought, assembly will be difficult, causing students to apply excess pressure to the key mechanism, which can cause keys and rods to bend.

Cork Grease

The corks of a new instrument will require grease for ease of assembly. It is wise to wipe old cork grease from used instruments with a cloth, then apply new grease. Show students how to apply a thin layer of cork grease. It should not be caked on; you should not see white on the corks. How often should one apply cork grease? On an as needed basis—frequently when corks are new and thick, less often as they become worn. Fox bassoons have a string wrap instead of cork at the tenons. It is best lubricated with wax.

Avoid Excessive Pressure on Keys and Rods

The goal in assembly and disassembly is to avoid putting excessive pressure on keys that stick out and on rods. These can bend. Damage will not occur if, in grasping the joints, you apply pressure to keys that are ordinarily closed or if you close keys that are ordinarily open.

Bridge Keys

Pay attention. In assembly, look at the bridge keys. Use smallish back and forth turns.

Wet the Reed First

In assembly of clarinet and saxophone, wet the reed, then assemble the small piece, then the instrument from bottom to top. For oboe and bassoon, wet the reed, then assemble the instrument from bottom to top.

In disassembly, take care of the reed first. Take it off the mouthpiece and store in a place where it will dry between playings.

FOUNDATIONS OF INSTRUMENT CARE

Swabs

The teacher and student should be cautious about pulling a swab through all or part of an instrument. Avoid forcing it. If a swab gets stuck, it can be difficult to remove, requiring an instrument repair technician. Some swabs are meant to be pulled through because they are made of a silk (and are thus sleek) or cotton that has been cut small enough.

Other swabs cannot be pulled through; they should be pulled until snug, then reverse pulled out. It is wise to also wipe dry tenon joints and receivers.

Time for Swabbing

If students do not swab the instrument after each playing, moisture from the bore of the instrument will stay moist longer inside the closed case, causing pads to deteriorate at a faster than normal rate. In addition, moisture will work its way into the unlined bore of the instrument (e.g., the U-tube area at the bottom of the bassoon boot joint) causing excessive expansion and contraction of the wood, which can lead to cracking. If you expect your woodwind players to swab regularly, you must provide time for this at the end of class or rehearsal. Monitor this activity until students become proficient, responsible, and independent.

Caring for the Mouthpiece

Many clarinet and saxophone mouthpieces are made of machine rod rubber. Periodically wash a mouthpiece in luke-warm water. Hot water will warp it.

Taking Extra Stuff on Stage

Be cognizant of the fact that oboist and bassoonists, in particular, have good reasons to take accessories with them on stage for performance and to have it ready for use each day in rehearsal. This includes reed case with an extra, working reed, water container, swab, and cigarette paper or something similar to help clear out water that gets hung up in a tone hole.

Traveling with Instrument

When traveling (walking) with instrument, things that stick out should be taken off for protection. That is, oboe and bassoon reeds should be placed in the mouth or in a case. The bassoon bocal should be removed and placed in the bell. The bassoon seat strap should not drag on the floor.

Instruments Left Unmonitored in Rehearsal Room

Store the instruments in their cases. Left lying on a chair or music stand, the instruments can easily be bumped or damaged, if not sat upon. If left on a chair, avoid having anything stick out beyond the chair edges. Separate flute, clarinet, and oboe into two parts. Keep reeds protected.

Instrument in Case

The instrument should fit snugly in its case. You should feel and hear no movement of instrument parts while transporting. If there is movement, lay an appropriately sized towel over the instrument for extra padding. To prevent keys and rods from bending, do not store pencils in the case. Instruments in cases that are dropped or fall to the floor will likely be damaged. The case protects the instrument under normal handling. Dropping the case is not normal handling.

Wood Instruments Will Crack if . . .

Wood instruments will crack due to drastic changes of temperature. Do not place or store in extremes of hot or cold (on a heater or in a car in cold weather). If an instrument gets extremely cold, warm it up gradually by cradling it in the hands and against the body. Don't be too quick to blow hot air (98.6°) into the bore.

The Best Care of a Woodwind Instrument Is . . .

Regular use of the instrument and disciplined swabbing make for a healthy woodwind instrument.

Instrument Vocabulary

- Tenon: the male end of an instrument joint.
- Receiver: the female end of an instrument joint.
- Rod: a bar-like mechanism on which keys are attached. In some cases, the rod rotates inside a metal casing. Alternatively, the metal casing itself rotates and serves as the rod.
- Post: nub-like protrusions found at both ends of a rod. Posts are attached to the body of the instrument. With the help of post screws, posts hold rods in place.
- Spring: a roughly 1 inch (2.5cm) long sturdy wire whose elasticity functions to return a key to an open or closed position after having been depressed and released by a finger.
- Seated pad: a pad that has been leveled with the tone hole. While the glue is heated and soft, the pad is *seated* securely and evenly in its cup.
- Key cork: a piece of cork attached to a key. The cork is cut to a size that allows a key to open to a correct height. Corks can come unglued, thus allowing keys to open too much. A key that opens too much or too little will cause certain notes to play out of tune.

Sticky Pad

Sticky pads (those that make a noise when in use or that stick shut) can result from students who eat lunch, chew gum, or drink soft drinks before playing the instrument. Sticky breath, which condenses in the bore, and sticky saliva eventually find their way to the pads. When sticky, the pads collect dirt, which becomes an added problem. In school scheduling, try to avoid the placement of rehearsal immediately after lunch. Encourage students to rinse their mouths with water as a way to minimize the negative effects of having eaten before playing.

Also, pads tend to stick when the instrument is not swabbed, causing humid conditions to build up in the case during storage.

To remove the sticky substance from a pad, place a dollar bill (or cigarette paper or regular paper) under the pad, close the pad on top of the bill, and pull the bill out. Repeat several times. The friction caused by pulling the bill should remove the stickiness.

Water in Tone Hole

Occasionally, moisture in the bore travels in a stream and collects in a tone hole. This water will cause one note to gurgle. For example, if the bassoon gurgles while playing third line D, water is in the open tone hole adjacent to D. It is in the C tone hole. There are two ways to deal with this problem—a quick, but temporary fix and a long-term fix that is time-consuming. The quick fix: Find the problem tone hole (look for water that has splashed), put your face close to the instrument, and blow a very fast, blast of air into the tone hole. This will force the water out of the tone hole and back into the bore. This can be done in the middle of a performance when there is no time to do anything else. However, the fix is usually temporary because the cause has not been dealt with. Water was in the tone hole because it ran in a stream inside the bore. As long as the stream is present, water will continue to enter the tone hole.

The long-term fix: If the bassoon gurgles on D, swab out the bore of the affected joint (in this case, the tenor joint). This removes the root cause of the problem, the stream of water in the bore. Take the tenor joint, plug the end, and close all keys/tone holes except the one with water in it (C). Blow hard through the joint forcing the water out of the tone hole.

Keys That Function Improperly

Keys that function improperly frequently require the attention of an instrument repair technician. Depending on circumstances, however, there are a few repairs that can be done without sending the instrument to the repair shop. They involve pivot screws, unhooked springs, simple key adjustments, and quick-fix pad replacement.

Pivot Screws

Screws on woodwind instruments function in two different ways: 1) To hold rods in place at posts (these are called pivot screws), and 2) as adjustment screws on keys. Periodically check to see that pivot screws are not backing out. If one falls out, the key mechanism connected to it will hang loose or fall off. Pivot screws should be snug, not tight. Over-tightening can cause the rod to bind, preventing the smooth operation of keys. Unless there are key adjustment problems, adjustment screws should be left alone. More information on adjustment screws can be found under "Leak in Key Mechanism."

Unhooked Spring

Often when a wrong pitch is produced by the correct fingering, the culprit is a spring that has come unhooked or broken off. Springs function to return a key to a closed or open position. If a key stays open when it should be closed, either a wrong pitch or no pitch will result. An unhooked spring is easily fixed by remounting it with a spring hook or acceptable substitute (pen, pencil, finger, small screw driver). It is not uncommon for either the first or second tone hole on the flute (nearest the head joint) to remain open because of an unhooked spring. In these cases, no distinct single pitch will sound regardless of fingering.

Leak in Key Mechanism

A leak in the key mechanism can result from a faulty key pad or faulty key adjustment.

- A pad will leak air when it does not seal completely around the tone hole. The problem may be caused by a worn or hardened pad or by faulty workmanship (e.g., a good pad that has not been seated correctly). Formal pad replacement involving the seating of pads is beyond the scope of this book. Quick-fix pad replacement is described below.
- A pad will leak because of faulty key adjustment. This kind of leak is not uncommon on student model flutes. Key adjustment is a more complex endeavor on the oboe. The clarinet typically has only one adjustment screw (on the front G-sharp). A flute example will be used to show simple key adjustment that can be performed quite easily with a small screw driver.

Key Adjustment: Flute Example

Notice that when you depress and release the G-sharp/A-flat key, only that key moves. When you depress and release the E key, however, two keys move—the E key (the primary key) and another key (a slave key). The E key and its slave are designed to move in tandem. In fact every key operated by fingers 1 through 3 on both hands moves in tandem with slave keys. If the movement of these key pairs is not synchronized, the instrument is said to be *out of adjustment* or *out of regulation*. Flutes have small adjustment screws that have one purpose—to allow the instrument to be adjusted or regulated when necessary. Adjustment screws, which are positioned near keys, should not be turned at random or tightened because they appear to need tightening. If the flute plays well, the adjustment screws should be left alone.

Back to the E key—if the slave key closes before or after the E key, or if it does not close completely, E will not speak correctly. Response will be difficult, pitch will be sharp, and tone quality will be fuzzy or unfocused. Tightening the screw near the E key will cause the slave key to close sooner. Loosening that screw will cause the slave key to close later. The amount of tightening and loosening will be quite small. Start with a quarter of a turn, then test the E by playing the flute. This concept is the same for all key pairs. The goal is that keys close precisely together. This is a relatively minor repair that can have major positive ramifications. A screw turned too far or not far enough can always be turned back.

Quick-Fix Pad Replacement

Many pads on woodwind instruments are held in place by glue or shellac. When glue looses its adhesiveness, pads fall out—and they are prone to during marching season when the weather can be rough on instruments. When one does fall out, a quick fix involves re-using the same pad, if it can be found. Place the old pad into the key cup. Heat the cup with a flame from a match or cigarette lighter such that the dried glue in the cup and on the pad melts. Hold the flame at an angle to the key so that the heat does not burn the body of the instrument. Close the key with your thumb and hold it shut for a minute or so, allowing the glue to dry. This is a quick fix best suited for emergency repairs associated with the marching band season. Because the pad has not been formally seated, the pad may leak, sometimes rendering this repair only temporary.

Repairs for the Instrument Repair Technician

Certain repairs are best done by an experienced instrument repair technician. They include the following:

- Key adjustment or regulation that involves bending keys or complicated screw manipulation (it gets complicated on the oboe)
- Pad replacement
- Key cork replacement—an individual key that does not open the correct height (which in many cases should be the same as that of adjacent keys) probably has a cork problem
- Head joint cork replacement (flute)
- Tenon cork replacement
- Loose post
- Stuck swab
- Spring replacement
- Neck screw that will not tighten enough (saxophone)
- Soldering loose braces and key guards (saxophone)
- Body dents (flute and saxophone) and cracks (oboe, clarinet, bassoon)
- Fixing a leaky embouchure plate (flute)
- Re-plating a worn finish (flute and saxophone).

FOUNDATIONS OF POSTURE, HANDS, AND HOLDING

Hand Digit Labels

In woodwind study, we refer to the hand digits as follows:

- Top hand (left): 1–2–3
- Bottom hand (right): 1–2–3
- Two thumbs
- Two pinkies.

Body Posture

As a starting point for addressing the "posture" of the hands, let's first think about the posture of the body. In order for the breathing system and moving parts (fingers, hands, arms, tongue) to function optimally, several body posture features should be established and maintained.

- Sit or stand tall.
- Hold the head erect. Bring the instrument to you; don't move the head to the instrument. For flute, the head may be tilted slightly to the right. For bassoon and saxophone held to the side, turn the reed and mouthpiece so that the head remains erect.
- Position the instrument at an optimal angle or angles to your body. For clarinet and oboe, establish a 35° angle. For bassoon and saxophone held to the side, create a slight forward lean of the upper torso to allow an upward approach of the bocal or neck to the face. For bassoon, the instrument crosses the body and the bell tips forward. For flute, the line of the instrument should be parallel to the line of the lips, and the instrument should form a right angle to the player's face.
- Arms should feel natural. Elbows should not be against the ribs, nor should they be unnaturally extended away from the ribs.

Soft and Flexible Body Parts

Your body should feel soft and flexible when you play. Hardness in your face, hands, or arms, in places that don't need to be hard, is an indication of unwanted tension.

Best Body Position

Ultimately the best body and instrument positions are the ones that permit the most comfort, the best tone, and the most facility. This way of thinking allows for some (but not much) variation of positioning among people and suggests that careful consideration be given in arriving at optimal positioning.

Finger Position

With few exceptions, which will be noted as they arise, the fingers should be moderately curved as if grasping a hand-sized ball. The fingerprint areas should contact or hover above the center of the keys. Avoid playing with fingers that overreach the keys.

Fingers: Relaxed, Efficient Motion

This goal is always relaxed, efficient motion. When lifting a finger from the depressed position, aim to maintain contact with the key, or if no key, lift only high enough that the new note sounds properly. In other words, do not allow fingers to fly away aimlessly from the instrument, a condition that promotes sloppy, "slappy" finger technique. Keep fingers close. To think of lifting is probably making too much of the action. Little more than a relaxation of the finger is necessary.

FOUNDATIONS OF TONGUING AND ARTICULATION

Relaxed, Efficient Motion Defined

The goal is always relaxed, efficient motion; that is, you should be as relaxed as possible and move as little as possible to accomplish whatever movement is necessary in playing your instrument. This principle pertains to movements of the fingers, arms (e.g., violin, percussion, and trombone) and tongue.

- The tongue is not literally relaxed but it can be as relaxed as possible, thus allowing for it to be pointed, that is, the tip is rigid for staccato/marcato and for fast tonguing. It is somewhat less rigid for legato tonguing.
- Confine movement to the front of the tongue. Avoid excessive movement of the jaw and throat while tonguing. Say "d-d-d-d" rather rapidly to show that only the front of the tongue moves.

Tongue Releases Tone

While tonguing, place the air far forward in the mouth. The tongue must press against the reed, then *release* the air into the mouthpiece. The tongue releases tone; it doesn't *attack*.

In Troubleshooting, Embouchure and Air Stream First, Tonguing Second

Tonguing should be viewed as something that occurs in conjunction with embouchure and air stream. The quality of one's articulation is affected by the ability to properly support the tone with a) proper embouchure pressures (lips, corners, teeth, cheeks), b) a sufficiently fast stream of air, and c) proper shape of oral cavity (voicing). The tongue cannot work optimally if embouchure and air stream are not optimal. So to troubleshoot, address embouchure and air first, tonguing second.

Why That Squeaking?

It is tempting to think that when a novice clarinet player squeaks, it is because of a faulty tongue. "Don't tongue so hard" is a common teacher response. Consider, however, that there are other causes of squeaking and a few that are more probable as culprits for novices:

1. An embouchure that is too soft (specifically a lower lip that is too soft) may not support the reed enough to prevent squeaking when the tongue is applied.
2. Faulty finger coverage will cause squeaking. Pay attention to Finger 3 in both hands (is it reaching enough for the floor?).
3. Too much mouthpiece in the mouth will cause squeaking. But be careful in this diagnosis; sometimes what appears to be a too-much-in-the-mouth problem is really a too-soft-lower-lip problem.

Does the Tongue Stop Tone?

The tongue is used to start the tone and, in certain situations (e.g., short, crisp staccato notes in fast passages), to stop the tone. Beginning instrumentalists, however, should know the tongue as a starting, not a stopping, agent. As a teacher, watch that students do not stop last notes of phrases or notes before rests with their tongues. Instead, they should stop these notes by stopping the air stream.

Establish Embouchure First; Bring Tongue to Embouchure

It is preferable that a ballpark accurate embouchure be established *before* tonguing is introduced. To teach embouchure and tonguing at the same time unnecessarily complicates the teaching and learning process and may in fact prevent both from developing optimally. The teacher's goal is to be skillful enough to establish in students this ballpark embouchure as quickly as possible. This embouchure combined with a fast air stream should result in a sustained, *forte*, unwavering tone that is relatively in tune. On most school schedules and with most students, the pre-tonguing procedure should not be continued much beyond one month of instruction. However, if a student continues to have difficulty producing the tone described above, it makes little sense to introduce tonguing, which complicates tone production.

No Rush to Tongue

In the *Habits of Musicianship* beginning band method book by Duke and Byo (URL provided in Preface), the first melodies are written so that they can be slurred by all instruments except of course trombone. There is no need to rush into tonguing. By structuring the melodies this way (no same-note repetitions) we build in time for embouchures and air streams to stabilize without the added complication of tonguing. The teacher is free to decide when ballpark embouchures are stable enough such that tonguing can be introduced. And tonguing can be approached more on an individual student readiness level. Everyone does not need to tongue today in order for the class to play "this here melody." Students who pick it up easily can do so now, while those who need more time can participate fully as yet-to-be tonguers or partial tonguers.

Legato is the Priority

Legato tongue should be taught and well established from the beginning. This is the beauty of the *Backward Approach to Teaching Tonguing*, which is based on a sort of "accidental" legato tongue. Do not allow beginners to puff at notes, that is, make a space or breathe after each note. This puffing is what causes elementary and middle school bands to sound like the stereotypical young band. They do not have to sound bad! Teach students to sustain through notes, to connect notes with their tongues, to play a line of music. They should in effect tongue the air, which is continually moving through, during, and between the notes. Marcato and staccato articulations should be introduced after students are adept at legato tonguing. If you want your young band to sound more rather than less mature, get them to legato tongue. They can do it!

Du to Model Legato

Traditionally, the D consonant (e.g., Du) is used as a vocal model for legato.

Teaching Tonguing: Two Alternatives

Traditional Approach to Teaching Tonguing

The traditional approach to teaching tonguing, to use terminology from psychology, is a holistic approach. Tonguing is kept intact; it is not broken into its component parts. Modeling by the teacher, with voice and instrument, is integrated with the admonition to say "Dah" or "Tah" into the instrument—tip of tongue to tip of reed or tip of tongue to contact point just above the front teeth (flute).

Backward Approach to Teaching Tonguing

The traditional approach works for many students. It doesn't for others. The problem is that some novices are unable to coordinate air stream, embouchure, and tongue. They can't put it all together at once. Or they unknowingly articulate from the throat (glottal tonguing). The *Backward Approach* teaches tonguing by starting with something that we know students can do successfully, that is, start a tone with a pre-tonguing technique (the P consonant for flute, a breath attack for other woodwinds), and progressing incrementally into unknown tonguing territory. The process, explained in full in the flute, clarinet, and saxophone chapters, provides experiences in finding tip of tongue and tip of reed and tonguing during a sustained air stream.

Assessment and Tonguing

I considered calling this section Addressing Problems in Tonguing, but it's actually about something bigger and more far reaching in your development as a music teacher. We'll call it assessment. Don't confuse this form of assessment with making up, giving, and grading tests. Assessment as I intend it here is one thing that good teachers do that makes them good.

Simply, assessment is collecting information. When I'm about to leave my office to walk across campus, I look outside my window to determine whether I should take an umbrella. I assess with my eyes. At my desk, my back is turned to the window, so frequently I hear thunder or rain before I see the visible effects. I assess with my ears.

Assessment is something that people do all the time in order to get along in life. In the music room and rehearsal hall, effective teachers are keen observers, taking in information, some obvious and some very subtle, in order to make wise moment-to-moment decisions about what to do. This recurring cycle of collect–decide–act is fundamental to the structured teaching/learning setting. The teacher's skills of observation and assessment are greatly enhanced when she knows what to look for and listen for relative to tonguing. The instrument chapters provide lists of things a teacher can see and hear that indicate faulty tonguing.

Bassoon Staccato

The bassoon produces a clear, crisp staccato. A student bassoonist can produce a good staccato far earlier in his development than a student clarinetist. Stated differently, the bassoon's natural tendencies allow it to emulate the string pizzicato in convincing fashion.

Multiple Tonguing

Multiple tonguing (double and triple tonguing) is possible on all woodwind instruments. It is a more or less standard performance technique depending on the instrument. The clarinet and saxophone are less conducive to multiple tonguing than flute and the double reed instruments. Many professional level woodwind players double and triple tongue with ease.

- *Double tongue.* Use an alternating "Tah-Kah" articulation. For a less percussive effect, use "Dah-Gah."
- *Triple tongue.* Use "Tah-Tah-Kah" ("Dah-Dah-Gah") or "Tah-Kah-Tah" ("Dah-Gah-Dah").

Flutter Tonguing

For flute and the single reed instruments, flutter tonguing is a contemporary performance technique. The player in effect rolls Rs while playing. It is more accurately thought of as a tonal or timbral effect than an articulation.

Vocal Modeling

The effective teacher models (sings) articulations as a teaching tool. He uses combinations of consonants and vowels that are instrumentally appropriate (e.g., "DU–DU" instead of "BAH–BAH"). No instrument is played with a "BAH" articulation. Part of teacher preparation entails developing your modeling skills and becoming increasingly more comfortable using this important teaching tool. For rapid figures, use double and triple tonguing in your model.

Spell "Tongue"

Tongue, tongued, tonguing.

FOUNDATIONS OF THE MECHANISM

In this section I include a broad range of information relating to the instruments as mechanical devices. Each device (instrument) is situated in historical and instrument-manufacturing contexts. Each is a member of a family of like-devices and is included in collections of devices (ensembles) for the performance of chamber music. Each is identified by a clef or clefs for its music, a relationship between written pitch and sounding pitch, a playing range, fingerings that change pipe length and blowing properties thus creating pitch tendencies that require special attention. Other devices (reeds) serve as sound sources.

Theobald Boehm

Boehm (1794–1881) was a flutist who patented a new fingering system for flute in 1847, the basis of which is intact today. The Boehm system today is relevant also to fingerings on clarinet and oboe.

Classical or Jazz

Clarinet and saxophone histories include formidable jazz components. In university music majors so dominated by the classical music idiom, it is easy to overlook the past and present place of the woodwind instruments in jazz.

Instrument Manufacturing

Be aware of distinctions between professional and student line models. Synthetic instruments by reputable manufacturers are very acceptable and certainly durable instruments. In this text, I do not make specific recommendations regarding instrument purchase. Your best bet is to heed the advice of those who have expert, specific, and current knowledge about the instrument in question before purchasing.

Families of Instruments

Instruments with the family (e.g., the clarinet family) have the same theoretical range and, for the most part, identical fingerings. Piccolo and E-flat soprano clarinet pose more intonation difficulties than do flute and B-flat soprano clarinet, respectively. The larger instruments (English horn, bass clarinets, baritone saxophone) are less accurate in upper register response and intonation than are oboe, B-flat soprano clarinet, and alto saxophone, respectively.

Woodwind Ensembles

Various combinations of woodwinds create a wide variety of woodwind ensembles: Flute trio, clarinet trio, flute–oboe–clarinet trio, miscellaneous woodwind trio, flute quartet, clarinet quartet, mixed clarinet quartet, clarinet choir, woodwind quartet and quintet, saxophone quartet and quintet, woodwind octet, and woodwind choir. For music organized by ensemble type, see Texas's University Interscholastic League "Prescribed Music List" at www.utexas.edu/uil/pml/browse.

Woodwind Quintet

A staple of the chamber music world is the woodwind quintet. It has two standard seating arrangements.

	Horn			Bassoon	
Oboe		Bassoon	Oboe		Horn
Flute		Clarinet	Flute		Clarinet
	Audience			Audience	

Saxophone Quartet

There are two standard saxophone quartet instrumentations. Two altos, tenor, and baritone are common for school chamber music. One of each (soprano, alto, tenor, and baritone) is called the French quartet.

The Saxophone in the Jazz Band

The standard big band instrumentation includes five players in the sax section (1st and 2nd alto, 1st and 2nd tenor, and baritone). Traditional seating left to right (from a conductor's perspective) across the front of the ensemble is:

Tenor 1   Alto 2   Alto 1   Tenor 2   Baritone

Audience

Most of the solo work is in the Tenor 1 part, so it is good to situate this player close to the rhythm section, which is located to the left of the ensemble.

Doubling

It is not uncommon in advanced jazz band literature to have saxophone parts call for doubling, that is, for the part to stipulate saxophone and flute, or saxophone and clarinet, or all three. Professional saxophonists with a jazz specialty are proficient doublers.

If flute or clarinet parts are called for in high school jazz literature, the most expedient approach is to have an accomplished flute or clarinet player join the band and cover the part. Alternatively, saxophone players can learn the flute or clarinet. This is a slow process, but educationally sound if there is time for the doubler to develop on these secondary instruments.

Transposition

With the exception of the piccolo and E-flat soprano clarinet, which *sound* up, the woodwinds instruments *sound* down.

Clefs

Music for every instrument in the clarinet and saxophone families is written in the treble clef. The player of the larger instruments reads in the treble clef while playing instruments that *sound down* into the tenor and bass ranges. Bassoon music is written in the bass, tenor, and treble clefs.

Playing Range

Playing range is viewed in two ways: possible range and practical range. The lowest possible notes on flute, oboe, saxophone, and bassoon are the same or similar in name: flute (C or B), oboe (B-flat), saxophone (B-flat), and bassoon (B-flat).

The lowest notes of the clarinet are easy to produce. The lowest notes of the flute, oboe, saxophone, and bassoon require extra effort to produce. They do not speak readily at *p* dynamic level or in the context of rapid tonguing.

Stimulus Notes and Fingerings

To help you learn and retain long term a limited number of common fingerings on each woodwind instrument, we will designate a stimulus note and fingering for each instrument and promote a process for recall of other fingerings, using the stimulus as a starting point. For this to happen, you must commit to memory the notes and fingerings shown in Figure 7.1.

FIGURE 7.1 Stimulus Notes and Fingerings

First Octave Notes and Their "Overblown" Counterparts: Fingerings

One arrives at "first octave" notes and fingerings by depressing one adjacent finger at a time, using the stimulus as the starting point. As pictured in Figure 7.2, on clarinet the stimulus note F is fingered with thumb depressed. For E, add finger 1 (Thumb–1). For D, add finger 2 (Thumb–1–2), etc. Notice in Figure 7.2 that for the double reeds the interval from finger 3 (top hand) to finger 1 (bottom hand) is a half step and for the single reeds and flute a whole step. For learning and remembering fingerings, this is a helpful fact.

One arrives at the overblown register (the right side of Figure 7.2) by applying knowledge from acoustics. Four instruments overblow an octave, so the same or similar fingering produces the same note in the upper octave. The saxophonist adds an octave key; the oboist uses a half-hole and two octaves keys; the bassoonist uses a whisper key and firmer embouchure; and the flutist covers more embouchure hole with the lower lip.

In contrast, the clarinetist uses a register key to overblow a 12th.

In summary, by learning the stimulus notes and fingerings and applying some fingering logic and basic acoustical knowledge, one can with relative ease derive fingerings for as many as 13 other notes per instrument without the help of a fingering chart.

Fingering Idiosyncrasies

On the flute, the right pinky depresses the E-flat key for most notes on the instrument.

On the clarinet, the clarion register E is raised a major 6th by lifting the 1st finger. Further, for clarion F and above, lift the 1st finger and add the E-flat key to create notes a major 6th above. The F to D relationship is notated in Figure 7.3. In effect, high register notes are built from clarion register notes.

As a teacher, be aware that first-year clarinet players have more notes/fingerings to learn than do first-year flute and saxophone players. At this level the clarinet has three fingering groups—the low register (roughly the F major scale), the upper register (roughly third space C up a fifth to G), and the throat register which bridges the low and upper registers. Flute and saxophone have a low octave of fingerings that largely stay the same in the second octave.

On the oboe and bassoon, the half-hole functions as an octave key.

On the bassoon, the top hand thumb depresses the whisper key (thus *closing* the vent hole on the bocal) for low notes. The thumb raises, thus *opening* the vent hole, for high notes. For the instruments with octave keys (oboe, saxophone) and a register key (clarinet), top hand thumb action is different. It depresses the key (thus *opening* a hole) for high notes and comes off the key, thus *closing* a hole, for low notes.

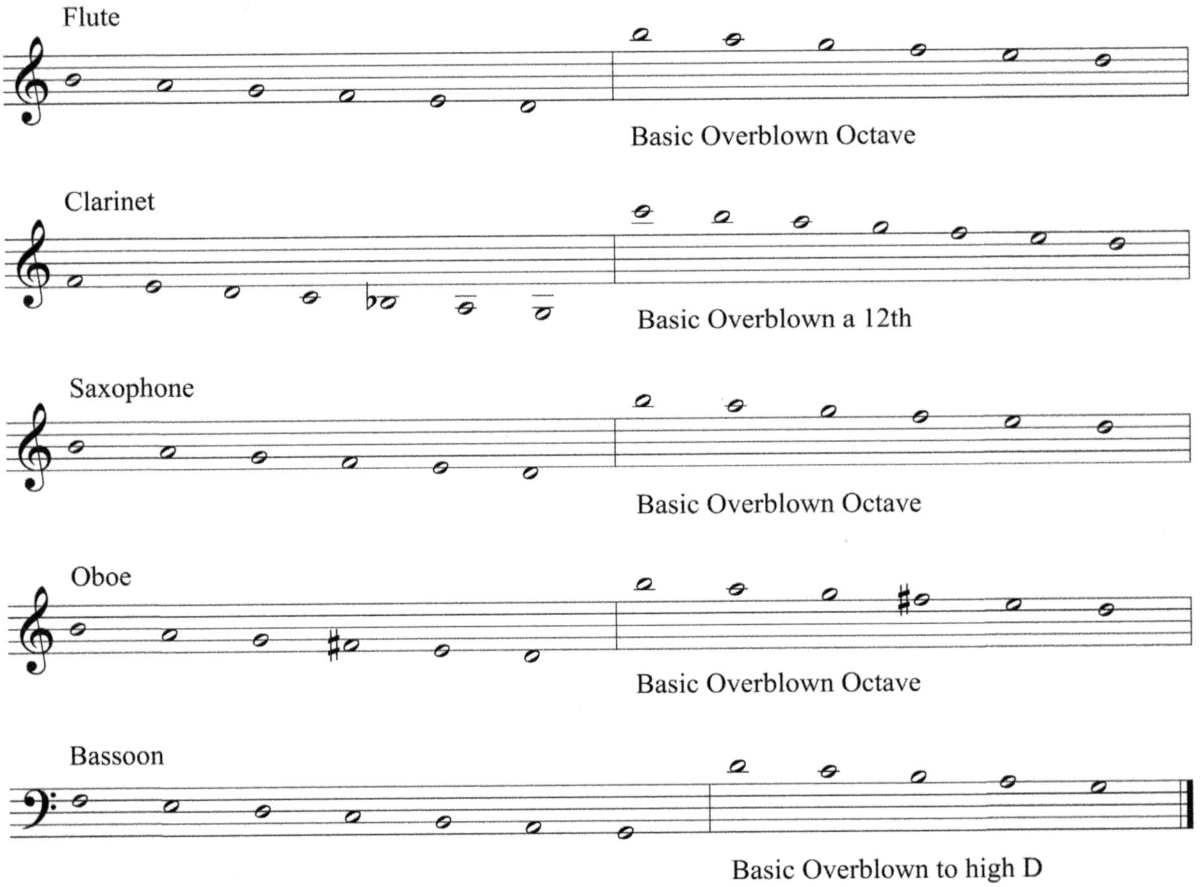

FIGURE 7.2 First Octave Notes and Their "Overblown" Counterparts

FIGURE 7.3 Clarinet 1st Finger up Major Sixth

Other Fingering Groups

The best among you will recognize the advantages to learning and remembering offered by notes whose fingerings are grouped together by some common trait. For example:

- flute—first-finger up notes
- clarinet—the throat register notes
- saxophone—palm key notes
- oboe and bassoon—half-hole notes
- oboe—back octave key notes, side octave key notes, three F fingerings
- bassoon—thumb up notes, two F-sharp fingerings, and two G-sharp fingerings.

The Break

Theoretically, all woodwind instruments have a "break" between a note at or near the top of the low register ascending to a note in the second register. Break implies differences between registers—differences in timbre and awkwardness in fingering (few fingers for the highest notes of the low register to many fingers for the lowest notes in the second register). This is best exemplified on the clarinet where the high note of the chalumeau (or low) register is B-flat (few fingers) and the lowest note of the clarion register is B (all fingers). C-sharp to D on both the flute and the saxophone constitute register breaks as well.

Alternate Fingerings: Three Kinds

Right-Hand-Down

On some notes for the flute, clarinet, and saxophone, the right-hand fingers (some or all) can be depressed even when they are not a part of the normal fingering in order to a) improve tone quality, b) lower the pitch, or c) make for less finger movement and consequently smooth out finger technique. The right-hand-down technique is most often associated with the clarinet throat register.

Cross-fingerings

Cross-fingerings is woodwind terminology that refers to use of the left and right pinkies in alternation on successive notes. The player looks to avoid using same-pinkies in succession because they make fluid technique difficult and slurring impossible in most instances. The cross-fingering concept and technique is common on the clarinet and oboe, and it comes in a slightly modified form on the bassoon. The bassoonist avoids using successive thumbs and successive pinkies in the right hand by opting for thumb to pinky pairings (or vice versa) situated on the front and back of the boot joint.

Trill Fingerings

Trill fingerings involving easy-to-trill normal fingerings are non-issues. When normal fingerings prove especially awkward or impossible to trill, refer to a trill fingering chart for special fingerings.

Comprehensive trill fingering charts are readily available on the Internet. Only common trill fingerings are charted in this book. Some trill fingerings are used in non-trill situations because the trill fingering sounds better, is better in tune, or allows for more fluid technique than a primary fingering—for example, clarinet alternate B-flat (throat tone) and saxophone side C.

FOUNDATIONS OF TUNING AND INTONATION

Tuning Note

Mass tuning in band class is not an issue in the first year of instrumental study. The priorities should be characteristic tone quality and correct use of air stream by individual students. From this, pitch accuracy will develop.

I wish it were this simple—that one tuning note works for all instruments of the school band or orchestra. In practice, however, there are different "tuning notes" for each instrument, the notes having been derived to satisfy unique needs.

1. Traditionally, accomplished orchestras tune to the oboe A.
2. School orchestras often tune to two notes—concert B-flat for the wind players and concert A for the strings.
3. Traditionally, bands tune to concert B-flat.
4. Young bands may tune to the lower concert F.
5. The following are best practices relative to tuning individual instruments (to avoid the compromise inherent in one tuning note for all instruments). For the flute, use an ascending, diatonic F to B-flat (above staff) slurred sequence. For the clarinet, use a three-register tuning process involving thumb F, top line F, and 3rd space C. The saxophone's best tuning note is top line F-sharp. Assuming a good embouchure, the best tuning "note" for the oboe and bassoon is the reed's crow (octave Cs for the oboe, loose rattle for the bassoon). For the oboe, the note A is a good tuning one, as is top line F. The bassoon does well with B-flats in octaves (2nd line and above staff). These notes function best as reed and embouchure checks, not as "how much to pull" checks, because pulling is such a limited option on the double reeds. The information in this paragraph is developed in each instrument chapter.

What's the point? The aim is for a player to use a note for "tuning up" that is more rather than less representative of the general tuning of the entire instrument. Some notes are better suited for this than others—and herein lies the point of using one note to make push or pull decisions. The note is supposed to give you an accurate picture of pitch on the entire instrument. In ensemble performance settings, everyone's best note cannot always be used, so compromises are made. Advanced-level musicians know how to handle the compromises; amateurs are more or less able to handle them—and this is where the knowledge and skill of the teacher/conductor must be counted on. Which brings us to. . .

A tuning note is one note. Many band directors spend inordinate amounts of rehearsal time with students playing and making adjustments to *one note*! The ongoing, many-noted nature of tuning and intonation gets lost. Let's not do that. Instead, let's use tuning notes primarily as "quick checks" for two groups—a) for students who have been taught how to use this quick check to adjust instrument length with the aim of getting into the right pitch ballpark, and b) for the conductor/teacher who uses this quick check format with individuals and groups to make decisions about how to proceed from there.

The meat of tuning and intonation is not at all in the tuning note. The meat is in noticing and caring—and the noticing and caring starts with tone quality. Do students recognize and achieve good tone quality? Do they care? Who teaches them to notice—and care? One's got to notice to do anything about anything. Do students listen for melodic intonation—the half steps and whole steps in a melody or a scale? Do students know their role in tuning a chord in a band or orchestra? Importantly, does the teacher/conductor listen and notice at a high level?

Tuning: Is It Instrument, Reed, or Embouchure?

That's the question. If tuning and intonation were just matters of adjusting instrument length, this would be easy. But pulling joints can mask to some extent an embouchure that is too tight. Excessive pinching of the embouchure can mask to some extent an oboe reed with a flat crow. Of course, these are not ideal circumstances. It is your job to know what's going on. How do you parse this stuff out? No really. Read on please.

Pitch Tendencies

Every wind instrument has pitch tendencies; certain notes, because of the design of the instrument, tend to be sharp, flat, or unstable (sharp and flat). By knowing the pitch tendencies of the clarinet, the effective music teacher is able to predict what might happen with regard to pitch before it actually happens in a lesson or rehearsal. These would be intonation problems imposed by the music. One's job in rehearsal is to listen and discern whether student performance is consistent with the tendencies. If it is, he must know what to do to solve the pitch problems.

Pitch Solutions

The following constitute physical solutions to pitch discrepancies. Keep in mind that the physical techniques do not address the ear, which is where pitch solutions must begin and end. On the flute, adjust the direction of the air stream by manipulating the position of the lower lip and or the head. On reed instruments, lip down or up or use an alternate fingering or both to adjust pitch.

Organizing Your Thoughts about Intonation Problems

When intonation is a concern, what should you consider first, second, third? Assuming that the embouchure is correct (F-sharp on the clarinet small piece, A concert on the saxophone mouthpiece), reed strength appropriate, and reed crows suitable (oboe Cs, bassoon loose rattle), organizing your approach as follows can be fruitful. Notice in these intonation what-to-dos that adjusting the length of the instrument (number 2) doesn't happen until after the instrument and player are warmed up. Number 3 shows that through score study one can anticipate intonation problems. Lipping generally occurs before alternate fingerings, though there are exceptions (e.g., the throat tones).

1. Allow for sufficient warm-up of instruments.
2. Adjust instrument length (this is a two- or three-step process for clarinet).

3. Know where to expect intonation problems imposed by the music. The clarinet serves as an example. Soft music may be sharp. A *decrescendo* may lead to sharpness. The low register or throat register may be sharp.

4. Lip pitch up or down.

5. Use alternate fingerings, including the right-hand-down technique.

FOUNDATIONS OF REED AND MOUTHPIECE

Reed Strength

Reeds come in different strengths along a soft to hard continuum (the blowing properties of a soft reed make it easy to make vibrate, sometimes too easy; the blowing properties of a hard reed make the player work harder to make it vibrate).

The actual feel of a reed of a certain strength reed (say a number 3 clarinet reed) will vary among number 3 reeds of the same brand and different brands, and depend on the characteristics of the mouthpiece.

The Reed Needs of Novices

Novice players should play softer reeds that have good response, pitch, and stability. These reeds are not necessarily the same as "soft reeds." A number 1 reed is soft, but too soft even for beginners. Beginners should start on number 2 or 2.5 reeds. They need reeds that are on the softer end of the soft to hard continuum, but not so soft that they are not relatively stable.

"There's So Much To Know"!

It is tempting for music teachers who are not woodwind majors to assume that "I can't possibly have much to offer my students about reeds. There is so much to know, including how to make and adjust them, I couldn't possibly learn all that."

It is not necessary to "learn all that" to be an effective teacher of the woodwinds. It is, however, reasonable to expect the non-woodwind major music teacher to be familiar with and use basic information about reeds. Take for example *Wetting, Storing, Rotating,* and *Crowing.* A teacher uses this information in one or both of two ways: By teaching it to his students and/or observing their "reed behaviors," noting what they do and don't do, and leading them to do what is suggested. If you use this information in your teaching, you will be pleasantly surprised at "how much you have to offer your students about reeds."

Evaluating Reed Quality

All reeds, both single and double, are evaluated on five criteria: 1) Response, 2) pitch, 3) stability, 4) dynamic range, and 5) tone quality. On single reed instruments, it is not the reed alone, but the mouthpiece and the reed relationship that creates these performance characteristics.

Single Reeds Can Warp

Fixing them is easy.

The Mouthpiece Facing Is . . .

The part of the mouthpiece that curves away from the reed. The facing has length and curvature, both of which vary from one make of mouthpiece to another. Length and curve determine the size of the tip opening. A larger tip opening requires a stronger embouchure because there is more distance for the reed to cover in order for it to make contact with the mouthpiece during vibration. A more open tip opening requires a softer reed. A more closed tip opening requires a harder reed.

Stock Versus Better Quality Mouthpiece

A beginning model clarinet or saxophone comes with what is called a stock mouthpiece. Stock means it came with the instrument. Implied is that this mouthpiece is not of good quality, though it is sufficient for the needs of a beginning level player. After a year or two, it is wise to encourage students and their parents to purchase a better quality mouthpiece in order to take advantage of the potential for enhanced response, intonation, dynamics, and tone quality. In some cases, school music teachers arrange with local music store dealers to include a better quality mouthpiece rather than the stock mouthpiece with rental instruments. In other instances, one make of mouthpiece is purchased with school funds so that every clarinet or saxophone player in the band is using the same step-up mouthpiece. The thinking is that if everyone uses the same make of mouthpiece, tone quality will tend to be more uniform across students than it would be if students were given no direction in mouthpiece selection.

Sources for Double Reeds

University teachers and their students. Private teachers. Online catalogs.

Oboe Reed: Short or Long Scrape?

Avoid a short (French) style of scrape. A short scrape reed looks like its name implies. The scrape (that which has been cut with a knife) is short, meaning about half of the wood part of the reed is scraped. The other half has not been scraped; the bark remains. An oboe tone of a short scrape reed is brighter, more lazer-beam like than that of the other style of scrape—the long scrape. The scraped portion of the long scrape reed extends farther back, almost to the string. This allows the vibrations of the reed to travel unobstructed farther into the back of the reed, promoting greater depth and darkness in the tone.

The Reed Crow

The player is at a real disadvantage if the oboe reed does not crow (a C in octaves) and the bassoon does not crow a loose rattle.

Tip Opening

The tip opening of the double reed has much to do with how well the reed works. If too wide, the reed will be hard to blow; response will be difficult. If too small an opening, the tone will be small and the pitch sharp. The size of the reed opening on the oboe and bassoon can be controlled to some degree. On the wet oboe reed, coax it open by gently squeezing from the sides or close it by holding the tip shut for 20 seconds or so. On the bassoon, use needle nose pliers to adjust the tip opening at the first wire.

FOUNDATIONS: PROFESSIONAL ORGANIZATIONS AND PERIODICALS

- Flute
    - The National Flute Association publishes *Flute Quarterly*. Access the journal online. www.nfaonline.org
    - *Flute Talk Magazine*. Published by *The Instrumentalist*. www.instrumentalistmagazine.com
- Clarinet
    - The International Clarinet Association publishes *The Clarinet*. Join ICA or access the journal at a major university library. www.clarinet.org
- Saxophone
    - The North American Saxophone Alliance publishes *The Saxophone Symposium*. Join NASA or access the journal at a major university library. www.saxalliance.org
- Oboe
    - The International Double Reed Society (IDRS) publishes the *The Double Reed*. Join IDRS or access the journal at a major university library. www.idrs.org
- Bassoon:
    - The International Double Reed Society (IDRS) publishes the *The Double Reed*. Join IDRS or access the journal at a major university library. www.idrs.org

Relevant articles about all instruments appear in *The Instrumentalist, Music Educators Journal, Bandworld,* and *School Band and Orchestra.*

Notes on the Author

James L. Byo is the Carl Prince Matthies Professor of Music Education and Head of Music Education at Louisiana State University in Baton Rouge. His research, which appears in major research journals and texts, centers on both sides of the podium—in teacher/conductor effectiveness and performer rhythm reading and aural discrimination. He has presented research in numerous states as well as England, Spain, Japan, and Austria. Byo has served as editor of *Update: Applications of Research in Music Education*, chair of the research division of the World Association of Symphonic Bands and Ensembles, and on the editorial committee of the *Journal of Research in Music Education*. Currently, he is the program evaluator for the National String Project Consortium and a member of the Executive Committee of the Society for Research in Music Education.

A former public school band and orchestra conductor in Wooster, Ohio, he holds music education and oboe performance degrees from Youngstown State University and a Ph.D. from Florida State University. He studied oboe with Loyal Mould and John Mack. For eight seasons he performed professionally with the Youngstown and Wooster Symphony Orchestras. More recently he was conductor of the 80-member Louisiana Junior Youth Orchestra and the LSU High School Honors Wind Ensemble.

Byo has co-authored the method book *The Habits of Musicianship: A Radical Approach to Beginning Band* with Bob Duke of the University of Texas-Austin. *The Habits of Musicianship* was released in the spring of 2007 and is distributed cost-free as a service to music education.

Notes on the Authors

Index

Entries in *italics* refer to figures; entries in **bold** refer to tables.

2 o clock position 64, *65*, 114, 135

action place 192
adding keys for pitch adjustment *130*
air stream: for bassoon 177–8, 194; for clarinet 56, 69; and embouchure 228; for flute 19–20, 34; practicing use of 11; for saxophone 105, 108, 111; as sound factor 4–5; and tonguing 243
alternate fingerings: for clarinet 87–8; for flute 41; for saxophone 126; three kinds of 251
altissimo register, on saxophone 118, 124–5
alto clarinet 77, 123
alto flute 40–1
alto saxophone 12, 95, 123–4, 130, 247
articulated G-sharp/A-flat *126*, *156*
articulation: for bassoon 195; for clarinet 73, 76; for flute 39; foundations of 243; for oboe 150; pre-tonguing 37, 39, 74, 76, 120, 122, 244; for saxophone 120, 122; and small piece 230
assembly and disassembly: of bassoon 179–85, *180–1*, *183*; of clarinet 62, *63*; of flute 26–7; foundations of 236–7; of oboe 112–13, 140–1
attrition rate 13
automatic behavior 9

backward approach to teaching tonguing 8; for clarinet 74, 75; for flute 37, *38*; and legato tongue 244; for saxophone 120, *121*
ballpark accuracy 58–9, 108–9, 233–4
ballpark embouchure: for bassoon 178, 195; for clarinet 58, 73–4; for oboe 150; prior to tonguing 244; for saxophone 111, 120
ballpark tone, for flute 21, 25, 33
band method books: for clarinet 66; for oboe *154*
baritone saxophone 124, 127, 130, 247
bass clarinet 77–8, 122–3, 247
bass clef 175–6, 197, 201, 248
bass flute 40–1
bass oboe 151
bassoon: accessories for 237; angle to body 242; breathing for 192; care of 186; fingering for 196, 198–202, *221–3*, 251; first notes on *189–90*; first sounds on 177; hand position for 186–9, *187*; history of 196; initial playing material for 211, 212–16; parts of *179*; pitch tendencies for 194; potential for success 175–6; professional organizations for 256; range of *197*, 198, 248; rote study for *190*, 191; staccato 245; tonguing 195–6; tuning and intonation 203–6, 252; water in tone hole 239
bassoon bocal: handling *182*, 184–5; leak at juncture with reed 211; manufacturing of 197; and pitch 203, 205; in playing position 188, 192–3; removing 237; in small piece 176–7; and tone quality 178
bassoon embouchure: changing 9; early stage 176; front view *177*; intentional deviations from normal 194; and pitch 204; side view *178*; teaching 177–8, 189, 191–3
bassoon hand rest 184, 187
bassoon reed: amount in mouth 178, 192, 204; for early students 178–9, 209; evaluating 207–8; extending life of 211; leak in 210–11; parts of *208*; purchasing 209–10; scraping 198, 204, 207, 209, 211; soaking 180, 183, 206; storing 207
bassoon small piece: assembling 176–7; pitch of 178, 193, 204
biting 157
bocal: for English horn 151; *see also* bassoon bocal
bocal vent hole 185, 197–8, 203, 250
body posture 242
Boehm, Theobald 40, 76, 151, 246
bore, cylindrical or conical 4
brass 3–4
brass instruments 122, 131
breathing, and early instruction 228
breathy tone 33–4
bridge keys 62, 68, 140–1, 180, 182, 236
Buffet, Louis-August 76

chalumeau register 15, 76, 81, 87–8, 233
characteristic tone: difference between soloists 5; practicing 11

clarinet: angle to body 242; care for 63–4, 238; cross-fingering on 81–3, *82*, 251; fingering for *79*, 80–3, *100*–1, 249–51, *250*; first sounds on 56–7; hand position 64–6, *65*; notes not speaking 68; notes that reveal on 233; potential for success in 59; professional organizations for 256; range and register *78*, 248; sound factors in 4; squeaking 68, 243; stimulus note for 249; tonguing 73–6; tuning and intonation 86–8, 252; voicing 72
clarinet embouchure: checkpoints 71; component skills of 9; improving 66–8, *67*; initial work 55–9, *58*; performance test for **61**; teaching 69–72
clarinet family 76–8
clarinet ligature: facts 95–6; and small piece assembly 53, *54*
clarinet mouthpiece: care of 237; compatible with reed 73, 89; curvature of *55*; facts 94–5; parts of *94*; placement in mouth 57, 67–72, 243; sanitizing 68
clarinet reed: care of 90–4; characteristics of 88–90, *89*, 92; evaluating quality 91; position adjustment *54*; removing from mouthpiece 63; softness of 72–3; wetting 237
clarinet screw heads *54*
clarinet small piece: assembly of *52*, 53–5; pitch of 67, 69, 71, 86, 106
clarion register 59, 72, 78–9, 81, 87–8, 249, 251
Coker, Jerry 131–2
component skills 9
conservatory system of fingering 151
contra-alto clarinet 77
contra-bass clarinet 77
contrabassoon 196
cooling soup aperture 74, 120
cork grease: for clarinet 53, 63; general comments on 236; for saxophone 103
cork replacement 241
correct repetitions, in learning 7, 9
cross-fingerings 12, 251

crossing the break 251; on clarinet 78, 81; on oboe 155; on saxophone 125
crowing the reed: for bassoon 176, 178, 203–4, 207; for oboe 139, 157–60, 162; and tuning 252
C-sharps: on bassoon *199*; short-fingered on flute 46
Cupid's bow formation 25–6

declarative memory 7
diaphragmatic vibrato 4, 35, 149, 194
disabilities: and clarinet 59; and flute 26; and saxophone 109
dizziness 34
double reed instruments: challenges of 12, 138–9, 175–6; half-hole technique on 250–1; pitch issues for 148, 194; sources of reeds 255; stimulus note for 249
double tongue 39, 246
doubling 77, 132, 248

E-flat, on bassoon *201*, 205
E-flat Rule 155
embouchure: component parts of 230; flexibility of 228; mental checklist of traits 60; one-on-one teaching 232; as primary concern 227; students' interactions with 6; and timbre 5; and tonguing 243–4
embouchure formation 7, 53, 102, 227–8
embouchure plate, leaky 241
English horn 151–2, 247
enharmonic equivalents 79, 81, 152
Evans, Bill 123, 131
experience before theory 8

feedback, personalized 31
fingering, awkward 12, 211
fingering groups 251
finger position 29, 242–3
first notes 15
first octave notes 249, *250*
flick key technique 200, *201*
flute: aligning embouchure hole with keys *26*; aligning foot joint and body *26*; contexts for tone production 6; fingering for 41–4, *42*, 50–1, 249–51; first sounds on 20–2; hand position for 27–9, *28*; how it works 3–4; key adjustment for 240; parallel to lips 24–5, 29, 31, *32*, 35, 242; potential for success with 25–6; professional organizations for 256; range of *41*, 248; refining tone for 30–1, 33–4; separating into parts 238; sound factors in 3–4; tonguing 37–9, *38*; tuning and intonation 44–6, 252
flute embouchure: characteristics of 19; early work on 6, 20–4; improving 30–1, 33–5
flute embouchure hole: air stream across 19, 44–5; aligning with keys 27; lip over *21*, 22–3, 31, 33–4, 40, 43
flute family 40–1
flute head joint: curved 41; early work with 19–23, *20*, *24*; performance test 24, **25**; pressure against lip 35; and tuning 44
flutter tonguing 246
fork F 151, *153*, 154–5, 158
fork F-sharp 126
Fox bassoons 196–7, 236
Fox oboes 152
French tonguing 37
F Rule 153

glottal tonguing: for clarinet 74–5; for flute 37, 39; for saxophone 120, 122
grenadilla wood 78, 152

half-hole technique: for bassoon 187, 198, *199*, 205; for clarinet 77; for oboe 152, *153*, 155
hand digits 241
hands, size of 176
harmonics, for flute *44*
harmonic series 4, *5*
Heckel, J. A. 196–7
high register: on bassoon 194, 198, 205; on oboe 148
hyperventilation 34

individual student teaching 21, 233–5
instrument care, foundations of 237–9
instrument demonstration 12, 14
instrument families 247

instrument manufacturing: bassoon 196–7; clarinet 78; flute 40–1; oboe 151–2; professional and student-line 247; saxophone 124
instrument parts: companies selling 95; naming 236
instrument repair technicians 41, 45, 63, 237, 239, 241
intonation problems: for bassoon 194, 203, 205; for clarinet 247; hearing 12; for oboe 148; troubleshooting 253–4

jaw down: for bassoon 191–2, 194; for clarinet 56, 58, 67, 70; for flute 35; and oral cavity 227; for saxophone 106, 108, 115
jaw drop, for oboe 148
jaw movement, excessive 39, 75, 122
jaw vibrato 4, 118
jazz, woodwind instruments in 247
jazz clarinet 4, 76, 132
jazz flute 132
jazz saxophone 131–2, 248

key mechanism: excess pressure on 236; leak in 239–40
keys: improper functioning 239–41; pressure on 236
Klosé, Hyacinthe 76
Kovar, Simon 196

labeling 9
leaky pads 6, 45, 68, 117
"no lean" 64, 66
learning: process of 10–12; and teaching 6–10
left F 153, *154*
legato tongue: for clarinet 74–5; for flute 39; relaxed tip for 243; for saxophone 120–1; teaching 8, 11, 229, 244
lip across technique 12, 22–3, 33, *34*, 43
lip down 130, 170
lip movement, for flute 22–3
lipping: for bassoon 194, 205; for clarinet 88; for oboe 148, 152, 157–8; for saxophone 130–1
lip pressure: for bassoon 176, 191–2, 194, 205; for oboe 139–40, 146, 148; for saxophone 118
"Little Bird" 10
longer-tube notes 15

lower lip: for clarinet 11–12, 55–61, 66–70; for flute 19–23, *21*, 33–4, 230, 249; for saxophone 105–7
low register: on bassoon 194, 198, 204–5; on clarinet 254; on oboe 148, 152, 157–8; on saxophone 116, 124

material, and tone quality 3
memory, enhancing 9
motor skills 7
mouthpiece facing 255
multiple tonguing 39, 246

neck strap: for bass clarinet 77; for bassoon 184; for English horn 151; for saxophone 108, 112–14
needs assessment **13**
nickel silver 4
nose breathing 229
notes that reveal 233

oboe: accessories for 237; angle to body 242; breathing for 147; care for 142, 238; fingering for *153*, 154–6, *155*, 173–4, 251; first notes on 143, *144*; first sounds on 140; hand position *143*; history of 150; playing material for 164, *165*–9; posture and holding 142–3; potential for success on 138–9; professional organizations for 256; range and octaves 152–3, 248; rote study for *145*; tonguing 150; tuning and intonation 157–9, 252
oboe d'amore 151
oboe embouchure: characteristics of *146*; flaws in 158; and reed quality 161; teaching 139, 143–4, 147–8
oboe family 151
oboe reed: evaluating quality 160–2; parts of 162, *163*; position in mouth 146, 158; scraping 152, 161–2; short or long scrape 255; sources of 164; storing and rotating 160; tip opening 163; travelling with 142; tuning 157; wetting 139–40, 159
octave key: on oboe 141–2, 152, *153*; and overblown register 249; on saxophone 112, 114
oral cavity 227, 243

overbite embouchure 192
overblowing 33, 44, 249, *250*

pad replacement 239–41
pads: height of 45; problems with 239–41; seated 238
palm keys *127*
pancake key 184, 188–9, 198, 205
partials, stimulating or dampening 5
peers, learning from 10
performance testing: for bassoon 219–20; for clarinet 60, **61**, 98–9; for flute 24, **25**, 48–9; for oboe 171–2; for saxophone 110, **111**, 134–5
Pestalozzi, Johann Heinrich 7
phrases, playing with eye towards 11
piccolo 12, 40–1, 248
pinky fingers: on bassoon *200*; successive 81, 126, 251
pipe, closed or open 3–4
pitch tendencies 253; for bassoon 205–6; for clarinet 86–7; for flute 45; for oboe 148, 158; for saxophone 129–30
pivot screws 239
positive habit strength 232–4
practice discipline 11
preparatory breath 147, 192, 228–9
procedural memory 7
puffed cheeks: and clarinet 59, 67, 71; and saxophone 109, 116, 118

reamer 211
recruiting 13–14, 138–9, 175–6
reed cases 90, 141–2, 160, 184, *185*, 237
reeds: and embouchure 4; evaluating quality 254; foundations of 254; optimal strength of 71–2, 229; rotating 90, 160, 207
reed style 5
register breaks 251
register key, on clarinet 64, 71, 76, 79, *80*, 198
re-teaching 9–10
right hand down 79, 125, 251, 254
rods, pressure on 236
rollers 126
rolling out flute 45
rote practice 144, 191, 232

saxophone: angle to body 242; care of 113; fingering for 125–7,

136–7, 250–1; first sounds on 106–7; hand position *114*; history of 122–3; potential for success 109; professional organizations for 256; range and register 124, *125*, 248; sound factors for 5; tonguing 120–2; tuning and intonation 127, 129–31, 252
saxophone embouchure *107*–8, *115*; performance test **111**; teaching 105–8, 115–18
saxophone family 123–4
saxophone ligature *103*; regular and inverted 104
saxophone mouthpiece: care for 237; compatibility with reed 119; jazz 131; pitch of 111, 116–17, 123; position in mouth 115, 117; and tuning 129
saxophone quartet 6, 123, 132, 247–8
saxophone reed: cost of 91; hardness of 119; placement in mouth 106–7; wetting 237
saxophone screw heads *104*
saxophone small piece: angle to face 107; assembly 102–5; pitch of 106
saxophone tone 5, 102, 119
scaffolding 9
seat strap for bassoon 179–80, 182, 184–6, 188, 219, 237
secondary instruments: performance testing 48, 98, 134, 171, 219; practicing 11; teacher developing performance skills 233
short-tube notes 15, 79, 125, 130, 233
slave keys 240
small aperture, for flute 19–20, 25, 30, *32*, 33–5, 230
small piece: and embouchure development 230; tone of 231–2
small piece practice: for bassoon 178; for clarinet 56–7, 59, *60*; and instrument selection 15; for saxophone 109, *110*; sustaining 230–1
small sound, on clarinet 57, 68
soprano clarinet 76–7, 95, 247–8
spring replacement 241
springs, unhooked 239–40

sterilization 68, 92, 117
stimulus notes *249*
stock mouthpiece 95, 255
structured environments 8
swabbing: for bassoon 184–6; for clarinet 55, 63; for flute 27; for oboe 141–2; for saxophone 105, 113; time for 237–8

teacher demonstration 22, 232
teaching/learning sequence: for clarinet 59, *60*, 61, 64; in embouchure instruction 230; for flute 8, 23–5, *24*; for saxophone 109, *110*
teeth on top: for clarinet 57–61, 66, 68, 70; for saxophone 107–9, 111, 115–17
tenor clef 197, *201*, 248
throat tones 78, *79*, 81, 86–8, 250, 252–4
thumb keys: for bassoon *181*, 187–8, *199*; for flute 28, 42
thumb rest 64–5, 98, 114, 141–3
timbre 4–5, 44, 251
tip opening: for bassoon reed 176, 180, 183, 193, *209*, 210; for double reeds 255–6; for mouthpiece 88–9, 94–5, 255; for oboe reed 140, 147–8, 152, 161; optimal size of 229
tone, controlling 11
tone development: for bassoon 189; for clarinet 66, 72–3; for flute 25, 30, 33; for oboe 143; practice on 11; for saxophone 115, 119
tone hole, water in 239
tone production, students' interactions with 6
tone quality: for bassoon 197, 205, 208; of clarinet reeds 91; foundations of 227–9; impact of material on 3; for jazz saxophone 131; and mouthpiece 255; noticing and caring about 253; for oboe 152, 158, 160–1; performers as models of **229**; positive habits for 7
tongue, shape of 227
tongue movement, isolating *39*, 75, 122

tonguing: and assessment 38, 75, 121–2, 245; in early teaching 229; foundations of 243–4
traditional approach to teaching tonguing 245; for clarinet 73–4; for flute 37; for saxophone 120
treble clef 78, 124, 196, 248
trill fingerings 251–2; for bassoon 202–3; for clarinet 83, *84*–5; for flute *43*; for oboe *156*; for saxophone 127, *128*
trill keys 43, 151, 156, 197, 202
triple tongue 39, 246
tuning and intonation, foundations of 252–3
tuning notes: for bassoon *203*; for clarinet *86*; for flute *44*; for oboe *157*; for saxophone 127, *128*
tuning rod 44
tuning the embouchure: for clarinet 86, 88; for saxophone 117, 127

upper lip, and flute 19, 21–2, 25
upper register, on flute 33

vibrato: on bassoon 194–5; on clarinet 4–5, 73; on flute 35, *36*; on oboe 149; on saxophone 118–19; on woodwinds 4–5
vocal modeling 246
voicing 71–2, 87, 129–30, 148, 227, 243
Vygotsky, Lev 9

warped reeds 62, 90, 93–4
whisper key on bassoon: in assembly and disassembly 182; hand position for 186, 189; lock mechanism 197; and overblown register 249–50; range *198*
whistle formation 70, 118, 148, 193
wood cracking 64, 142, 186, 238, 241
Woods, Phil 123, 131
woodwind ensembles 247
woodwind quintet 247
woodwinds: matching students to instruments 12–15; sound factors of 3, **4**; teaching in K-12 schools 5–6; vocabulary for 238